EUROPEAN POLITICAL FACTS
1648–1789

In the same series

Chris Cook and John Paxton
EUROPEAN POLITICAL FACTS 1789–1848
EUROPEAN POLITICAL FACTS 1848–1918
EUROPEAN POLITICAL FACTS 1918–1973

EUROPEAN POLITICAL FACTS 1648–1789

JACK BABUSCIO
Lecturer in History, Kingsway-Princeton College, London

and

RICHARD MINTA DUNN
Senior Lecturer in History, Polytechnic of North London

M

MACMILLAN

First published 1984 by
THE MACMILLAN PRESS LTD
London and Basingstoke
Companies and representatives
throughout the world

Filmsetting by Vantage Photosetting Co. Ltd
Eastleigh and London
Printed in Hong Kong

British Library Cataloguing in Publication Data
Babuscio, Jack
European political facts 1648–1789
1. Europe – Social conditions – 17th century   2. Europe – Social
conditions – 18th century
I. Title   II. Dunn, Richard Minta
940.2′5   HN373
ISBN 0–333–32111–1

To our parents
Elizabeth and Minta Dunn
and
Miriam and John Babuscio

CONTENTS

PREFACE

This is the fourth volume to appear in the *European Political Facts* series. Hence this book has been designed to be a companion to the existing *European Political Facts 1789–1848, European Political Facts 1848–1918* and *European Political Facts 1918–1973*. As with the preceding volumes, the authors have gathered in a single volume as many of the important political facts as possible for one of the most crucial periods of modern history.

Inevitably, for a period as far back as 1648 to 1789, reliable sources become ever more scarce. Dates are often difficult to give with absolute precision. Reliable economic or social statistics are even more difficult to find. Facts on Turkey have been excluded because of the difficulty of collating reliable information. The authors would like to be informed of error or inconsistency so that these may be taken into account in planning future editions of this book.

Jack Babuscio
Richard Minta Dunn

London

1 HEADS OF STATE AND KEY MINISTERS

AUSTRIA:
see under Habsburg Empire*

DENMARK–NORWAY

HEADS OF STATE

4 Apr 1588	Christian IV, son of Frederick II (House of Oldenburg), b. 12 Apr 1577
28 Feb 1648	Frederick III, son, b. 18 Mar 1609
9 Feb 1670	Christian V, son, b. 15 Apr 1646
26 Aug 1699	Frederick IV, son, b. 21 Oct 1671
12 Oct 1730	Christian VI, son, 10 Dec 1699
6 Aug 1746	Frederick V, son, b. 31 Mar 1723
14 Jan 1766	Christian VII, son, b. 20 Jan 1749
13 Mar 1808	Frederick VI, son, b. 28 Jan 1768

KEY MINISTERS

1643–51	Corfitz Ulfeldt, Steward of the Court
1660	Hannibal Sehested, Treasurer
1664–99	U. F. Gyldenløve, Statholder in Norway
1673–11 Mar 1676	Peder Schumacher, Count Griffenfeld, Chancellor
Mar 1676	Frederick Ahlefeld, Chancellor
1721	Ditler Vibe, Statholder in Norway
12 Oct 1730	Baron Iver Rosenkrans, Chancellor; Count Christian Ranteau, Statholder in Norway
6 Aug 1746–1770	Adam Gottlob Moltke, Master of the Royal Household

* This applies to all chapters.

1751–13 Sep 1770	Johann Hartwig Ernst (from 1767: Count) Bernstorff, Foreign Minister
13 Sep 1770–17 Jan 1772	Johann Friedrich (from 1771: Count) Struensee, Foreign Minister (from 13 Sept 1770) and Secretary of State and Regent (from 1771)
Jan 1772–1784	Ove Høegh-Guldberg
13 Apr 1784–21 Jun 1979	Andreas Peter, Count Bernstorff, Foreign Minister

FRANCE

HEADS OF STATE

4 May 1643	Louix XIV, son of Louis XIII (House of Bourbon), b. 5 Sep 1638
1 Sep 1715	Louis XV, great-grandson, b. 15 Feb 1710 (Duke of Orleans Regent from 1715–23)
10 May 1774	Louix XVI, grandson, b. 23 Aug 1754; d. (guillotined) 21 January 1793
	Monarchy abolished 10 Aug 1792

KEY MINISTERS

1643–9 Mar 1661: Mazarin

Chief Minister	Jules Mazarin (Cardinal)
Finance	Nicholas Fouquet, 1653–Sep 1661

1661–6 Sep 1683: Colbert

Chief Minister	Jean Baptiste Colbert, Marquis de Seignelay, Controller-General of Finance
Foreign Affairs	Hugues de Lionne, Marquis de Berni, 1661–Jun 1671
	Simon Arnauld, Marquis de Pomponne, Jun 1671–Nov 1679
	Charles, Marquis Colbert de Croissy, 1679–96
Justice	Voysin, 1661–(?)
War	François Michel Le Tellier, Marquis de Louvois, 1666–91

1699–1715: Torcy

Chief Minister	Jean Baptiste Colbert, Marquis de Torcy

1718–10 Aug 1723: Dubois

Chief Minister	Guillaume Dubois (Cardinal)

Lord Chancellor   Marc René, Marquis d'Argenson, 1718–20
Controller-General John Law of Lauriston, Jan–July 1720
  of Finances
Minister of State   Louis Hector, Duc de Villars, 1718–33

22 Aug–2 Dec 1723: Orléans
Chief Minister   Philippe, Duc d'Orléans (Regent)

1724–11 Jun 1726: Bourbon et Condé
Chief Minister   Louis Henri, Duc de Bourbon et de Condé

1726–29 Jan 1743: Fleury
Chief Minister   André Hercule de Fleury (Cardinal)
Foreign Affairs   Jean Jacques Amelot de Chaillou, 1737–44
Minister of State   Camille, Comte de Tallard, Marquis de la Baume
    d'Hostun, 1726–20 Mar 1728

18 Nov 1744–10 Jan 1747: Argenson
Chief Minister   René Louis de Voyer de Paulmy, Marquis d'Argenson
    (Foreign Affairs)
War   Marc Pierre, Comte d'Argenson, Feb 1743–1 Feb
    1751
Finance   Jean Baptiste de Machault d'Arnounville, 6 Dec
    1745–28 Jul 1754
Navy   Antoine Louis Rouillé, Comte de Juoy, 3 May
    1749–Aug 1754

1754–25 Jun 1757: Jouy
Chief Minister   Antoine Louis Rouillé, Comte de Jouy (Foreign
    Affairs)
War   Charles Louis Auguste Fouquet, Duc de Belle-Isle,
    1751–26 Jan 1761
Navy   Jean Baptiste de Machault d'Arnounville, 28 Jul
    1754–1 Feb 1757
Intendant of   Jean Claude Marie Vincent de Gournay, 1747–59
  Commerce

25 Jun 1757–1758: Bernis
Chief Minister   François Joachim de Pierres de Bernis
Home Affairs and Louis Prélypeaux, Comte de St Florentin, 1757–75
  Administration
  of Paris

1758–Dec 1770: *Choiseul*

Chief Minister and Foreign Affairs*	Étienne François, Duc de Choiseul
Finance	Étienne de Silhouette, 4 Mar–21 Nov 1759
Home Affairs	Louis Prélypeaux, Comte de St Florentin, 1757–75

1770–74: *Triumvirate (Aiguillon/Maupeou/Terray)*

Foreign Minister	Armand Vigerol-Duplessis-Richelieu, Duc d'Aiguillon
Chancellor	René Nicolas Charles Augustin de Maupeou, 1768–74
Finance	Joseph-Marie Terray, 23 Dec 1769–24 Aug 1774

1774–88: *Maurepas*

Chief Minister	Jean-Frédéric Phélippeaux, Comte de Maurepas, 1774–21 Nov 1781
	Charles Gravier, Comte de Vergennes, 1781–7
	Étienne Charles de Loménie de Brienne (Cardinal), 1787–8
Foreign Affairs	Charles Gravier, Comte de Vergennes, 1774–13 Feb 1787
	Armand Marc, Comte de Montmorin St-Hérem, 1787–12 Jul 1789
Finance	Anne Robert Jacques Turgot, Baron de l'Aulne, 24 Aug 1774–12 May 1776
	Jacques Necker, Jun 1777–12 May 1781
	Jean François Joly de Fleury, 1781–Mar 1783
	Henri François de Paule Le Fèvre d'Ormesson, Marquis d'Amboile, 30 Mar–3 Nov 1783
	Charles Alexandre de Calonne, Nov 1783–7
	Étienne Charles de Lomenie de Brienne, 1 May 1787–25 Aug 1788
Home Affairs	Chrétien Guillaume de Lamoignon de Malesherbes, 1775–12 May 1776
	Charles Louis François de Paul de Barentin, May 1776–16 Jul 1789
Justice	Armand Thomas Duc de Miromesnil, 1774–87
	Chrétien François de Lamoignon, 1787–8
War	Charles Louis, Comte de St-Germain, 25 Oct 1775–1777

*Choiseul succeeded by his cousin, fifth Duke of Choiseul-Praslin, 13 Oct 1761, as Foreign Minister, but took ministries of marine and war.

Lord Chamberlain   Louis Auguste Le Tonnelier, Baron de Breteuil, 1783–7

Aug 1788–90: Necker

Chief Minister   Jacques Necker, Aug 1788–11 Jul 1789
  and Finance   Louis Auguste Le Tonnelier, Baron de Breteuil, 11–14 Jul 1789
Chief Minister   Jacques Necker, 14 Jul 1789–Sep 1790

GERMAN STATES

HEADS OF STATE
Holy Roman Emperors
House of Habsburg (1439–1740 and 1745–1806)

12 Feb 1637–2 Apr 1657   Ferdinand III, son of Ferdinand II, b. 13 Jul 1608
18 Jul 1658   Leopold I, son, b. 9 Jun 1640
 5 May 1705–17 Apr 1711 Joseph I, son, b. 26 Jul 1678
12 Oct 1711–20 Oct 1740 Charles VI, brother, b. 1 Oct 1658

House of Bavaria (Wittelsbach)

24 Jan 1742–20 Jan 1745 Charles VII, son of Elector Maximilian (Maximilian II) of Bavaria; b. 6 Aug 1697

House of Habsburg

13 Sep 1745   Francis I, son of Duke Leopold Joseph Hyacinth of Lorraine, b. 8 Dec 1708
18 Aug 1765–20 Feb 1790 Joseph II, son, b. 13 Mar 1741

1 *Baden*

HEADS OF STATE
Margraves
Baden–Durlach line (Protestant from 1555)

12 Apr 1622   Friedrich V, son of Georg Friedrich, b. 6 Jul 1594
 8 Sep 1659   Friedrich VI, son, b. 16 Nov 1617
31 Jan 1677   Friedrich VII, Magnus, son, b. 23 Sep 1647
25 Jun 1709   Karl III, Wilhelm, son, b. 17 Jan 1679
12 May 1738   Karl Friedrich, grandson; from 8 May 1803: Elector; from 5 May 1806: Duke; b. 22 Nov 1728

2 *Bavaria*

HEADS OF STATE
Dukes
15 Oct 1597	Maximilian I, son; from 25 Feb 1623: Elector; b. 15 Apr 1573

Electors
27 Sep 1651	Ferdinand, son, b. 31 Oct 1636
26 May 1679	Maximilian II, son; Stadholder of the Spanish Netherlands 1691, expelled from Bavaria 1704, restored 1714; b. 11 Jul 1662
26 Feb 1726	Karl Albert, son; from 24 Jan 1742: Holy Roman Emperor Charles VII; b. 6 Aug 1697
20 Jan 1745	Maximilian III, son, b. 28 Mar 1727
30 Dec 1777	Karl Theodor, son of Johann Christian of Pfalz-Sulzbach; from 1742: Elector Palatine; b. 11 Dec 1742

3 *Brandenburg–Prussia*

Brandenburg

HEADS OF STATE
Electors (from 1618 also Dukes of Prussia)
House of Hohenzollern
1 Dec 1640	Frederick William, son of George William, b. 16 Feb 1620
29 Apr 1688–	Frederick III, son; from 18 Jan 1701: King of Prussia; b. 11
25 Feb 1713	Jul 1657

Prussia

HEADS OF STATE
Regents of the House of Hohenzollern
18 Aug 1618–	The Electors of Brandenburg were also Dukes of Prussia
18 Jan 1701	

Kings
18 Jan 1701	Frederick I, previously Elector of Brandenburg
25 Feb 1713	Frederick William I, son, b. 4 Aug 1688
31 May 1740	Frederick II, the Great, son, b. 24 Jan 1712
17 Aug 1786	Frederick William II, nephew, b. 25 Sep 1744
16 Nov 1797	Frederick William III, son, b. 3 Aug 1770

KEY MINISTERS (BRANDENBURG–PRUSSIA)
*Prime Ministers**

1619–40	Adam, Count Schwarzenberg
1653–8	Georg Friedrich, Count (from 1682: Prince) Waldeck
1658–4 Nov 1679	Otto, Baron Schwerin
1695–Dec 1697	Eberhard, Baron Danckelmann
1697–early 1711	Johann Kasimir (from 1699: Count) Kolbe von Wartenberg
early 1711–16 Dec 1728	Heinrich Rüdiger von Ilgen
1728–18 Mar 1739	Friedrich Wilhelm von Grumbkow
Jun 1749–3 Jan 1800	Karl Wilhelm, Count Finck von Finckenstein
1749–20 Oct 1753	Georg Dietlof von Arnim-Boitzenburg, in similar capacity
1777–15 May 1802	Friedrich Anton, Baron Heinitz, Secretary of State and head of various departments
8 Nov 1786–1798	Friedrich Wilhelm, Count Arnim, Secretary of State

Foreign Affairs

1728–May 1741	Adrian Bernhard, Count Borck
1728–30	Friedrich Ernst, Baron Inn-und-Knyphausen
1730–29 July 1760	Heinrich Count Podewils
27 Nov 1731–4 Aug 1740	Wilhelm Heinrich von Thulemeir
1741–8 Mar 1747	Caspar Wilhelm von Borcke
10 Mar 1747–24 Jun 1748	Axel von Mardefeld
Jun 1749–3 Jan 1800	Karl Wilhelm, Count Finck von Finckenstein
5 Apr 1763–Jul 1791	Ewald Friedrich, Baron (from 1787: Count) Hertzberg

Lord High Chancellors and Ministers of Justice

1746–4 Oct 1755	Samuel, Baron von Cocceji; Minister of Justice from 1738
(?)–9 Nov 1770	Philipp Joseph von Jarriges
1770–11 Dec 1779	Karl Joseph Maximilian, Baron Fürst und Kupferberg
1770–89	Karl Abraham, Baron Zedlitz; Minister of Education, 1771–88
1779–14 Feb 1795	Johann Heinrich Kasimir (from 1798: Count) von Carmer

*There were often two or more chief ministers at the same time.

4 *Brunswick*

HEADS OF STATE
Dukes
1635–66	August II
1666–1704	Rudolf August
1685–1714	Anton Ulrich (co-ruler)
1714–31	August Wilhelm
1731–5	Ludwig Rudolf
1735	Ferdinand Albrecht
1735–80	Karl
1780–1806	Karl Wilhelm Ferdinand

5 *Cologne*

HEADS OF STATE
Electors and Archbishops
12 May 1612–13 Sep 1650	Ferdinand, Prince of Bavaria, son of Duke Wilhelm V; from 18 Dec 1596: co-adjutor; b. 6 Oct 1577
26 Oct 1650–3 Jun 1688	Maximilian Heinrich, Prince of Bavaria, nephew; from 17 May 1642: co-adjutor
19 Jul 1688	Josef Klemens, Prince of Bavaria, brother of the Elector Maximilian II, b. 5 Dec 1671
6 Feb 1761	Maximilian Friedrich, Count Königseck und Rothenfels
15 Apr 1784–27 Jul 1801	Maximilian Franz, Archduke of Austria, son of the Emperor Francis I, b. 8 Dec 1756

6 *Courland and Semigallia*

HEADS OF STATE
28 Nov 1561	After Livonia was annexed by Poland, the territory south of the Duna was made a hereditary duchy under the last Master of the Teutonic Knights, who did homage on 5 March 1562

Dukes
House of Kettler
17 Aug 1641	Jakob, son of William, b. 28 Oct 1610
1 Jan 1682	Friedrich Kazimir, son, b. 1650

22 Jan 1698	Friedrich Wilhelm, son, b. 19 Jul 1692
1698–1710	Council of Regency under the leadership of:
	1698–1701: Christoph Heinrich von Puttkamer
	1701–8: Friedrich von Brackel-Kuckschen, b. 1634
	1708–10: Heinrich Christian von der Bricken-Sessilen
21 Jan 1711– 1737	Ferdinand, uncle of Friedrich Wilhelm, b. 1655

House of Biron

| 13 Jul 1737 | Ernst Johann (originally Bühren), exiled 1740–63; b. 1 Dec 1690 |
| 24 Nov 1769– 28 Mar 1795 | Peter, son, b. 15 Feb 1724 |

7 *East Friesland*

HEADS OF STATE

Counts

1628–48	Ulric II
1648–60	Enno Ludwig
1660–5	Georg Christian
1665–1708	Christian Eberhard
1708–34	Georg Albricht
1734–44	Carl Edzard, Prince of East Friesland

8 *Hanover*

HEADS OF STATE

Dukes

2 Dec 1641	Frederick, brother of George; from 1 Oct 1636–10 Dec 1648: Duke of Celle; b. 24 Aug 1574
10 Dec 1648	George William, nephew, from 15 Mar 1665–28 Aug 1705: Duke of Celle; b. 16 Jan 1624
15 Mar 1665	John Frederick, brother, Duke of Calenberg and Hanover; b. 25 Apr 1625
20 Dec 1679	Ernest Augustus I, brother; from 1692: Elector; b. 20 Nov 1630

Electors

| 23 Dec 1698 | George I, son; from 1 Aug 1714: King of England, through mother, Sophia, granddaughter of James I of England; b. 28 May 1660 |

22 Jun 1727   George II, son, King of England, b. 30 Oct 1683
25 Oct 1760   George III, grandson; from 1815: King of Hanover; b. 4 Jun
               1738

9 Hesse–Cassel

HEADS OF STATE
Landgraves
1637–63   Wilhelm VI
1663–70   Wilhelm VII
1670–1730   Karl
1730–51   Friedrich I
1751–60   Wilhelm VIII
1760–85   Friedrich II
1785–1803   Wilhelm IX

10 Hesse–Darmstadt

HEADS OF STATE
Dukes
27 Jun 1626   Georg II, son of Ludwig V, b. 7 Mar 1605
11 Jun 1661   Ludwig VI, son, b. 25 Jan 1630
24 Apr 1678   Ludwig VII, son, b. 22 Jun 1658
31 Aug 1678   Ernst Ludwig, brother, b. 15 Dec 1667
12 Sep 1738   Ludwig VIII, son, b. 5 Apr 1691
17 Oct 1768   Grand Duke Ludwig IX

11 Mainz

HEADS OF STATE
Electors and Archbishops
19 Nov 1647–12 Feb 1673   Johann Philipp, Count Schönborn
13 Feb 1673   Lothar Friedrich, Baron Metternich
 3 Jul 1675–6 Dec 1678   Damian Hartrad von der Leyen
 9 Jan–26 Sep 1679   Karl Heinrich, Baron Metternich
 7 Nov 1679   Anselm Franz von Ingelheim
30 Mar 1695–30 Jan 1729   Lothar Franz, Count Schönborn
 7 Apr 1729–18 Apr 1732   Franz Ludwig, brother of Elector Palatine
                           Karl Philipp
 9 Jun 1732–20 Mar 1743   Philipp Karl, Baron Eltz

22 Apr 1743–4 Jun 1763	Johann Friedrich Karl, Count Ostein
5 Jul 1763–11 Jun 1774	Emmerich Josef, Baron Breidbach
18 Jul 1774–25 Jul 1802	Friedrich Karl Josef, Baron Erthal

12 *Mecklenburg*

HEADS OF STATE
Duke

1636–95	Gustav Adolf

13 *Mecklenburg–Schwerin*

HEADS OF STATE
Dukes

1592–1658	Adolf Friedrich I
1658–88	Christian Ludwig I
1688–1713	Friedrich Wilhelm
1713–47	Carl Leopold
1747–56	Christian Ludwig II
1756–85	Friedrich
1785–1837	Friedrich Franz I

14 *Mecklenburg–Strelitz*

HEADS OF STATE
Grand Dukes

1658–1708	Adolf Friedrich
1708–52	Friedrich III
1752–94	Adolf

15 *Rhenish Palatinate*

HEADS OF STATE
Electors
Pfalz–Simmern line

23 Feb 1623– 24 Oct 1648	The Palatinate subject to the Elector Maximilian I of Bavaria until the Peace of Westphalia
24 Oct 1648	Karl I, son of Friedrich V, b. 22 Dec 1617
28 Aug 1680	Karl II, son, b. 31 Mar 1651

Pfalz–Neuburg line

16 May 1685	Philip Wilhelm, son of Wolfgang Wilhelm of Pfalz-Neuburg, ruled in Neuburg from 20 Mar 1653; b. 25 Nov 1615
2 Sep 1690	Johann Wilhelm, son, b. 19 Apr 1658

Pfalz–Sulzbach line

31 Dec 1742	Karl Theodor, son of Johann Christian of Pfalz-Sulzbach, ruled in Sulzbach from 20 Jul 1733 and inherited Bavaria on the death of Maximilian III, 30 Dec 1777; b. 11 Dec 1724

16 *Saxony*

HEADS OF STATE

Electors

Albertine line

26 Jun 1611	John George I, brother of Christian II, b. 6 Mar 1585
8 Oct 1656	John George II, son, b. 31 Mar 1613
22 Aug 1680	John George III, b. 20 Jun 1647
12 Sep 1691	John George IV, son, b. 18 Oct 1668
27 Apr 1694	Frederick Augustus I, brother; King Augustus II, the Strong, of Poland from 17 Jun 1696; b. 12 May 1670
1 Feb 1733	Frederick Augustus II, son; King Augustus III of Poland from 14 Aug 1733; b. 17 Oct 1696
5 Oct 1763	Frederick Christian, son, b. 5 Sep 1722
17 Dec 1763	Frederick Augustus III, the Just, son; King Frederick Augustus I from 11 Dec 1806; b. 23 Dec 1750
	17 Dec 1763–15 Sep 1768: Prince Xavier, uncle, Regent

17 *Württemberg*

HEADS OF STATE

Dukes

18 Jul 1628	Eberhard III, son of Johann Friedrich, b. 16 Aug 1614
2 Jul 1674	Wilhelm Ludwig, son, b. 7 Jan 1647
23 Jun 1677	Eberhard Ludwig, son, b. 18 Sep 1676; Regency of his uncle, Duke Frederick Charles, 1677–93
31 Oct 1733	Karl Alexander, cousin, b. 24 Jan 1684
12 Mar 1737	Karl Eugen, son, b. 11 Feb 1728
24 Oct 1793	Ludwig Eugen, brother, b. 6 Jan 1731

GREAT BRITAIN*

HEADS OF STATE
Kings and Queens
House of Stuart

27 Mar 1625–30 Jan 1649	Charles I, son of James I, b. 19 Nov 1600; d. (executed) 30 Jan 1649
30 Jan 1649–12 Dec 1653	All powers exercised by Parliament, which abolished the monarchy 19 Mar 1649

Lord Protectors

16 Dec 1653–3 Sep 1658	Oliver Cromwell, b. 25 Apr 1559
3 Sep 1658–25 May 1659	Richard Cromwell, son, b. 4 Oct 1626; d. 12 Jul 1712; resigned
1 May 1660	Parliament resolved to restore the monarchy

Kings and Queens
House of Stuart

1 May 1660	Charles II, son of Charles I, b. 29 May 1630; king in exile from 30 Jan 1649; returned to England 29 May 1660
6 Feb 1685–Dec 1688	James II, brother, b. 14 Oct 1633; d. 16 Sep 1701; left England 25 Dec 1688 and declared by Parliament to have abdicated
12 Feb 1689–8 Mar 1702	William III of Orange, Stadholder of Holland (b. 4 Nov 1650) and his wife, Mary II, daughter of James II (b. 30 Apr 1662, d. 28 Dec 1694)
8 Mar 1702–1 Aug 1714	Anne, sister of Mary II, b. 6 Feb 1665; also Queen of Scotland
1 May 1707	Union of England and Scotland to form Great Britain

House of Hanover

1 Aug 1714–11 Jun 1727	George I, b. 28 May 1660; Elector of Hanover, great-grandson of James I
11 Jun 1727–25 Oct 1760	George II, son, b. 30 Oct 1683, Elector of Hanover

*England, Scotland, Ireland, Wales (England until 1707). Dates before 14 Sep 1752 are given according to the Julian calendar but the year begins at all times on 1 Jan ('new style').

25 Oct 1760–29 Jan 1820   George III, grandson, b. 4 Jun 1738; Elector (from 1815: King) of Hanover; incurably ill from 1811, the Prince of Wales (later King George IV) acting as Regent

KEY MINISTERS
Date of taking office
Chancellors and Keepers of the Great Seal

30 Aug 1645	Sir Richard Lane, Lord Keeper
6 Apr 1653	Sir Edward Herbert
13 Jan 1658	Sir Edward Hyde, 1st Lord Hyde (1660), 1st Earl of Clarendon (1661)
1642–60	The Parliamentary and Protectorate great seal was in the hands of various commissioners who were neither chancellors nor keepers.
1660	Lord Hyde
30 Aug 1667	Sir Orlando Bridgman, Lord Keeper
17 Nov 1672	Anthony Ashley Cooper, 1st Lord Ashley (1661), 1st Earl of Shaftesbury (April 1672)
9 Nov 1673	Sir Heneage Finch, 1st Lord Finch of Daventry (1674), Earl of Nottingham (1681), Lord Keeper until 19 Dec 1675 when he became Lord Chancellor
20 Dec 1682	Sir Francis North, Lord Keeper, created Lord Guilford (1683)
1685	Lord Guilford remained in office until his death on 4 Sep 1685
28 Sep 1685	George Jeffreys, 1st Lord Jeffreys (May 1685)
1689–93	The seal in commission
23 Mar 1693	Sir John Somers, 1st Lord Somers 1697, Lord Keeper until 22 Apr 1697 when he became Lord Chancellor
27 Apr 1700	The seal in commission
21 May 1700	Sir Nathan Wright, Lord Keeper
11 Oct 1705	William Cowper, Lord Keeper, 1st Lord Cowper (1706), created Viscount Fordwiche and Earl Cowper (1718)
4 May 1707	Lord Cowper became 1st Lord Chancellor of Great Britain. (Act of Union came into force 1 May 1707)
29 Sep 1708	The seal in commission.
19 Oct 1710	Sir Simon Harcourt, Lord Keeper, 1st Lord Harcourt (1711), 1st Viscount Harcourt (1721)
7 Apr 1713	Lord Harcourt became Lord Chancellor
21 Sep 1714	Lord Cowper
Apr 1718	The seal in commission

12 May 1718	Thomas Parker, 1st Lord Macclesfield (1716), created Earl of Macclesfield (1721). Impeached in 1725
1 Jun 1725	Peter King, 1st Lord King (29 May 1725)
29 Nov 1727	Charles Talbot, 1st Lord Talbot of Hensol (5 Dec 1733)
21 Feb 1737	Philip Yorke, 1st Lord Hardwicke (1733), 1st Earl of Hardwicke (1754)
20 Nov 1756	The seal in commission
30 Jun 1757	Sir Robert Henley, Lord Keeper, 1st Lord Henley (1760), 1st Earl of Northington (1764)
16 Jan 1761	Lord Henley, who had remained in office, delivered up the seal and received it back with the title of Lord Chancellor
30 Jul 1766	Charles Pratt, 1st Lord Camden (1765), 1st Earl Camden (1786)
17 Jan 1770	Hon. Charles Yorke
20 Jan 1770	The seal in commission
23 Jan 1771	Henry Bathurst, 1st Lord Apsley (24 Jan 1771), 2nd Earl Bathurst (1775)
3 Jun 1778	Edward Thurlow, 1st Lord Thurlow (3 June 1778) until 7 Apr 1783
9 Apr 1783	The seal in commission
23 Dec 1783	Lord Thurlow reappointed
Jun 1792	The seal in commission

Lord Treasurers and Lord Commissioners of the Treasury
Civil War and Interregnum
(Financial system in abeyance, 1642–54)

1654–8	*Commissioners*: John Lisle; William Matham; Edward Montagu; Henry Rolle; Oliver St John; William Sydenham; Bulstrode Whitelocke; Sir Thomas Widdrington
1658–9	*Commissioners*: Edward, Lord Montagu; William, Lord Sydenham; Bulstrode, Lord Whitelocke; Sir Thomas Widdrington
1659–60	*Parliamentary Commissioners*: John Blackwell; John Clerke; John Disbrowe; Cornelius Holland; Richard Salway; William Sydenham

Charles II

1660	*First Lord*: Sir Edward Hyde (afterwards Earl of Clarendon, 1661)
	Commissioners: Thomas, Lord Colepepper; George Monck (afterwards Duke of Albemarle); Admiral Edward Montagu (afterwards Earl of Sandwich); Sir William Morrice; Sir Edward Nicholas; John, Lord Robarts; Thomas, Earl of Southampton

1660–7   *Lord Treasurer*: (from 8 Sep 1660) Thomas, Earl of Southampton

1667–9   *First Lord*: George Monck, Duke of Albemarle
         Commissioners: Anthony, Lord Ashley; Sir Thomas Clifford; Sir William Coventry; Sir John Duncombe

1669–72   Same, but without Sir William Coventry

1672–3   *Lord Treasurer*: (from 28 Nov 1672) Thomas, Lord Clifford

1673–9   *Lord Treasurer*: (From 19 Jun 1673) Sir Thomas Osborne, Viscount Latimer (later Earl of Danby, 1674)

1679   *First Lord*: (Mar–Nov) Arthur, Earl of Essex
         Commissioners: Sir Edward Dering; Sir John Ernley; Sidney Godolphin; Hon. Laurence Hyde

1679–84   *First Lord*: (from 19 Nov 1679) Laurence Hyde (afterwards Earl of Rochester, 1682)
         Commissioners: Sir Edward Dering; Sir John Ernley; Sir Stephen Fox; Sidney Godolphin

1684–5   *First Lord*: (from 25 Aug 1684) Sidney, Lord Godolphin
         Commissioners: Sir John Ernley; Sir Stephen Fox; Sir Dudley North; Henry Frederick Thynne

James II

1685–6   *Lord Treasurer*: (from 16 Feb 1685) Laurence, Earl of Rochester

1687–8   *First Lord*: (from 5 Jan 1687) John, Lord Belasyse
         Commissioners: Henry, Lord Dover; Sir John Ernley; Sir Stephen Fox

William III

1689–90   *First Lord*: (from 8 Apr 1689) Charles, Earl of Monmouth
         Commissioners: Sir Henry Capell; Henry, Lord Delamere; Sidney, Lord Godolphin; Richard Hampden

1690   *First Lord*: (19 Mar–Nov) Sir John Lowther (later Viscount Lonsdale, 1696)
         Commissioners: Sir Stephen Fox; Richard Hampden; Thomas Pelham

1690–1   *First Lord*: (from 15 Nov 1690) Sidney, Lord Godolphin
         Commissioners: same as above

1691–4   *First Lord*: Sidney, Lord Godolphin
         Commissioners: Sir Stephen Fox; Richard Hampden; Charles Montague; Sir Edward Seymour

1694–5   *First Lord*: Sidney, Lord Godolphin
         Commissioners: Sir Stephen Fox; Charles Montague; John Smith; Sir William Trumbull

1695   The same, without Sir William Trumbull.

1696   The same, with Sir Thomas Lyttleton.

1697–9   *First Lord*: (from 1 May 1697) Charles Montague (afterwards Earl of Halifax, 14 Oct 1714)

               Commissioners: Sir Stephen Fox, John Smith, Sir Thomas Lyttleton

1699–   *First Lord*: (from 15 Nov 1699) Ford Grey, 1st Earl of Tanker-
1700   ville

1700–1   *First Lord*: (from 12 Dec 1700) Sidney Godolphin

1701–2   *First Lord*: (from 27 Dec 1701) Charles Howard, Earl of Carlisle

Anne

1702–10   *Lord Treasurer*: (from 6 May 1702) Sidney, Lord Godolphin

1710–11   *First Lord*: (from 11 Aug 1710) John, Earl of Paulett

               Commissioners: Robert Benson, Robert Harley, Sir Thomas Mansell; Hon. Henry Paget

1711–14   *First Lord*: (from 29 Mar 1711) Robert Harley, Earl of Oxford

1714   *First Lord*: (30 Jul) Charles Talbot, Duke of Shrewsbury

George I

1714–15   *First Lord*: (from 11 Oct 1714) Charles Montagu, Earl of Halifax (died 19 May 1715)

1715   *First Lord*: (23 May) Charles Howard, Earl of Carlisle

1715–17   *First Lord*: (from 12 Oct 1715) Sir Robert Walpole

1717–18   *First Lord*: (from 12 Apr 1717) James, Viscount (afterwards Earl) Stanhope

1718–21   *First Lord*: (from 21 Mar 1718) Charles Spencer, 3rd Earl of Sunderland

1721–42   *First Lord*: (from 4 Apr 1721) Sir Robert Walpole (afterwards first Earl of Orford, 1742)

George II (from 1727)

1742–3   *First Lord*: (from 16 Feb 1742) Spencer Compton, Earl of Wilmington

1743–54   *First Lord*: (from 27 Aug 1743) Henry Pelham

1754–6   *First Lord*: (from 16 Mar 1754) Thomas Pelham, Duke of Newcastle

1756–7   *First Lord*: (from 16 Nov 1757) William Cavendish, 2nd Duke of Devonshire

1757–62   *First Lord*: (from 2 July 1757) Duke of Newcastle

George III (from 1760)

1762–3   *First Lord*: (from 26 May 1762) James Stuart, 3rd Earl of Bute

1763–5	*First Lord*: (from 16 Apr 1763) George Grenville
1765–6	*First Lord*: (from 13 Jul 1765) Charles Wentworth, 2nd Marquess of Rockingham
1766–8	*First Lord*: (from 30 Jul 1766) William Pitt, Earl of Chatham
1768–70	*First Lord*: (from 14 Oct 1768) Augustus Henry Fitzroy, 3rd Duke of Grafton
1770–82	*First Lord*: (from 28 Jan 1770) Frederick, Lord North
1782	*First Lord*: (27 Mar) Marquess of Rockingham
1782–3	*First Lord*: (from 11 Jul 1782) William Petty-Fitzmaurice, 2nd Earl of Shelburne
1783	*First Lord*: (2 Apr) William Cavendish-Bentinck, 3rd Duke of Portland
1783– 1801	*First Lord*: (from 19 Dec 1783) William Pitt and Younger

Chancellors and Under-Treasurers of the Exchequer from 1714

1714	Sir William Wyndham
1714–15	(from 13 Oct 1714) Sir Richard Onslow (afterwards first Lord Onslow)
1715–17	(from 12 Apr 1715) Sir Robert Walpole
1717–18	(from 15 Apr) James Stanhope (afterwards Earl of Stanhope)
1718–21	(from 21 Mar) John Aislabie
1721	(21 Feb) Sir John Pratt
1721–42	(from 3 Apr 1721) Sir Robert Walpole
1742–3	(from 12 Feb 1742) Samuel Sandys, first Lord Sandys
1743–54	(from 12 Dec 1743) Henry Pelham
1754	(8 Mar) Sir William Lee
1754–5	(from 6 Apr 1754) Henry Bilson Legge
1755–6	(from 25 Nov 1755) Sir George Lyttleton (afterwards first Lord Lyttleton)
1756–7	(from 16 Nov 1756) Henry Bilson Legge
1757	(13 Apr) William Murray, first Lord Mansfield
1757–61	(from 2 Jul 1757) Henry Bilson Legge
1761–2	(from 19 Mar 1761) William Wildman Barrington-Shute, 2nd Viscount Barrington
1762–3	(from 29 Mar 1762) Sir Francis Dashwood (afterwards Lord le Despencer)
1763–5	(from 16 Apr 1763) George Grenville
1765–6	(from 16 Jul 1765) William Dowdeswell
1766–7	(from 2 Aug 1766) Charles Townshend
1767	(11 Sep) Lord Mansfield (Chancellor of Exchequer only)
1767–82	(from 6 Oct) Frederick, Lord North (afterwards 4th Earl of Guildford, 1790)

1782	(1 Apr) Lord John Cavendish
1782–3	(from 13 Jul 1782) William Pitt the Younger
1783	(5 Apr) Lord John Cavendish
1783– 1801	(from 27 Dec 1783) William Pitt the Younger

1 *England*

KEY MINISTERS

Principal Secretaries of State

1643	George Digby, 2nd Earl of Bristol (1653)
	INTERREGNUM
1 Jun 1660	Sir Edward Nicholas
30 Jun 1660	Sir William Morice
20 Oct 1662	Sir Henry Bennet, 1st Lord Arlington (1665), 1st Earl of Arlington (1672)
Sep 1668	Sir John Trevor (Northern department)
8 Jul 1672	Henry Coventry (Northern till 1674), then Southern till 1680)
Sep 1674	Sir Joseph Williamson (Northern)
20 Feb 1679	Robert Spencer, 2nd Earl of Sunderland (Northern till Apr 1680, then Southern till 1681)
26 Apr 1680	Sir Leoline Jenkins (Northern till Feb 1681, then Southern till 1684)
2 Feb 1681	Edward Conway, 1st Earl of Conway (Northern)
28 Jan 1683	Earl of Sunderland (Northern till Apr 1684, then Southern till 1688)
14 Apr 1684	Sidney Godolphin, 1st Lord Godolphin (1684), 1st Earl of Godolphin (1706) (Northern)
24 Aug 1684	Charles Middleton, 2nd Earl of Middleton (Scot., 1673) (Northern till 1688, S. Oct 1688)
28 Oct 1688	Richard Graham, 1st Viscount Preston (Scot.) (Northern)

The official division into Northern and Southern departments begins here

	Northern	*Southern*
14 Feb 1689		Charles Talbot, 12th Earl of Shrewsbury; Duke of Shrewsbury (1694); vacated office 2 Jun 1690
5 Mar 1689	Daniel Finch, 2nd Earl of Nottingham; 7th Earl of Winchilsea (1729)	

2 Jun 1690	Earl of Nottingham sole Secretary	
26 Dec 1690	Henry Sydney, 1st Viscount Sydney of Sheppey; 1st Earl of Sheppey (1694)	Earl of Nottingham
3 Mar 1692	Earl of Nottingham sole Secretary	
23 Mar 1693	Sir John Trenchard	Earl of Nottingham, dismissed Nov 1693
Nov 1693	Sir John Trenchard sole Secretary	
2 Mar 1694	Earl of Shrewsbury	Sir John Trenchard, died 27 Apr 1695
3 May 1695	Sir William Trumbull	Duke of Shrewsbury, appointed late Apr; vacated office 12 Dec 1698
2 Dec 1698	James Vernon	
12 Dec 1698	James Vernon sole Secretary	
14 May 1699	James Vernon	Edward Villiers, 1st Earl of Jersey; dismissed 27 June 1700
27 Jun 1700	James Vernon sole Secretary	
5 Nov 1700	Sir Charles Hedges; dismissed 29 Dec 1701	James Vernon
4 Jan 1702	James Vernon; dismissed 1 May 1702	Charles Montagu, 4th Earl of Manchester; 1st Duke of Manchester (1719); dismissed 1 May 1702
2 May 1702	Sir Charles Hedges	Earl of Nottingham; vacated office on or shortly before 22 Apr 1704
18 May 1704	Robert Harley, 1st Earl of Oxford and Mortimer (1711). Vacated office 13 Feb 1708	Sir Charles Hedges; dismissed Dec 1706
3 Dec 1706		Charles Spencer, 3rd Earl of Sunderland; dismissed 13–14 Jun 1710
13 Feb 1708	Henry Boyle, 1st Lord Carleton (1714). Vacated office Sep 1710	

15 Jun 1710		William Legge, 2nd Lord Dartmouth, 1st Earl of Dartmouth (1711); vacated office 6–13 Aug 1713
21 Sep 1710	Henry St John, 1st Viscount Bolingbroke (1712)	
17 Aug 1713	William Bromley; dismissed Sep 1714	Viscount Bolingbroke; dismissed 31 Aug 1714
17 Sep 1714	Charles Townshend, 2nd Viscount Townshend; dismissed early in Dec 1716	
27 Sep 1714		James Stanhope, 1st Viscount Stanhope (1717), Earl of Stanhope (1718)
22 Jun 1716		Paul Methuen; appointed to act in Stanhope's absence; remained S. Sec. after 12 Dec 1716
12 Dec 1716	James Stanhope	Paul Methuen; vacated office 10 Apr 1717
15–16 Apr 1717	Earl of Sunderland; vacated office 2 Mar 1718	Joseph Addison; vacated office 14 Mar 1718
16 Mar 1718		James Craggs; died 16 Feb 1721
18–21 Mar 1718	Viscount Stanhope; died 5 Feb 1721	
10 Feb 1721	Viscount Townshend; vacated office 16 May 1730 (Sir Robert Walpole, appointed 29 May 1723, acted in the king's absence 5 Jun–28 Dec 1723)	
5 Mar 1721		John Carteret, 2nd Lord Carteret; 2nd Earl of Granville (1744); dismissed 3 Apr 1724
6 Apr 1724		Thomas Pelham-Holles, 1st Duke of Newcastle upon Tyne (1715); vacated office 10 Feb 1746
19 Jun 1730	William Stanhope, Lord Harrington (1730), Earl of Harrington (1742); vacated office 12 Feb 1742	

21

12 Feb 1742	Lord Carteret; vacated office 24 Nov 1744	
24 Nov 1744	Earl of Harrington; vacated office 10 Feb 1746	
10 Feb 1746	Earl of Granville sole Secretary	
14 Feb 1746	Earl of Harrington; vacated office 28 Oct 1746	Duke of Newcastle
29 Oct 1746	Philip Dormer Stanhope, 4th Earl of Chesterfield; vacated office 6 Feb 1748	
6–12 Feb 1748	Duke of Newcastle; vacated office Mar 1754	John Russell, 7th Duke of Bedford; vacated office 13 Jun 1751
18 Jun 1751		Robert Darcy, 4th Earl of Holdernesse
23 Mar 1754	Earl of Holdernesse; vacated office 9 Jun 1757	Sir Thomas Robinson, 1st Lord Grantham (1761); vacated office Oct 1755
14 Nov 1755		Henry Fox, 1st Lord Holland of Foxley (1763); vacated office 13 Nov 1756
4 Dec 1756		William Pitt, 1st Earl of Chatham (1766); dismissed 6 Apr 1757
27 Jun 1757		William Pitt reappointed; vacated office 5 Oct 1761
29 Jun 1757	Earl of Holdernesse reappointed; vacated office 12 Mar 1761	
25 Mar 1761	John Stuart, 3rd Earl of Bute (Scot.); vacated office May 1762	
9 Oct 1761		Charles Wyndham, 2nd Earl of Egremont; died 21 Aug 1763
27 May 1762	George Grenville; vacated office on or about 9 Oct 1762	
14 Oct 1762	George Montague-Dunk, 2nd Earl of Halifax	
9 Sep 1763	John Montagu, 4th Earl of Sandwich; dismissed July 1765	Earl of Halifax; dismissed 10 July 1765

10–12 Jul 1765	Augustus Henry FitzRoy, 3rd Duke of Grafton; vacated office 14 May 1766	Henry Seymour Conway
23 May 1766	Henry Seymour Conway; vacated office 20 Jan 1768	Charles Lennox, 8th Duke of Richmond; dismissed 29 July 1766
30 Jul 1766		William Fitz-Maurice Petty, 2nd Earl of Shelburne (Irish) and 2nd Lord Wycombe; 1st Marquess of Lansdowne (1784); vacated office 19–20 Oct 1768
20 Jan 1768	Thomas Thynne, 3rd Viscount Weymouth; 1st Marquess of Bath (1789)	
21 Oct 1768	William Henry Nassau de Zuylestein, 4th Earl of Rochford	Viscount Weymouth; vacated office 12–17 Dec 1770
19 Dec 1770	Earl of Sandwich; vacated office 12 Jan 1771	Earl of Rochford; vacated office 9 Nov 1775
22 Jan 1771	Earl of Halifax; died 6 Jun 1771	
12 Jun 1771	Henry Howard, 12th Earl of Suffolk and 5th Earl of Berkshire; died 7 Mar 1777	
9 Nov 1775		Viscount Weymouth
7 Mar 1779	Viscount Weymouth sole Secretary until 27 Oct	
27 Oct 1779	David Murray, 7th Viscount Stormont (Scot.); vacated office Mar 1782	Viscount Weymouth; vacated office 24 Nov 1779
24 Nov 1779		Wills Hill, Earl of Hillsborough, 1st Marquess of Downshire (Irish, 1789); vacated office Mar 1782

In Mar 1782 the secretariat was reorganised.

Secretaries of State for the Home Department
27 Mar 1782   William Petty, 3rd Earl of Shelburne (Irish) and 2nd Lord Wycombe

10 Jul 1782   Thomas Townshend, 1st Lord Sydney of Chiselhurst (1783)
2 Apr 1783   Frederick North, commonly called Lord North
19 Dec 1783   George Nugent-Temple-Grenville, 3rd Earl Temple
23 Dec 1783   Lord Sydney
5 Jun 1789   William Wyndham Grenville, 1st Lord Grenville (1790)
8 Jun 1791   Henry Dundas

Secretaries of State for Foreign Affairs

27 Mar 1782   Charles James Fox
17 Jul 1782   Thomas Robinson, 2nd Lord Grantham
2 Apr 1783   Charles James Fox
19 Dec 1783   George Nugent-Temple-Grenville, 3rd Earl Temple
23 Dec 1783   Francis Godolphin Osborne, commonly called Marquess of Carmarthen, 5th Duke of Leeds (1789)
8 Jun 1791   William Wyndham Grenville, 1st Lord Grenville (1790)

2 Scotland

KEY MINISTERS
Chancellors
30 Sep 1641   John Campbell, 1st Earl of Loudoun
19 Jan 1661   William Cunningham, 8th Earl of Glencairn; died 30 May 1664
14 Oct 1664   John Leslie, 7th Earl of Rothes, 1st Duke of Rothes (1680)
16 Apr 1667   Earl of Rothes appointed chancellor, died 27 Jul 1681
1 May 1682   Sir George Gordon of Haddo, 1st Earl of Aberdeen (1682)
13 Jun 1684   James Drummond, 4th Earl of Perth (remained in office until the Revolution)
1689–92   Seal in commission
5 Jan 1692   John Hay, 2nd Earl of Tweeddale, 1st Marquess of Tweeddale (1694)
2 May 1696   Patrick Hume, 1st Lord Polwarth, 1st Earl of Marchmont (1697)
21 Nov 1702   James Ogilvy, 1st Earl of Seafield
17 Oct 1704   John Hay, 2nd Marquess of Tweeddale
9 Mar 1705   James Ogilvy, 1st Earl of Seafield, remained in office after the Union until appointed Lord Chief Baron of Exchequer in Scotland 25 May 1708, given title of chancellor again 14 Sep 1713; died 15 Aug 1730

HABSBURG EMPIRE*

HEADS OF STATE
Archdukes
House of Habsburg

15 Feb 1637–2 Apr 1657	Ferdinand III; from 7 Dec 1625: King of Hungary; from 12 Dec 1636: King of the Romans; from 12 Feb 1637: Holy Roman Emperor; b. 13 Jul 1608
18 Jul 1658–5 May 1705	Leopold I, son; from 27 Jun 1655 to 9 Dec 1687: King of Hungary; from 18 Jul 1658: Holy Roman Emperor; b. 9 Jun 1640
5 May 1705–17 Apr 1711	Joseph I, son; from 9 Dec 1687: King of Hungary; from 24 Aug 1690: King of the Romans; from 5 May 1705: Holy Roman Emperor; b. 26 Jul 1678
17 Apr 1711–20 Oct 1740	Charles VI, brother; from 12 Oct 1711: Holy Roman Emperor Charles VI; from 22 May 1712: King Charles III of Hungary; b. 1 Oct 1685
20 Oct 1740–29 Nov 1780	(Archduchess) Maria Theresa, daughter; from 20 Oct 1740: Queen of Hungary; married to Francis of Lorraine, subsequently Holy Roman Emperor Francis I; b. 13 May 1717

House of Habsburg–Lorraine

29 Nov 1780–20 Feb 1790	Joseph II, son; from 27 Mar 1764: King of the Romans; from 18 Aug 1765: Holy Roman Emperor; from 29 Nov 1780: King of Hungary; b. 13 Mar 1741

KEY MINISTERS

1634–50	Max, Count Trauttmannsdorff, Head of Privy Council
1650–7	Johann Weikard, Prince Auersperg
1669–74	Václar Euseb, Count Lobkovic, President of State Council
1683–93	Theodor, Count Strattmann, Lord Chancellor
1698–1706	Ferdinand Bonaventura, Count Harrach, Lord Chamberlain and Head of State Council

*Includes Austria, Bohemia, Silesia and Serbia-Croatia; Hungary and Italian possessions treated separately.

1705-12   Jan Václav, Count of Vratislav, Chancellor of Bohemia and member of State Council

1727-53   Anton Corfiz, Count Uhlefeld, Lord Chancellor

1753-92   Wenzel Anton, Count Kaunitz (from 1764: Prince) Kaunitz-Rietburg, Lord Chamberlain and Chancellor

HOLLAND (UNITED PROVINCES)

HEADS OF STATE
House of Orange

14 Mar 1647–6 Nov 1650	William II, son of Frederick Henry, b. 27 May 1626
2 Jul 1672–8 Mar 1702	William III, son; from 12 Feb 1689 King of England in conjunction with his wife Mary; b. 4 Nov 1650
4 May 1747	William IV, son of Prince John William of Nassau, of the line of the Stadholder of Friesland; b. 1 Sep 1711
22 Oct 1751	William V, son, b. 8 Mar 1748
16 May 1795	Batavian republic (under control of France)

Stadholders of Friesland

2 Jul 1640	William Frederick (from 1654: Prince of Nassau–Diez), brother of Henry Casimir I; b. 7 Aug 1613
21 Oct 1664	Henry Casimir II, son, b. 18 Jan 1657
15 Mar 1696	John William, son, b. 4 Aug 1687
1711–22 Oct 1751	William (from 1747: William IV, Hereditary Stadholder of the Netherlands) (see above)

Stadholders of the Burgundian, from 1504 Spanish, and from 1714 Austrian Netherlands

1647–1656	Leopold Wilhelm, son of Emperor Ferdinand II, b. 6 Jan 1614
1656–Mar 1659	John of Austria, son of King Philip IV of Spain, b. 7 Apr 1629
1659–Sep 1664	Luis de Benavides Carillo, Marquis Franiata, d. 1668
1664–Sep 1668	Francisco de Moura-Cortereal, Marquis of Castel Rodrigo, d. 1675
1668–Jul 1670	Inigo Fernández de Valesco y Tovar, Duke of Feria

1670–Feb 1675	Juan Domingo de Maro Duke of Monterrey, d. 1716
1675–Dec 1677	Carlos de Aragón de Gurrea Borja y Aragón, Duke of Villahermosa, d. 14 Aug 1692
1678–82	Alessandero, son of Duke Odoardo I of Parma, b. 1635
1682–85	Ottone Hernrico dal Carreto, Marquis of Grana
1685–92	Francisco Antonio de Agurto, Marquis of Gastañaga
1692–1706	Maximilian II of Bavaria, son of Duke Ferdinand of Bavaria, b. 11 Jul 1662
22 Mar 1701–7 Oct 1704	Isidor de la Cueba, Marquis of Bedmar, Deputy of the foregoing
1706–7 Mar 1714	Administration by a Council of State
1716–Dec 1724	Eugene, Prince of Savoy, son of Prince Eugene Maurice of Savoy, b. 18 Oct 1663
1725–26 Aug 1741	Marie Elisabeth, daughter of Emperor Leopold I, b. 13 Dec 1680
1741–4 Jul 1780	Friedrich August, Count Harrach-Rohrau
1744–4 Jul 1780	Marie Anna, daughter of Emperor Charles VI; from 7 Jan 1744 married to Karl Alexander Emanuel, brother of Emperor Francis I; b. 14 Sep 1718
1781–93	Christine, daughter of Emperor Francis I, from 8 Apr 1766 married to Albert, Duke of Teschen, son of Prince Friedrich August II of Saxony; b. 13 May 1742

KEY MINISTERS
Grand Pensionaries

4 Jun 1636–1651	Jacob Cats (for 2nd time), b. 10 Nov 1577
27 Sep 1651–21 Feb 1653	Adriaan Pauw (for 2nd time), b. 1 Nov 1585
23 Jul 1653–4 Aug 1672	Johan de Witt, b. 24 Sep 1625
20 Aug 1672–15 Dec 1688	Caspar Fagel, b. Jan 1634
23 Dec 1688	(acting:) Michel ten Hove
24 Mar 1689–3 Aug 1720	Anthonie Heinsius, b. 23 Nov 1641
12 Sep 1720–17 Jun 1727	Isaak van Hoornbeek, b. 1653/6
17 Jul 1727–1 Dec 1736	Simon van Slingelandt, b. 14 Jan 1664
4 Apr 1737–1746	Anthonie van der Heim, b. 1693
23 Sep 1746–1749	Joacob Gilles
12 Jun 1749–5 Nov 1772	Pieter Steyn, b. 6 Oct 1706

1 Dec 1772–Nov 1787   Pieter van Bleiswijk, b. 1724
9 Nov 1787–Jan 1795   Laurens Pieter van de Spiegel, b. 19 Jan 1737

HUNGARY

HEADS OF STATE

Kings

House of Habsburg

16 Jun 1647– 9 Jul 1654	Ferdinand IV, son of Ferdinand III, b. 8 Sep 1633
27 Jun 1655	Leopold I, brother, b. 9 Jun 1640
9 Dec 1687– 17 Jun 1711	Joseph I, son, b. 26 Jul 1678
17 Jun 1711	Charles III, brother, b. 1 Oct 1685
20 Oct 1740	Maria Theresa, daughter (Queen), b. 13 May 1717
29 Nov 1780	Joseph II, son, b. 13 Mar 1741
20 Feb 1790	Leopold II, brother, b. 5 May 1747

Voivodes of Transylvania

1630–48	Prince (Governor) George Rakoczi, son of Sigismund, b. 1591
1648–60	Prince (Governor) George II, son of George Rakoczi, b. 1621
1658–60	Prince (Governor) Achatius Bocskai
1662–90	Governor (Turkish) Michael Apafi, b. 1632
1682–90	Prince (Governor) Emerich Tököli
1690–99	Governor (Turkish) Michael II Apafi, son of Michael Apafi, b. 1680

To Habsburg Hungary, 1699

1704–11	Prince Francis Rakoczi, b. 1676

Transylvania under Austria, 1711–1918

ITALY

1 *Genoa*

HEADS OF STATE

Doges

1646	Giambattista Lomellini	1656	Giulio Sauli
1648	Jacope de' Franchi	1658	Giambattista Centurione
1650	Agostino Centurione	1660	Giovanni Bernardo
1652	Geronimo de' Franchi		Frugoni
1654	Alessandro Spinola	1661	Antonio Invrea

1663	Stefano Mari	1732	Domenico Maria Spinola
1665	Cesare Durazzo	1734	Gianstefano Durazzo
1667	Cesare Gentile	1736	Nicolò Cantaneo
1669	Francesco Garbarini	1738	Costantino Balbi
1671	Alessandro Grimaldi	1740	Nicolò Spinola
1673	Agostino Saluzzo	1742	Domenico Maria Canevaro
1675	Antonio Passano	1744	Lorenzo Mari
1677	Giannettino Odone	1746	Giovan Francesco Maria
1679	Agostino Spinola		Brignole Sale
1681	Luca Maria Invrea	1748	Cesare Cataneo
1683	Francesco Maria	1750	Agostino Viali
	Imperiale-Lercaro	1752	Stefano Lomellini
1685	Pietro Durazzo	1752	Giambattista Grimaldi
1687	Luca Spinola	1754	Giovanni Jacopo Stefano
1689	Oberto Torre		Veneroso
1691	Giambattista Cataneo	1756	Giovanni Jacopo Grimaldi
1693	Francesco Maria Invrea	1758	Matteo Fransone
1695	Bandinelli Negrone	1760	Agostino Lomellini
1697	Francesco Maria Sauli	1765	Maria Gaetano Della
1699	Geronimo Mari		Rovere
1701	Federigo de' Franchi	1767	Marcellino Durazzo
1703	Antonio Grimaldi-Cebà	1769	Giambattista Negrone
1705	Stefano Onorio Feretto	1771	Giovanni Battista Cam-
1707	Domenico Maria Mari		biaso
1709	Vincenzo Durazzo	1773	Alessandro Pietro Frances-
1711	Francesco Maria Imperiale		co Grimaldi
1713	Giannantonio Giustiniani	1775	Brizio Giustiniani
1715	Lorenzo Centurione	1777	Giuseppe Lomellini
1717	Benedetto Viali	1779	Giacomo Maria Brignole
1719	Ambrogio Imperiale	1781	Marcantonio Gentile
1721	Cesare de' Franchi	1783	Giambattista Airoli
1723	Domenico Negrone	1785	Gian Carlo Pallavicini
1726	Geronimo Veneroso	1787	Rafaele Ferrari
1728	Luca Grimaldi	1789	Alerame Maria Pallavicini
1730	Francesco Maria Balbi		

2 *Mantua*

HEADS OF STATE

Dukes

House of Gonzaga

21 Sep 1637   Carlo II, grandson of Carlo I and of Francesco II, b. 3 Oct
1629

14 Aug 1665– 1707	Ferdinando Carlo, son, b. 31 Aug 1652
1707	Mantua occupied by Imperial troops
5 Jul 1708	Fief reverted to the Emeror

3 *Modena, Reggio and Ferrara*

HEADS OF STATE
Dukes
House of Este

11 Dec 1628	Alfonso III, son of Cesare V, abdicated; b. 22 Oct 1591
1629	Francesco I, son, b. 5 Sep 1610
13 Oct 1658	Alfonso IV (II), son, b. 13 Feb 1634
16 Jul 1662	Francesco II, son, b. 6 Mar 1660
7 Sep 1694	Rinaldo, uncle, b. 25 Apr 1655
26 Oct 1737	Francesco III, son, b. 2 Jul 1698
22 Feb 1780	Ercole III, son, b. 22 Nov 1727

4 *Naples – Sicily*

HEADS OF STATE

Sicily and Naples were ruled by Spain between 1504 and 1713, as the Kingdom of the Two Sicilies

1713–20	Victor Amadeus II, Duke of Savoy, b. 14 May 1666
1720–35	Austrian rule

Spanish Bourbon rulers

3 Oct 1735	Charles VII, brother of King Ferdinand VI of Spain; from 10 Aug 1759 as Charles III, King of Spain; b. 20 Jun 1716
6 Oct 1759	Ferdinand IV, son, brother of King Charles IV of Spain (for 1st time); b. 12 Jan 1751

5 *The Papacy*

Popes

15 Sep 1644–7 Jan 1655	Innocent X (Pamphili), b. 6 May 1575
7 Apr 1655–22 May 1667	Alexander VII (Chigi), b. 13 Feb 1599
20 Jun 1667–9 Dec 1669	Clement IX (Rospigliosi), b. 28 Jan 1600
29 Apr 1670–22 Jul 1676	Clement X (Albieri), b. 13 Jul 1590

21 Sep 1676–12 Aug 1689	Innocent XI (Odescalchi), b. 16 May 1611
6 Oct 1689–1 Feb 1691	Alexander VIII (Ottoboni), b. 22 Apr 1610
12 July 1691–27 Sep 1700	Innocent XII (Pignatelli), b. 13 Mar 1615
23 Nov 1700–19 Mar 1721	Clement XI (Albani), b. 22 Jul 1649
8 May 1721–7 Mar 1724	Innocent XIII (de'Conti), b. 13 May 1655
29 May 1724–21 Feb 1730	Benedict XIII (Orsini), b. 2 Feb 1649
12 Jul 1730–6 Feb 1740	Clement XII (Corsini), b. 7 Apr 1652
17 Aug 1740–3 May 1758	Benedict XIV (Lambertini), b. 31 Mar 1675
6 Jul 1758–2 Feb 1769	Clement XIII (de la Torre de Rezzonico), b. 20 Dec 1693
19 May 1769–22 Sep 1774	Clement XIV (Ganganelli), b. 31 Oct 1705
15 Feb 1775–29 Aug 1799	Pius VI (Braschi), b. 27 Nov 1717

KEY MINISTERS
Cardinal Secretaries of State

1644–3 Sep 1651	Giovanni Giacomo Panciroli
Dec 1651–7 Apr 1655	Fabio Chigi
1655–22 May 1667	Giulio Rospigliosi
1667–70	Decio Azzolini
1670–19 Feb 1673	Ghiberto Borromeo
1673–6	Francesco Nerli
23 Sep 1676–89	Alderano Cibo
1689–91	Pietro Ottoboni
14 Jul 1691–1700	Fabrizio Spada
1700–21	Fabrizio Paolucci
1721–4	Giorgio Spinola
1724–12 Jun 1726	Fabrizio Paolucci
1726–30	Niccoló Maria Lercari
1730–3	Antonio Banchieri
1733–40	Giuseppe Firrao
1740–29 Sep 1756	Silvio Valenti Gonzaga
Sep 1756–30 Sep 1758	Alberico Archinto
Oct 1758–69	Luigi Torrigiani
1769–23 Feb 1785	Opizio Pallavicini
Jun 1785–Sep 1789	Ignazio Boncompagni
1789–Aug 1796	Francesco Saverio Zelada

6 *Parma*

HEADS OF STATE
Dukes
House of Farnese
12 Sep 1646   Ranuccio II, son of Odoardo I; b. 17 Sep 1630

8 Dec 1694	Francesco, son, b. 19 May 1678
26 May 1727– 20 Jan 1731	Antonio Francesco, brother, b. 29 Nov 1679
1735	Parma ceded to Austria by the Treaty of Vienna
3 Oct 1735	Charles I, German Emperor as Charles VI from 1711–40; b. 1 Oct 1685
20 Oct 1740	Maria Theresa, daughter, married to Emperor Francis I, b. 13 May 1717
18 Oct 1748	Philip, son of King Philip V of Spain, b. 15 Mar 1720
18 Jul 1765	Ferdinand, son; from 9 Feb 1801: Archduke of Tuscany; b. 20 Jan 1741

7 *Piedmont – Savoy (Sardinia)*

HEADS OF STATE
Dukes

4 Oct 1638	Charles Emmanuel II, brother of Francis Hyacinth, b. 20 Jun 1634
12 Jun 1675– 3 Sep 1730	Victor Amadeus II, son; King of Sicily 1713–20; b. 14 May 1666
1718–24 Aug 1720	Piedmont – Savoy merged in the newly formed Kingdom of Sardinia
3 Sep 1730	Charles Emmanuel III, son, b. 27 Apr 1701
20 Feb 1773	Victor Amadeus III, son, b. 26 Jun 1726

8 *Tuscany*

HEADS OF STATE
Grand Dukes of Tuscany
House of Medici

28 Feb 1621	Ferdinando II, son of Cosimo II, b. 14 Jul 1610
23 May 1670	Cosimo III, son, b. 14 Aug 1642
31 Oct 1723	Gian Gastone, son, b. 26 May 1671

House of Lorraine – Habsburg

9 Jul 1737	Francis II, son of Duke Leopold Joseph Hyacinth of Lor- raine; from 13 Sep 1745: Holy Roman Emperor Francis I; married to Maria Theresa, Archduchess of Austria; b. 8 Dec 1708

18 Aug 1765   Leopold I, son; from 20 Feb 1790: King Leopold II of
               Hungary; from 30 Sep 1790: Archduke Leopold II of
               Austria and Holy Roman Emperor Leopold II; b. 5 May
               1747

9 *Venice*

HEADS OF STATE
Doges

20 Jan 1646–27 Feb 1655	Francesco Molino
27 Mar 1655–1 May 1656	Carlo Contarini
17 May 1656–5 Jun 1656	Francesco Cornaro
15 Jun 1656–29 Mar 1658	Bertuccio Valier
8 Apr 1658–30 Sep 1659	Giovanni Pesaro
16 Oct 1659–26 Jan 1675	Domenico Contarini II
6 Feb 1675–14 Aug 1676	Niccolò Sagredo
26 Aug 1676–15 Jan 1684	Aloise Contarini II
26 Jan 1684–23 Mar 1688	Marc Antonio Giustinian
3 Apr 1688–6 Jan 1694	Francesco Morosini
25 Feb 1694–5 Jul 1700	Silvestro Valier
16 Jul 1700–6 May 1709	Aloise Mocenigo II
22 May 1709–12 Aug 1722	Giovanni Corner
24 Aug 1722–21 May 1732	Aloise Mocenigo III (Sebastiano)
2 Jun 1732–5 Jan 1735	Carol Ruzzini
17 Jan 1735–17 Jun 1741	Aloise Pisani
30 Jun 1741–7 Mar 1752	Pietro Grimani
18 Mar 1752–19 May 1762	Francesco Loredano
31 May 1762–31 Mar 1763	Marco Foscarini
19 Apr 1763–31 Dec 1778	Aloise Mocenigo IV
14 Jan 1779–13 Feb 1789	Paolo Renier
9 Mar 1789–12 May 1794	Luigi Manin
1797–1805 and from 1814	Under Austrian rule

LIECHTENSTEIN

HEADS OF STATE
Princes
Gundakar Dynasty
11 Feb 1686   Jacob Moritz, son of Prince Hartmann of Liechtenstein,
               b. 25 Jul 1641

21 Apr 1709   Anton Florian, brother, b. 4 May 1656
         1719   Vaduz and Schellenberg united with the Principality of Liechtenstein
11 Oct 1721   Josef, son, b. 27 May 1690
17 Dec 1732   Johann Nepomuk Karl, son, b. 6 Jul 1724
22 Dec 1748   Josef Wenzel Lorenz, cousin of Josef, b. 9 Aug 1696

Franz Dynasty
10 Feb 1772   Franz Josef I, nephew, b. 29 Nov 1726
11 Aug 1781   Alois I, son, b. 14 May 1759

POLAND – LITHUANIA

HEADS OF STATE
Elected Kings

30 Apr 1632 – 10 May 1648   Wladyslaw IV, son of Sigismund III, b. 9 Jun 1595
10 May 1648 – 16 Sep 1668   John II, Casimir, son, b. 22 May 1609
19 Jun 1669 – 10 Nov 1673   Michael Wiśniowiecki, son of Jeremias Michael Wiśniowiecki, b. 18 Jun 1640
19 May 1674 – 17 Jun 1696   John III, Sobieski, son of John Sobieski, Protector of Krakow, b. 9 Jun 1624
17 Jun 1696 – 1 Feb 1733   Augustus II, the Strong; from 27 Apr 1694: Elector Frederick Augustus I of Saxony; exiled from Poland in 1703 by King Charles XII of Sweden, reinstated in 1710; b. 12 May 1670
12 Aug 1704 – Aug 1709   Stanislaw I, Leszczynski, son of Rafael Leszczynski, chosen as King in 1733 but banished by the Russians, died as Duke of Lorraine; b. 23 Oct 1677
14 Aug 1733 – 5 Oct 1763   Augustus III, son of Augustus II; from 1 Feb 1733: Elector Frederick Augustus II of Saxony; b. 17 Oct 1696
7 Sep 1764 – 22 Nov 1795   Stanislaw II, Augustus Poniatowski, son of Stanislaw Poniatowski, b. 17 Jan 1732
         1795   Partition of Poland and end of the old Polish Kingdom

PORTUGAL

HEADS OF STATE
Kings
House of Braganza

15 Dec 1640 John IV, son of Duke Theodore II of Braganza, b. 18 Mar 1604

 6 Nov 1656 Alfonso VI, son, b. 12 Aug 1643 (deposed 23 Nov 1667 and replaced by Regency of brother, Pedro; d. 12 Sep 1683)

12 Sep 1683 Pedro II, brother, b. 26 Apr 1648

 9 Dec 1706 John V, son, b. 22 Oct 1689

31 Jul 1750 José I, son, b. 6 Jun 1714

24 Feb 1777 Maria I, daughter; from 6 Jun 1760 married to Pedro III, her uncle, b. 17 Dec 1734

20 Mar 1816 John VI, son, Regent from 1792; lived with his mother in Brazil while Portugal was occupied by the French, 27 Nov 1807–3 Jul 1821, b. 13 May 1767

KEY MINISTERS

Jul 1662–7 Sep 1667	Count Castelo-Melhor, 'Secret' Secretary
1667–1706	Duke of Cadaval, Chief Minister
1706–36	Diogo de Mendonça Corte Real, Secretary of State
1730–50	Alexandre de Gusmão, King's Private Secretary
1736–47	Cardinal da Mota, Secretary of State
1749–50	Frei Gaspar da Encarnacão, Chief Minister
5 Aug 1750–1 Mar 1777	Sebastião José de Carvalho e Melo (Marquis of Pombal, 1770), Minister of Foreign Affairs and War (Chief Minister)
1770–95	Martinho de Melo e Castro, Chief Minister
1777–1800	Viscount of Vila Nova de Cerveira (later Marquis of Ponte de Lima)

RUSSIA

HEADS OF STATE
Tsars
House of Romanov

12 Jul 1645 Alexis, son of Michael III, b. 10 Mar 1629

8 Feb 1676   Fyodor III, son, b. 30 May 1661

27 Apr 1682   Peter I, the Great, half-brother, from 2 Nov 1721: Emperor; b. 30 May 1672

Regents:

Apr – May 1682: Natalia Naryshkina, mother

May 1682–1689: Sofia Aleksyeevna, sister of Fyodor III

Co-ruler, in name only:

26 May 1682–29 Jan 1696: Ivan V, brother of Fyodor III, b. 27 Aug 1666

Emperors and Empresses

2 Nov 1721   Peter I, previously Tsar

8 Feb 1725   Catherine I (Marta Skowronska), second wife, b. 1684

18 May 1727   Peter II, grandson of Peter I, b. 25 Oct 1715

28 Jan 1730   Anna, daughter of Ivan V, b. 25 Jan 1693

28 Oct 1740   Ivan VI, son of Prince Anton Ulrich of Brunswick and great-nephew of Empress Anna, deposed; b. 23 Aug 1740

Regents:

28 Oct – Nov 1740: Ernest Johann Biron, Duke of Courland

Nov 1740–5 Dec 1741: Anne, mother of Ivan VI and niece of Peter I

5 Dec 1741   Elizabeth, daughter of Peter I, b. 29 Dec 1709

House of Romanov – Holstein – Gottorp

5 Jan 1762   Peter III (Karl Peter Ulrich, Duke of Holstein-Gottorp), nephew, probably assassinated 6 Jul 1762; b. 21 Feb 1728

9 Jul 1762   Catherine II, the Great, wife of Peter III and daughter of Duke Christian August of Anhalt-Zerbst, b. 2 May 1729

17 Nov 1796   Paul, son, assassinated 24 May 1801; b. 1 Oct 1754

KEY MINISTERS

1696–1727   Prince Aleksandr Danilovich Menshikov, Chief Minister

1721–41   Heinrich J. F. Ostermann, Foreign Minister

1730–40   Ernst Johann Biron, Duke of Kurland, Chief Minister

1732–41   Burkhard Christoph von Münnich, Field Marshal

1742–57   Count Bestuzhev-Riumin, Foreign Minister

1762–67   Burkhard Christoph von Münnich, Field Marshal

1762–81   Nikita Ivanovich Panin, Chief Minister

1774–91   Grigory Aleksandrovich Potemkin, Chief Minister

SPAIN

HEADS OF STATE

Kings

House of Habsburg

30 Mar 1621	Philip IV, son of Philip III, b. 8 Apr 1605
17 Sep 1665	Charles II, son, b. 6 Nov 1661

House of Bourbon

1 Nov 1700	Philip V, grandson of King Louis XIV of France (for 1st time), b. 19 Dec 1683
14 Jan 1724	Luis, I, son, b. 25 Aug 1707
7 Sep 1724	Philip V (for 2nd time)
9 Jul 1746	Ferdinand VI, son, b. 17 Sep 1713
10 Aug 1759	Charles III, brother, b. 20 Jun 1716
13 Dec 1788	Charles IV, son, b. 12 Nov 1748
19 Mar 1808	Ferdinand VII, son, b. 14 Oct 1784

KEY MINISTERS

1643–26 Nov 1661	Luis de Haro, Prime Minister
26 Nov 1661–1665	Count of Castrillo and Duke of Medina de las Torres, Ministers to the King
22 Sep 1666–25 Feb 1669	Johan Everard Nithard, Prime Minister
1673–23 Jan 1677	Fernando Valenzuela, Chief Adviser and, after 1676, Prime Minister
21 Feb 1680–Apr 1685	Pedro, Duke of Medinaceli, Prime Minister
Apr 1685–25 June 1693	Fernandez, Count of Oropesa, Prime Minister
Feb 1701–Mar 1705	Cardinal Portocarrero, Chief Adviser
Jun 1701–Oct 1703	Jean Orry, Secretary of Finance
Jul 1705	José de Grimaldo, Secretary of War and Finance
Sep 1715–5 Dec 1719	Giulio Alberoni (Cardinal from 1717), Prime Minister
1724–14 May 1726	Baron Jan Willem Ripperda, Prime Minister
14 May 1726–Nov 1736	José Patiño, Prime Minister
Nov 1736–1741	Villarias Marquis de Laquadra, Prime Minister
1741–11 Apr 1743	José del Campillo, Prime Minister
11 Apr 1743–20 Jul 1754	Marqués de Ensenada, Prime Minister
Dec 1746–8 Apr 1754	José de Carvajal, Secretary of State
8 Apr 1754–17 May 1754	Marqués de Ensenada, Prime Minister

17 May 1754	Ricardo Wall (for 1st time), Prime Minister
11 Aug 1759	Ricardo Wall (for 2nd time)
11 Oct 1763–7 Nov 1776	Geronimo, Count Grimaldi, Prime Minister
1766–73	Conde de Aranda, President of Council of Castile
7 Nov 1776–1792	José Moñino, Count Floridablanca, Prime Minister

SWEDEN–FINLAND

HEAD OF STATE

Kings

House of Vasa

16 Nov 1632   (Queen) Christina, daughter of Gustav II Adolf, abdicated; b. 8 Dec 1626

House of Pfalz–Zweibrücken–Kleeburg

6 Jun 1654   Charles X (Gustav), grandson on mother's side of Charles IX, b. 8 Nov 1622

13 Feb 1660   Charles XI, son, b. 24 Nov 1655

15 Apr 1697   Charles XII, son, b. 17 Jun 1682

11 Dec 1718   (Queen) Ulrika Eleonora, sister, abdicated; b. 23 Jan 1688

House of Hessen–Kassel

26 Mar 1720   Frederick I, son of Duke Charles I of Hesse–Cassel, husband of Ulrika Eleonora from 4 Apr 1715; b. 28 Apr 1676

House of Holstein–Gottorp

5 Apr 1751   Adolf Frederick, son of Duke Christian August of Holstein-Gottorp, b. 14 May 1710

12 Feb 1771   Gustavus III, son, b. 24 Jan 1746; d. 1792

KEY MINISTERS

1611–54   Axel Oxenstierna, Chancellor

1653–60   Herman Klasson Fleming, President of Treasury Board

1660–72   Magnus Gabriel de la Gardie, Chancellor

1660–72   Peter Brahe, Steward

1660–72   Gustavus Bonde, Minister of Finance

1672–9   Johan Gyllenstierna, Council member and principal adviser to Charles XI

1680–1702	Bengt Gabrielsson Oxenstierna, Chancellor
1680–5	Klas Hermansson Fleming, President of the Treasury Board
1685–97	Fabian Wrede, President of Estates Restitution Board
1697–1709	Count Charles Piper, principal adviser
1700–9	Karl Gustav Rehnsköld, principal military adviser
1710–19	Count Arvid Bernhard Horn, Chancellor and Foreign Minister
1715–18	Baron Georg Henrik von Görtz, principal adviser
1719–20	Gustav Cronhjelm, Chief Minister
1720–38	Count Arvid Bernhard Horn, Chancellor and Foreign Minister
1738–46	Carl Gyllenborg, Chancellor
1747–51	Count Karl Gustavus Tessin, Chancellor
1752–61	Anders Johan von Höpken, Chancellor
1761–5	Klas Ekeblad, Chancellor
1765–8	Karl Gustavus Lowenheilm, Chancellor
1769–71	Klas Ekeblad, Chancellor
1772	Joachim von Duben, Chancellor
1772–83	Ulrik Scheffer, Chancellor
1783–5	Gustavus Philip Creutz, Chancellor
1785–7	Emanuel De Geer, Chancellor
1787–9	Johan Gabriel Oxenstierna, Chancellor
1789–90	Carl Wilhelm von Duben, Chancellor

2 POLITICAL CHRONOLOGY

DENMARK–NORWAY

1645 *14 Aug*: Treaty of Brömsebro, signed after defeat by Sweden, which gained Gothland and two Norwegian provinces.

1648 *28 Feb*: Death of King Christian IV. Succession of Frederick III, who was forced by the nobility to sign charter limiting royal prerogatives.

1658 *26 Feb*: Treaty of Roskilde, by which Denmark was forced to cede to Sweden three Scanian provinces and Norwegian provinces of Baahus and Trondhjem.

1660 *6 Jun*: Treaty of Copenhagen, signed after valiant defence of that city, by which Denmark–Norway regained Trondhjem from Sweden.

16 Sep: Burgher and clerical Estates of Rigstad (parliament) agree to renounce privileges if nobility did same.

30 Sep: Nobility, under heavy public pressure, agreed to renounce privileges.

13 Oct: Constitutional revolution produced by collusion by King Frederick III, clergy and burghers against nobility. King made hereditary monarch and released from restrictive charter of 1648 in return for assurance to recognise rights of three Estates. Signalled onset of absolute monarchy in Denmark.

1660 *4 Nov*: Frederick III established Privy Council and five Administrative Colleges to manage state bureaucracy.

Hannibal Sehested, former Statholder of Norway, appointed Treasurer.

1661 *10 Jan*: Instrument or Pragmatic Sanction recognised King as hereditary heir to throne and granted him all royal prerogatives and sovereign privileges.

27 May: Norwegian Estates summoned to ratify constitutional changes.

7 Aug: Norwegian Estates approved new fundamental law introducing royal absolutism, ending dominion of Danish nobility, and placing Norway directly under King with same constitution as Denmark. Post of Statholder in Norway retained with authority to supervise all subordinate officials.

1664   U. F. Gyldenløve, illegitimate son of Frederick III, appointed Statholder in Norway.

       23 Sep: Death of Hannibal Sehested.

1665   *14 Nov*: Secret promulgation of King's Law, drafted by Peder Schumacher (later Count Griffenfeld), carrying royal absolutism to extremes. King declared supreme authority due to Estates' surrender of power, with right to make, change, and annul laws, appoint all higher officials, make war and peace, and coin money. King bound only by will of God, Augsburg Confession and King's Law itself. Law not revealed until after death of Frederick III.

1670   *9 Feb*: Death of Frederick III. Succession of Christian V.

       Norwegian local government rationalised and taxation reduced, following scheme of Gyldenløve.

1673   Peder Schumacher, now Count Griffenfeld, appointed Chancellor, with complete supervision over administrative and diplomatic affairs.

1674   Alliance with United Provinces against France should Louis XIV receive additional aid.

1675   *Aug*: War with Sweden broke out.

1676   *11 Mar*: Griffenfeld dismissed as Chancellor and arrested. Later tried for high crimes and imprisoned for 22 years. Frederick Ahlefeld appointed Chancellor.

1677   Danes defeated at Landskrona by Charles XI of Sweden, but later reconquered Gothland and Rügen.

1678   Defeat of Sweden by Denmark–Norway at Uddevalla.

1679   *23 Aug*: Peace of Fontainebleau, dominated by Louis XIV, forced Denmark to return captured Swedish possessions.

1682   First Chief of Police appointed in Copenhagen, with authority to maintain law and order, supervise servants and clean and light streets.

1683   'Code of Christian V', new law code, promulgated in Denmark.

1685   Visit of Christian V to Norway.

1687   New law code promulgated in Norway.

1698   Alliance against Sweden formed by Christian V with Augustus II of Saxony–Poland.

1699   New alliance made between Denmark–Norway and Peter I of Russia.

       26 Aug: Death of Christian V. Succession of Frederick IV.

       Retirement of Gyldenløve in Norway; no new Stateholder appointed.

1700 *Apr*: Danes attacked Swedish territory of Gottorp.
       18 Aug: Peace of Traventhal between Sweden and Denmark, recognising autonomy of Gottorp.
1702 Serfdom officially abolished by Frederick IV, but decree virtually negated by revival of system of compulsory military service controlled by nobility.
1704 Slotshoven – new civil and military administrative council – created in Norway to assist Vice-Statholder and perform former functions of Statholder.
1709 Frederick IV made new alliance with Saxony with aim of recovering Polish throne for Augustus II and former Danish provinces from Sweden.
       Nov: Denmark–Norway entered Great Northern War in alliance with Saxony and Russia against Sweden.
1710 *28 Feb*: Danes suffered crushing defeat by Swedes at battle of Helsingborg. Reversal led to appointment of new Statholder, Løvendal, in Norway.
1715 *23 Dec*: Danish–Prussian force captured Pomeranian city of Stralsrund from Sweden.
1716 *9 Mar*: Norway invaded by Charles XII of Sweden.
       21 Mar: Christian captured by Swedes.
       Jul: Charles XII forced to withdraw from Norway after naval defeat.
1718 *11 Dec*: Charles XII killed at Frederickshall, after launching second invasion of Norway; followed by ragged retreat of Swedish army.
1720 *3 Jul*: Peace of Fredericksborg ended war between Denmark–Norway and Sweden.
1721 Slotshoven, Norwegian administrative council, abolished, and Ditler Vibe appointed Statholder.
1730 Frederick issued Sabbath Ordinance reinforcing religious conformity. (*See* Chapter 6: The Church).
       12 Oct: Death of Frederick IV. Succession of Christian VI, followed by appointment of Baron Iver Rosenkrans as Chancellor and Count Christian Rantzau as Statholder of Norway (but latter office was soon afterwards abolished).
1733 Journey of Christian VI to Norway.
1735 New Sabbath Ordinance provided stricter penalties for religious and moral offences.
1739 *29 Jan*: Ordinance laid foundations for public school system, enforcing compulsory attendance between years of seven and twelve.
1742 Treaty with France brought subsidy of 400,000 riksdalers per annum.
1746 *6 Aug*: Death of Christian VI. Succession of Frederick V. Adam Gottlob Moltke appointed Master of Royal Household (–1770).

1750   Denmark territories of Oldenburg and Delmenhorst exchanged for Gottorp possessions in Holstein, rounding out southern boundary. Boundary dispute settled with Sweden.

1751   Johann Bernstorff appointed Minister of Foreign Affairs.

1756–63   Bernstorff maintained Danish–Norwegian neutrality in Seven Years' War.

1762   Extensive rioting provoked new tax levy.

1766   *14 Jan*: Death of Frederick V. Succession of Christian VII.

1770   *13 Sep*: Dismissal of Bernstorff and appointment of Johann Friedrich Struensee, at instigation of Queen Carolina Mathilda.

5 Dec: Privy Council and Administrative Colleges abolished and replaced by government by 'cabinet orders' – directives issued by Struensee and signed by King. Struensee then launched far-reaching programme of reforms, including freedom of religion and press.

1771   Struensee made Regent with unlimited powers, as Christian VII lapsed towards imbecility.

1772   *17 Jan*: Fall of Struensee as reactionary Ove Høegh-Guldberg secured his arrest. Prince Frederick, Christian's brother, made Regent; Privy Council restored and freedom of press abolished.

18 Apr: Struensee executed.

1773   *13 Apr*: Andreas Peter Bernstorff appointed Minister of Foreign Affairs.

12 Aug: Mutual defence treaty signed between Denmark–Norway and Russia.

1780   *13 Nov*: Bernstorff dismissed by Høegh-Guldberg after Russian complaints that he had undermined alliance.

1784   *14 Apr*: Crown Prince Frederick came of age, dismissed Høegh-Guldberg and reappointed Bernstorff.

6 Aug: C. D. F. Reventlow, progressive reformer, appointed head of Commission of Agriculture.

1786   Reventlow established commission to enquire into condition of peasantry, leading to numerous liberal reforms.

1788   *6 Jun*: Abolition of villeinage, greatly improving lot of peasantry.

Sep: Sweden invaded by Denmark–Norway in alliance with Russia, but armistice secured in October.

FRANCE

1643   *4 May*: Death of Louis XIII; succeeded by four-year-old Louis XIV (–1715).

18 May: Anne of Austria, Queen Mother, invested with supreme

43

power in France: Mazarin confirmed as chief minister and Duke of Orleans appointed lieutenant-general.

1643– Numerous peasant risings occur in Armagnac, Normandy, Dauphiné
4 and Languedoc; nobles began conspiracies in Saintonge, Angoumois and Poitiers. In response to opposition Mazarin reduced taxation.

1644 *Apr*: Arrival of French envoys at Congress of Münster.
Aug–Sep: French troops occupied Rhineland and captured Philippsburg, Mainz, Worms, Speyer and Oppenheim.
French forces driven out of Aragon by Spain.

1645 *Mar*: Many opposition members of Parlement of Paris imprisoned by Mazarin.
1 Jun: Peace negotiations opened between France and Empire at Münster.
Aug–Sep: French victory at Nördlingen (*3 Aug*) strengthened government position; Lit de Justice (*Sep*) forced Parlement to yield to Mazarin.

1646 *Dec*: Death of Henry, Prince of Condé.

1647 *Sep*: French campaign failed in Netherlands.
1 Sep: Marzarin made treaty with Duke of Modena for invasion of Duchy of Milan.
Nov: Serious illness of Louis XIV.

1648 *Aug*: Insurrection of Fronde assumed serious proportions.
20 Aug: Victory of Condé at Lens hastened conclusion of Peace of Westphalia.
24 Oct: Peace of Westphalia concluded Thirty Years' War. By treaty, France gained (1) definite possession of Metz, Toul and Verdun; (2) Breisach and Austrian possessions of Alsace; and (3) right to garrison Philippsburg while no fortresses were to be built on right bank of Danube from Basle to Philippsburg.

1649 *15 Jan*: French court forced to leave Paris; opening of 'twelve weeks' war' in Fronde.
11 Mar: Peace of Rueil ended First or Parlementary Fronde.
18 Aug: Return of court to Paris.
Dec: Unrest in provinces and riots in Paris marked outbreak of Second Fronde; Condé charged leaders of old Fronde with attempted murder.

1650 *18 Jan*: Arrest of Fronde leaders including Condé, Conti and Longueville by Mazarin, who now allied court with leaders of first Fronde.
30 Apr: Turenne concluded treaty between French rebels and Spain.
Sep: Siege of Bordeaux, stronghold of Fronde, by royalist forces.
29 Sep: Peace of Bordeaux imposed by Parlement and Mazarin.

1651   *6 Feb*: Parlement voted for release of Fronde leaders, forcing Mazarin to flee from Paris during night.

13 Feb: Despite agreeing to release Fronde leaders, Mazarin failed to regain support, subsequently forced to retire to Cologne.

17 Aug: Queen Anne of Austria allied court with new Fronde against Condé.

5 Sep: Louis XIV attained his majority; charges against Condé dropped, although he later left Paris and made alliance with Spain. Turenne refused to fight against Louis now that regency had ended. Rebellion of Condé began.

Dec: Condé attainted of treason by Parlement of Paris.

1652   *24 Jan*: Duke of Orleans joined rebels on recall of Cardinal Mazarin, but court strengthened by support of Turenne.

29 Mar: Victory of Turenne and royalist forces over Frondeurs at Jargeau.

7 Apr: Royal army defeated at Bleneau by Condé.

4 May: Frondeurs, aided by Condé's Spanish mercenaries, defeated at Etampes by Turenne and royalist forces.

2 Jul: Turenne defeated Condé in Faubourg St Antoine, Paris, but forced to retire to defend frontier against Spanish. Mazarin again compelled to flee. Fronde government set up in Paris after June rising.

21 Oct: Return of Louis XIV to Paris and re-establishment of royal government; leading Frondeurs exiled; Cardinal Mazarin recalled.

1653   *3 Feb*: Return of Mazarin to Paris.

7 Feb: Nicholas Fouquet appointed Superintendent of Finances.

31 Jul: Surrender of Bordeaux ended Provincial Fronde.

1654   *7 Jun*: Coronation of Louis XIV at Rheims.

1656   *Aug*: Cardinal Mazarin and Duke of Orleans reconciled.

1657   *May*: Louis XIV put forward as candidate for Holy Roman Emperor.

1659   *7 Nov*: Marriage between Louis XIV and Maria Theresa, eldest daughter of Philip IV of Spain, arranged by Peace of Pyrenees, which ended war between France and Spain.

1660   *Jan–Mar*: Louis XIV visited Toulon and South of France and was reconciled with Condé.

Mar: Territory of Orange forced to recognise royal sovereignty.

6 Jun: Marriage of Louis XIV and Maria Theresa, Infanta of Spain.

1661   *9 Mar*: Death of Cardinal Mazarin at age 59. Louis XIV began his personal rule.

1 Apr: Marriage of Philip of Orleans, brother of Louis XIV, to Henrietta, sister of Charles II of England.

5 Sep: Nicholas Fouquet stripped of office and arrested. Emergence of Jean Baptiste Colbert as principal financial minister.

1661–2 Pirates attacked southern coasts of France.

1662 Widespread famine and unrest.

1663 *26 Jul*: Louis declared Venaissin united with France after quarrel with papacy; Avignon also seized.

Colbert began reform of financial, commercial, naval and colonial systems of France. Many internal tariff duties abolished.

1664 Establishment by Colbert of French East and West India Companies, Company of the West, and companies to trade in North and Levant.

1665 Council of Commerce reorganised.

1666 Marquis of Louvois appointed Minister of War in succession to his father, Michel Le Tellier.

Colbert re-established Gobelin tapestry workshops in Paris.

1667 *20 Jan*: Death of Queen Mother, Anne of Austria.

Colbert extended state manufacture of fine arts (Manufacture Royale des Meubles de la Couronne).

National Observatory founded in Paris.

1667–8 War of Devolution between France and Spain. (*See* Chapters 4 and 5: Defence and Warfare, and Treaties and Diplomacy.)

1669 Colbert made minister of navy, commerce, colonies and royal buildings.

Vaublan published *La Conduite des Siéges*.

1670 Uniforms introduced into French army by Louvois.

1 Jun: Secret Treaty of Dover between Louis XIV and Charles II.

30 Jun: Death of Henrietta of Orleans.

Aug: Louis occupied Lorraine as result of Duke of Lorraine's intrigues with United Provinces.

1671 *Sep*: Vauban began construction of fortresses in Netherlands.

1 Sep: Death of Hugues de Lionne, Foreign Minister from 1661 to June 1671.

Foundation of Senegal Company.

1672 French postal services farmed to private contractors (1790).

1672–8 Franco-Dutch War.

1673 *Feb*: Edict of Louis XIV suppressed right of Parlement of Paris to object to royal edicts until they had been registered.

1675 *27 Jul*: Death of Turenne, marking end of great French victories against Grand Alliance.

Dec: Retirement of Prince of Condé from military affairs.

1678   Dispute with Pope Innocent XI about régale breaks out in open. (*See* Chapter 6: The Church.)

1679   Colbert required French merchants to be examined in book-keeping and commercial law.
       Louis XIV issued stringent edict against duelling; extracted agreement from nobility not to engage in duels under any provocation.
       Oct: 'Chambers of Reunion' set up in Metz, Breisach, Besancon and Tournai to adjudge for France certain towns on left bank of Rhine.

1680   Chamber of Reunion in Breisach claimed French sovereignty in Upper and Lower Alsace.

1681   *18 Sep*: French troops seize Strasbourg and Casale in time of peace.

1682   Assembly of French clergy endorse Louis XIV's Declaration of Four Articles to secure independence of Gallican church. (*See* Chapter 6: The Church.)

1683   *6 Sep*: Death of Colbert; succeeded by his son as Minister of Marine; Le Peletier made chief finance minister.

1684   *12 Jan*: Louis XIV married Madame de Maintenon after death of his wife Maria Theresa in 1683.

1685   *18 Oct*: Revocation of Edict of Nantes. (*See* Chapter 6: The Church.)

1686   College of St Cyr founded by Madame de Maintenon.
       11 Dec: Death of Prince of Condé.

1688   *Oct*: Avignon seized by Louis XIV in reply to Pope's refusal to receive Lavardin, French ambassador to Rome.

1688– War of League of Augsburg.
97

1689   Le Peletier succeeded by Pontchartrain as Controller-General of Finances. Protestant insurrection in Cévennes.

1690   Avignon restored once more to papacy.
       13 Nov: Death of Seignelay, Minister of Marine; succeeded by Pontchartrain.

1691   Death of Louvois; succeeded by inexperienced Barbézieux.

1693   Gallican church reconciled with papacy. (*See* Chapter 6: The Church.)

1695   *4 Jan*: Death of Duke of Luxemburg, Marshal of France; succeeded by Duke of Villeroi.

1696   *28 Jul*: Death of Colbert de Croissy; succeeded by Torcy as Minister of Foreign Affairs.

1699   Chamillard succeeded Pontchartrain as Controller-General of Finances; later made Chancellor of France and Minister of Marine and of the Royal Household.

1701   Death of Barbézieux; Chamillard given War Department in addition to his control of finances.

1702 Outbreak of rebellion of Protestant peasants in Cévennes. (*See* Chapter 6: The Church.)

1704 Revolt of Cévennes Protestants crushed by forces under Duke of Villars; however, guerrilla activity lingered until 1711.

1707 Vauban, in *Dîme Royal*, attacked exemptions from taxation and urged uniform land and income taxes; book proscribed and burned on Louis XIV's orders.

1708 *20 Feb*: Chamillard succeeded by Desmarets as Controller-General.

1709 *Jan–Mar*: Great distress caused by extreme cold weather.
Retirement of Chamillard from administration of war; succeeded by Voysin.

1710 Destruction of Jansenist convent of Port Royal at order of Louis XIV.
Fénélon recommended summoning of Estates General.

1711 *14 Apr*: Death of the Dauphin, heir to the French throne.

1712 *18 Feb*: Louis, Duke of Burgundy, heir to French throne, died. Youngest son of Duke of Burgundy became Dauphin and later Louis XV.
15 Nov: Philip V of Spain renounced claim to French throne and Dukes of Berry and Orleans subsequently gave up claims to Spanish throne.

1713 *Mar*: Solemn meeting of Paris Parlement held to register renunciations by Dukes of Berry and Orleans.

1714 *14 Feb*: Parlement of Paris registered under compulsion Bull *Unigenitus* which condemned Jansenism. (*See* Chapter 6: The Church.)
Louis XIV made his last will, appointing his nephew, Duke of Orleans, Regent; his illegitimate son, Duke of Maine, Guardian; Villeroy, Governor; Le Tellier, Confessor; and Fleury, Bishop of Fréjus, the Preceptor of the Dauphin.

1715 *7 Jan*: Death of Fénélon, whose political aspirations had been overthrown by death of Duke of Burgundy.
1 Sep: Death of Louis XIV after unprecedented reign of 72 years; succeeded by his five-year-old great-grandson Louis XV. Duke of Orleans assumed regency although Louis XIV had decreed power was to be shared between Orleans and Maine. Aspirations of Philip V, still hopeful despite his renunciation, were disappointed.
15 Sep: Government placed in hands of seven councils under Regent and Council of Regency (Commerce, finance, war, navy, foreign affairs, interior and religion).

1716 John Law established Banque Générale (in 1718 made Banque Royale).
Chamber of Justice established to check financial corruption.

1717 *Aug*: John Law's Mississippi Company given monopoly of trade with Louisiana.

Chamber of Justice closed.

1718 *Jan*: Disgrace of Noialles and d'Aguesseau, who were replaced by d'Argenson, Lieutenant of Police.

Regent, Duke of Orleans, acted to stop religious disputes.

26 Aug: Lit de Justice held which checked Paris Parlement's oppositions to John Law; its pretensions curtailed.

21 Sep: Councils suppressed; d'Huxelles removed and replaced as Foreign Minister by Dubois (*24 Sep*).

Dec: Rising planned in Brittany failed to occur; Cellanare conspiracy discovered. Duke and Duchess of Maine and others imprisoned.

Law's Banque Générale made Banque Royale.

Abbe Charles Saint-Pierre, in *Discours sur la Polysynodie*, recommended system of concilliar government and attacked reputation of Louis XIV.

1719 *15 Apr*: Death of Madame de Maintenon.

1720 Parlement of Paris exiled to Pontoise. John Law made Controller-General of Finances after his conversion to Roman Catholicism.

Horrible outbreak of bubonic plague killed c. 40,000 people in Marseilles.

Dec: John Law forced to flee France, the collapse of his financial schemes having brought the nation to the verge of bankruptcy.

Government established department of technical civil servants to oversee roads and bridges.

1721 *Oct*: Fall from power of Torcy, Superintendent of all the Ports.

1723 *15 Feb*: Louis XV attained his majority; end of Regency. Dubois made First Minister and Orleans President of the Council, which included Dubois, Duke of Bourbon, and Bishop Fleury of Fréjus.

10 Aug: Death of Dubois; succeeded as First Minister by Duke of Orleans with Count de Morville as Foreign Minister.

2 Dec: Death of Orleans; Duke of Bourbon made First Minister.

1725 *Jan*: Louis XV dismissed Spanish Infanta who was engaged to marry him, greatly angering Spain.

5 Sep: Marriage of Louis XV to Maria Leszczynska, daughter of exiled King of Poland, then resident in Alsace.

1726 *11 Jun*: Cardinal Fleury made First Minister after dismissal of Duke of Bourbon. Voltaire, banished from France, visited England.

1727 *Oct*: Chauvelin, member of anti-British faction, succeeded Morville as Foreign Minister.

Count de Boulainvilliers investigated history of local government to support his demand that the nobility be given greater power.

1729 *Sep*: Birth of the Dauphin.

1730 *Sep*: Louis XV ordered Paris Parlement not to interfere in politics after its refusal to accept Bull *Unigenitus*.

1731 *Sep*: Parlement of Paris decreed temporal power independent of all other powers and placed clergy under crown jurisdiction. Cardinal Fleury annulled decree and exiled eleven advocates.

1732 *Jul*: Truce made between court and Parlement, but struggle renewed with attempt of court to prevent Parlement's discussion of church matters. Parlement declared Lit de Justice, which was pronounced illegal by Louis XV. 139 magistrates exiled but, due to approach of war, recalled in December, producing apparent triumph for Parlement.

1737 *20 Feb*: Chauvelin dismissed as Foreign Secretary through antagonism with Fleury.
Corvée, system of forced labour to construct and repair main roads, organised throughout France by Orry, Controller-General.

1743 *29 Jan*: Death of Cardinal Fleury signalled change to more aggressive foreign policy.

1744 *Nov*: Marquis d'Argenson succeeded Amelot as Foreign Minister.

1745 *Sep*: Madame de Pompadour installed at Versailles as recognised mistress of Louis XV.

1747 *Jan*: Puysieulx succeeded d'Argenson as Foreign Minister.

1748 Montesquieu published *The Spirit of the Laws*.

1749 Imposition by Machault of tax of one-twentieth on all incomes but collection blocked by opposition of clergy.

1751 Puysieulx succeeded by St Contest as Foreign Minister.
École Supériere de Guerre, an officers' training school, founded in Paris.

1752 Parlement of Paris, resisting ecclesiastical policy of Archbishop of Paris, seized his temporal possessions.

1753 Louis XV, supporting Archbishop of Paris, exiled Paris Parlement. Provincial parlements backed Parlement of Paris.

1754 *Jul*: With Paris on verge of civil war, Louis XV recalled Parlement to end dispute over ecclesiastical causes.
28 Jul: Machault d'Arnounville made Minister of Navy.

1756 Struggle between parlements and church renewed, with Parlement of Paris posing as opponent to tyranny.
Dec: Louis XV coerced Paris Parlement, curtailing its jurisdiction in ecclesiastical cases; but struggle between parlements and government continued for next four years.

1757 *5 Jan*: Attempted assassination of Louis XV by J.-F. Damiens, who was subsequently executed.

1758 Choiseul made Minister of Foreign Affairs.

1759   Forced resignation of Étienne de Silhouette, Controller-General of Finances, through public opposition to his land tax; name became synonym for figure reduced to a shadow.

1761   Choiseul made Minister of War and Navy; Duke of Choiseul-Praslin appointed Foreign Minister.

1762   Jean-Jacques Rousseau published *Du Contrat Social*.

1763   *25 May*: Declaration of Louis XV established freedom of internal corn trade.

1764   Death of Madame de Pompadour.

1765   *Dec*: Death of Dauphin; Louis Augustus (future Louis XVI) became heir to throne.

1766   Choiseul again made Foreign Minister (–70), retaining War; Choiseul-Praslin became Minister of Navy.
       Mar: Louis XV attacked Parlement of Paris and declared that sovereignty resided in himself.

1767   Foundation of Society of Economists, of which Turgot was member.

1769   *22 Apr*: Madame Dubarry recognised as official mistress of Louis XV.
       15 Aug: Birth in Corsica of Napoleon Bonaparte (–1821).

1770   *16 May*: Marriage of future Louis XVI to Marie Antoinette, daughter of Maria Theresa of Austria.
       24 Dec: Choiseul ousted through intrigues of Madame Dubarry and Duke of d'Aiguillon, who succeeded as Foreign Minister. Choiseul's fall marked new attack on Parlement of Paris.

1771   *Jan*: Overthrow of parlements. Government of triumvirate of Maupeou, Terray and Aiguillon, 'Parlement Maupeou' set up and court system simplified.
       May: Duc de la Vrilliére made Foreign Minister.

1772   *Essai sur la Despotisme* published by Count Mirabeau.

1774   Terray abrogated law of 1763 permitting free internal circulation of corn (law in fact suspended in 1766).
       10 May: Death of Louis XV. Accession of Louis XVI, who appointed Jean Maurepas First Minister and Vergennes Foreign Minister.
       Aug: Recall of parlements and appointment of Turgot as Controller-General of Finances by Louis XVI.
       13 Sep: Turgot reintroduced free internal circulation of corn (law re-abolished in 1776).

1775   *19 Jul*: Chrétien Malesherbes appointed Interior Minister and initiated programme of reforms.

1776   *6 Jan*: Abolition of corvée (forced labour for building and repairing roads).
       5 Feb: Jurandes (privileged corporations) abolished by Turgot.

12 May: Resignation of Malesherbes; Turgot dismissed by Louis XVI after attempted to carry out further financial reforms. Turgot succeeded by Clugny, who died in October, being succeeded as Controller-General by Taboreaux de Réaux.

Aug: Corvée and Jurandes restored.

Sep: Corn law abrogated once more.

Oct: Jacques Necker made Director of Finances; appointed Minister of Finances in 1777.

1781   *Jan*: 'Compte rendu' published by Necker.

       12 May: Necker dismissed by Louis XVI.

       Death of Maurepas marked beginning of feudal reaction.

1783   Parlement of Besançon demanded convocation of Estates General.

       Nov: Calonne made Controller-General in succession to d'Ormesson and Joly de Fleury.

1785   Parliament of Paris began series of attacks on Calonne.

       15 Aug: Mysterious affair of diamond necklace brought suspicion and shame on Queen Marie Antoinette; Cardinal de Rohan arrested.

1787   *13 Feb*: Death of Comte de Vergennes; appointment of Armand Comte de Montmorin as Foreign Minister.

       22 Feb–25 May: Meeting of notables at Versailles rejected Charles de Calonne's proposals for financial reform.

       17 Apr: Calonne banished to Lorraine and succeeded as Finance Minister by Loménie de Brienne, Archbishop of Toulouse.

       6 Jul: Parlement of Paris opposed Brienne and demanded calling of Estates General.

       14 Aug: Paris Parlement banished to Troyes.

       24 Sep: Parlement recalled to Paris by Louis XVI.

       20 Nov: Declaration by Louis XVI that Estates General will be convened in July 1792.

1788   *20 Jan*: List of grievances presented by Parlement of Paris.

       May: Brienne secured registration of six edicts suppressing Paris Parlement and establishing Plenary Court.

       8 Aug: Estates General summoned to meet on 5 May 1789.

       25 Aug: Necker reappointed Finance Minister.

       Nov: Louis XVI summoned notables to Versailles; discussions ensued on questions of proposed double representation of third estate (bourgeoisie) and of whether to vote by head or by order.

1789   *24 Jan*: Necker issued final règlement for elections to Estates General.

       28 Apr: Success of riot at Réveillon showed political potential of mob action.

       5 May: Opening of the Estates General at Versailles.

       (For subsequent events see *European Political Facts 1789–1848*.)

GERMANY

1 *Bavaria*

1623 Duke Maximilian I achieved rank of Elector of Holy Roman Empire.

1632 Elector Maxmilian levied taxes by decree and collected them by military force, after Estates refused to pay sums demanded – thus rendering Elector's power virtually absolute.

1648 *24 Oct*: Peace of Westphalia, by which Bavaria retained electoral dignity acquired in 1623. Subsequently most of Bavarian army of 20,000 men were disbanded.

1651 Maximilian refused to summon Diet to discuss means of paying off war debts, forcing Estates' committee to yield to imposition of taxes.
27 Sep: Death of Elector Maximilian I. Succession of Ferdinand Maria.

1658 *15 Aug*: Bavaria joined Rhenish League, alliance of several German states with France and Sweden.

1667 *Apr*: Elector Ferdinand Maria signed defensive League of the Rhine with Louis XIV, Sweden, Brunswick, Hesse–Cassel, etc.

1669 *Jan*: Bavarian Diet, summoned to meet after interval of 57 years, granted 372,000 guilders a year for nine years, and was never called again.

1670 Decree regulating urban administration, empowering 'Rentmeisters' or electoral intendants to supervise election of councillors, taxation and police within towns.

1671 Elector Ferdinand Maria joined in alliance with rulers of Brandenburg, Cologne, Palatinate–Neuberg, etc., to aid each other if their estates resisted them by force of arms or if they refused to grant what was requested for defence.

1679 *26 May*: Death of Elector Ferdinand Maria. Succession of Maximilian II Emmanuel.

1682 *Jun*: Bavaria joined Austria, Sweden and others in pact to limit aggression of Louis XIV.

1687 Bavaria joined League of Augsburg against Louis XIV.

1689 Treaty of alliance with Austria in face of French threat.

1692 Elector Maximilian Emmanuel relieved Charleroi, under siege by French.

1699 *6 Feb*: Death of Joseph Ferdinand, son of Elector Maximilian and grandson of Emperor Leopold, designated heir of Charles II of Spain.

1701 *9 Mar*: Treaty of alliance with France in preparation for War of Spanish Succession.

53

1704 *Aug*: Bavaria overrun by allies and Elector Maximilian Emmanuel forced to flee to France after battle of Blenheim, where Marlborough and Eugene of Savoy crushed Bavarian and French armies.

1706 *29 Apr*: Elector Maximilian placed under ban of Empire and deprived of dominions.

1712 Imperial ban against Elector Maximilian allowed to lapse.

1714 *7 Mar*: Peace of Rastatt, which restored Maximilian Emmanuel to his electoral dominions. Thereafter Maximilian paid scant heed to Estates' committee and levied taxes by decree.

1722 Archduchess Amelia, daughter of Emperor Joseph I, on marriage to electoral heir Karl Albert renounced all claims to Austrian inheritance.

1724 Electors of Bavaria and Palatinate made pact for mutual support.

1726 *26 Feb*: Death of Elector Maximilian II Emmanuel. Succession of Karl Albert.

1732 Bavaria refused to ratify Pragmatic Sanction after its acceptance by Imperial Diet of Ratisbon.

1741 *8 May*: Treaty of Nymphenburg with France, which promised to back Elector Karl Albert's candidature as Holy Roman Emperor.
28 May: Treaty with Spain to partition Habsburg lands.
1 Nov: Treaty with Prussia and Saxony for partition of Austrian possessions.

1742 *24 Jan*: Elector Karl Albert elected Holy Roman Emperor (Charles VII, crowned 12 Feb).

1743 *27 Jun*: Convention of Niederschönfeld handed whole of Bavaria to Austria (which had occupied it) until end of war.

1744 *May*: Union of Frankfurt between Emperor Charles VII (Karl Albert), Frederick II, Elector Palatine, etc., to compel Austria to restore Bavaria, make peace and restore constitution of Empire.

1745 *20 Jan*: Death of Emperor Charles VII. Succession as Elector of Bavaria of Maximilian III Joseph, who subsequently agreed to support candidature of Grand Duke Francis as Emperor.
22 Apr: Peace of Füssen with Austria, which restored all Bavarian conquests to Elector Maximilian Joseph, who renounced claims to Empire.

1768 Diet summoned but never met because of conflict between maximilian Joseph and Estates, over administration of revenues.

1777 *30 Dec*: Death of Elector Maximilian Joseph, last of Bavarian Wittelsbach line. Succession of Elector Palatine Karl Theodor.

1778 *Jan*: Karl Theodor made convention with Emperor Joseph II, ceding much of Bavaria to Austria. Heir presumptive Karl Augustus of Zweibrücken protested, and in July Frederick the Great declared war on Austria, starting War of Bavarian Succession.

1779   *13 May*: Peace of Teschen, by which Austria received Inn quarter of Bavaria and the rights of Karl Augustus were confirmed.

1785   Joseph II, in collusion with Elector Karl Theodor, tried unsuccessfully to arrange exchange of Bavaria for Southern Netherlands.

2 *Brandenburg–Prussia*

1640   *Dec*: Death of Elector George William. Succession of Frederick William, subsequently known as 'Great Elector'.

1648   *24 Oct*: Peace of Westphalia, by which Brandenburg gained territories of Halberstadt, Minden, Kammin and Magdeburg, but failed to secure Western Pomerania.

1651   Privy Council made representative of all electoral dominions.

1653   *Aug*: Brandenburg Diet induced to vote Elector Frederick William revenue for six years, thus greatly reducing fiscal and political powers of nobility.

1655   *27 Jul*: Brandenburg invaded East Prussia to stem Swedish advance at outbreak of First Northern War.

1656   *17 Jan*: Treaty of Königsberg with Sweden, whereby East Prussia became fief of Charles X.
       20 Nov: Treaty of Labiau, by which Sweden ceded Prussia to Brandenburg.

1657   *19 Sep*: Treaty of Wehlau, whereby Poland renounced suzerainty of Prussia in favour of Brandenburg.
       10 Nov: Alliance with Denmark against Sweden.

1658   *Sep*: Frederick William marched to aid of Denmark, then besieged by Charles X of Sweden.

1659   Swedish forces driven from electoral territories and Pomerania by Great Elector.

1660   *3 May*: Peace of Oliva, ending first Northern War, by which Brandenburg gained recognition of sovereignty in East Prussia.

1661   *Jul*: Frederick William summoned Diet in Prussia, which attacked his authority and was dismissed.

1662   Frederick William invaded Königsberg with 2000 troops, forcing submission of Prussian Diet.

1666   *16 Feb*: Treaty of alliance with Holland.
       Dec: Elector Frederick William and Duke of Neuburg signed Treaty of Cleves, providing for partition of Jülich–Cleves; Brandenburg was to receive Cleves, Mark and Ravensburg, while Neuburg retained Jülich and Berg.

1667   Excise tax on consumption imposed in towns and cities, subsequently collected by General War Commissary – mainly for use of standing army.

1668 Marriage of Frederick William and widowed Duchess Dorothea of Brunswick.

1669 *31 Dec*: Secret treaty of alliance with France.

1672 *2 May*: Frederick made alliance with Holland, promising 22,000 troops, leading to First Coalition against France. Colonel von Kalckstein, leader of Prussian opposition to Great Elector, executed.

1673 *10 Apr*: Great Elector made preliminary peace with France (confirmed in June), ending First Coalition.

1674 *Jul*: Brandenburg–Prussia rejoined alliance against Louis XIV.

1675 *5 Jan*: Defeat of Brandenburg forces at Colmer by French led by Turenne.
      28 Jun: Great Elector defeated Swedes decisively at battle of Fehrbellin.

1677 *12 Dec*: Brandenburg army captured Stettin, followed in 1678 by conquest of Rugen and retreat of Swedes to Riga.

1678 *Nov*: Brandenburg captured remaining Swedish possessions in Pomerania.

1679 *29 Jun*: Treaty of St Germain-en-Laye, whereby Brandenburg was forced to return Pomerania and other conquests to Sweden.

1680 First Brandenburg expedition to West Africa.

1681 *11 Jan*: New defensive alliance with France.
      Apr: Treaty of Finsterwalde, providing for defensive alliance with Sweden.

1683 Brandenburg East African Company built fortress of Gross-Friedrichsburg on Guinea Coast.

1684 *Feb*: Great Elector offered refuge to French Huguenots in electoral dominions.

1686 *1 Apr*: Alliance with Austria, by which Brandenburg gained Schweibus and promise of East Friedland, in return for Frederick William's renunciation of claim to Silesia.
      9 Jul: Brandenburg joined League of Augsburg against Louis XIV.

1688 *29 Apr*: Death of Great Elector Frederick William. Succession of Elector Frederick III, later King Frederick I (–1713).

1688– Prime Ministry of Eberhard von Danckelmann.
97

1689 'Geheime Hofkammer' founded to provide financial supervision of electoral domains.

1692 Foundation of University of Halle (opened 1694).

1694 *20 Dec*: Frederick III restored Schweibus to Austria, thereby reviving claim to Silesia.

1700 *16 Nov*: Treaty with Emperor Leopold I, who agreed to recognise Elector Frederick III as King Frederick I of Prussia, on provision that he supply troops for expected war against France, support Austrian Habsburgs in future Imperial elections, and vote with Habsburgs in Imperial Diet.

1701 *18 Jan*: Elector Frederick III crowned as King Frederick I of Prussia.

1702– Prime ministry of Kolbe von Wartenberg.
11

1707 *Aug*: 'Perpetual' Alliance signed with Sweden, pledging mutual military support in event of third-party attack.
Acquisition of Neuchatel, Tecklenburg and Valengrin.

1713 *25 Feb*: Death of King Frederick I. Succession of Frederick William I (–1740).
31 Mar: Peace of Utrecht, ending War of Spanish Succession, recognising Prussian acquisition of Neuchatel and Upper Gelderland.
13 Aug: Ordinance of King Frederick William I that all royal domains and property were inalienable and indivisible.
Establishment of General Finance Directory, which assumed administration and control of all electoral domains.

1715 *Apr*: Prussia joined Saxony, Poland, Hanover and Denmark in alliance and declared war on Sweden.
24 Dec: Stralsund captured from Sweden.

1717 Beginning of compulsory education in Prussia.

1720 *1 Feb*: Treaty of Stockholm with Sweden, whereby Prussia gained Western Pomerania, including Stettin, for two million thalers.

1723 General Directory of War, Finance and Domains established, uniting functions of General War Commissary and General Finance Directory.

1725 *23 Aug*: Treaty of Herrenhausen with Britain and France, guaranteeing Prussian claim to Jülich–Berg.

1726 *17 Oct*: Treaty of Wusterhausen with Austria, whereby Prussia abandoned alliance of Herrenhausen and recognised Pragmatic Sanction. Prussia agreed to aid Austria in any war with 10,000 troops, while Emperor gave vague support to Prussian claims to succession in Jülich–Berg and Ravenstein.

1728 *23 Dec*: Treaty of Berlin, by which Emperor Charles VI recognised Prussian claim to Jülich–Berg, while Prussia guaranteed Pragmatic Sanction.
Establishment of Prussian Foreign Ministry.

1730 *4 Aug*: Crown Prince Frederick imprisoned after unsuccessful attempt to flee to England.
Prussia divided into military cantons for purposes of recruitment and each district ordered to provide soldiers for its local regiment.

1738   *26 Feb*: Baron Samuel von Cocceji appointed Minister of Justice.

1740   *31 May*: Death of King Frederick William I. Succession of Frederick II, later known as Frederick the Great.

       16 Dec: King Frederick II invaded Silesia, breaking Pragmatic Sanction and launching War of Austrian Succession.

       Torture abolished and limited freedom of press granted by Frederick II.

1741   *15 Jun*: Treaty of Breslau with France, providing for partition of Habsburg lands.

       10 Jun: Frederick II captured Breslau.

       9 Oct: Treaty of Klein Schnellendorf with Maria Theresa, who ceded Lower Silesia to Prussia.

       1 Nov: Frederick II broke Treaty of Klein Schnellendorf by invading Neisse and signing treaty for partition of Habsburg lands with Bavaria and Saxony.

1742   *17 May*: Frederick II defeated Austrians at Chotusitz.

       28 Jul: Peace of Berlin with Maria Theresa, whereby Prussia gained Silesia and Glatz and agreed to withdraw from coalition against Austria.

1744   *25 May*: Prussia acquired East Friesland on death of last prince, Charles Edward.

       May: Union of Frankfurt with Bavaria, Elector Palatine, and Hesse–Cassel to force Maria Theresa to restore Bavaria, make peace, and uphold Imperial constitution.

       6 Jun: Alliance with France, which guaranteed Union of Frankfurt.

       15 Aug: Frederick invaded Saxony, beginning second Silesian War.

1745   *25 Dec*: Peace of Dresden with Austria and Saxony, by which Prussia retained Silesia in return for recognition of Pragmatic Sanction and support in election of Francis I as Emperor.

1746   Baron von Cocceji appointed Grand Chancellor.

1748   *7 Oct*: Peace of Aix-la-Chapelle, ending War of Austrian Succession and recognising Prussian conquest of Silesia.

       'Codex Fredericanus' drawn up by Baron von Cocceji and imposed by Frederick II, creating foundation of uniform judicial system in Prussia.

1755   Death of Baron Samuel von Cocceji.

1756   *16 Jan*: Treaty of Westminster with Britain, by which Frederick II guaranteed neutrality of Hanover, signalling Anglo-Prussian *rapprochement*.

       29 Aug: Frederick II invaded Saxony on learning of Franco–Austrian alliance, starting Seven Years' War.

1757   *17 Jan*: Austria declared war on Prussia and was followed by Russia, Poland and Sweden.

5 Nov: Frederick II defeated French and Imperial forces at Rossbach.

1758 *Jan*: Russia occupied East Prussia.

1759 *23 Jul*: Prussian army crushed by Russians under Soltykov at Key.

1760 *9–13 Oct*: Russians burned Berlin, which they briefly occupied jointly with Austria.

1762 *Apr*: Britain cut off subsidy to Prussia.
5 May: Treaty of St Petersburg with Russia, whereby Tsar Peter III restored all Russian conquests and entered alliance with Prussia (formally concluded 8 June).

1763 *15 May*: Peace of Hubertusburg with Austria, ending Seven Years' War, with Prussia retaining Silesia in return for undertaking to support election of Archduke Joseph as King of Romans.

1768 *7 Nov*: Frederick II completed his *Political Testament.*

1769 *Aug*: Frederick II met Joseph II at Neisse to discuss partition of Poland.

1771 *Jan*: Prince Henry visited Russia to discuss partition of Poland with Catherine II.

1772 *5 Aug*: First partition of Poland, with Prussia obtaining West Prussia (except Danzig and Ermland).

1778 *3 Jul*: Prussia declared war on Austria, beginning conflict known as War of Bavarian Succession.

1779 *13 May*: Peace of Teschen, ending War of Bavarian Succession, whereby Austria gained Inn district of Bavaria and Prussia acquired reversionary right to Ansbach and Bayreuth.

1786 *17 Aug*: Death of King Frederick II. Succession of Frederick William II (–1797).

1787 *Sep*: Prussian troops invaded Holland at invitation of Prince of Orange to assist his restoration to power.

3 *Hanover*
(Brunswick–Lüneburg–Celle–Calenberg)

1610 Seven sons of Duke William of Brunswick-Lüneburg made pact that only one of them should marry and continue family of Guelph, lot falling on sixth son, George (1582–1641).

1636 *27 Jan*: George became Duke of Calenberg.
1 Oct: Duke Frederick, elder brother of George, became Duke of Celle.

1641 *2 Dec:* Death of Duke George, with Calenberg, and its capital Hanover, passing to his eldest son Christian Louis.

1648   *10 Dec*: Death of Duke Frederick, with Lüneburg–Celle passing to Duke Christian Louis, whose younger brother, George William, now became Duke of Calenberg.

1658   Marriage of Duke Ernest Augustus, youngest brother of Christian Louis and George William, to Sophia, daughter of Frederick V, Elector Palatine, and Elizabeth, daughter of James I of England, thus laying future Hanoverian claim to British throne.

1665   *15 Mar*: Death of Duke Christian Louis. Succession of George William in Lüneburg–Celle, while his younger brother John Frederick, a Roman Catholic convert, assumed government in Calenberg, where he established standing army and attempted to rule in absolute fashion.

1672–   John Frederick supported Louis XIV in Franco-Dutch War, while
   9   George William backed Austria and Holland under guidance of Chancellor Schütz.

1679   *20 Dec*: Death of Duke John Frederick, with Calenberg passing to his younger brother, Ernest Augustus, previously Protestant Bishop of Osnabrück.

1682   Duke Ernest Augustus, in violation of family pact, introduced principle of primogeniture into Calenberg.

1692   After lavish promises of assistance to Habsburgs, Ernest Augustus was granted title of Elector of Brunswick–Lüneburg by Emperor Leopold I (despite fact that Duke George William held Lüneburg–Celle, largest of family possessions).

1698   *23 Dec*: Death of Duke Ernest Augustus. Succession in Calenberg of George Louis.

1701   *12 Jun*: Act of Settlement placed Electress Sophia (mother of Duke George Louis) and her Protestant heirs next in succession after Princess Anne to throne of Great Britain and Ireland.
Both George William of Lüneburg–Celle and George Louis of Calenberg joined Grand Alliance against France in approaching War of Spanish Succession, subsequently furnishing more than 10,000 troops.

1705   *28 Aug*: Death of Duke George William. George Louis, who had married Sophia Dorothea, only child of George William, thus inherited Lüneburg–Celle, uniting all territories of house of Guelph and forming what became known as Electorate of Hanover.

1708   Imperial Diet, after 16 years of resistence, finally recognised Duke George Louis as Elector of Holy Roman Empire.

1709   Baron Andreas Gottlieb von Bernstorff appointed chief minister by Elector George Louis.

1714   *28 May*: Death of Electress Sophia.

1 Aug: Death of Queen Anne. Succession of George Louis as King George I, first Hanoverian ruler of Great Britain and Ireland.

George I, before leaving Hanover for London, issued Ordinance determining conduct of government in Hanover after Elector's accession to British throne. Power delegated to Board of Privy Councillors, whose actions were co-ordinated by George through 'minister in attendance' to King and by establishment of 'German Chancery' in London. Ordinance remained basis of Hanoverian system of government until accession of King Ernest Augustus in 1837.

Appointment of Philip von Hattorf as 'minister in attendance' to George I (–1737).

1716   *20 Sep*: Treaty of Hanover between Britain–Hanover and France.

1718   *25 Dec*: Alliance of Vienna between Britain, Hanover, Saxony–Poland and Austria against Russia and Prussia.

1719   *20 Nov*: Peace of Stockholm between Sweden and Hanover, which bought Bremen and Verdun for 1,000,000 thalers.

1720   Fall of Bernstorff from power, although he remained nominally in Hanoverian government until 1723.

1725   *23 Aug*: Treaty of Herrenhausen (or Hanover) between Britain–Hanover, France and Prussia, aimed against Treaty of Vienna between Empire and Spain, guaranteeing Prussia's claim to Jülich–Berg.

1727   *22 Jan*: Death of George I. Succession of George II as King of Great Britain and Elector of Hanover.

1731   Baron G. A. Münchhausen, subsequently chief minister, appointed to Hanoverian Privy Council (–1770).

1741   *Sep*: George II attempted, unsuccessfully, to secure neutrality of Hanover in War of Austrian Succession by signing treaty with France.

1742–   Hanoverian troops served in British pay, in alliance with Austria.
8

1743   *16 Jun*: George II personally led defeat of French at Dettingen, but did not implement plans to invade France.

1749   Philip Adolph Münchhausen, brother of chief Hanoverian minister, made 'minister in attendance' to George II (–1762).

1756   *16 Jan*: Treaty of Westminster between Britain and Prussia, by which Frederick II guaranteed neutrality of Hanover in design to foil French attempts to seize German possessions of George II.

Jun: Hanoverian troops dispatched to England to strengthen defences against France.

1757   *8 Sep*: Duke of Cumberland, commanding Hanoverian, Brunswicker and Hessian troops, surrendered to French at Kloster Seven, allowing occupation of Hanover and Brunswick. George II, refusing to ratify Convention of Kloster Seven, replaced Cumberland as commander by Duke of Brunswick.

Oct: William Pitt rejected terms of Kloster Seven Convention.

1758 *Mar*: Hanover entirely freed from French occupying forces.

1760 *25 Oct*: Death of George II. Succession of George III as King of Great Britain and Elector of Hanover.

1785 *23 Jul*: Hanover joined Frederick II's *Fürstenband* (League of German Princes) to oppose Joseph II's scheme to exchange Austrian Netherlands for Bavaria.

4 *Hesse–Cassel*

1567 Division of Hesse into landgraviates of Hesse–Cassel and Hesse–Darmstadt.

1637 *21 Sep*: Succession of Landgrave Wilhelm VI, a minor.

1648 *24 Oct*: Peace of Westphalia, by which Hesse–Cassel received larger part of countship of Schaumburg and abbey of Hersfeld. (*See* Chapter 6: The Church).

1650 Landgravine Amalia Elisabeth resigned regency and Landgrave Wilhelm VI assumed government. Dispute between court and nobles over latter's traditional privilege of free meetings.

1653 Diet at which nobles left meeting, so that *Recess*, or subsidy, could only be negotiated with towns.

1655 Compromise between nobles and Landgrave, forming basis of Hessian 'constitution' and strengthening Landgrave's powers. Nobles renounced claim to meet without Landgrave's permission; taxes for country and army to be voted by diet, while those for Empire were voted by local assemblies.

1663 *16 Jul*: Death of Wilhelm VI. Succession of Wilhelm VII.

1670 *21 Sep*: Death of Wilhelm VII. Succession of Landgrave Karl.

1682 Diet voted additional taxes and agreed to increase army to 16 companies of cavalry and 31 of infantry, plus life guards.

1688 Outbreak of War of League of Augsburg, which brought increase in size of Hessian army to 41 companies of cavalry and 75 of infantry, numbering over 10,000 men. Increased forces subsidised by United Provinces and Venice.

1727 King George II took entire Hessian army of 12,000 men into service and pay of Great Britain.

1730 *23 Mar*: Death of Landgrave Karl. Succession of Friedrich I, during whose rule size of Hessian army was greatly reduced.

1751   *25 Mar*: Death of Friedrich I. Succession of Wilhelm VIII.

1756– Hessian army fought with Britain against France during Seven
63   Years' War, earning millions of thalers in subsidies.

1760   *1 Feb*: Death of Wilhelm VIII. Succession of Friedrich II, convert to
       Roman Catholicism.

1764   Estates voted extension of excise tax until 1802.

1776   Landgrave Friedrich II concluded new alliance with Britain, under-
       taking to supply 12,000 men to fight in suppression of American
       rebellion.

1776– Mercenary services of Hessian soldiers under British command
84   earned 19,056,778 thalers for Hesse–Cassel, enabling Landgrave
       Friedrich II to lower taxes and maintain amicable relations with
       Estates.

1785   *31 Oct*: Death of Friedrich II. Succession of Wilhelm IX.

1786   Meeting of Diet at which Estates refused new contribution which
       would have lessened their financial powers, due to which no further
       Diet was summoned for eleven years.

5 *Saxony*

1635   *30 May*: Peace of Prague, ending conflict between Empire and
       Saxony, whose possession of Lusatia (180 square miles and
       c. 500,000 inhabitants) was recognised; Lutheran predominance in
       Saxony confirmed.
       Estates granted excise and imposed property tax.

1646   Committees of Estates extended property tax and excise and intro-
       duced new poll tax and levies on trade and enterprise for support of
       army, known subsequently as 'quarter tax'.

1648   *24 Oct*: Peace of Westphalia confirmed provisions of Treaty of
       Prague concerning Saxony.

1653   Committees of Estates extended existing taxes for four years and
       suggested 4000 mercenaries be retained instead of militia, proposal
       accepted by Elector John George I.

1656   *8 Oct*: Death of Elector John George I. Succession of his son, John
       George II. Will of John George I bequeathed territories of
       Saxe–Weissenfels, Saxe–Merseburg and Saxe–Zeitz to younger
       sons.

1657   Estates opposed division of Saxon territories, although matters of
       defence left in Elector's control; excise and 'quarter tax' for army
       continued.

1660   Meeting of Diet, at which Estates extended property and 'quarter'
       taxes, allowing Elector to maintain small standing army, in return for

electoral promise to cut excise taxes and consult Estates on all important matters.

1666 Estates complained that revenues from secularised church lands were being alienated by officials and appointed committee to investigate.

1670 Diet revived opposition to excise, but secured only abolition of excise levies on home-produced products. Funding of army increased to 228,000 guilders per annum (from 112,000 in 1660).

1676 Size of standing army increased to 8260 men and military spending rose to 457,000 guilders.

1680 *22 Aug*: Death of Elector John George II. Succession of John George III.

1681 Meeting of Diet at which Estates reintroduced excise on home-produced goods, voted 800,000 guilders to support army of 10,000 men, and tried unsuccessfully to prevent purchase of noble estates by merchants and other commoners.

1683 Saxon forces joined Imperial army in expulsion of Turks from Habsburg lands.

1691 *12 Sep*: Death of Elector John George III. Succession of John George IV.

1694 Threat issued by John George to Estates that he would introduce general excise on consumption by decree unless Diet approved his proposal.

1694 *27 Apr*: Death of Elector John George IV, before implementing threat to impose excise on consumption. Succession of Frederick Augustus I, also known as Augustus the Strong.

2 Jun: Elector Frederick Augustus announced his conversion to Roman Catholicism as means of obtaining Polish crown.

17 Jun: Election of Augustus as King of Poland in succession to John Sobieski.

1699 Meeting of Diet, at which Estates made strong objections to Frederick Augustus's conversion to Catholicism and complained about holding of Popish services. Estates, after hard bargaining with Elector, voted 1,143,000 guilders to support 20,000-man standing army in return for abolition of 'council of revision' – prerogative court with unlimited powers of investigation and punishment.

1700 *May*: Saxon troops invaded Swedish Livonia, marking start of Great Northern War.

Saxon army increased to 30,000 men and taxes levied without consent of Estates.

1702 'Excise inspection' established and charged with transformation of existing taxes into general excise on consumption in towns desiring this change. By end of 1703, 112 towns joined scheme.

1704   Estates, protesting against general excise, refused to vote money and were dismissed by Elector.

1705   General excise extended by decree to rural areas.

1706   Swedish invasion of Saxony.
    24 Sep: Peace of Altrandstadt with Sweden, which agreed to withdraw its army from Saxony in return for Frederick Augustus's renunciation of Polish throne.

1707   Comprehensive regulation of general excise promulgated, with towns promised surplus.

1709   New poll and property taxes levied by Frederick Augustus without Estates' consent.
    Frederick Augustus regained Polish crown after Russian defeat of Charles XII at Poltava.

1717   Announcement that Frederick Augustus's son and heir had converted to Roman Catholicism.

1718   Meeting of Diet, at which Estates, concerned because of conversion of crown prince to Catholicism, reaffirmed loyalty to Augsburg Confession and limited membership of Estates to Lutherans.

1722   Estates unsuccessfully demanded abolition of general excise.

1725   Estates granted 940,000 guilders to support army of 26,000.

1729   Army recruitment by drawing of lots introduced.

1733   *1 Feb*: Death of Elector Frederick Augustus I. Succession of Frederick Augustus II.
    14 Aug: Frederick Augustus recognised as King Augustus III of Poland.

1733– War of Polish Succession, with Saxon involvement.
5

1740– War of Austrian Succession.
8

1741   *19 Sep*: Saxony joined alliance with France against Maria Theresa.
    1 Nov: Treaty with Prussia and Bavaria for partition of Habsburg lands.

1743   *Dec*: Peace treaty signed with Austria.

1745   *May*: Treaty of Warsaw between Saxony–Poland and Austria for partition of Prussia.

1756   *29 Aug*: Frederick II invaded Saxony, beginning Seven years' War, during which Elector Frederick Augustus and Saxon ministers fled to Poland, leaving Saxony to occupation by Prussia and Austria.

1759   *Aug*: Dresden taken by Austria from Prussians.

1763   *15 Feb*: Peace of Hubertusburg, by which Prussia evacuated Saxony. Diet established sinking fund to pay off massive debts.
    5 Oct: Death of Elector Frederick Augustus II. Succession of Frederick Christian.

17 Dec: Death of Frederick Christian. Succession of Frederick Augustus III, with his uncle Prince Xavier as Regent.

1770   Torture abolished by Elector Frederick Augustus III, subsequently termed Frederick the Just.

6 *Württemberg*

1648   *24 Oct*: Peace in Westphalia confirmed Protestant ascendancy and formally recognised Württemberg's independence from Emperor.

1651–   *May–Jan*: Meeting of Württemberg Diet, at which Estates ex-
2   tended excise on foreign imports, salt, wine, beer, etc. (first levied in 1638); assumed 3,000,000-guilder government debt; granted Duke Eberhard III 40,000 guilders; but refused to pay for fortresses and garrisons.

1659   Estates granted 50,000 guilders for three years, but only on condition that Duke Eberhard would not join Rhenish Alliance against Habsburg Emperor or build new fortresses.

1660   *Jan*: Duke Eberhard joined Rhenish Alliance, despite his contrary promise to Estates, which were at length persuaded to grant additional money, which was employed to support small force of standing guards.

1672   Estates agreed to pay for small contingents of infantry and cavalry to aid Imperial forces against French.

1673   Estates persuaded by Duke Eberhard to raise and pay for additional 200 horse and 1000 foot soldiers to resist French threat.

1674   *2 Jul*: Death of Duke Eberhard III. Succession of his son, Duke Wilhelm Ludwig.

1675   Estates consented to maintain Württemberg contingent with Imperial army, in addition to five companies conceded in 1673 which formed nucleus of standing force.

1677   *23 Jun*: Death of Duke Wilhelm Ludwig. Succession of Eberhard Ludwig, aged nine months, with his uncle, Duke Frederick Charles as Regent.

1680   Estates voted 86,000 guilders for defence and other purposes in addition to 200,000 for repayment of debts, allowing 400 additional standing troops to be recruited.

1689   French threat forced Estates to agree to support 2500 mercenaries and 8000 militiamen during War of League of Augsburg.

1691   Württemberg militia 'transformed' by Regent Frederick Charles into standing army of 6000 men, despite protests of Estates.

1693   *Jan*: Duke Eberhard Ludwig declared to have obtained his majority at age 16.

Aug: French occupied Württemberg, burned and looted several towns, and exacted tribute of 600,000 guilders and further 150,000 per year during war.

1695– Duke Eberhard Ludwig claimed right to administer Estates' con-
6   tributions, to maintain standing army, and to collect extraordinary taxes.

1698– *Sep–Jan*: Only meeting of Diet during reign of Eberhard Ludwig, at
9   which Estates refused to vote supply unless standing army was disbanded. Duke Eberhard Ludwig refused and Diet ended in open rupture.

1699 Duke collected taxes despite refusal of Estates and their permanent committees to grant approval.

1704 Treaty with Holland, which agreed to pay 300,000 guilders per annum for upkeep of expanded army during War of Spanish Succession.

1706 Permanent Committee of Estates protested against standing army and absolute government, but was finally induced to grant supply.

1713 *31 Mar*: Peace of Utrecht, ending War of Spanish Succession, whereupon Württemberg troops temporarily passed into pay of Empire.

1715 Permanent Committee of Estates persuaded to grant 195,000 guilders, thus indirectly conceding maintenance of peacetime standing army.
      Jul: Duke Eberhard Ludwig extended taxes on wine and corn by decree.

1719 Duke Eberhard Ludwig established *Generalkriegscommisariat* on Prussian model, with responsibility for military administration and finances.

1724 Permanent Committee of Estates voted 367,000 guilders a year for maintenance of ducal standing army (at that time 1800 strong), in return for abolition of one-thirtieth tax on corn and wine.

1733 *31 Oct*: Death of Duke Eberhard Ludwig. Succession of his cousin, Karl Alexander, convert to Roman Catholicism.

1734 Taxes on salaries, property, church, etc., introduced and collected by ducal decree.

1735 Permanent Committee of Estates agreed to recruitment of standing army of 12,100 men.

1737 *12 Mar*: Death of Duke Karl Alexander. Succession of Karl Eugen, aged nine, and collapse of schemes for imposing absolutist government.
      Jul: Meeting of first Württemberg Diet for 39 years, at which standing army was reduced to 500 men and taxes lowered.

1744 Duke Karl Eugen assumed government of duchy at age 16.

1752 Treaty with France, whereby Louis XV promised to pay 387,000 guilders a year for maintenance of 6000 infantrymen during peace (479,000 during war), making Karl Eugen more financially independent of Estates.

1759 Estates' house in Stuttgart surrounded by ducal troops and Estates' receivers forced to pay 30,000 guilders – procedure repeated six months later.

1762 New military plan published which required collection of increased taxes by force.

1763 Diet convened, at which Estates refused to support army or illegal taxation and were speedily dismissed.

1764 *Mar*: Annual tax of 920,000 guilders decreed by Duke Karl Eugen, to be collected by army.

1770 Compromise between Estates and Duke suggested by Aulic Council of Empire, by which Estates retained financial powers but agreed to fund standing army of 3000.

1793 *24 Oct*: Death of Duke Karl Eugen.

GREAT BRITAIN AND IRELAND

1 *England*

1648 *1 May*: Invasion of Scottish army marks start of second Civil War.

17–20 Aug: Scots defeated at Preston by Oliver Cromwell.

27 Aug: General Fairfax captured Colchester after lengthy siege.

18 Sep: Negotiations between Charles I and Parliament opened at Newport.

28 Sep: Charles offered slight concessions regarding command of army and religion.

2 Oct: Charles's concessions rejected by Parliament, and, on 27 Oct, refused King's offer of further concessions.

27 Nov: Parliamentary commissions broke off negotiations with Charles I and left Newport.

6 Dec: Colonel Pride's purge of House of Commons, expelling members thought hostile to army, including many Presbyterians. Parliamentary remnant, known thereafter as the 'Rump', subsequently voted to abandon negotiations with Charles I.

23 Dec: Rump Parliament voted to put Charles I on trial.

John Lilburne published *The Foundations of Freedom*.

1649 *19 Jan*: Trial of Charles I began.

30 Jan: Execution of Charles I: Prince of Wales assumed title of Charles II in exile at The Hague.

17 Mar: House of Lords abolished by Rump Parliament.

19 Mar: English monarchy abolished.

28 Mar: Leveller leaders arrested.

15 May: Levellers defeated at Burford.

19 May: England declared Commonwealth by Rump.

John Milton's *The Tenure of Kings and Magistrates* defended execution of Charles I.

Eikon Basilike, by John Gauden, based partly on notes of Charles I, defended institution of monarchy and reputation of Charles I; began martyr cult of slain king.

John Lilburne wrote *An Agreement of the Free People of England* and *The Legall, Fundamental Liberties of the People of England* ...

English replaced Latin as language of legal documents (until 1660).

Diggers established settlement at St George's Hill, Surrey, and attempted to till common land, denouncing institution of private property.

1650   *1 Aug*: Permanent economic council established.

3 Sep: Cromwell and New Model defeated Scots at Dunbar.

24 Dec: Surrender of Edinburgh to English army.

1651   *3 Sep*: Cromwell defeated Charles II and Scottish forces at Worcester. Charles II escaped to continent after flight disguised in female clothing (*17 Oct*).

9 Oct: First Navigation Act passed to secure monopoly of English trade for native vessels; specifically aimed against Dutch.

Leviathan published by Thomas Hobbes.

1652   *Feb*: Act of Pardon and Oblivion passed by Rump Parliament to reconcile royalists.

2 Aug: Army rejected Perpetuation Bill, demanding new parliamentary elections and further reforms.

1653   *20 Apr*: Cromwell 'interrupted' Rump Parliament, expelling members by force.

29 Apr: Ten-member Council of State established by Cromwell.

4 Jul: Meeting of 'Barebones' Parliament.

16 Dec: Instrument of Government proclaimed England a Protectorate, with Council of State and Oliver Cromwell as Protector, following vote of Barebones Parliament to dissolve itself (manipulated by Cromwell's supporters).

1654   *12 Apr*: Union of Scotland and Ireland with England.

3 Sep: Meeting of first Protectorate Parliament.

12 Sep: 100 republicans excluded from Parliament by Cromwell who, however, later readmitted them when they accepted certain of his proposals.

1655   *22 Jan*: Dissolution by Cromwell of first Protectorate Parliament.

11–14 Mar: Abortive royalist rising in Wiltshire led by Colonel John Penruddock, subsequently executed. Penruddock's rebellion scuttled Cromwell's conciliatory schemes and launched anti-royalist reaction.

9 Aug: Rule of Major-Generals began; England divided into 11 military districts, each governed by a major-general.

1656   *17 Sep*: Meeting of second Protectorate Parliament.

James Harrington, in *Commonwealth of Oceana*, advocated republic ruled by landed oligarchy, with educational, electoral and parliamentary reforms.

1657   *31 Mar*: Parliament, in Humble Petition and Advice, offered title of King to Oliver Cromwell.

3 Apr: Cromwell rejected offer of crown.

25 May: New Humble Petition and Advice created new house of peers and increased Cromwell's power.

26 Jun: Further Petition and Advice expanded power of Parliament; Cromwell reconfirmed as Protector.

Cromwell authorised foundation of Durham College (dissolved 1660).

1658   *20 Jan*: Parliament reconvened.

4 Feb: Cromwell dissolved second Protectorate Parliament after revelation of intrigues between republican MPs and army officers.

17 Mar: Discovery of royalist plot.

3 Sep: Death of Oliver Cromwell. Succession of his eldest son Richard Cromwell as Lord Protector according to Humble Petition and Advice.

1659   *27 Jan*: Meeting of Richard's Parliament, called to vote supplies and confirm Protectorate but debates stymied by republican intransigence. Army alienated by anti-militarist attacks by MPs.

22 Apr: Richard Cromwell forced to dissolve Parliament by army, which now seized reins of government.

7 May: Rump Parliament recalled by army; scarcely concealed struggle for power commenced between military and civilian authorities.

25 May: Richard Cromwell forced to resign as Lord Protector, thwarting army hierarchy which planned to use him as figurehead. Commonwealth reproclaimed by Rump Parliament.

Aug: Royalist rebellion in Cheshire led by Sir George Booth crushed by Major-General John Lambert.

13 Oct: Army expelled Rump Parliament after parliamentary attempts to purge army hierarchy and establish supremacy of civil authority. Parliament supported by General George Monck, commander of army in Scotland.

26 Dec: Rump Parliament restored after defection of Portsmouth garrison and rising in Yorkshire.

1660   *1 Jan*: General Monck led his army, purged of radicals, across R. Tweed into England and began march south towards London.

Jan: Rump purged army hierarchy and hundreds of lesser officers.

3 Feb: General Monck led his forces into London, having received many petitions for 'Free Parliament' and having forced Rump to remove contingents of English army from capital.

16 Feb: Monck declared for 'Free Parliament', involving dissolution of Rump and fresh elections.

21 Feb: Monck removed guard from Parliament allowing Presbyterian members of Long Parliament excluded by Colonel Pride in 1648 to resume their seats.

Feb–Mar: Further purge of army by General Monck.

Mar: New militia act empowering Monck and Council of State to purge militia of republican elements.

16 Mar: Long Parliament (first met November 1640) dissolved itself and provided for new elections, supposedly excluding royalists.

4 Apr: Charles II, after learning of General Monck's intention to restore monarchy, issued Declaration of Breda, promising amnesty, religious toleration and payment of army arrears.

25 Apr–29 Dec: Convention Parliament met at Westminster and subsequently invited Charles II to return to England and resume crown.

1 May: Charles II proclaimed King of England.

29 May: Charles II entered London amidst tumultuous celebrations.

Jun–Jul: Army again purged and royalist officers appointed; Anglican hierarchy restored by royal prerogative.

29 Aug: Act of Indemnity and Oblivion signed by Charles II.

8 Sep: Thomas, Earl of Southampton, appointed Lord Treasurer.

Sep: Convention voted for dissolution of army.

Sep–Dec: Army gradually disbanded, leaving only two regiments of foot and one of horse by end of year.

29 Dec: Dissolution of Convention Parliament.

1661   *7 Jan*: Council for Foreign Plantations first met.

20 Jan: Venner's Rebellion, abortive Fifth Monarchist uprising in London, providing royal government with excuse to retain and expand standing army.

20 Apr: Edward Hyde, Lord Chancellor, created 1st Earl of Clarendon.

23 Apr: Coronation of Charles II.

8 May: Second Parliament of Charles II first met; overwhelmingly royalist, it became known as 'Cavalier Parliament' (–Jan 1679)

20 Dec: Charles II signed Corporation Act, which compelled all town officials in England and Wales to take Anglican sacrament, swear oaths of allegiance and supremacy, and renounce use of force against King. Commissions of gentry and aristocracy appointed in each county to administer act, which resulted in many expulsions.

1662   *Mar*: A Bill is introduced in the House of Commons for the introduction of a Hearth Tax at the rate of two shillings on each fireplace or stove.

      19 May: Act of Uniformity passed by Parliament. (*See* Chapter 6: The Church.)

      21 May: Marriage of Charles II and Catherine of Braganza.

      27 Oct: Dunkirk sold by Charles II to France for 2½ million livres (£400,000).

1663   *10 Jan*: Royal African Company granted charter.

      Aug–Oct: Derwentdale or Yorkshire plot exposed, implicating former Cromwellian officers.

1664   *May*: Passage of Conventicle Act directed against meetings of Nonconformists. (*See* Chapter 6: The Church.)

      Jun: Undeclared war breaks out in colonies and at sea with Holland (United Provinces).

1665   *4 Mar*: Declaration of war against Holland.

      Great Plague of London, reaching peak in September.

      9–31 Oct: Fifth session of Cavalier Parliament held at Oxford because of plague in London; passage on 30 Oct of Five-Mile Act. (*See* Chapter 6: The Church.)

1666   *2–6 Sep*: Great Fire of London destroyed much of city, including old St Paul's Cathedral.

1667   *21 Jul*: Peace of Breda ended second Dutch war.

      30 Aug: Earl of Clarendon, accused of mismanagement of war and absolutist counsel, forced to resign. Clarendon's fall followed by gradual emergence of Clifford, Arlington, Buckingham, Ashley Cooper and Lauderdale, known collectively as the Cabal.

      29 Nov: Earl of Clarendon fled to France to escape impeachment.

1670   *1 Jun*: Secret Treaty of Dover between Charles II and Louis XIV; England to aid France in new war against Holland and Charles II to receive subsidies of £150,000 p.a. (£225,000 during war) in return for announcing his conversion to Roman Catholicism; French troops to be sent to impose Catholicism if necessary.

1671   *22 Apr*: Parliament prorogued by Charles II (until February 1673). Crown resumed direct control of customs (farmed since 1605).

1672   *2 Jan*: Stop of the Exchequer, whereby the government suspended payment of interest on loans advanced by London financiers, bankrupting many. Economic council organised with Ashley Cooper as president and John Locke as secretary.

15 Mar: Declaration of Indulgence to Catholics and Protestant dissenters, in which Charles II suspended penal laws against religious noncomformity.

17 Mar: Declaration of war against Holland, inaugurating third Dutch War.

17 Nov: Anthony Ashley Cooper, new Earl of Shaftesbury, appointed Lord Chancellor.

1673 *4 Feb*: Parliament met for the first time since April 1671.

19 Feb: Commons resolution that King could not suspend laws in ecclesiastical matters.

8 Mar: Charles II withdrew Declaration of Indulgence.

29 Mar: First Test Act, excluding Roman Catholics from office, given royal assent.

19 Jun: Sir Thomas Osborne, later Earl of Danby, replaced Lord Clifford as Lord Treasurer.

12 Jun: James, Duke of York, forced to resign as Lord High Admiral by Test Act.

21 Nov: Marriage of Duke of York and Mary of Modena, Roman Catholic princess, hastily performed by Nathaniel Crewe, Bishop of Oxford.

1674 *9 Feb*: England withdrew from Dutch war due to intense parliamentary pressure.

Jun: Earl of Arlington made Lord Chamberlain, after selling his secretaryship of state to Joseph Williamson under duress.

1675 *Apr*: Danby introduced Non-Resisting Test Bill in House of Lords, which would have required all members of Parliament and all office-holders to swear to oppose any alterations in government; Test failed due to conflict between Lords and Commons over procedural matters.

22 Nov: Charles II, armed with £100,000 p.a. subsidy from Louis XIV, prorogued Parliament (−15 Feb 1677).

1677 *15 Feb*: Parliament met after 15-month prorogation. Lords Shaftesbury, Buckingham, Salisbury and Wharton imprisoned in Tower for having argued that long prorogation had in fact dissolved Cavalier Parliament.

28 May: Declaration by Charles II that foreign policy was part of royal prerogative.

4 Nov: Marriage of William of Orange and Princess Mary, Protestant daughter of Duke of York. Marriage an attempt by Earl of Danby to wean Charles II from French alliance towards Dutch one.

1678 *Feb*: Earl of Shaftesbury released from Tower.

73

English troops recalled from French service and contingent dispatched to Flanders, in aid of Dutch.

4 Jun: Suspecting Charles II's motive in expanding army was not to make war against France but establish absolutism in England, Parliament voted £200,000 to disband forces. King subsequently used money to keep troops standing.

13 Aug: Popish Plot, in which it was alleged that Pope Innocent XI had instructed Jesuits to murder Charles II, overthrow his government and re-establish Roman Catholicism with French and Spanish aid, first revealed to King.

6 Sep: Titus Oates deposed his version of the Popish Plot before Sir Edmund Berry Godfrey, London magistrate.

17 Oct: Sir Edmund Berry Godfrey found murdered on Primrose Hill.

30 Nov: Charles II vetoed Militia Bill which would have disbanded army, claiming it invaded royal prerogative.

1 Dec: Charles II signed second Test Act, which excluded Roman Catholics from both houses of Parliament.

21 Dec: Earl of Danby impeached by Commons for counselling arbitrary government, rule by a standing army, making clandestine agreements with France, being 'Popishly affected' and concealing the Popish Plot. Lords refused to commit Danby or proceed in case.

1679 *24 Jan*: Dissolution of Cavalier Parliament, first elected in 1661.

4 Mar: Duke of York sent into exile by Charles II in attempt to pacify opposition.

6 Mar: Meeting of First Exclusion Parliament (−27 May).

21 May: Exclusion Bill to ban Duke of York from succession passed in Commons by vote of 207 to 128.

27 May: Parliament prorogued by King to stop Exclusion Bill; Charles II passed Habeas Corpus Act.

22 Jun: Duke of Monmouth defeated Scottish Covenanters at Bothwell Bridge.

12 Jul: Dissolution of First Exclusion Parliament.

7 Oct: Second Exclusion Parliament prorogued on day it was to have first met.

15 Oct: Earl of Shaftesbury dismissed from Privy Council; subsequently Lords Essex and Halifax resigned.

1680 Robert Filmer's *Patriarcha; or the Natural Power of Kings* first published posthumously.

21 Oct: Second Exclusion Parliament finally met.

4 Nov: First reading of Exclusion Bill barring James, Duke of York, from throne and making it treasonous for him to enter Britain.

11 Nov: Exclusion Bill passed Commons.

15 Nov: House of Lords rejected exclusions by vote of 63 to 30.

29 Dec: Earl of Stafford executed for alleged implication in Popish Plot.

1681 *7 Jan*: Commons resolved that no further supplies would be granted until Exclusion was passed.

18 Jan: Second Exclusion Parliament dissolved.

21 Mar: Third Exclusion or Oxford Parliament met at Oxford, London having been deemed too turbulent.

28 Mar: Oxford Parliament dissolved after introduction of a third Exclusion Bill.

Chelsea Hospital founded by Charles II for wounded and retired soldiers.

2 Jul: Earl of Shaftesbury accused of high treason and sent to Tower.

1681 *Nov*: John Dryden published *Absolom and Achitophel*, part 1, poetic allegory of Exclusion crisis.

Dec: Writ of *quo warranto* against city of London launched campaign by crown to remodel borough corporations.

1682 *Feb*: Shaftesbury released from Tower on bail.

Mar: Duke of York allowed to return to England.

Jun–Sep: Tories captured control of London after intervention of crown in disputed sheriffs' election.

19 Oct: Shaftesbury fled to exile in Holland on hearing of his imminent rearrest.

1683 *21 Jan*: Death of Shaftesbury in Holland.

28 Jan: Earl of Sunderland appointed Secretary of State, North (–1684: then South till 1688).

12 Jun: Discovery of Rye House Plot to assassinate Charles II and Duke of York and put Duke of Monmouth on throne.

21 Jul: William Russell executed for alleged implication in Rye House Plot.

4 Oct: Judgement delivered against London for forfeiture of its charter.

7 Dec: Algernon Sydney executed for alleged plotting against King.

25 Dec: Flight of Duke of Monmouth to Holland following arrest and execution of Whig leaders.

1684 *May*: Charles II granted Duke of York dispensation from Test Act, reappointing him Lord High Admiral.

Remodelling of charters of London and 65 provincial towns accelerated; King given power to appoint some officials, veto election of others and thus indirectly control election of borough MPs.

Garrison of Tangiers abandoned by English forces, which were ordered home by Charles II and incorporated in domestic standing army.

1685   *6 Feb*: Death of Charles II. Succession of James II.

16 Feb: Earl of Rochester appointed Lord Treasurer, and (*18 Feb*) Lord President of Council.

19 May: Meeting of James's Parliament, overwhelmingly Tory and loyalist in composition; Earl of Danby released from Tower.

11 Jun: Outbreak of Monmouth's Rebellion.

30 Jun: Earl of Argyle executed for role in rebellion.

6 Jul: Monmouth defeated at Sedgemoor and captured.

15 Jul: Monmouth executed.

Sep: Judge Jeffreys conducted 'Bloody Assizes' in West Country, sentencing hundreds to death or exile.

28 Sep: Jeffreys appointed Lord Chancellor.

12–19 Nov: Parliament refused to approve repeal of Test Acts.

4 Dec: Earl of Sunderland appointed Lord President of Council.

1686   *Apr*: Godden *vs* Hales, collusive case in which judges ruled that James II could dispense with Test Acts; King then proceeded to introduce Roman Catholics into army, universities and Anglican Church.

Jul: Court of Ecclesiastical Commission set up by James to control church.

10 Dec: Earl of Rochester dismissed as Treasurer.

1687   *4 Apr*: James II granted extensive indulgence to Protestant dissenters and Roman Catholic recusants.

2 Jul: Parliament, prorogued since 20 November 1685, was dissolved.

July–Aug: King dismissed many Tory Anglicans from municipal corporations and appointed nonconformists and Catholics. Lord and deputy lieutenants questioned about willingness to repeal Test Acts; most gave negative responses and many were removed from office.

1688   *27 Apr*: Declaration of Indulgence reissued.

4 May: James II ordered Anglican clergy to read Declaration of Indulgence from pulpit on two consecutive Sundays.

18 May: Archbishop of Canterbury Sancroft and six other bishops refused to read Declaration and petitioned against order.

8 Jun: Seven bishops arrested and sent to Tower to await trial.

10 Jun: Birth of a son to James II and Mary of Modena, giving rise to rumour that infant had been smuggled into palace in warming pan.

29–30 Jun: Trial and acquittal of seven bishops.

30 Jun: Prominent Whigs and Tories led by Danby, Shrewsbury, Devonshire, Compton, Sidney Lumley and Robinson invited William of Orange to invade England in defence of 'liberties'.

30 Sep: William of Orange accepted invitation to invade England and issued manifesto (*1 Oct*).

5 Nov: William of Orange landed at Torbay in Devon with 15,000

Dutch troops. Risings followed in Midlands and North led by Lords Devonshire and Danby.

19 Dec: William entered London.

25 Dec: James II allowed to escape to France.

29 Dec: Convention Parliament summoned.

1689   *22 Jan*: Convention Parliament met.

28 Jan: Convention declared that James II had abdicated and that throne was vacant.

12 Feb: William and Mary proclaimed King and Queen for life; Declaration of Rights claimed suspension of laws without Parliament illegal.

13 Feb: Bill of Rights drawn up by parliamentary committee.

5 Mar: Earl of Nottingham made Secretary of State, South.

12 Apr: Toleration Act passed by Parliament. (*See* Chapter 6: The Church.)

Jul: Bill of Rights enacted.

1690   *6 Feb*: Convention Parliament dissolved.

20 Mar: Second Parliament of William and Mary met (−3 May 1695).

1692   *10 Jan*: Earl of Marlborough (John Churchill) dismissed for alleged communication with James II.

3 Mar: Earl of Nottingham became sole Secretary of State.

5 May: Marlborough imprisoned in Tower, but released soon afterwards.

1693   *23 Mar*: Lord Somers made Lord Keeper as head of Whig 'Junto'.

7 Nov: Earl of Nottingham, Tory Secretary of State, dismissed.

1694   *2 Mar*: Earl of Shrewsbury, member of Whig Junto, appointed Secretary of State.

May: Ministry remodelled leaving Whig Junto – Somers, Shrewsbury, Wharton, Russell and Montague – in control; all Tories except Danby and Godolphin removed.

27 Jul: Bank of England founded.

3 Dec: Parliament passed Triennial Act, providing for new parliament to be elected every three years; royal assent conferred 22 Dec.

28 Dec: Queen Mary died of smallpox.

1695   *6 May*: Duke of Leeds (formerly Earl of Danby) forced to resign as Lord President of Council for accepting bribe.

22 Nov: William's third Parliament met with large Whig majority (−5 July 1698).

1696   *14 Feb*: William III revealed to Parliament plot to kill him by Sir John Fenwick and Jacobites.

27 Feb: Oath of Association to defend William and Protestant succession taken throughout England and Wales (– May).

1697   *21 Jan*: Sir John Fenwick executed.

22 Apr: Lord Somers made Lord Chancellor; Bank of England's charter renewed (–1711).

1 May: Resignation of Sidney Godolphin as First Lord of Treasury, leaving ministry wholly Whig; appointment of Charles Montague as First Lord.

Sep: Treaty of Ryswick signed, ending War of League of Augsburg.

Dec: Robert Harley's motion to disband all forces raised since 1680 approved by both houses of Parliament; Earl of Sunderland resigned from royal service.

1698   Parliament established Civil List to supplement crown income from hereditary sources.

Sep–Oct: William III committed England to Partition Treaty dividing Spanish possessions without consulting ministers or Parliament.

6 Dec: Meeting of William's fourth Parliament (–11 Apr 1700).

1699   *Jan*: Parliament forced William to reduce drastically the size of the English army and disband Dutch guards.

1700   *14 Mar*: Second Partition Treaty (of June 1699) ratified.

11 Apr: Parliament prorogued.

17 Apr: William III forced to dismiss Somers as Lord Chancellor.

12 Dec: Sidney Godolphin rejoined ministry as Treasurer.

1701   *6 Feb*: Parliament resumed sitting; Robert Harley elected Speaker of Commons.

14 Apr: Commons began impeachment proceedings against Whig ministers Somers, Orford and Montague for failing to consult Parliament over Partition Treaties.

12 Jun: Act of Settlement provided that Protestant succession be safeguarded by making Electress Sophia of Hanover, granddaughter of James I, next in line to throne after Princess Anne. Act also outlawed royal pardon of those impeached by Parliament and prevented removal of judges by monarch.

11 Nov: Parliament dissolved.

30 Dec: Sixth Parliament of William III met (–2 July 1702).

1702   *20 Feb*: Act for attainder of Pretender, James Edward Stuart.

24 Feb: Act of Abjuration of Pretender, requiring oath of loyalty to King and heirs according to Act of Settlement.

8 Mar: Death of William III. Succession of Queen Anne.

24 Mar: Marlborough made Captain-General of armed forces.

23 Apr: Coronation of Queen Anne; new coronation oath pledged monarch to obey parliamentary statutes and uphold Anglican settlement.

4 May: Declaration of war against France and Spain.

6 May: Sidney Godolphin appointed Lord Treasurer.

20 Oct: Meeting of Anne's first Parliament (–5 Apr 1705).

1703   *16 Jan*: Tory bill requiring frequent communion for office-holders defeated in Lords despite Queen's backing.

Mar: Queen persuaded by Earls of Nottingham and Rochester to dismiss several Whig lord and deputy lieutenants, sheriffs and justices of the peace.

7 Dec: Second bill against occasional conformity defeated in Lords after Commons' approval.

1704   *20 Apr*: Henry St John named Secretary of War.

18 May: Robert Harley, moderate Tory, made Secretary of State, North.

14–15 Dec: Bill to outlaw occasional conformity, 'tacked' to money bill by High Church Tories, defeated in Parliament.

1705   *5 Apr*: Dissolution of Anne's first parliament

25 Oct: Anne's second Parliament met with pronounced Whig majority.

1706   *3 Dec*: 3rd Earl of Sunderland appointed Secretary of State, South.

1707   *6 Mar*: Act of Union joining Kingdoms of England and Scotland under name of Great Britain given royal assent; Act provided for Hanoverian succession, one Parliament at Westminster where Scotland would be represented, security of Anglican Church in England and Presbyterian Church in Scotland, and adoption of common flag – the Union Jack.

1 May: Union of England and Scotland effected.

Oct: Second Parliament of Anne reconvened as first Parliament of Great Britain.

1708   *13 Feb*: Whig pressure forced Queen Anne to dismiss Robert Harley as Secretary of State, North.

25 Feb: Robert Walpole, Whig, appointed Secretary at War.

16 Nov: Queen Anne's third Parliament, with Whig majority, first met.

1709   *5 Nov*: Dr Henry Sacheverell preached fiery sermon condemning toleration of nonconformists and praising divine right of monarchy before lord mayor and alderman of London at St Paul's Cathedral.

13 Dec: Dr Sacheverell impeached by Whig majority in Commons.

1710   *27 Feb–20 Mar*: Trial of Sacheverell; (*23 Mar*) Sacheverell suspended from preaching for three years; lightness of sentence seen as reversal for Whig ministry. On 28 February began pro-Sacheverell riots in which London mobs sacked several nonconformist meeting houses, finally suppressed by army.

14 Jun: Sunderland dismissed as Secretary of State, South.

8 Aug: Queen dismissed Godolphin and Whig ministry; Robert Harley, as Chancellor of Exchequer, and Henry St John, as Secretary of State, North, formed Tory ministry.

21 Sep: Dissolution of Parliament, followed by elections.

25 Nov: Fourth Parliament of Anne met with Tory majority.

1711 *22 Feb*: Parliament passed Landed Property Qualification Act, which provided that knights of shire own property worth £600 p.a. and borough MPs property worth £300.

29 Mar: Robert Harley made Lord Treasurer.

23 May: Harley created Earl of Oxford.

15 Dec: New bill against occasional conformity introduced in Lords by Nottingham.

31 Dec: Queen, bowing to Tory pressure, dismissed Duke of Marlborough as Commander-in-Chief.

1712 *1 Jan*: Twelve new Tory peers created by Anne to assure success of government peace initiative in Lords.

17 Jan: Robert Walpole imprisoned in Tower for alleged corruption as Secretary at War.

1713 *8 Aug*: Anne's fourth Parliament dissolved, followed by elections.

Earl of Mar appointed Secretary of State for Scotland.

1714 *16 Feb*: Fifth Parliament of Queen Anne convened.

15 Jun: Passage of Schism Act, which provided that anyone keeping or teaching in a private school must be an Anglican licensed by a bishop.

27 Jul: Earl of Oxford dismissed as Lord Treasurer following manoeuvrings by Bolingbroke.

1 Aug: Death of Queen Anne shortly after appointment of Shrewsbury as Lord Treasurer. Succession of George Louis, Elector of Hanover, as George I.

17 Sep: Ministry dominated by militant Whigs formed with Townshend and Stanhope as Secretaries of State, Walpole as Paymaster-General, and Shrewsbury as Lord Chamberlain.

17 Sep: George I landed in England.

20 Oct: Coronation of George I.

1715 *5 Jan*: Parliament dissolved, followed by elections.

17 Mar: First Parliament of George I met with large Whig majority.

27 Mar: Bolingbroke, fearing arrest, fled to France.

10 Jun: Impeachment of Bolingbroke for high treason followed by that of Oxford.

9 Jul: Earl of Oxford imprisoned in Tower for his part in peace negotiations with French. Passage of Riot Act due to fears of Jacobite disturbances, followed on 12 Jul by suspension of Habeas Corpus Act.

23 Jul: Bolingbroke joined court of Stuart Pretender as adviser.

18 Aug: Act of Attainder against Bolingbroke passed.

6 Sep: Jacobite rebellion to restore Stuarts to British throne began at Braemar in Scotland, under Earl of Mar.

12 Oct: Robert Walpole appointed First Lord of Treasury and Chancellor of Exchequer following death of Lord Halifax (Charles Montagu).

13 Nov: Jacobites defeated at Sheriffmuir and Preston.

22 Dec: Pretender James Edward Stuart finally landed at Peterhead in Scotland.

1716   *10 Feb*: Pretender returned to France in flight from Scotland and subsequently dismissed Bolingbroke.

26 Apr: Septennial Act passed by Whig majority, extending life of Parliament from three to seven years; royal assent given on 7 May.

12 Dec: Lord Townshend dismissed as Secretary of State, North, for opposing French alliance favoured by George I for defence of Hanover.

1717   *10 Apr*: Walpole resigned as First Lord of Treasury and Chancellor of Exchequer and was succeeded by Stanhope; Joseph Addison made Secretary of State, South, and Sunderland Secretary of State, North.

1 Jul: Oxford acquitted of secret dealings with France and released from Tower.

Walpole's scheme to consolidate national debt at lower interest put into operation by Stanhope by means of General Fund Act, Bank Act and South Sea Act. 'Sinking Fund' then established from surplus obtained by reducing interest.

1718   *21 Mar*: Sunderland, with royal approval, remodelled ministry, making Stanhope Secretary of State, North, and John Aislabie Chancellor of Exchequer. Sunderland became First Lord of Treasury.

17 Dec: Britain declared war on Spain.

1719   *7 Jan*: Whigs led by Stanhope repealed Schism Act and Act of Occasional Conformity despite Walpole's opposition.

28 Apr: Peerage Bill to fix number of peers in House of Lords, originally sponsored by ministry, defeated in Commons largely due to opposition of Walpole faction.

8 Dec: Peerage Bill, reintroduced by Duke of Buckingham, defeated again in Commons.

1720   *7 Apr*: royal assent given to act empowering South Sea Company to manage national debt, followed by sharp escalation in value of South Sea stocks.

11 Jun: Robert Walpole and Charles Townshend return to office from their 'political wilderness' as Paymaster-General and Lord President of Council respectively.

Oct–Nov: 'South Sea Bubble' began to burst. Wild speculation in South Sea and other stocks led to panic selling, collapse of prices and ruin for thousands of investors.

1721   *24 Jan*: Knight, cashier of South Sea Company, fled with register, obstructing parliamentary investigation. Thereafter company's directors detained and five holding government posts dismissed. John Aislabie forced to resign as Chancellor of Exchequer.

      5 Feb: Earl of Stanhope died of brain haemorrhage.

      10 Feb: Townshend appointed Secretary of State, North.

      5 Mar: John Lord Carteret named Secretary of State, South.

      8 Mar: House of Commons unanimously voted Aislabie guilty of fraud, expelled him from Parliament, and imprisoned him in Tower.

      15 Mar: Earl of Sunderland acquitted of charges of corruption, but weakened by scandal and soon forced to resign.

      4 Apr: Robert Walpole appointed First Lord of the Treasury and Chancellor of Exchequer.

      19 Oct: Speech from the throne announced Walpole ministry's intentions to reduce export duties on manufactures and import duties on raw materials.

1722   *10 Mar*: Dissolution of George I's first Parliament.

      9 Oct: George I's second Parliament met with huge Whig majority.

1723   *May*: Lord Bolingbroke pardoned; returned to England in June but barred from sitting in House of Lords.

      June: System of bonded warehouses established to prevent smuggling and increase revenues on tea and coffee.

1724   *3 Apr*: Carteret dismissed as Secretary of State, South, for political intrigues against Walpole and Townshend, and made Lord Lieutenant of Ireland.

      6 Apr: Thomas Pelham-Holles, Duke of Newcastle appointed Secretary of State, South, and his brother, Henry Pelham, named Secretary at War.

      Professorships of modern history and languages founded by George I at Oxford and Cambridge.

1725   *Jul*: Tax on beer provoked serious riots in Glasgow.

      Office of Secretary of State for Scotland abolished.

1726   *24 Nov*: *The Craftsman*, journal edited by Bolingbroke and Pulteney to attack Walpole ministry, first appeared.

1727   *Feb*: Undeclared war broke out between Britain and Spain when latter began siege of Gibraltar.

      11 Jan: Death of George I. Succession of son, George II (–1760).

      27 Jun: Walpole reappointed First Lord of Treasury and Chancellor of Exchequer by George II, who had originally planned to dismiss him; in return Walpole raised Civil List to £800,000 p.a.

      17 Jul: George I's second Parliament formally dissolved.

1728   *23 Jan*: First Parliament of George II met.

1730   *15 May*: Resignation of Lord Townshend as Secretary of State,

North, after quarrel with Walpole over direction of foreign policy; succeeded by William Stanhope, Earl of Harrington, after refusal of office by Pulteney.

Walpole lowered land tax to two shillings in pound.

1731   *11 Jul*: Britain joined Empire, Holland and Spain in Treaty of Vienna upholding Pragmatic Sanction and preserving peace in Italy.

1733   *11 April*: Walpole forced to withdraw Excise Bill, which would have established system of bonded warehouses to regulate excise collections on wine and tobacco, after fierce controversy. Afterwards, office-holders opposing scheme were dismissed.

1734   *16 Apr*: Dissolution of first Parliament of George II, followed by elections.

1735   *14 Jan*: Second Parliament of George II met.

1736   *Mar*: Repeal of Test Act defeated 251 to 123 in Commons, Walpole opposing.

Passage of Gin Act imposing 20 shilling a gallon tax on spirits and £50 licence for selling them, to take effect 29 September.

Aug–Sep: Outbreak of Gin Riots in London in anticipation of Gin Act coming into force; became anti-Irish in character.

7 Sep: Porteus Riots in Edinburgh in which mob lynched Captain Porteus, who, as head of town guard, had in April fired on crowd protesting against arrest of smugglers.

1737   *20 Nov*: Death of Queen Caroline, pillar of support for Walpole.

1738   *24 Jan*: Opposition in Commons denounced Spain for attacks against British shipping.

16–21 Mar: Commons committee examined one Captain Jenkins who alleged that Spanish Guardas Costas had in 1731 pillaged his ship and cut off his ear.

30 Mar: Carteret succeeded in passing resolution in House of Lords condemning Spanish right to search British ships in Spanish American waters after Walpole had defeated similar resolution in Commons.

1739   *Jan*: Convention of Pardo approved to heal disputes between Britain and Spain. (*See* Chapter 5: Treaties and Diplomacy.)

8 Mar: Address approving Pardo Convention carried by Walpole in Commons against opposition of William Pitt and 'Patriots', who demanded war with Spain.

19 Oct: War against Spain declared when Spain refused to honour Convention of Pardo, despite determined opposition of Walpole.

1741   *8 Apr*: King's speech invited Parliament to aid him in support of Pragmatic Sanction and £300,000 was voted in subsidies for Queen Maria Theresa of Austria.

25 Apr: Second Parliament of George II dissolved.

1 Dec: George II's third Parliament met (after prorogation from 25 June).

1742   *11 Feb*: Sir Robert Walpole resigned all his offices, having been created Earl of Orford on 9 February. Pulteney asked to form ministry but declined office himself, thinking mistakenly to guide the government from behind scenes.

16 Feb: New ministry formed including Earl of Wilmington as First Lord of Treasury, Samuel Sandys as Chancellor of Exchequer, and Carteret as Secretary of State, North. Newcastle remained as Secretary of State, South.

7 Nov: Carteret negotiated defence pact with Frederick II's Prussia, which had made a separate peace with Austria.

1743   *16 Jun*: George II led British forces to victory over French at Dettingen; but abandoned planned invasion of France.

27 Aug: Henry Pelham appointed First Lord of Treasury by George II, acting on advice of Walpole, whose friends gradually regained control of ministry.

12 Dec: Henry Pelham made Chancellor of Exchequer.

1744   *29 Mar*: Britain declared war on France.

24 Nov: Carteret (now Earl of Granville) forced to resign due to unpopularity and expense of war and despite support of King. Duke of Newcastle and Henry Pelham remodelled cabinet to include major Whig factions.

28 Dec: Formation of Quadruple Alliance of Britain, Austria, Saxony–Poland and Holland against Prussia.

1745   *18 Mar*: Death of Walpole.

2 Apr: British subsidy to Maria Theresa raised from £300,000 to £500,000.

23 Jul: Charles Edward Stuart, the 'Young Pretender', landed in Scotland signalling outbreak of Jacobite rebellion known as 'The '45'; British troops subsequently recalled from Netherlands.

11 Sep: Edinburgh captured by Jacobite forces.

4 Dec: Pretender's Jacobite army reached as far south as Derby, but was forced to retreat on 6 December, beginning collapse of rebellion.

1746   *10 Feb*: Pelham ministry resigned *en bloc* on George II's refusal to name William Pitt Secretary of War, but Lords Bath and Granville, called by King to form new cabinet, failed to do so.

14 Feb: Bath and Granville abandoned attempt to form ministry; George II grudgingly turned again to Newcastle and Pelham, but still vetoed Pitt's presence in cabinet, although on 22 February Pitt was given minor office as Joint Vice-Treasurer for Ireland.

16 Apr: Duke of Cumberland finally crushed Jacobite rebels at

Culloden, beginning ruthless suppression of Highland clans, thus earning nickname of 'Butcher'.

6 May: William Pitt appointed Paymaster-General on death of Thomas Winnington; Henry Fox subsequently named Secretary at War.

1747   *18 Jun*: Dissolution of George II's third Parliament.

10 Nov: Fourth Parliament of George II met.

1748   *6 Feb*: Duke of Newcastle shifted to Secretary of State, North, with Duke of Bedford becoming Secretary of State, South.

7 Oct: Peace of Aix-la-Chapelle ended War of Austrian Succession. (*See* Chapter 5: Treaties and Diplomacy.)

Heritable jurisdiction abolished in Scotland, reducing power of clan chiefs.

1751   *Jan*: Henry Fielding's *An Inquiry into the Causes of the Late Increase of Robbers* published.

20 Mar: Death of Frederick, Prince of Wales, creating consternation among opposition.

Calendar altered to coincide with Western European reckoning, being moved 11 days forward, effective 3 September 1752; also provided year should begin on 1 January instead of 7 March.

Nugent's Bill, commonly known as 'the Tippling Act', passed to suppress unlicensed retailing of gin and other spirits. Gin consumption reduced from 8.5 million gallons in 1751 to 2.1 million by 1760.

1752   Lords passed measure transferring to crown Scottish estates forfeited in '45 rebellion, with revenues allocated to improvement of Highlands.

14 Sep: Gregorian Calendar came into force in Britain (3–13 September omitted).

1753   'Bow Street Runners' established by Henry and Sir John Fielding, Middlesex magistrates, to attack crime in Westminster.

1754   *6 Mar*: Death of Henry Pelham.

16 Mar: Duke of Newcastle, Pelham's brother, appointed First Lord of Treasury.

Apr: Thomas Robinson made Secretary of State, South, after Henry Fox and William Pitt declined office; Henry Legge named Chancellor of Exchequer.

8 Apr: Fourth Parliament of George II dissolved.

Nov: George II's fifth Parliament convened.

1755   *Jun*: William Pitt opened correspondence with Lord Bute, tutor of future George III, with eye to joining 'reversionary interest'.

14 Nov: Newcastle ministry remodelled, with Henry Fox becoming Secretary of State, South, and Leader of House of Commons.

20 Nov: William Pitt dismissed as Paymaster-General.

1756   *16 Jan*: Treaty between Britain and Prussia, securing Hanoverian neutrality – first stage of so-called 'Diplomatic Revolution' completed when France allied with Austria.
17 May: Britain declared war on France.
11 Nov: Resignation of Duke of Newcastle and Henry Fox after serious reverses in war with France.
16 Nov: Duke of Devonshire made First Lord of Treasury with nominal power to form new ministry.
4 Dec: William Pitt appointed Secretary of State, South, dominating new ministry, although Holdernesse remained Secretary of State, North.

1757   *14 Mar*: Admiral Byng shot for neglect of duty in loss of Minorca to French, despite defence by Pitt.
6 Apr: Pitt dismissed from office by George II after Duke of Cumberland had refused to take command in Germany unless Pitt was replaced.
29 Jun: New ministry formed after three months of confusion, with Newcastle as First Lord of Treasury in alliance with Pitt as Secretary of State, South.
Pitt's Militia Act reorganised British militia, although reducing numbers to 32,340 against Pitt's wishes.

1758   *20 Apr*: Convention of London, by which Pitt obtained £670,000 p.a. subsidy to Frederick II of Prussia and undertook to maintain British army in Germany.

1759   *17 Aug*: Admiral Boscawen defeated French off Cape St Vincent.
18 Sep: British took Quebec from French, but both Montcalm and Wolfe were killed.
20 Nov: Admiral Hawke defeated French navy at Quiberon Bay, preventing invasion of Britain.

1760   *May*: Secret negotiations with French broken off.
25 Oct: Death of George II. Succession of his grandson, George III, with Pitt and Newcastle retained as leaders of ministry despite expectations to contrary.

1761   *19 Mar*: George II's last parliament dissolved, followed by elections.
25 Mar: Earl of Bute appointed Secretary of State, North, replacing Holdernesse.
8 Sep: Marriage of George III and Princess Charlotte of Mecklenburg-Strelitz.
5 Oct: William Pitt resigned as Secretary of State, South, due to George III's and Lord Bute's opposition to his war policies. Succeeded by Charles Wyndham, Earl of Egremont.
3 Nov: First Parliament of George III met.

1762   *4 Jan*: Britain declared war on Spain after publication of new 'Family Compact' between Spain and France.

      Apr: British subsidies to Prussia cancelled.

      26 May: Duke of Newcastle, angered by loss of patronage powers, resigned; Lord Bute succeeded as First Lord of Treasury, George Grenville becoming Secretary of State, North.

      9 Dec: Pitt attacked provisions of peace treaty in Commons.

      First appearance of *The North Briton*, edited by John Wilkes and Charles Churchill (–1763).

1763   *10 Jan*: Peace of Paris officially ended Seven Years' War.

      7 Apr: Lord Bute resigned following outcry against terms of Paris Treaty; George Grenville became First Lord of Treasury and Chancellor of Exchequer.

      19 Apr: George III prorogued Parliament and claimed peace was honourable to his crown.

      23 Apr: John Wilkes attacked King's speech defending Peace of Paris in no. 45 of *North Briton*.

      30 Apr: John Wilkes arrested on general warrant.

      6 May: Chief Justice Pratt of Common Pleas freed Wilkes on grounds of parliamentary privilege and declared general warrants illegal.

      7 Oct: Grenville ministry issued Proclamation providing government for Quebec and forbidding American colonial expansion west of Allegheny Mountains.

      23 Nov: House of Commons reversed Judge Pratt's ruling, maintaining that parliamentary privilege did not extend to seditious libel.

      3 Dec: London mob attacked sheriff and rescued no. 45 of *North Briton* from public burning.

1764   *19 Jan*: John Wilkes expelled from Commons for seditious libel; more London riots in his favour.

      Feb: Parliament declared general warrants legal, thus overturning Pratt's decision.

      21 Feb: Court of King's Bench found Wilkes guilty of reprinting no. 45 of *North Briton* and publishing *Essay on Women*, condemned as obscene and blasphemous. Following Wilkes's flight to France he was outlawed.

1765   *23 Mar*: Stamp Act passed to increase taxes on American colonies defied in America.

      May: Riots of London silkweavers.

      16 Jul: Removal of Grenville by George III, who reluctantly made Marquess of Rockingham First Lord of Treasury.

1766   *12 Jul*: Dismissal of Rockingham. William Pitt, elevated to Lords as

Earl of Chatham, formed new administration as Lord Privy Seal. Duke of Grafton appointed First Lord of Treasury; Earl of Shelburne made Secretary of State, South; Charles Townshend named Chancellor of Exchequer.

Aug–Oct: Widespread food riots resulting from harvest failures and profiteering.

1767   *Mar*: Chatham stricken by physical and mental illness forcing his virtual retirement.

Jun: Townshend's Enumerated Articles levying import duties on glass, paint, paper and tea in American colonies passed by Parliament.

Sep: Death of Charles Townshend; Lord North appointed Chancellor of Exchequer, aged 25.

1768   *20 Jan*: Office of Secretary of State for Colonies first created and Lord Hillsborough appointed, assuming colonial responsibilities formerly held by Secretary of State, South.

Feb: John Wilkes returned to London.

11 Mar: George III's first Parliament dissolved, followed by general election.

28 Mar: Wilkes elected MP for Middlesex.

Apr–Jun: Sporadic Wilkesite riots in London.

10 May: Second Parliament of George III met amidst pro-Wilkes riot in Westminster.

8 Jun: Chief Justice Mansfield of King's Bench sentenced Wilkes to 22 months' imprisonment for seditious libel, but reversed his outlawry, allowing him to retain seat in Commons.

19 Oct: Resignation of Chatham and Shelburne from ministry. Duke of Grafton became head of administration, with Lords Weymouth and Rochford as Secretaries of State.

1769   *Jan*: John Wilkes elected an alderman of London. *Letters of Junius* launched attacks against George III, Grafton, Mansfield and other ministers.

3 Feb: Wilkes expelled from Commons by vote of 219 to 137; subsequently he was re-elected twice and twice expelled.

13 Apr: Wilkes re-elected again over court candidate Colonel Luttrell, but under pressure from King, Commons declared that Luttrell 'ought to have been elected' and seated him (*15 Apr*).

1770   *28 Jan*: Resignation of Duke of Grafton. Lord North appointed First Lord of Treasury to lead ministry of 'King's Friends'.

3 Mar: Five people killed by British troops in so-called 'Boston Massacre'.

Apr: Edmund Burke published *Thoughts on the Causes of the Present Discontents*.

Apr: Parliament repealed import duties on lead, paper, glass and dyestuffs but retained duty on tea in American colonies.

13 Jun: Printers and publishers of *Letters of Junius* accused of seditious libel.

1772 *24 Mar*: Parliament placed all descendants of George III under terms of Royal Marriage Act, following marriage to commoners of Dukes of Gloucester and Cumberland.

13 Apr: Warren Hastings appointed Governor of Bengal.

Somerset's Case, in which Lord Chief Justice Mansfield ruled that any slave landing in Britain was freed.

1773 *Jun*: Lord North's British East India Company Regulating Act provided for governor-general and council in India, extended Treasury audit to cover Company accounts, and authorised Company to ship tea directly to American colonies without duty.

16 Dec: Boston Tea Party, when Samuel Adams and his 'Patriot' friends dumped 340 chests of East India tea into Boston harbour.

1774 *28 Mar*: Passage of Coercive Acts against Massachusetts, which closed Boston harbour, moved colonial capital to Salem, and quartered troops in Boston.

Apr: Passage of Quebec Act which established Roman Catholicism and Roman Law in Canada and allowed Canadians to extend borders south to Ohio, blocking westward expansion of American colonies.

27 May: Virginia House of Burgesses passed resolution calling for Continental Congress.

5 Sep–26 Oct: Meeting of first Continental Congress in Philadelphia.

30 Sep: Second Parliament of George III dissolved.

Nov: John Wilkes became Lord Mayor of London.

1 Dec: Non-importation order against British goods passed by American Continental Congress came into force.

1775 *20 Jan*: Chatham's resolution for recall of troops from Boston defeated.

1 Feb: Chatham introduced bill to conciliate American colonies overwhelmingly rejected. Further repressive measures subsequently carried by Lord North.

19 Apr: American Revolution began in Massachusetts with defeat of British troops by colonial forces at Lexington and Concord.

10 May: Second Continental Congress met at Philadelphia.

31 May: Continental Army formed out of colonial troops surrounding Boston.

15 Jun: George Washington appointed Commander-in-Chief of Continental Army.

9 Nov: Duke of Grafton resigned from ministry, disapproving war; replaced by Lord Dartmouth. Lord George Germain, violent enemy of Americans, made Colonial Secretary.

1776 *4 Jul*: American Declaration of Independence, drawn up by Thomas Jefferson, with revisions by Benjamin Franklin and John Adams, passed by Continental Congress.

1777 *3 Jan*: British troops defeated by Washington at Princeton, New Jersey.

11 Sep: British forces under Home defeated Americans at Brandywine, Pennsylvania.

7 Oct: General Burgoyne and British troops surrendered to Americans at Saratoga, New York.

15 Nov: Articles of Confederation adopted by Continental Congress, providing first constitution of United States of America, and sent to states for ratification (completed in 1781).

1778 *6 Feb*: Britain declared war on France after France had signed offensive and defensive alliance with American forces.

17 Feb: Lord North, with grudging approval of George III, presented bill of conciliation to Parliament.

5 Apr: British commissioners appointed to negotiate with American Congress; repressive legislation suspended in meantime.

17 Jun: British peace initiative rejected by American Congress.

1779 *27 Oct*: Viscount Stormont succeeded Suffolk as Secretary of State, North.

24 Nov: Earl of Hillsborough replaced Weymouth as Secretary of State, South.

1780 *8 Feb*: Christopher Wyvill, champion of landed interest, presented Yorkshire petition for increasing parliamentary representation of English counties.

6 Apr: Dunning's Resolution declaring 'that the influence of the Crown has increased, is increasing, and ought to be diminished', passed by Parliament.

May: Edmund Burke introduced 'economical reform' bill to reduce royal power of patronage by abolishing some sinecures and minor offices. Measure killed in committee.

2–8 Jun: Gordon Riots raged in London after Lord George Gordon led demonstration against Catholic relief. Riots began as anti-Catholic but extended to general assault on property. Some 285 rioters killed by army, called in by George III to suppress tumults.

1 Sep: George III dissolved his third Parliament.

13 Dec: Britain granted free trade to Ireland.

1781 *Jan*: Americans under Daniel Morgan defeated British at battle of Cowpens, South Carolina.

15 Mar: Cornwallis and British defeated Americans at Guildford Courthouse, North Carolina.

19 Oct: Cornwallis and 8000 British troops surrendered to Americans at Yorktown; British evacuated Charleston and Savannah, greatly curtailing land operations.

1782   *22 Feb*: Motion to end American war lost by only one vote in Commons; subsequently a similar motion passed and government introduced bill to enable King to make peace.

15 Mar: Motion of no confidence in North's ministry defeated by nine votes in Commons, after George III had unsuccessfully sounded out Marquess of Rockingham.

20 Mar: Lord North resigned, together with Secretaries Stormont and Hillsborough.

27 Mar: George III forced to accept coalition Whig ministry headed by Marquess of Rockingham as First Lord of Treasury. Old secretarial system abolished and duties divided into home and foreign spheres. Earl of Shelburne appointed Home Secretary; Charles James Fox, Foreign Secretary; Lord Cavendish, Chancellor of Exchequer.

30 May: Motion for recall of Warren Hastings passed by Parliament.

1 Jul: Death of Marquess of Rockingham.

11 Jul: Earl of Shelburne asked to form ministry as First Lord of Treasury; William Pitt the Younger appointed Chancellor of Exchequer and Leader of Commons. Fox, however, left office.

27 Sep: Britain acknowledged American independence.

30 Nov: Peace preliminaries accepted by Britain and America to end war.

1783   *21 Feb*: Terms of peace preliminaries censured in Commons by vote of 207 to 190.

24 Feb: Lord Shelburne resigned; lengthy negotiations ensued for formation of new ministry after Pitt's refusal to lead administration.

1 Apr: George III forced to accept Fox–North coalition under nominal leadership of Duke of Portland.

7 May: William Pitt introduced parliamentary reform bill to redistribute seats in Commons, backed by Fox, opposed by North.

3 Sep: Peace of Paris officially ended war between Britain and America, France and Spain. American independence formally recognised.

17 Dec: Fox's bill to reform government of India defeated in Lords after personal intervention by George III. Fox–North coalition resigned.

19 Dec: William Pitt, appointed First Lord of Treasury and Chancellor of Exchequer by George III, formed new ministry with Lord

Sydney as Home Secretary and Marquess of Carmarthen as Foreign Secretary.

1784   *Jan–Feb*: Concerted attacks by Foxite Whigs on Pitt ministry and alleged abuse of royal prerogative; opposition refused to renew Mutiny Act or vote supplies.

8 Mar: Opposition resolution drafted by Burke passed by only one vote; in days following majority against Pitt reversed, with supplies voted.

24 Mar: George III, sensing triumph over Fox and Whigs, dissolved Parliament after only three years. In ensuing general election, Pitt secured strong majority in large part due to King's influence.

13 Aug: Pitt's India Act placed East India Company under government Board of Control.

Aug: Dundas's motion for restoration of Scottish estates forfeited after '45 rebellion unanimously passed by Commons.

1785   *18 Apr*: Pitt's proposal to reform House of Commons by disenfranchising 36 rotten boroughs and adding 72 members for London and the counties defeated by 248 votes to 174.

1786   *29 Mar*: Pitt's bill for establishing new Sinking Fund to reduce national debt enacted.

Jun: Reform of customs and excise duties and collection; consolidation of militia.

1787   *11 May*: Edmund Burke impeached Warren Hastings for high crimes and misdemeanours.

Beaufoy's attempt to repeal Test and Corporation Acts defeated by 78 votes, Pitt opposing.

13 Feb: Trial of Warren Hastings opened before Lords in Westminster Hall (–1795).

5 Nov: Onslaught of George III's first prolonged bout of madness.

10 Dec: Commons accepted Pitt's motion that regency should be determined by Parliament, not automatically assumed by Prince of Wales, as advocated by Fox.

1789   *13 Feb*: House of Commons passed Regency Bill vesting Regency in Prince of Wales, but not conferring power to grant offices or create peers.

27 Feb: George III sufficiently recovered from illness that bulletins were discontinued.

10 Mar: Speech from the throne, delivered by commission, announced that King had fully resumed his authority.

Beaufoy's second attempt to repeal Test and Corporation Acts defeated by vote of 122 to 102.

2 *Ireland*

1648   *Sep*: Duke of Ormond returned to Ireland.

1649   *Jan*: New treaty signed between Ormond and Catholic Confederates; Confederacy formally dissolved and government in name of Charles I entrusted to twelve commissioners.
Feb: Charles II proclaimed as King of Ireland, with Ormond as Lord Lieutenant. Irish rebellion against England renewed.
2 Aug: Ormond and Irish forces routed by Jones near Dublin.
15 Aug: Oliver Cromwell landed with New Model Army to begin reconquest of Ireland.
11 Sep: Cromwell crushed Irish troops and sacked Drogheda, massacring garrison.
11 Oct: Sack of Wexford by Cromwell.

1650   *26 May*: Cromwell returned to England.
Aug: Waterford surrendered to English army.

1651   *27 Nov*: Surrender of Limerick to English forces.
Nov: Offices of Lord Lieutenant and Lord Deputy abolished and entire government of Ireland given to commissioners appointed by English Parliament.

1652   *12 Aug*: Act of Settlement passed by English Parliament, providing for confiscation of estates of landowners acting against Parliament since 1641 according to degree of delinquency. Delinquent proprietors to be transplanted in Connaught and Clare.
Reconquest of Ireland completed.

1653   *26 Sep*: Act of Satisfaction passed by English Parliament to distribute 'forfeited lands' in Ireland, setting aside ten counties for adventurers and soldiers.

1654   *2 Mar*: English Parliament voted for union of Ireland with England and Scotland, promising free trade and 30 parliamentary representatives at Westminster.

1657   *26 Jun*: Act for attainder of rebels in Ireland declared that all rebels and papists who had transplanted to Connaught were pardoned of high treason but that those not transplanted by 24 Sep 1657 would forfeit claim to benefit.

1660   *7 Feb*: Convention representing old parliamentary constituencies met in Dublin, preparing way for restoration of Charles II in Ireland.
14 May: Charles II proclaimed King in Ireland.
30 Nov: Charles II's Declaration for Settling the Affairs of Ireland, proposing board of commissioners to adjudicate land disputes.

1661   *8 May*: Restored Irish Parliament, entirely Protestant in composition, met.
Nov: Duke of Ormond appointed Lord Lieutenant.

1662   *27 Sep*: Royal Assent given to Act of Settlement, providing for resumption of crown lands and compensation of Catholics never in revolt against Charles I. Soldiers and adventurers allowed to retain two-thirds of Cromwellian grants. Court of claims set up to administer act.

1665   *Nov*: Explanatory Act, requiring soldiers and adventurers to surrender one-third of holdings in order to accommodate claims of other protestants and 'innocent' Catholics.

1666   Export of Irish cattle and sheep to England forbidden.

1669   *Mar*: Lord Robartes replaced Ormond as Lord Lieutenant (–1670).

1670   John, Lord Berkeley of Stratton appointed Lord Lieutenant (–1672).
        Navigation Act barred direct imports from colonies but continued to allow direct exports.

1672   *May*: Earl of Essex appointed Lord Lieutenant (–1677).

1677   *May*: Duke of Ormond reappointed Lord Lieutenant (–1685).

1681   *Jul*: Execution of Oliver Plunket, Roman Catholic Archbishop of Armagh, for alleged high treason.

1685   *Feb*: Ormond dismissed as Lord Lieutenant after death of Charles II; government of Ireland entrusted to Lords Justices by James II; Roman Catholic Richard Talbot appointed colonel of horse.
        Jun: Richard Talbot created Earl of Tyrconnell and given actual, though not official, command of Irish army and militia.
        Sep: Henry Hyde, second Earl of Clarendon, appointed Lord Lieutenant (–1687).

1686   *Jun*: Tyrconnell, formally appointed commander of Irish armed forces, began replacing Protestant with Catholic officers and soldiers. Army greatly increased in size.

1687   *8 Jan*: Earl of Clarendon recalled.
        Feb: Tyrconnell appointed Lord Lieutenant.
        Borough Corporations remodelled to ensure Catholic control of town governments; Catholic sheriffs, judges and privy councillors appointed.

1688   *Oct*: Irish troops dispatched to England in defence of James II.
        7 Dec: Londonderry refused new garrison of Catholic troops loyal to James II.

1689   *Jan*: Following James II's expulsion from England, Ulster Protestants organised county defence associations and raised troops.
        Feb: William and Mary proclaimed King and Queen in Ulster by Protestants.
        12 Mar: James II arrived in Ireland, finding Tyrconnell still in control of most of country.
        20 Apr: James II's siege of Londonderry began.

7 May: Meeting of James II's Irish Parliament, which recognised him as King, provided for return to Roman Catholic supremacy, cut ties with English Parliament, and repealed acts of Settlement and Explanation.

30 Jul: Siege of Londonderry broken.

13 Aug: Duke of Schomberg arrived in Ireland with 20,000 English troops.

1690   *Mar*: 7000 French troops dispatched in aid of James II.

1 Jul: William and English forces defeated James II's Catholic army at Battle of Boyne (anniversary now celebrated on 12 July of Julian Calendar).

6 Jul: Dublin fell to William III.

1691   *3 Oct*: Surrender of Limerick to English after month's siege. Treaty of Limerick provided surrender of all Jacobite forces in Ireland, in return for which English crown promised to secure Catholic officers and soldiers in their possessions on their taking oath of allegiance. Religious toleration promised but not guaranteed.

Nov: English Parliament, ignoring Treaty of Limerick, imposed oaths of allegiance and supremacy and declaration against transubstantiation for all Irish office-holders and members of Parliament.

1692   *Mar*: Henry Viscount Sydney appointed Lord Lieutenant.

Oct: Meeting of Irish Parliament with Roman Catholics excluded legally for first time. William and Mary recognised as legitimate monarchs; Lord Sydney forced to abandon bill to endorse Treaty of Limerick and promised to remove Catholics from army.

3 Nov: Parliament prorogued for refusal to pass money bill.

1693   *26 Jun*: Parliament dissolved by order of William and Mary.

1695   *27 Jul*: First meeting of William III's second Irish Parliament, which disarmed all Catholics and prohibited them from teaching in schools or private houses.

1697   Parliament expelled all Catholic prelates and monastic clergy from Ireland and forbade marriage between Protestants and Catholics.

1698   All Catholics excluded from legal practice except those taking oaths of allegiance and abjuration of papal authority.

1699   Export of Irish woollen manufactures restricted to England, where heavy duties prevented their competition. Act led to collapse of woollen industry and rise of linen manufacture.

1702   *8 Mar*: Death of William III. Succession of Anne as Queen of Ireland.

1703   Parliament met for first time in five years.

1704   *Mar*: Further 'Act to Prevent Growth of Popery', which provided that estates belonging to Protestants could not pass to Catholics, who could only inherit land from one another; further, law of 'gravelkind' provided that land must be divided at owner's death amongst all sons. Act also excluded Protestant dissenters from office.

1707 Earl of Pembroke succeeded second Duke of Ormond as Lord Lieutenant.

1708 Catholics forbidden to sit on grand juries although still allowed on petty juries.

1709 Catholic priests required by law to abjure papal authority; few obeyed and law was not generally enforced.

1713 Duke of Shrewsbury appointed Lord Lieutenant.

1719 Act of Toleration granted religious freedom to Protestant dissenters in Ireland, but Test Acts retained.

1720 *Mar*: English Parliament passed act stating that Irish House of Lords had no appellate jurisdiction and that appeals must be made to British Lords at Westminster.

1721 Duke of Grafton appointed Lord Lieutenant.

1722 *Jul*: William Wood granted patent to coin money for Ireland.

1723 *27 Sep*: Irish Parliament passed six resolutions deploring the coinage patent of William Wood and protesting the inferiority and irregularity of the coins.

1724 *3 Apr*: Lord Carteret replaced Duke of Grafton as Lord Lieutenant, in response to outcry over 'Wood's half pence'.
   'Drapier's Letters' published anonymously by Jonathan Swift satirising currency scandal and appealing to Irish national spirit.

1725 *Sep*: Wood's coinage patent revoked.

1727 Roman Catholics debarred from voting for members of Parliament in both counties and boroughs.

1731 *Sep*: Duke of Dorset succeeded Carteret as Lord Lieutenant.

1733 System of 'Charter Schools' founded by Archbishop Boulter of Armagh to give technical training to poor Roman Catholic children and educate them as Protestants.

1737 Duke of Devonshire appointed Lord Lieutenant.

1742 Death of Archbishop Boulter.

1745 Appointment as Lord Lieutenant of Earl of Chesterfield, who began suspension of penal laws against Catholics.

1747 Charles Lucas of Dublin began publishing *Citizen's Journal* (–1749), in which he denounced restrictions on Irish trade and asserted rights of Ireland as separate kingdom.
   Sep: Earl of Harrington replaced Chesterfield as Lord Lieutenant.

1751 *Sep*: Duke of Dorset appointed Lord Lieutenant.

1753 Defeat of money bill in Irish Parliament due to proposed allocation of Irish surplus to English national debt. Henry Boyle, Speaker of Commons, dismissed as Chancellor of Exchequer along with other officials. Parliament prorogued.

1755   *Apr*: Marquess of Hartington appointed Lord Lieutenant with instructions to secure compromise in money bill dispute. Boyle given earldom and other officials reinstated to secure approval of supply.

1757   *Jan*: Duke of Bedford named Lord Lieutenant.

1759   *Dec*: Riots in Dublin by mobs which sacked Parliament on hearing rumours of union with Britain.

1761   Earl of Halifax appointed Lord Lieutenant.
Whiteboys Societies formed due to discontent caused by evictions.

1763   'Whiteboys' rose against agrarian hardships.

1767   Lord Townshend appointed Lord Lieutenant with instructions from George III to reside continuously in Ireland.

1768   Octennial Act limited life of Irish Parliament to eight years.

1769   *Nov–Dec*: Bill to augment army and money bill first defeated and then passed by refractory session of Parliament.
26 Dec: Lord Townshend prorogued Parliament, making formal complaint against Commons' claim to initiate all money bills.

1771   Bogland Act enabled Roman Catholics to take leases of 61 years on unprofitable land, free of taxes for 7 years.

1772   Lord Townshend resigned as Lord Lieutenant, confident he had broken power of 'undertakers', and was replaced by Earl of Harcourt.

1773   *Nov*: Government proposal to levy tax of two shillings in pound on rents of absentee landlords defeated.

1775   English government laid embargo on all Irish goods destined for American colonies; Irish Parliament voted supplies and raised 4000 troops to be used in American war.

1776   Parliament dissolved followed by elections.
Nov: Lord Harcourt resigned as Lord Lieutenant.

1777   Earl of Buckinghamshire appointed Lord Lieutenant.

1778   Gardiner's Relief Act allowed Catholics to take indefinite leases and inherit land on same terms as Protestants.

1779   40,000 Protestant Volunteer forces raised to deter French invasion.
25 Nov: Irish Parliament, defying Britain, voted supplies for only six months.
Dec: Lord North carried through British Parliament measures permitting free export of Irish wool, cloth and glass and allowing free trade with colonies.

1780   Earl of Carlisle appointed Lord Lieutenant.

1781   Habeas Corpus Act for Ireland passed.

1782   Convention of Protestant Volunteers asserted Irish right to legislative freedom and unconstitutionality of Poyning's Law.
16 Apr: House of Commons unanimously approved Henry Grattan's resolution demanding legislative independence of Ireland,

following appointment of Whig Duke of Portland as Lord Lieutenant.

17 May: Charles James Fox introduced bill in British Parliament granting legislative independence to Irish Parliament, subsequently passed.

1783   *Jan*: Renunciation Act passed by British Parliament reaffirming autonomy of Irish Parliament.

Apr: Earl of Northington replaced Portland as Lord Lieutenant.

29–30 Nov: Henry Flood's bill for reform of representation refused by Parliament.

Dec: Duke of Rutland appointed Lord Lieutenant.

1784   Foster's Corn Law gave bounties for expansion of tillage.

1785   *12–13 Aug*: Bill to establish complete freedom of trade between Ireland and Britain defeated due to Irish fears that accompanying measures would erode legislative autonomy.

1787   Marquess of Buckingham appointed Lord Lieutenant.

1789   *5 Feb*: Gratton and 'Patriots' carried address calling for Prince of Wales to take regency of Ireland during George III's illness, but Lord Lieutenant refused to send address.

3 *Scotland*

1648   *1 May*: Berwick and Carlisle Castles seized by English royalists in collusion with Hamiltonian party, dominant in Scotland, starting second Civil War.

13 Jul: Duke of Hamilton invaded England with 15,000 Scottish troops.

17–20 Aug: Scottish forces defeated by Oliver Cromwell and New Model Army at Preston.

1649   *23 Jan*: Act of Classes excluded from state and church offices those who had taken the Engagement or accompanied Hamilton's invasion of England; and barred other malignants and 'sinners' from office for one to ten years.

5 Feb: Charles II proclaimed King of Scotland, following Charles I's execution.

9 Mar: Execution of Duke of Hamilton.

1650   *27 Apr*: Earl of Montrose defeated at Carbiesdale and captured.

21 May: Montrose executed.

23 Jun: Charles II took the Covenant and landed at Speymouth.

3 Sep: Scottish army defeated by Cromwell at Dunbar.

17 Oct: Remonstrants called for strict enforcement of Act of Classes and rigorous purge of army.

14 Dec: Moderate majority in commission of assembly resolved that all but excommunicated men and obstinate enemies of Covenant should be allowed to fight with Scottish army.

24 Dec: Edinburgh captured by Cromwell.

1651   *1 Jan*: Coronation of Charles II at Scone.

Jun: Act of Classes rescinded.

2 Aug: Perth captured by Cromwell.

3 Sep: Defeat of Charles II and Scottish forces at Worcester.

Oct: English government appointed commissions, for the administration of Scotland, announcing that England and Scotland were to be one commonwealth.

19 Nov: All public meetings for exercise of any jurisdiction not sanctioned by English Parliament forbidden.

1652   *Apr*: Scottish shires and burghs called upon to elect representatives to discuss nature of union with England.

1653   *Jul*: General Assemblies of Presbyterian clergy forbidden.

1654   *12 Apr*: Ordinance of Union, joining Scotland with England and Ireland and promising free trade and representation at Westminster Parliament (not passed by Parliament until 1657).

May: General George Monck appointed commander of army in Scotland.

Ordinance abolished baron courts held by landlords and replaced them with public courts.

1655   *Sep*: Right of burghs to hold elections restored, with persons refusing loyalty oath to Protectorate excluded.

1656   *Jan*: Justices of the peace appointed in all shires with jurisdiction over assault, riot and vagrancy, and powers to repair roads and fix wages and prices.

1659   *Jul*: Bill of union introduced on Scottish initiative in recalled Rump of Long Parliament, but not passed before Parliament's interruption in October.

Oct: General Monck, commander of army in Scotland, opposed expulsion of Rump Parliament by English army and supported supremacy of civilian government.

Nov–Dec: Monck purged army in Scotland of most radical elements.

1660   *1 Jan*: General Monck's march with his army south into England.

Aug: Earl of Glencairn, appointed Chancellor, sent to Scotland to restore royalist government with aid of committee of estates; Earl of Middleton appointed Lord High Commissioner, Lord Rothes President of Council and Earl of Lauderdale Secretary of State.

1661   *1 Jan*: Meeting of restored Parliament in Edinburgh, which subsequently revised Committee of Articles and proclaimed royal prerogative to choose ministers and councillors and command army and militia.

28 Mar: Rescissory Act passed by Scottish Parliament. (*See* Chapter 6: The Church.)

27 May: Marquess of Argyle beheaded.

1662 *8 May*: Scottish bishops readmitted to Parliament and Lords of Articles; episcopal church re-established. (*See* Chapter 6: The Church.)

9 Sep: Act of Indemnity passed.

1663 *May*: Middleton dismissed and replaced by Lord Rothes as High Commissioner.

Jun: Method of electing Lords of Articles first adopted in 1633 restored. Bishops chose eight nobles; nobles chose eight bishops; and 16 thus selected chose eight barons and eight burgesses. High Commissioner added officers of state.

Jul: Parliament offered to raise an army of 20,000 foot and 2000 horse to serve annually for forty days; field preaching and attendance at field conventicles outlawed.

9 Oct: 'Restoration Parliament' dissolved.

1666 *28 Nov*: Covenanter rebellion suppressed; 40 rebels executed, many others exiled or imprisoned.

1667 *Jun*: Lord Rothes forced to resign High Commission; treasury entrusted to commission of Lauderdale's friends.

Aug: Army disbanded except for two troops of lifeguards and eight companies of foot.

1669 *7 Jun*: Charles II's 'first indulgence' in Scotland ordered the restoration of livings to penitent evicted ministers; 40 accepted.

Oct: Lauderdale sent to Scotland as High Commissioner.

19 Oct: Charles II's second Scottish Parliament met.

16 Nov: Royal assent given to act declaring royal supremacy in church government, and militia act providing for 20,000 men under King's command.

1670 'Clanking Act' imposing severe fines on those attending field conventicles.

1671 Lauderdale appointed President of Council in Scotland, thus uniting all leading offices in one man.

1672 *2 May*: Lauderdale created Duke of Lauderdale.

3 Sep: Charles II's second 'Scottish indulgence' restored livings to further 80 ministers.

1673 *Nov*: Lauderdale faced serious opposition in Scottish Parliament from Hamilton, Tweeddale, Kincardine and their allies.

1674 Parliament first prorogued and then dissolved; not called again until 1681.

1674– Persecution of Covenanter dissenters stepped up.
   5

1677 *2 Aug*: Privy Council, under influence of Archbishop Sharp, required all Scottish landowners to enter into bond that they, their families, servants and tenants would attend parish churches and not frequent conventicles. Following this order, Lauderdale sent a 10,000-man army into western Scotland to impose bond and disarm inhabitants.

1679 *3 May*: Assassination of Archbishop Sharp by Covenanters.
   29 May: Covenanters' rebellion, ending with Duke of Monmouth's defeat of rising at Bothwell Bridge on 22 June.
   24 Nov: Duke of York took up residence in Edinburgh.

1680 *Oct*: Duke of Lauderdale resigned as Secretary of State after being stricken by apoplexy.

1681 *28 Jul*: Charles II's third Scottish Parliament met, with James, Duke of York, as High Commissioner.
   Aug: Passage of act binding Scotland to recognition of 'next legitimate heir' – James, Duke of York – on death of Charles II.
   31 Aug: Test Act passed.

1685 *6 Feb*: Death of Charles II. Succession of James II.
   Apr: James II and VII's Parliament met with profuse expressions of loyalty.

1686 *Mar*: Duke of Queensbury removed as Treasurer and office put into commission.
   29 Apr: Second session of Parliament opened, with Earl of Moray as High Commissioner in place of Queensbury.
   14 Jun: Parliament prorogued after refusal to grant indulgence to Roman Catholics.

1687 *12 Feb*: James II issued declaration of indulgence to Roman Catholics and Quakers.
   28 Jun: Second declaration of indulgence extended religious toleration to all sects, including Presbyterians.
   Scottish burghs ordered to cease elections and to await royal nominations.

1688 *Dec*: Upon news of James II's flight, mobs sacked Holyrood chapel and drove out Jesuits from Edinburgh, while in south-west Scotland extreme Presbyterians expelled Episcopalian clergy from their churches and manses.

1689 *Jan*: Assembly of Scottish nobles and gentry in London asked William to assume administration of Scotland, whereupon William accepted, issuing a circular letter calling for convention.
   14 Mar: Convention met in Edinburgh.
   11 Apr: Convention declared William and Mary joint monarchs,

while approving Claim of Right, which limited royal prerogative and strengthened Parliament.

13 Apr: Convention passed 'Articles of Grievance', which condemned Lords of Articles and other legislative committees not freely elected, 1669 Act of Supremacy and arbitrary powers to levy import duties and maintain standing army.

11 May: William and Mary accepted crown of Scotland, implying acquiescence in terms of Claim of Right and Articles of Grievance.

5 Jun: Convention met as Parliament, with Duke of Hamilton as High Commissioner, Sir John Dalrymple as Lord Advocate, and Earl of Melville as Secretary of State.

Jul: Episcopacy abolished.

27 Jul: Jacobites defeated at Killiecrankie.

2 Aug: Parliament prorogued after stalemate over character of new Lords of Articles.

1690　*15 Apr*; Parliament reconvened with Melville as Commissioner.

8 May: Lords of Articles abolished and replaced by system of standing and *ad hoc* committees chosen by Parliament.

7 Jun: Presbyterian Church established.

1691　*Aug*: William offered indemnity to all Highland clans still in rebellion which would take oath of allegiance by end of year.

1692　*13 Feb*: Massacre of MacDonalds of Glencoe despite their oath of allegiance.

1695　Act establishing Company of Scotland, authorised to trade with and plant colonies in America, Africa and Asia.

1698　Attempts by Scotland Comapny to establish colony of New Caledonia on isthmus of Darien or Panama plagued by disease and food shortages.

1699　Second Darien expedition.

1700　*Mar*: Scottish colonies forced to withdraw from Darien after defeat by Spanish.

1701　*1 Feb*: Close of last session of William's Parliament, after failure of opposition to pass act declaring legality of Scottish claim to Darien.

1702　*Jun*: Parliament, convened two months late, proclaimed Anne Queen of Scotland and, after withdrawal of Hamilton's faction, passed act nominating commissioners to treat for union with England.

1703　*13 Aug*: Parliament passed Act of Security claiming right to name Protestant successor to Queen Anne and safeguard parliamentary privilege, religion and trade from English domination. Royal assent refused.

1703–
4　*Dec–Feb*: Anti-prelate and anti-government mobs rioted in Edinburgh.

1704 *6 Jul*: New Session of Parliament opened with Earl of Tweeddale replacing Duke of Queensberry as Commissioner.
Aug: Amended version of Act of Security given royal assent in order to gain supply.

1705 *Apr*: Duke of Argyle appointed High Commissioner.
Sep: Parliament approved act empowering Queen to appoint commissioners to negotiate treaty of union with England.

1706 *27 Feb*: Scottish commissioners named by Queen Anne, meeting first with English commissioners at Westminster on 16 April.
22 Jul: Articles of Union signed by Scottish and English commissioners, providing union of parliaments with 16 Scottish peers and 45 commoners to sit in House of Commons, common coinage, free trade with England and colonies, preservation of Presbyterian Church in Scotland, and Scottish recognition of English Act of Succession.

1707 *16 Jan*: Scottish Parliament ratified Articles of Union by 110 votes to 67.
28 Apr: Final dissolution of Scottish Parliament by proclamation of Queen Anne.
1 May: Formal union of Scotland and England.

(Hereafter, Scottish political chronology is merged with English under 'Britain'; separate Scottish ecclesiastical chronology given in Chapter 6: The Church.)

HABSBURG EMPIRE

1648 *24 Oct*: Peace of Westphalia, by which Habsburg Emperor recognised independence of German states, which could thereafter make treaties with foreign powers so long as they were not directed against Empire.

1655 Archduke Leopold elected King of Hungary.

1656 Election of Leopold I as King of Bohemia.

1657 *2 Apr*: Death of Emperor Ferdinand III.
18 Jul: Leopold I elected Holy Roman Emperor.

1663– War with Turkey fought over issue of suzerainty of Transylvania,
4   ended (*10 Aug 1664*) by Peace of Vasvár (Eisenburg) which ceded south-east central Hungary to Turks and recognised their continued overlordship of Transylvania.

1668 *19 Jan*: Emperor Leopold I signed treaty with Louis XIV for future partition of Spanish possessions in event of death of Charles II of

103

Spain without heirs, by which Austria would acquire Spain itself and its American Empire.

1672 *23 Jun*: Alliance with Brandenburg–Prussia to prevent extension of French power.

27 Oct: Treaty of alliance with Dutch republic concluded; strengthened 11 Aug 1673.

1673 Establishment of royal governor's office in Hungary, which was treated as captured province.

16 Sep: Leopold I declared war against France.

1675 Leopold I seized Leignitz, Brieg and Wohlau after death of Duke George William, last Piast of Lower Silesia, despite claims of Brandenburg–Prussia.

1681 *9 Nov*: Diet of Odenburg, at which Leopold acknowledged traditional constitutional privileges of Hungarian nobility, revived office of Palatine and restored religious freedom of Protestants in northern Hungary.

1682 *Dec*: Turks proclaimed Emeric Tokoly King of Hungary.

1683 Turkish invasion of Habsburg lands.

14 Jul–12 Sep: Turkish siege of Vienna, broken after two months under leadership of King John Sobieski of Poland and Duke Charles of Lorraine.

1684 *5 Mar*: Holy League of Linz between Austria, Poland and Venice against Turks.

15 Aug: Truce of Ratisbon with Louis XIV providing for 20-year peace, whereby France kept all places assigned to it by Chambers of Reunion.

1686 *9 Jul*: League of Augsburg formed with Spain, Sweden, Saxony, Palatinate and Brandenburg–Prussia against France.

Sep: Buda captured from Turks.

1687 *12 Aug*: Turks defeated at battle of Nágy-Harsany, establishing Austrian control of central Hungary.

9 Dec: Joseph I, eldest son of Leopold I, crowned King of Hungary.

1687– Diet of Pozsony (Pressburg) at which Hungarian Estates were
8 induced to recognise hereditary Habsburg succession in male line, but retained right of election should male line become extinct. Hungarian nobles gave up right of resistence but retained 'ancient constitutional liberties'.

1688 Religious toleration confirmed in Transylvania.

1689 *May*: Leopold I made treaties of alliance with Holland and Bavaria.

Bloody assizes of Eperjes, which launched campaign against Hungarian collaborators with Turkey and against Protestants. Thereafter, landowners suspected of disloyalty or nonconformity lost their estates, and many Protestant townsmen were executed or lost their property.

1691   *Diploma Leopoldinum* recognised special status of Transylvania under Emperor, including religious liberties.

1697   *11 Sep*: Austrian forces under Prince Eugene of Savoy defeated Turks at Zenta.

       30 Oct: Peace of Ryswick with France, ending War of League of Augsburg.

1699   *26 Jan*: Peace of Karlowitz signed by Austria, Russia, Poland and Venice with Turkey, by which Habsburgs gained all of Hungary, Croatia, Transylvania and Slavonia.

1700   *16 Nov*: Treaty with Brandenburg–Prussia in anticipation of war with France.

1701   *27 Aug*: Grand Alliance against France formed at The Hague by Austria, Holland and England.

1702   *23 Apr*: Austria, together with England and Holland, declared war on France.

1703   *12 Sep*: Leopold I and his eldest son Joseph renounced all claims to Spanish Empire in favour of Archduke Charles, who gave up all claims to Habsburg lands. However, on death of either Joseph or Charles without heirs, each was to inherit entire possessions of other.

       19 Sep: Archduke Charles proclaimed Charles III of Spain.

1703– Hungarian rebellion led by Francis II Rákózi, with French support.
11

1705   *5 May*: Death of Emperor Leopold I. Succession of Joseph I.

       Oct: Archduke Charles recognised as King Charles III of Spain in Catalonia, Aragon and Valencia.

1709   Single supreme advisory body called the Konferenz established to coordinate central government committees; confirmed in its functions by ordinance of 1721.

1711   *17 Apr*: Death of Joseph I. Succession of Charles VI.

       1 May: Peace of Szatmár by which moderate Hungarian rebels submitted to Emperor Charles VI, who in turn confirmed traditional Hungarian constitution.

       12 Oct: Charles VI elected Holy Roman Emperor.

1712   Diet of Pozsony: Hungarian Chancery and *Camera* to be kept separate from Austrian equivalents; establishment of standing army to be paid for by Hungarian nobles but controlled from Vienna; nobles to retain freedom from direct taxation.

1713   *19 Apr*: Charles VI issued Pragmatic Sanction, which proclaimed that at his death all his lands should pass undivided to his male heir; should no son survive, his eldest daughter should inherit all Habsburg lands and kingdoms.

1714   *7 Mar*: Peace of Rastatt, by which Austria kept Italian possessions of Lombardy, Mantua, Naples and Sardinia and acquired Southern Netherlands.

1716   *13 Apr*: Charles VI declared war on Turkey.

1717   *13 May*: Birth of Maria Theresa.

       17 Aug: Belgrade recaptured from Turks.

       Finanzkonferenz created to supervise all financial institutions of Habsburg Empire.

1718   *21 Jul*: Peace of Passarowitz, by which Austria gained formal possession of Belgrade, part of Serbia, Banat of Temesvár and whole of Hungary.

       2 Aug: Austria adhered to Quadruple Alliance, Charles VI renouncing claims to Spain, recognising succession of Don Carlos in Tuscany and Parma-Piacenza, and exchanging Sardinia for Sicily with Piedmont-Savoy.

1719   *Jun*: Austrian troops expelled Spanish from Sicily.

1720   *6 Feb*: Peace of The Hague, which confirmed Austrian possession of Sicily in exchange for Sardinia.

       Austrian and Bohemian estates accepted Pragmatic Sanction, recognising right of Maria Theresa to inherit entire possessions of Habsburg Empire. Croatia followed suit in 1721, while Hungarian and Croatian Estates confirmed Sanction in 1722–3.

1722   Charles VI granted patent to Austrian East India (Ostend) Company to compete with Dutch and English in Africa and Far East.

1724   *6 Dec*: Pragmatic Sanction solemnly proclaimed by Charles VI after receiving assent from all territories.

1725   *30 Apr–1 May*: Treaty with Spain which recognised Pragmatic Sanction and granted privileges in Spanish ports to Ostend Company.

1726   *6 Aug*: Russia recognised Pragmatic Sanction in return for alliance against Turks.

1731   *11 Jul*: Treaty of Vienna, whereby Charles VI agreed to abolish Ostend Company in return for recognition of Pragmatic Sanction by Britain and Holland.

1732   *Jan*: Imperial Diet recognised Pragmatic Sanction, with Saxony ratifying agreement in 1733.

1733–   War of Polish Succession.
5

1734   Austrian forces defeated throughout Italy.

1736   *12 Feb*: Marriage of Maria Theresa and Duke Francis of Lorraine.

       May: Outbreak of new war against Turkey.

1738   *18 Nov*: Treaty of Vienna, formally ending War of Polish Succession, by which Austria gained French recognition of Pragmatic Sanction and duchies of Parma – Piacenza, but gave up Naples and Sicily to Don Carlos, heir to Spanish throne; Francis of Lorraine, husband of Maria Theresa, to inherit Tuscany on death of last Medici Grand Duke.

1739   *1 Sep*: Peace of Belgrade, by which Austria was forced to relinquish Belgrade and Serbian conquests to Turkey.

1740   *20 Oct*: Death of Charles VI. Succession of Maria Theresa, which was disputed by Bavaria, Saxony and Spain. Britain and Holland supported Maria Theresa, Russia remained neutral, while France indicated opposition.

        16 Dec: Frederick II of Prussia invaded Silesia, provoking First Silesian War and in fact igniting War of Austrian Succession.

1741   *25 Jun*: Coronation of Maria Theresa as Queen of Hungary.

        21 Sep: Hungarian Diet accepted Grand Duke Francis as co-Regent.

        9 Oct: Treaty of Klein Schnellendorf, ceding Lower Silesia to Frederick II of Prussia, who promptly broke treaty.

        1 Nov: Frederick II broke Treaty of Klein Schnellendorf by entering Neisse and signing treaty for partition of Habsburg Empire with Bavaria and France.

        Establishment of Commerce Directory for all Habsburg lands.

1742   *28 Jul*: Peace of Berlin, ending first Silesian War, whereby Austria ceded Silesia to Prussia, which withdrew from coalition against Maria Theresa.

        Sep: Count Uhlefeld appointed Chancellor, following death of Count Zinzendorf.

        Court Chancery divided into Court and State Chancery, primarily concerned with conduct of foreign affairs, and Austrian Court Chancery, with control over domestic administration.

1743   *18 Jan*: Count Wilhelm Friedrich Haugwitz appointed state chancellor (–1761).

        Apr: Maria Theresa crowned Queen of Bohemia at Prague.

        27 Jun: Bavaria placed under Austrian rule until end of war by Convention of Niederschönfeld.

        2 Sep: Treaty of Worms with Britain and Piedmont – Sardinia to expel Spanish from Italy, to obtain part of Lombardy for Piedmont, and guaranteeing continuation of British subsidy.

1744   *26 Apr*: France finally declared war on Austria.

        15 Aug: Second Silesian War began with Frederick II's invasion of Saxony.

        28 Dec: Quadruple Alliance of Austria, Britain, Saxony – Poland and Holland formed against Prussia.

1745   *22 Apr*: Peace of Füssen with Bavaria, whereby Elector Maximilian Joseph renounced claims to Empire and supported candidature of Grand Duke Francis, husband of Maria Theresa, as Emperor; Austria restored all Bavarian conquests.

1745   *May*: Austria and Saxony – Poland signed Treaty of Warsaw for parition of Prussia.

        4 Jun: Austrians invading Silesia defeated at Hohenfriedberg.

13 Sep: Grand Duke Francis elected Holy Roman Emperor.

25 Dec: Peace of Dresden with Prussia, whereby Frederick II retained Silesia, but recognised Pragmatic Sanction and election of Francis I as Emperor.

1746 *2 Jun*: Alliance with Russia for recovery of Silesia.

1748 *7 Oct*: Peace of Aix-la-Chapelle ended War of Austrian Succession, confirming Pragmatic Sanction and Francis I's election as Holy Roman Emperor, restoring Southern Netherlands to Austria, and recognising Prussia's possession of Silesia.

1748– Reorganisation of Bohemian local government displaced landlords'
51 authority with that of paid officials.

1748– Nobility and clergy first subjected to direct taxation; Estates of
60 Bohemia, Moravia and Upper Austria submitted in full to proposals of Haugwitz, but in Carinthia subsidy was eventually collected by royal decree.

1749 *14 May*: Austrian and Bohemian Chanceries united in single Directorium dealing with political and financial matters in both kingdoms, following death (in 1748) of Wilhelm Kinsky, Bohemian Chancellor. Supreme Court for Habsburg Monarchy (excluding Hungary) established, clearly separating judicial and administrative functions.

1753 Prince Wenzel Anton Kaunitz-Rietburg (1711–1794), formerly Austrian envoy at Peace of Aix-la-Chapelle, appointed Court Chamberlain and State Chancellor.

All Bohemian lands joined in single tariff system.

1755 *Aug*: Failure of negotiations for Austro-British alliance, whereupon discussions for alliance with France, favoured by Kaunitz, were begun.

1756 *1 May*: 'Diplomatic Revolution', engineered by Chancellor Kaunitz, consummated by Treaty of Versailles with France. Austria to remain neutral in any Anglo-French war, but each side would aid other in conflict with Prussia.

29 Aug: Frederick II invaded Saxony, beginning Seven Years' War. Statute defining limits of labour services (*Robot*) owed by peasants to landlords and state issued in Slavonia.

1757 *17 Jan*: Declaration of war against Prussia.

Feb: New treaty with Russia, whereby parties agreed not to make peace with Prussia until Silesia and Glatz were conquered.

1 May: Second Treaty of Versailles with France, for partition of Prussia.

1759 *12 Aug*: Austro-Russian force under Laudon captured Dresden from Prussians.

1760 *26 Jul*: Silesian fortress of Glatz recovered from Prussia.

3 Nov: Frederick II defeated Austrian troops under Daun at Torgau, which forced Austria to evacuate all of Saxony except Dresden.

1761   Council of State (*Staatsrat*) established at insistence of Kaunitz to act as central policy-making body of Habsburg Empire.

1762   Directorium abolished, with financial functions given to Court Treasury and political matters (including taxation) assigned to new Austro-Bohemian Chancery.

1763   *15 Feb*: Peace of Hubertusburg with Prussia, ending Seven Years' War, whereby Austria restored Silesia to Frederick II, who secretly pledged to support election of Archduke Joseph as King of Romans. Enactment of poll tax, with population divided into 24 classes.

1764   *Mar*: Joseph II crowned King of Romans at Frankfurt.

1765   *18 Aug*: Death of Emperor Francis I. Succession of Joseph II as Holy Roman Emperor and his brother Leopold as Grand Duke of Tuscany.
        17 Nov: Declaration of co-regency of Maria Theresa and Joseph II, whereby Maria Theresa retained ultimate sovereignty over Habsburg lands but shared responsibility of governing with Joseph.

1767   *Urbarium* (protocol) set maximum labour services owed by peasants to landlords in Hungary and Croatia.

1768   *3 Dec*: Chancellor Kaunitz suggested to Joseph II practicability of partitioning Poland.

1769   *Feb*: Austria occupied Lemberg and Zips region of Poland.

1770   Marie Antoinette, daughter of Maria Theresa, married Louis, Dauphin of France.

1772   *5 Aug*: First partition of Poland, with Austria taking East Galicia and Lodomercia, containing 83,000 sq. km. and 2,650,000 inhabitants.

1773   Jesuit estates confiscated in Habsburg lands (but only after dissolution of order by Pope Clement XIV) and proceeds used to establish extensive system of primary education.

1774   *Sep*: Austria occupied Bukovina, formerly held by Turkey.

1775   *Feb*: revolt of Bohemian peasants against labour services owed to nobles.
        7 May: Turkey formally ceded Bukovina to Austria.
        Austrian and Bohemian territories combined in single customs union with, however, Hungary, Lombardy and Austrian Netherlands excluded.
        Maria Theresa converted peasants' labour services into money rental on royal estates, paving way for abolition of serfdom.

1777   *30 Dec*: Joseph II laid claim to Lower Bavaria, despite succession of Elector Palatine Karl Theodor.

1778   *3 Jan*: Palatinate recognised Austrian claim to Lower Bavaria.

3 Jul: Prussia declared war on Austria over Bavarian succession, which continued intermittently until May 1779.

1779   *13 May*: Peace of Teschen, ending War of Bavarian Succession, whereby Austria gained Inn quarter of Bavaria.

1780   *7 Oct*: Serfdom abolished in Bohemia and Hungary.

29 Nov: Death of Queen Maria Theresa. Succession of Joseph II.

1781   *Feb*: Austro-Russian treaty concluded for driving Turks out of Europe and dividing their European possessions.

13 Oct: Joseph II issued patent of religious toleration and allowed limited freedom of press. (For all Theresian and Josephine ecclesiastical reforms, *see* Chapter 6: The Church.)

26 Nov: Joseph II abolished serfdom in Austria.

1782   *Mar*: Visit of Pope Pius VI to Vienna failed to convince Joseph II to reverse religious policies.

Jul: Monopoly of guilds abolished, allowing freedom of enterprise.

1783   Joseph II imposed German language in Bohemia and suppressed permanent committee of Bohemian Estates.

1784   *4 Jul*: Abrogation of Transylvanian constitution following revolution there; subsequently Joseph transferred Hungarian crown to Vienna, suppressed feudal courts, and ordered all government business to be conducted in German.

Oct: Joseph II severed diplomatic relations with Holland when Dutch fired on two Austrian ships ordered to navigate Scheldt.

Issuance of protective tariff (strengthened in 1788), which virtually cut off import of luxury goods.

1785   Joseph II promulgated 'Physiocratic' tax law, equalising methods of tax assessment, on basis of land possessed by owner, and ordered all lands in Empire surveyed; not enforced until 1789.

1786   Emperor's order creating single theological seminary for Austrian Netherlands at Louvain provoked wave of clerical protests.

1787   *Jan*: Riots in Louvain and Brussels, led by Van der Noot, in reaction to Joseph II's conversion of Austrian Netherlands to province of Austrian monarchy.

Feb: Joseph II visited Catherine II in Crimea to sign defensive pact with Russia.

Promulgation of new civil law code which abolished primogeniture, introduced civil marriage and outlawed torture and death penalty.

1788   *9 Feb*: War declared against Turkey.

Promulgation of reformed penal code, abolishing crimes of witchcraft and apostasy, and legitimising marriage between Christians and non-Christians; code also distinguished between civil and political crimes.

1789   *10 Feb*: Tax decree enforced tax law first devised in 1785, thus abolishing basis of feudalism in Habsburg state.

1790   *20 Feb*: Death of Joseph II. Succession of Leopold II as Holy Roman Emperor (– 1792).

HOLLAND (UNITED PROVINCES)

1648   *30 Jan*: Peace of Münster ended war with Spain, which recognised complete independence of United Provinces. River Scheldt to remain closed.
24 Oct: Peace of Westphalia brought general recognition of Dutch independence.

1650   *30 Jul*: Six leading members of States (assembly) of Holland arrested by Stadholder William II of Orange, following Holland's insistence on disbanding army forces in its pay. Consequently, States of Holland submitted to wishes of States-General to retain reduced standing force.
6 Nov: Death of William II of Orange, aged 24, of smallpox at The Hague.
14 Nov: Birth of Prince William III of Orange.

1651   *18 Jan*: Great Assembly, composed of delegates from all provinces, met to consider state of union, army and religion. After lengthy deliberations, Assembly decided to continue in force the religious settlement of the Synod of Dort (1619) and to divide responsibility for army among Council of State, States-General and provincial States. There was to be no captain-general of army. Holland and four other provinces left position of Stadholder vacant. Prince William Frederick of Nassau remained Stadholder of Friesland and Groningen.

1652   *8 Jul*: First Anglo-Dutch War broke out due to commercial rivalry.

1653   *Feb*: Johan de Witt appointed Grand Pensionary in Holland on death of Adrian Pauw.

1654   *5 Apr*: Treaty of Westminster ended First Anglo-Dutch War. Dutch recognised English Navigation Acts and agreed to exclude Prince of Orange from civil or military office.

1656   *Nov*: Conflict with Portugal over colonial claims in Brazil and East Indies.

1660   Act of Exclusion against Prince of Orange repealed after restoration of Charles II in England.

1661   *6 Aug*: Treaty with Portugal whereby United Provinces abandoned claims in Brazil but retained captured eastern possessions of Ceylon and Macassar.

111

1664   *Jun*: Informal war breaks out with England in colonies and at sea.

1667   *22 Jun*: Admiral de Ruyter burned English fleet anchored in River Medway.

       21 Jul: Peace of Breda ended second Anglo-Dutch War.

       5 Aug: Office of Stadholder abolished in Holland.

1668   *13 Jan*: United Provinces joined Triple Alliance with England and Sweden.

       Jul: de Witt re-elected Grand Pensionary and his salary doubled.

1672   *25 Feb*: William III of Orange appointed Captain-General of armed forces for one campaign and with responsibility to States-General.

       17 Mar: England declared war on United Provinces followed by French declaration of war and invasion.

       21 Jun: Unsuccessful assassination attempt against Johan de Witt.

       2 Jul: William of Orange appointed Stadholder of Zeeland.

       3 Jul: States of Holland repealed Eternal Edict and (*4 Jul*) appointed William of Orange Stadholder of Holland.

       8 Jul: States-General made William III Captain and Admiral-General of United Provinces.

       4 Aug: Resignation of Johan de Witt as Grand Pensionary and appointment of Caspar Fagel.

       20 Aug: Johan and Cornelius de Witt murdered by enraged mob at The Hague.

1673   *Dec*: French troops driven out of United Provinces by William III.

1674   *2 Feb*: First Holland and then Zeeland declared the stadholdership of their provinces hereditary in male line of family of Orange. Subsequently, States-General offices of Captain and Admiral-General made hereditary.

       9 Feb: Separate peace signed with England at Westminster, with Dutch recognising English ownership of New Netherlands (New York).

1676   *29 Apr*: Death of Admiral de Ruyter.

1677   *4 Nov*: Marriage of William III and Princess Mary, daughter of James, Duke of York.

1678   *10 Aug*: Peace of Nijmegen between France and Holland; Maastricht restored to United Provinces.

1686   *Aug*: Anti-French alliance formed by William III with Austria, Spain, Brandenburg, Sweden, and several small German states.

1688   *Jun*: Coalition of anti-Catholic English Whigs and Tories issued William invitation to invade England, which he accepted.

       5 Nov: William landed in England with 15,000 Dutch troops.

       Dec: Death of Grand Pensionary Fagel.

1689   *12 Feb*: William and Mary made King and Queen of England.

       12 May: Grand Alliance against France signed at Vienna, followed by so-called War of League of Augsburg (–1697).

1691 *18 Jan*: William III returned to Holland to concert actions of Alliance.

1694 *28 Dec*: Death of Queen Mary.

1696 *May–Oct*: William III again in United Provinces campaigning against French; but Dutch domestic affairs still managed almost entirely by States-General.

1697 *10 Sep*: Peace of Ryswick ended War of League of Augsburg; Dutch given right to garrison chief fortresses in Netherlands.

1701 *7 Sep*: New Grand Alliance against France forged by William III after accession of Louis XIV's grandson, Philip of Anjou, to Spanish throne.

1702 *8 Mar*: Death of William III. Holland, Zeeland, Utrecht, Gelderland and Overijssel elected no stadholder to replace William, the claims of his heir John William of Nassau, a boy of 14, although stadholder in Friesland and Groningen, being ignored. Control of foreign and domestic affairs reverted to States-General, led by Anthonie Heinsius, Pensionary of Holland, and Jan Hop, Treasurer-General of United Provinces.

     4 May: States-General declared war on France and Spain, followed by England and Austria, beginning War of Spanish Succession.

1703– Disputes in Utrecht and Gelderland between nobles and burgher
9 magistrates over control of town governments.

1711 *14 Jul*: Death of John William of Nassau.

1713 *31 Mar*: Peace of Utrecht, by which Southern Netherlands were ceded by Spain to Austria and Dutch given right to erect permanent barrier against France.

1715 *15 Nov*: Antwerp Barrier Treaty signed with Austria, giving Dutch right to garrison fortresses of Namur, Tournai, Ypres and others.

1716– *28 Nov–14 Sep*: Great Assembly discussed troops, finances and
17 coordination of provinces, but little was accomplished.

1720 *3 Aug*: Death of Heinsius. Appointment of Isaak van Hoornbeek as Grand Pensionary.

     5 Oct: Popular rising in Amsterdam against English coffee-houses where speculation in stocks was centred, after collapse of John Law's Mississippi scheme.

1722 William IV of Orange (son of John William of Nassau) designated Stadholder of Drenthe and Gelderland with limited powers.

1723 Holland, Zeeland, Utrecht and Overijssel confirmed principle of government without stadholder.

1727 *17 Jul*: Simon van Slingelandt appointed Grand Pensionary following death in June of van Hoornbeek.

1729 William IV became of age and assumed stadholderate of Groningen, Drenthe and Gelderland.

1731 William assumed office of Stadholder of Friesland.

11 Jul: Treaty of Vienna by which Habsburg Emperor agreed to dissolve Ostend East India Company in return for Dutch recognition of Pragmatic Sanction.

1734 *25 Mar*: Marriage of William IV and Princess Anne, eldest daughter of George II of Britain.

1736 *1 Dec*: Death of Grand Pensionary Slingelandt.

1737 Anthonie van der Heim appointed Grand Pensionary.

1743 *22 Jun*: States-General agreed to support Maria Theresa of Austria with 20,000 men under command of Prince Maurice of Nassau-Ouwerkerk.

1745 *Jan*: United Provinces joined with England, Saxony and Austria in alliance to maintain Pragmatic Sanction.

1746 *15 Aug*: Death of Anthonie van der Heim, followed by selection of Joacob Gilles as Grand Pensionary.

1747 *25 Apr*: William IV of Nassau and Orange proclaimed Stadholder and Captain and Admiral-General of Zeeland, following French conquests in Belgium and Dutch Flanders.

3 May: William IV made Stadholder and Captain and Admiral-General of Holland, an example followed by Utrecht on 5 May and Overijssel on 10 May.

4 May: States-General appointed William IV Captain and Admiral-General of United Provinces.

Oct: Province of Holland made dignities of Stadholder and Captain and Admiral-General hereditary in both male and female lines of house of Nassau-Orange; other provinces followed suit.

1748 *26 Jun*: Farming of revenue abolished in Holland, following abolition in other provinces.

28 Aug: City council of Amsterdam forced to accept reforms after intense public agitation. Prince of Orange given control of post offices; abuses in official appointments curtailed; privileges of guilds restored; and militia colonels and captains to be appointed from citizenry. 17 of 36 members of city council subsequently dismissed.

7 Oct: Peace of Aix-la-Chapelle, by which France agreed to evacuate Brabant and Austrian Netherlands.

Dec: William IV declared hereditary Stadholder of generality lands and hereditary Captain and Admiral-General by States-General.

1749 *3 May*: Jaacob Gilles, adherent of regent party, forced to resign as Grand Pensionary; replaced by Haarlem financier, Pieter Steyn, who was instructed to report all matters of state to Stadholder.

Oct: Lewis Ernest, Duke of Brunswick-Wolfenbüttel, made Field-Marshal of United Provinces and entrusted with reform of army.

1751 *22 Oct*: Sudden death of Prince William IV of Orange and succession of minor William V; Anne of England made Regent and Duke of Brunswick made acting Captain-General.

1756– United Provinces preserved neutrality during Seven Years' War,
63 indicating weakening of military and naval capacity.

1763 *25 Jul*: Failure of firm of De Neufville in Amsterdam, followed by financial panic.

1766 *8 Mar*: Prince William V of Orange assumed hereditary rights on reaching age of 18.
3 May: Act of Consultation, secret agreement between William V and Duke of Brunswick, providing that Brunswick would assist Stadholder in all affairs of state.

1767 *4 Oct*: Marriage of William V and Princess Wilhelmina of Prussia.

1772 *5 Nov*: Death of Pieter Steyn and appointment as Grand Pensionary of Pieter van Bleiswijk, follower of Duke of Brunswick.

1779 *Apr*: End of Anglo-Dutch alliance due to refusal of United Provinces to cease trade with American colonies; followed extensive build-up of Dutch fleet.

1780 *20 Dec*: Great Britain declared war against United Provinces.

1781 Dutch possessions in West Indies, South America and India fell to British.

1784 *20 May*: Peace treaty between Britain and United Provinces, the latter ceding Indian territory of Negapatam.
May: Ultimatum from Joseph II of Austria to open River Scheldt to navigation, refused by United Provinces.
Oct: Dutch fired on two ships ordered to navigate Scheldt by Joseph II, who broke off relations with United Provinces, sparking European crisis.
Sep: States of Holland deprived Stadholder of command of troops at The Hague after 'patriot' riot there.
8 Nov: Mediation by Louis XVI led to Treaty of Fontainebleau, whereby Joseph II renounced demand for free navigation of Scheldt and abandoned claims to Maastricht, in return for 9,500,000 florins.

1786 Growth in strength all over United Provinces of Patriot party, opposed to rule of both Stadholder and Regents and favouring democratic government.
Aug: States of Holland removed Prince of Orange as Captain-General of army.

1787 *28 Jun*: Demand by Frederick William II of Prussia that Dutch punish officials who had offended his sister refused. Followed by Prussian invasion.
17 Sep: Prussian troops entered The Hague amid popular celebrations of 'Orange' victory over 'Patriots'.

115

3 Oct: Surrender of Amsterdam to Prussian troops.

6 Oct: States-General, at demand of Princess Wilhelmina and Orange party, agreed to punish persons involved in her 'arrest', to disband 'Patriot' defence corps, and purge town councils of persons of democratic principles.

21 Nov: Amnesty proclaimed by William V, but containing many exceptions, so that numerous 'Patriots' fled to France. Followed by withdrawal of Prussian troops.

Nov: Removal of Pieter van Bleiswijk and appointment of Laurens Pieter van der Spiegel as Grand Pensionary.

1788   *15 Apr*: Treaties signed with Britain and Prussia, both of which agreed to protect hereditary stadholdership in United Provinces.

HUNGARY: *see under* Habsburg Empire

ITALY

1 *Lombardy*

1535–   Spanish rule in Lombardy from the extinction of the Sforza dynasty
1713   to the Peace of Utrecht.

1713   *31 Mar*: Peace of Utrecht, by which Lombardy passed from Spanish to Austrian control.

1745   Lombardy overrun by French and Spanish forces.

1746   *16 Jun*: Battle of Piacenza, after which Austria and Piedmont drove Franco-Spanish forces out of Lombardy.

1748   *7 Oct*: Peace of Aix-la-Chapelle, at which Austria ceded to Piedmont Vigevanesco, Oltrepò Pavese and Val d'Ossola areas of Lombardy.

1755–   Major reform of provincial and communal administrations carried
8   out by Beltrame Cristiani, by which leading role of landowners was reinforced.

1757   Cadastral register imposed new measurement and valuation of most lands subject to taxation.

Abolition of Council of Italy, last symbol of Spanish influence, tightening Austrian control of Lombardy.

1765   Creation of Supreme Economic Council to survey and make proposals about all aspects of Lombard economic policy.

1770   Abolition of tax farms and assumption by central government of direct collection of taxes.

1781   Edict of Toleration issued by Joseph II (*See* Chapter 6: The Church).

1787   Abolition of craft guilds.

2 *Naples and Sicily*

1504– Sicily and Naples were ruled by Spain in this period as the Kingdom
1713   of the Two Sicilies.

1647   *7 Jul*: Naples revolted against Spanish rule under leadership of Masaniello.

      16 Jul: Masaniello assassinated.

      1 Oct: Don John of Austria entered Bay of Naples with Spanish forces.

1648   Naples restored to Spanish rule by Don John.

1707   Austrian troops captured Naples, ending 203 years of Spanish rule.

1713   *31 Mar*: Peace of Utrecht, by which Naples remained under Austrian rule while Sicily was ceded by Spain to Piedmont under King Victor Amadeus II.

1718   *Jul*: Sicily recaptured by Spain.

1719   *Jun*: Austrian forces expelled Spanish troops from Sicily.

1720   *6 Feb*: Peace treaty between Quadruple Alliance and Spain, whereby Austria gained possession of Sicily.

1734   *May*: Spanish army under Don Carlos reconquered Naples.

1735   *3 Oct*: Peace preliminaries at Vienna, by which Don Carlos of Spain received both Naples and Sicily, becoming King Charles VII.

1739   Bernardo Tanucci reorganised local tribunals, ordering them to submit reports on homicides to higher courts, and established Supreme Magistry for trade to expedite commercial lawsuits.

1744   Reform of local tribunals largely abandoned due to hostility of nobility.

1746   Supreme Magistry for trade severely restricted in competence.

1752   Compendium of legislation, reducing contradictions, promulgated.

1759   *10 Aug*: Accession of Charles VII to Spanish throne as King Charles III. Succession in Sicily–Naples of his son, Frederick IV (–30 Mar 1806).

      Tanucci introduced measures to limit autonomy of baronial jurisdictions, augmented in 1773.

1776   Fall of Tanucci from power, engineered by Queen Maria Carolina, daughter of Maria Theresa of Austria.

1781   Domenico Caracciolo made Viceroy of Sicily.

1782   John Acton made Minister of Finance and Commerce.

      Creation of Supreme Council of Finances.

1786 Caracciolo appointed chief minister, with Prince Francesco Caramanico becoming Viceroy of Sicily.

1789 John Acton replaced Caracciolo as chief minister.

3 Papal States

See Chapter 6: The Church, under 'The Papacy'.

4 Piedmont–Savoy

1638 *4 Oct*: Accession as Duke of Charles Emmanuel II, a minor, under the regency of his mother, Princess Christina, a daughter of Henry IV and sister of Louis XIII of France.

1648 Assumption of government by Charles Emmanuel.

1675 *12 Jun*: Death of Duke Charles Emmanuel II. Succession of Victor Amadeus II (d. 31 Oct 1732).

1691 Duke Victor Amadeus invaded Dauphiné.

1694 Waldensian Protestants readmitted to Alpine valleys and granted limited religious toleration.

1696 *29 Jul*: Victor Amadeus abandoned Grand Alliance, signing treaty with Louis XIV, by which Piedmont regained Savoy, Nice, Susa, Casale and Pignerolo.

1706 *7 Sep*: Prince Eugène defeated French at Turin, after which they were driven from Piedmont.
Piedmont gained Alessandrino, Lomellina and part of Novarese from Lombardy.

1713 *31 Mar*: Peace of Utrecht, by which Piedmont gained Sicily and Victor Amadeus was granted title of King.

1717 Council of State reorganised and given responsibility for judicial matters.

1718 *Jul*: Sicily lost to Spanish invading force.
Nov: Victor Amadeus renounced Sicily in return for promise of Sardinia by signatories of Quadruple Alliance.

1719 Secretariat of State divided into separate departments for internal affairs, foreign affairs and war.

1720 *6 Feb*: Piedmont gained Sardinia from Austria in exchange for Sicily; Victor Amadeus made King of Sardinia.

1723 and 1729 Royal constitutions supplied compendium of laws, eliminating contradictions of previous legislation and strengthening royal authority.

1729 Foundation of provincial colleges to train new bureaucracy.

1730 *3 Sep*: Abdication of King Victor Amadeus II in favour of his son, Charles Emmanuel III.

Four *aziende* or departments created to administer finances, war, artillery and fortifications, and royal household.

1731 Cadastral register promulgated, imposing new measurement and valuation of almost all Piedmontese land subject to taxation.

1733 Local administration reorganised (followed by further adjustments in 1738 and 1742).

26 Sep: League of Turin with France and Spain against Austria, by which Piedmont was to gain Lombardy while ceding Savoy to France.

1735 *3 Oct*: Peace preliminaries at Vienna by which Piedmont received Tortonese and remainder of Novarese.

1742 *1 Feb*: King Charles Emmanuel III signed alliance with Austria for defence of Lombardy against Spain.

1743 *2 Sep*: Treaty of Worms with Austria and Britain to expel Bourbons from Italy, by which Piedmont was promised part of Lombardy.

1746 *16 Jun*: Battle of Piacenza, after which Austria and Piedmont expelled Franco-Spanish forces from Lombardy and Sardinia.

1748 *7 Oct*: Peace of Aix-la-Chapelle, by which Piedmont obtained Vigevanesco, Oltrepò, Pavese and Val d'Ossola in return for support of Maria Theresa.

1773 *20 Feb*: Death of King Charles Emmanuel III. Succession of Victor Amadeus III (−16 Oct 1796).

5 *Tuscany*

1621 *28 Feb*: Succession of Ferdinando II Medici.

1670 *23 May*: Death of Grand Duke Ferdinando II. Succession of Cosimo III.

1723 *31 Oct*: Death of Grand Duke Cosimo III. Succession of Gian Gastone.

1735 *3 Oct*: Peace preliminaries at Vienna, by which Francis of Lorraine is promised succession to Medici in Tuscany.

1737 *9 Jul*: Death of Grand Duke Gian Gastone, last of Medici rulers. Succession of Francis of Lorraine, husband of Maria Theresa, as Grand Duke.

1739 Pompeo Neri succeeded in creating grand-ducal court to diminish judicial conflicts and expedite justice.

1758– Pompeo Neri served as chief minister.
77

1765   *18 Aug*: Death of Francis of Lorraine. Succession of his second son Leopold as Grand Duke.

1768   Tax farms and privileged tax exemptions abolished.

1771   Abolition of tariffs on imported grain.

1774   Reform of provincial and communal administrations carried out by Francesco Maria Gianni (extended in 1776 and 1779).

1775   Free export of grain, regardless of internal shortages, allowed.

1779   Abolition of Florentine guilds.

1786   Adoption of new criminal code, abolishing torture and death penalty.

6 *Venice*

1645   War with Turkey broke out after Sultan Ibrahim began attack on Crete.

1646   *3 Jan*: Death of Doge Francesco Erizzo.

      2 Jan: Election of Francesco Molino as Doge.

1655   *27 Feb*: Death of Doge Francesco Molino.

      27 Mar: Election of Carlo Contarini as Doge.

      1 May: Death of Doge Carlo Contarini.

      17 May: Election of Francesco Cornaro as Doge.

1656   *5 Jun*: Death of Doge Francesco Cornaro.

      15 Jun: Election of Bertuccio Valier as Doge.

1657   Islands of Lemnos and Tenedos lost to Turkey.

1658   *29 Mar*: Death of Doge Bertuccio Valier.

      8 Apr: Election of Giovanni Pesaro as Doge.

1659   *30 Sep*: Death of Doge Giovanni Pesaro.

      16 Oct: Election of Domenico Contarini II as Doge.

1667   *24 May*: Turks began siege of Candia, capital of Crete (–Sep 1669).

1669   *6 Sep*: Surrender of Crete to Turks after 24-year-long war.

1675   *26 Jan*: Death of Doge Domenico Contarini II.

      6 Feb: Election of Niccolò Sagredo as Doge.

1676   *14 Aug*: Death of Doge Niccolò Sagredo.

      26 Aug: Election of Aloise Contarini II as Doge.

1684   *15 Jan*: Death of Doge Aloise Contarini.

      26 Jan: Election of Marc Antonio Giustinian as Doge.

      5 Mar: Venice joined Empire and Poland in Holy League of Linz against Turkey.

1685   Francesco Morosini captured ports of Morea (in Greece) and Dalmatia for Venice.

1687   *26 Sep*: Venetian bombardment of Athens seriously damaged Parthenon.

28 Sep: Athens surrendered by Turkey, followed by Venetian subjugation of Morea.

1688 *23 Mar*: Death of Doge Marc Antonio Giustinian.
 3 Apr: Election of Francesco Morosini as Doge.

1694 *6 Jan*: Death of Doge Francesco Morosini.
 25 Feb: Election of Silvestro Valier as Doge.

1700 *5 Jul*: Death of Doge Silvestro Valier.
 16 Jul: Election of Aloise Mocenigo II as Doge.

1709 *6 May*: Death of Doge Aloise Mocenigo II.
 22 May: Election of Giovanni Corner as Doge.

1716 Venice expelled from Morea by Turks.

1718 *21 Jul*: Peace of Passarowitz, by which Venice retained Corfu and conquests in Albania and Dalmatia, but acknowledged loss of Morea to Turkey.

1722 *12 Aug*: Death of Doge Giovanni Corner.
 24 Aug: Election of Aloise Mocenigo III as Doge.

1732 *21 May*: Death of Doge Aloise Mocenigo
 3 Jun: Election of Carol Ruzzini as Doge.

1735 *5 Jan*: Death of Doge Carol Ruzzini.
 17 Jan: Election of Aloise Pisani as Doge.
 Level of taxation unified within each administrative district.

1741 *17 Jun*: Death of Doge Aloise Pisani.
 30 Jun: Election of Pietro Grimani as Doge.

1752 *7 Mar*: Death of Doge Pietro Grimani.
 18 Mar: Election of Francesco Loredano as Doge.

1762 *19 May*: Death of Doge Francesco Loredano.
 31 May: Election of Marco Foscarini as Doge.

1763 *31 Mar*: Death of Doge Marco Foscarini.
 19 Apr: Election of Aloise Mocenigo IV as Doge.

1778 *31 Dec*: Death of Doge Aloise Mocenigo IV.

1779 *14 Jan*: Election of Paolo Renier.

1789 *13 Feb*: Death of Doge Paolo Renier.
 9 Mar: Election of Luigi Manin (d. 23 Oct. 1802) as Doge.

1797–1805 and from 1814: Under Austrian rule.

POLAND–LITHUANIA

1648 *10 May*: Death of King Wladyslaw IV.
 23 Sep: Cossacks under Bogdan Chmielnicki defeated Polish army at Piławce.
 20 Nov: Election of King John II, Casimir.

121

1649   *Aug*: Chmielnicki accepted Zborów agreement, which increased number of registered Cossack troops to 40,000 and restored rule of gentry in Polish Ukraine.

1651   *28–30 Jun*: Battle of Beresteczko, at which Cossacks were defeated by Polish army.

1652   *Jan*: Sejm (Parliament) broken up by first individual use of *Liberum Veto*, right of nobles to obstruct parliamentary proceedings, previously exercised only by regional blocks.

1654   War with Russia, after Cossacks recognised Tsar's overlordship of Ukraine (suspended in 1657).

1655   *Jul*: Swedish invasion, facilitated by collusion of Polish gentry; followed by conquest of Warsaw (*30 Aug*) and Cracow (*8 Oct*).
       Dec: Resistance to Swedish invaders began.

1656   *1 Apr*: King John Casimir promised to improve condition of serfs.

1657   Treaties of Wehlau and Bydgoszczcz, by which Poland ceded suzerainty over Prussia to Brandenburg in return for assistance against Sweden.

1658   Arians (Anti-trinitarians) expelled from Poland.

1659   Renewed hostilities with Russia over Ukraine.

1660   *3 May*: Peace of Oliva, ending war with Sweden. John Casimir gave up claims to Swedish throne while Sweden relinquished claims to Polish provinces.

1661– Proposals for reform of Sejm, providing for simple rather than
2   two-thirds majority, defeated by conservative nobles and gentry.

1665– Rebellion led by Jerzy Lubomirski, ultimately suppressed.
6

1667   *20 Jan*: Treaty of Andruszov, ending war with Russia, which gained extensive Ukranian territories, including Smolensk and Kiev.

1668   *16 Sep*: Abdication of King John Casimir.

1669   *18 Jun*: Michael Wiśniowiecki elected King after turbulent nine-month election, forestalling French attempt to extend influence over Poland.

1669– Peasant rebellions in district of Cracow and other regions.
72

1672   Invasion of Poland by Turkey.
       18 Oct: Treaty of Buczacz, by which Poland was forced to cede Podolia and remaining Ukranian territories to Turkey.

1673   *11 Nov*: John Sobieski defeated Turks at Chocim (Khorzim).

1674   *19 May*: John III, Sobieski, elected king.
       21 May: John Sobieski concluded secret treaty with France, with aim of recovering Prussian and Ukranian lands.

1676   *27 Oct*: Peace of Zurawno with Turkey, providing for division of Podolia and return of some Ukranian provinces.

1683   *12 Sep*: King John Sobieski and Polish army raised Turkish siege of Vienna.

1684   *5 Mar*: Poland joined Austria and Venice in Holy League against Turks.

1686   Alliance with Russia against Turkey.

1696   *16 Jun*: Death of King John Sobieski.
       17 Jun: Elector Augustus of Saxony elected King Augustus II.

1699   *26 Jan*: Peace of Karlowice, by which Poland regained Podolian and Ukranian possessions.
       22 Nov: Treaty of Preobrazhenskoe with Russia, Denmark and Saxony for partition of Swedish empire.

1700   *May*: Augustus II's invasion of Livonia began Great Northern War.

1701   Sweden invaded Courland and Poland, demanding deposition of Augustus II.

1702   *14 May*: Charles XII and Swedish army captured Warsaw.
       9 Jul: Cracow fell to Swedes.

1704   *12 Aug*: Aristocratic faction opposed to Augustus II declared an interregnum and elected Stanislaw Leszczynski King at Warsaw at instigation of France and Sweden, creating 'two Polands' with rival rulers.

1706   *24 Sep*: Augustus II forced by Sweden to renounce Polish throne and recognise Stanislaw Leszczynski.

1709   Augustus II returned to Poland after Russia's defeat of Sweden at Poltava.

1710   *Feb*: Augustus II again recognised as King by General Assembly in Warsaw.

1713   Saxon troops brought into Poland, ostensibly because of Turkish threat, but actually to strengthen royal authority of Augustus II.

1714– Gentry-led uprisings in Little Poland, followed by wider rebellion
15   against presence of Saxon troops.

1715   *Apr*: Poland joined Russia, Denmark and other states in new coalition against Sweden.
       25 Nov: General Confederation of Tarnogród under Presidency of Stanislaw Ledchowski backed by army, directed at King's attempt to increase royal power with Saxon troops and against arbitrary actions of 'Hetmen' – regional governors.

1716   Russian mediation agreed by gentry, King and Hetmen, with Czar's envoy, Grigory Dolgoruki acting as arbitrator; 18,000 Russian troops sent into Poland to strengthen authority of Dolgoruki.

1717   *1 Feb*: 'Dumb Sejm', one-day parliament so-called because no one was allowed to speak, approved Treaty of Warsaw, compromise secured by Russian mediation. King was henceforth allowed only 1200 Saxon guards; regular army of 12,000 established; power of

123

local diets limited; and authority of Hetmen somewhat reduced. Afterwards, Russia claimed right to enforce Warsaw Treaty, by force if necessary.

1720   Russian troops left Poland after four years of occupation. Peter I of Russia concluded treaties with Turkey and Prussia to ensure free election of Polish kings, aimed against plans of Augustus II for his son's succession. Followed by similar treaties with Sweden in 1724 and Austria in 1726.

1733   *1 Feb*: Death of King Augustus II, setting off struggle for Polish Succession between factions favouring Stanislaw Leszczyński, backed by France, and that supporting Elector Augustus of Saxony, backed by Russia, Austria and Prussia.

12 Sep: Stanislaw Leszczyński elected King by faction led by Potocky family. Followed by Russian invasion and counter-election of Augustus III.

1734   *Jan*: Russian siege of Gdansk, where Leszczyński had taken refuge.
28 Jun: Surrender of Gdansk, after flight of Leszczyński.

1736   *Jun–Jul*: Pacification Sejm, which formally recognised Augustus III as King of Poland, signalling end of hostilities. Only Seym not to be broken up during reign of Augustus III, which was characterised by weakening of royal authority, growth of aristocratic autonomy, and domination by foreign powers.

1738   Emergence of Henry Brühl as chief minister in Poland.

1743   *Jan*: Brühl made alliance with Austria against Prussia.

1744   *Feb*: Russo-Polish alliance formed to limit Prussian ambitions.

1756– Poland, through impotence and near anarchy, remained neutral
63   during Seven Years' War, but her territory violated by belligerents.

1757   Russia occupied parts of eastern Poland, with encouragement of Brühl and Augustus III, to put pressure on East Prussia, but were never afterwards withdrawn.

1763   *5 Oct*: Death of Augustus III.

1764– Convocation Sejm slightly limited power of *Liberum Veto*, reduced
6   authority of oligarchic ministers, abolished internal customs and established general customs of country's frontiers (abolished under Prussian pressure in 1765).

1764   *7 Sep*: Stanislaw Poniatowski, candidate of Catherine II of Russia, elected King of Poland, largely due to pressure of Russian troops.

1765   Periodical 'Monitor', sponsored by King Stanislaw, criticised ignorance, proposed religious toleration, and advocated reform of industry and agriculture.

1767   Additional Russian troops enter Poland and establish two dissenting confederations, one for Lithuania at Stuck and one for the Crown in Warsaw.

Oct: Confederate Sejm meeting in Warsaw, surrounded by Russian troops, refused to grant equal rights to dissenters, whereupon Russians blockaded Warsaw forcing parliament's adjournment.

1768   Reconvened Sejm agreed on five 'eternal principles': (1) free election of kings; (2) *Liberum Veto*; (3) right of renouncing allegiance to king; (4) aristocracy's exclusive right to own land and hold office; and (5) landowners' dominion over peasants. Resolutions of Sejm were to be guaranteed by Russia, reducing Poland to vassal status.
       29 Feb: Formation of armed Confederation of Bar by Polish gentry against Russians, followed by insurrections.

1769   Formation of 'Generality' of opposition gentry, supported by France and Saxony.
       Oct: Austria occupied Polish county of Zips.

1770   'Generality' of gentry proclaimed dethronement of King Stanislaw.

1771   *Jun*: Frederick II surrounded Polish provinces coveted by Prussia with military cordon, ostensibly to keep out cattle plague.

1772   *6 Feb*: Treaty between Russia and Prussia for partition of Poland.
       5 Aug: Austria joined Russia and Prussia in treaty providing for first partition of Poland. Russia received north-east Poland including Vitebsk and Minsk (92,000 sq. km. and 1,300,000 inhabitants); Prussia annexed northern Poland, except Gdansk (36,000 sq. km. and 580,000 inhabitants); and Austria took East Galicia and Lodomercia (83,000 sq. km. and 2,650,000 inhabitants).

1773   *30 Sep*: Confederation Sejm forced to ratify partition treaties.
       Commission of National Education founded and endowed with estates of recently dissolved Jesuit order.

1775   *Mar*: Poland forced to sign commercial treaty with Prussia, which imposed heavy duties on Polish exports passing through Prussian territory.
       Confederation Sejm approved new constitution, which preserved elective kingship and *Liberum Veto* but established permanent council composed of 18 senators and 18 deputies chosen biennially by Sejm. Council presided over by King and divided into five administrative departments – foreign affairs, police, military, finance and justice.

1776   Opposition deputies excluded from Sejm, which abolished military commission, deprived Hetmen of military commands, and entrusted Andrzej Zamoyski with preparing codification of Polish law.

1778   Russia allowed anti-royalist magnates to obtain seats in Council to curb King's aspiration for independent foreign policy.

1780   Zamoyski's draft law code, which included social and political reforms, rejected by Sejm.

1788   *7 Oct*: Confederation Sejm met in Warsaw, beginning aristocratic revolution.
       20 Oct: Sejm voted to increase Polish army to 100,000 and (*3 Nov*)

abolished War Department, entrusting command to War Commission elected by parliament. Russia protested, but Prussia declared she had no intention of restricting Poland's freedom to legislate.

9 Dec: Sejm abolished Department of Foreign Affairs and established Seym Deputation for Foreign Affairs.

1789 *19 Jan*: Sejm abolished Permanent Council, prolonged its powers indefinitely, and decided to govern by itself.

Mar: Sejm imposed 10% tax on income from aristocratic estates and 20% tax on ecclesiastical lands, followed by state confiscation of latifundia of bishopric of Cracow.

PORTUGAL

1640 Portugal revolted from Spanish rule and re-established independence, though war with Spain continued.

15 Dec: John IV crowned King of Portugal in Lisbon, inaugurating Braganza dynasty.

1648 Loss of Muscat to Arabs.

1654 *10 Jul*: Treaty of alliance with England, granting concessions to English merchants.

Portugal re-established control of Brazil with expulsion of Dutch.

1656 *6 Nov*: Death of John IV. Succession of Alfonso VI, with Queen Mother Luisa as Regent.

1659 *14 Jan*: Spanish invaders defeated at Elvas.

1661 *23 Jun*: Marriage alliance between Charles II of England and Catherine of Braganza, whose dowry included two million cruzados and cession of Tangier.

6 Aug: Treaty with Holland, by which Portugal retained Brazil but Dutch gained Ceylon.

1662 *21 May*: Marriage of Charles II and Catherine of Braganza.

Jul: Alfonso VI assumed control of government, dismissing Queen Luisa as Regent and appointing Count Castelo-Melhor as 'secret' secretary.

1665 *6 Jun*: Spanish defeated at Montes Claros by Portugese and British forces, followed by victory at Villa Viciosa which assured Portugal's independence.

1667 *7 Sep*: Dismissal of Castelo-Melhor by Alfonso VI.

23 Nov: Alfonso VI forced to surrender government to his brother Pedro, who assumed title of Prince Regent.

1668 *Jan*: Cortes supported deposition of Alfonso and accession of Pedro to power.

126

13 Feb: Treaty of Lisbon, whereby Spain recognised Portugese independence.

Marriage of Prince Regent Pedro and Maria Francisca, whose previous marriage to Alfonso VI had been annulled.

1669   Re-establishment of relations with papacy, allowing for appointment of new bishops.

1683   *12 Sep*: Death of Alfonso VI finally allowed Prince Regent to assume title of King Pedro II.

Dec: Death of Queen Maria Francisca.

1687   Marriage of Pedro II and Maria Sophia, daughter of Elector-Palatine Philip William of Neuberg.

1689   *Oct*: Birth of future John V.

1698   Last meeting of Portugese Cortes.

1703   *21 Apr*: Portugal concluded treaty with Britain and joined Grand Alliance, in return for promise of territorial expansion at Spain's expense.

16 Dec: Methuen Treaty with Britain, by which Portugal agreed to admit woollen goods from Britain, which in turn would import Portugese wines for one-third less duty than on French.

1706   *9 Dec*: Death of Pedro II. Succession of King John V (–1750).

1708   Marriage of John V and Maria Ana of Austria, sister of Charles VI.

1715   *6 Feb*: Second Peace of Utrecht ended war between Spain and Portugal (ratified by Portugal on 9 March).

1720   Emigration from Portugal forbidden because of flood of fortune-hunters to Brazil, which threatened to ruin Portugese agriculture.

1729   *19 Jul*: Double marriage alliance between Spain and Portugal sealed, with Prince José of Portugal to wed Maria Ana of Spain and Prince Fernando of Asturias to wed Maria Barbara of Braganza.

1735– Diplomatic rupture with Spain despite marriage alliances.
7

1736   Number of secretaries of state increased from two to three and official work divided into internal affairs, foreign affairs and war, and colonies and navy.

1747   Deaths of Chief Minister, Cardinal da Mota, and Minister of Colonies, Antonio Pereira.

1749   Frei Gaspar da Encarnacão became Chief Minister.

1750   *31 Jul*: Death of John V. Succession of King José I.

5 Aug: Sebastião José de Carvalho e Melo, future Maquis of Pombal, named Minister of Foreign Affairs and War, and in fact became Prime Minister.

1755   *1 Nov*: Severe earthquake devastated city of Lisbon, killing some 30,000 people and wrecking over 10,000 buildings.

1756   Pombal detected plot of clergy and nobles against his ministry, imprisoning or exiling ringleaders.

'Junta do Comércio', with power to regulate all commercial matters, established by Pombal.

Sep: General Company for Wine Culture in Uppper Douro created to regulate port-wine trade.

1757   *23 Feb*: Riots in Oporto against wine monopoly, instigated by taverners; harshly suppressed, with 25 executed and 188 deported.

May: Jesuits purged from civil government in Brazil.

1758   *3 Sep*: King José I wounded in assassination attempt.

13 Dec: Marquis of Távora and his wife, Count of Atouguia, and Duke of Aveiro arrested and charged with attempted assassination of King and revolution.

1759   *12 Jan*: Execution, after torture, of would-be assassins; arrest of 10 Jesuits, including Gabriel Malagrida, allegedly implicated in assassination plot.

13 Jan: Decision to confiscate property of Society of Jesus, taken at insistence of Pombal.

Jun: System of free secular schools established in Lisbon.

3 Sep: Expulsion of Jesuits and confiscation of their property begun.

1760   Relations with papacy broken off by Pombal.

1761   Foundation of College of Nobles.

1762   *23 Apr*: Franco-Spanish ultimatum to Portugal, instructing closure of ports to British; rejected by Pombal, followed by Spanish invasion and capture of Braganza and Almeida.

18 May: King José I forced by invasion to declare war on Spain.

1763   *3 Feb*: Peace of Paris led to restitution of Portugese territories.

1768   Royal Board of Censorship established with right to approve all books and other publications.

1771   Royal Board of Censorship granted direction of primary education.

1773   Reorganisation of University of Coimbra by Pombal, adding faculties of mathematics and natural sciences.

1775   Spanish repulsed attempt by Portugese fleet to recapture Montevideo in Uruguay.

1777   *24 Feb*: Death of José I. Succession of Queen Maria I.

25 Feb: Unofficial dismissal of marquis of Pombal as Prime Minister by Queen Maria. Followed by order liberating over 800 political prisoners.

1 Mar: Official 'resignation' of Pombal, accepted by Queen on 3 Mar.

14 Mar: Marquises of Angeja and Cerveira appointed to lead ministry.

1781   Acquisition of Delagoa Bay, E. Africa, from Austria.

1782   *8 May*: Death of Pombal.

Jul: Portugal joined League of Armed Neutrality.

1786 Death of King consort Pedro III.

1788 Death of Don José, heir to throne, causing Queen Maria to drift towards insanity.

RUSSIA

1645 *Jul*: Death of Michael Romanov. Succession of Tsar Alexis.

1648 *Jun*: Severe rioting in Moscow and other towns against increased prices and taxation

1649 New legal code, which legalised serfdom and defined the relationship of social classes.

1650 Rebellion of cities of Novgorod and Pskov crushed after three months.

1652 Election of Patriarch Nikon as leader of Russian Orthodox Church. Re-establishment of German settlement in Moscow.

1654 Incorporation of Ukraine into Russia after Cossack rebellion against Poland.
      Patriarch Nikon ordered 'correction' of Orthodox liturgy, ceremony and icons according to Greek practice.

1654– Russo-Polish War.
  67

1658 Split between Tsar Alexis and Patriarch Nikon, who retired to monastary of New Jerusalem.

1662 'Copper rebellion' in Moscow, caused by substitution of copper for silver coins, followed by rapid depreciation and spiralling inflation. Silver coins restored in 1663.

1666 Nikon removed as Patriarch but his reforms confirmed. (*See* Chapter 6: The Church.)

1667 *20 Jan*: Treaty of Andruszov, ending Russo-Polish War, by which Russia annexed Kiev, Smolensk and other territories.

1667– Uprising of Stenka Razin, who formed a pirate horde of fugitive serfs
  71 and other desperate elements which savaged Ukraine and southern Russia until finally suppressed.

1671 *6 Jun*: Execution of Stenka Razin.

1676 Death of Alexis. Succession of Tsar Fyodor III.

1676– War with Turkey, which confirmed Russian possession of Ukranian
  80 territories.

1682 *27 Apr*: Death of Tsar Fyodor. Peter, younger son of Alexis, proclaimed Tsar by Patriarch Joakhim.
      May: Revolt of the streltsy militia led by Tsarevna Sophia, which proclaimed Alexis's retarded son Ivan first Tsar and Peter second

Tsar, with Sophia made Regent and entrusted with government. Prince Vasili Golitsin, favourite and adviser of Sophia, made Minister of Foreign Affairs.

17 Sep: Execution of streltsy leader Prince Khovansky, who had led subversive campaign against Sophia, followed by new streltsy revolt finally subdued on 8 Oct.

1686   'Eternal peace' signed with King John Sobiecki of Poland, confirming Russian possessions acquired by Treaty of Andruszov.

1687   Unsuccessful campaign against Crimean Tartars; further unsuccessful campaigns in 1689.

1689   Treaty of Nerschinsk with China.
        Aug: Overthrow of Regency of Sophia and exile of Prince Golitsin. Assumption of Regency by Tsarina Natalia, Peter's mother.

1694   Death of Tsarina Natalia.

1695   Peter's formation of a river flotilla, followed by first, unsuccessful assault on Azov.

1696   *29 Jan*: Peter I became sole Tsar on death of his brother Ivan.
        29 Jul: Azov captured from Turks.

1697–   Peter travelled incognito through Prussia, Holland, England and
8   Austria to acquire western military and scientific expertise and engage foreign artisans and advisers.

1698   *25 Jul*: Return of Peter to Moscow after receiving news of streltsy rising, which was punished with savagery, Peter himself executing five accused insurgents.

1699   Reorganisation of army into regiments on western model.

1700   *4 Jul*: Truce with Turkey, which ceded Azov.
        19 Aug: Russia declared war against Sweden, thus entering great Northern War.
        30 Nov: Charles XII of Sweden defeated Russians at Narva.
        Death of Patriarch Adrian, whose position was thereafter left vacant, beginning Peter's extension of state control over Orthodox Church. (*See* Chapter 6: The Church.)

1701   Foundation of Navigation School at Moscow.
        Establishment of Monastary Prikaz to oversee church property.

1703   *29 Jun*: Peter founded new capital city of St Petersburg after taking Ingria and Livonia from Sweden.

1705   System of army recruiting extended, with levy of recruits ordered at rate of one man from each twenty peasant households.

1707   Invasion of Russia by Charles XII and Swedish army.

1708   *Sep*: Russian army under Menshikov crushed Swedes at Lesnaia.
        Oct: Charles XII captured Mogilev and invaded Ukraine.

1708–   Division of Russia into eight administrative provinces (later ten),
11   each headed by appointed governor.

1709   *8 Jul*: Peter defeated Swedish army at Poltava, forcing Charles XII to take refuge in Turkey.

1710   *27 Jan*: Introduction of first national budget in Russia.

1710– War with Turkey.
11

1711   *1 Aug*: Tsar Peter, surrounded by Turks, made peace by restoring Azov and enabling Charles XII to return to Sweden.
Creation of Senate by Peter began reform of central administration. All classes allowed to engage in trade.

1714   Limited system of elementary education established for sons of landowners and officials.
Distinctions between land held by traditional tenure or for service abolished.

1715   Russian Naval Academy established in St Petersburg.

1717– Prikaz system of central government replaced by nine administrative
19   colleges, which dealt with commerce, mines and manufactures, foreign affairs, army, navy and justice – following Swedish model.

1718   *26 Jun*: Execution of Peter's son and heir, Tsarevitch Alexis, allegedly for plotting overthrow of his father and repeal of reforms.

1719   Abolition of most state monopolies, except that on salt.

1721   *10 Sep*: Treaty of Nystad with Sweden, ending Great Northern War, by which Russia gained Baltic provinces of Livonia, Ingria, Estonia and East Karelia, but restored Finland.
Abolition of Orthodox Patriarchate, which was replaced by Holy Synod, wholly subordinated to secular authority.

1721   Peter assumed title of 'Emperor of all the Russias', and, as sovereign, was allowed to name successor.

1722   Holy Synod placed under direction of lay procurator, selected from 'good and courageous' army officers.
'Table of Ranks' established, which divided army and navy officers into 14 distinct grades and assigned each to an equivalent in civil service.

1722– War with Persia, by which Russia acquired south-west shores of
3   Caspian sea (*Sep 1723*), including towns of Baku and Derbent.

1723   *9 Jan*: Poll tax imposed on entire servile male population, eliminating distinctions between serfs and other bondsmen.

1724   All imports subjected to heavy tariffs.
7 May: Coronation of Catherine, Peter's second wife, as Empress.

1725   *28 Jan*: Death of Peter I. Succession of Empress Catherine, supported by imperial guards and most ministers. Government assumed by Prince Menshikov and other aristocratic courtiers.

1726   *Feb*: Establishment of Supreme Privy Council as central executive organ, dominated by Princes Menshikov and Golitsin.

> *6 Aug*: Military alliance with Austria against Turkey, with guarantee of mutual aid for 30 years.

1727   *6 May*: Death of Empress Catherine I. Succession (18 May) of Peter II, grandson of Peter I and son of Alexis. Government to be exercised during Peter's minority by Supreme Privy Council, now completely dominated by Menshikov.

      8 May: Arrest and exile of Menshikov, at instigation of Dolgoruky family and Count Andrew Ostermann.

1730   *19 Jan*: Death of Peter II from smallpox. Succession of Anne, Duchess of Courland, daughter of Tsar Ivan V, upon acceptance of 'conditions' imposed by oligarchic Supreme Privy Council.

      25 Feb: Coup by palace guards allowed Empress Anne to tear up 'conditions' and resume autocratic rule; followed by abolition of Supreme Privy Council and execution of two of Dolgoruky family.

1731   *Mar*: Secret police, abolished by Peter I, re-established, subsequently unleashing reign of terror.

      10 Nov: Cabinet established as chief executive, dominated by German favourites, including Ostermann and Count Biron.

1733– War of Polish Succession, in which Russian intervention helped
5   secure accession of King Augustus III.

1735– War with Turkey, ended by Treaty of Belgrade, by which Russia
9   regained Azov.

      6 May: Police powers of landowners over serfs extended.

1736   *31 Dec*: Edict limited term of aristocratic service to state to 25 years and one male member of each family to manage estates.

1737   *1 Aug*: Decree depriving serfs of right to buy land, except in name of his lord.

1740   *17 Oct*: Death of Empress Anne and succession of her great-nephew, infant Ivan VI, under regency of Count Biron.

      9 Nov: Palace coup led by Field-Marshall Münnich exiled Biron and made Ivan VI's mother, Anna Leopoldovna, Regent.

1741   *25 Nov*: Palace revolution resulting in deposition of Ivan VI, exile of Anna Leopoldovna, and accession of Empress Elizabeth, daughter of Peter I and Catherine I.

      12 Dec: Cabinet abolished and Senate and colleges restored to control central administration. Elizabeth's private chancery in fact assumed direction of government policy.

1741– War with Sweden, ended by Peace of Åbo (17 Aug 1743), by which
3   Russia acquired part of south Finland.

1744   *17 May*: Empress Elizabeth decreed abolition of death penalty.

      Count A. P. Bestuzhev-Riumin appointed Chancellor, subsequently dominating foreign affairs.

1745   *21 Aug*: Marriage of Charles Peter, Duke of Holstein, nephew of

Empress Elizabeth and heir to Russian throne, to Princess Sophia Augusta (later Catherine) of Anhalt – Zerbst.

1746   Alexander Shuvalov appointed head of secret police.

1747   *Jun* and *Dec*: Treaties with Austria and Britain providing for commitment of 60,000 Russian troops in War of Austrian Succession in return for £300,000 subsidy. However, war ended in April 1748 before Russian army reached front.

1749   Ivan Shuvalov became official favourite of Empress Elizabeth.

1753   *7 May*: Creation of State Nobility Bank established to extend mortgage credit to aristocratic families.

Abolition of internal customs and charges on movement of domestic merchandise.

1754   Establishement of Commercial Bank in St Petersburg.

University of Moscow founded at instigation of Ivan Shuvalov.

1754–   Winter Palace built at St Petersburg by Rastrelli.
62

1756   *14 Mar*: 'Conference' of ten members, including Grand Duke Peter, established, which subsequently became supreme organ of government.

31 Dec: Russia acceded to Treaty of Versailles between France and Austria in alliance against Prussia.

1757   *22 Jan*: Secret treaty with Austria, both countries pledging to field 80,000 troops against Prussia, and not to conclude separate peace until Austria regained Silesia. Russia to receive one-million-ruble subsidy.

1758   *Jan*: Russian army captured East Prussia.

14 Feb: Count Bestuzhev arrested and deprived of all offices and titles, followed by appointment of Count M. J. Vorontsov as Chancellor.

Edict provided for state confiscation of all estates farmed by servile labour which was not owned by service (Dvoriane) nobility.

1759   *23 Jul*: Defeat of Prussian army at Kay.

1760   *9–13 Oct*: Russians burned Berlin, which they occupied until return of Prussian army from Silesia.

1762   *5 Jan*: Death of Elizabeth. Succession of Peter III, who, as an admirer of Frederick II of Prussia, moved to withdraw Russia from Seven Years' War.

29 Jan: 'Conference' of ten abolished.

18 Feb: Peter III issued decree freeing nobility (Dvoriane) from compusory service to state, allowing them to travel freely, and to enter service of foreign powers.

21 Feb: Abolition of secret police.

5 May: Treaty of St Petersburg with Prussia, by which Russia restored all conquests and formed offensive and defensive alliance with Frederick II.

28 Jun: Palace revolution which deposed Peter III and proclaimed his wife, Catherine, as Empress.

6 Jul: Assassination of Peter III, probably on orders of Catherine II.

1763   Count N. I. Panin made Minister of Foreign Affairs.

15 Dec: Senate divided into six departments, each subordinated to Procurator General.

Occupation of Courland, legally a fief of Polish crown.

1764   *26 Feb*: Catherine issued decree providing for secularisation of church properties, which were to be administered by College of Economy.

11 Apr: Treaty with Prussia, with aim to prevent constitutional changes in Prussia and to intercede with Polish government on behalf of religious minorities.

7 Sep: Election of Stanislaw Poniatowski, former lover of Catherine II, as King of Poland, following Poland's occupation by Russian troops.

1765   *17 Jan*: Landowners given right to sentence unruly serfs to penal servitude in Siberia and to reclaim them at will.

1767   Catherine II issued her 'Instruction', which proposed that Russia should be governed by enlightened principles, with absolute monarchy resting on foundation of law. Followed convening in July of Legislative Commission to draft new legal and judicial code. Commission met until Dec 1768 but never completed its project.

Sep: Polish nobility of Confederation of Radom occupied Warsaw with support of Russia, which overran Poland with additional troops.

1768   *Feb*: Polish parliament ratified Russo-Polish treaty confirming existing Polish constitution, which was placed under Russian guarantee.

Mar: Confederation of Bar organised by dissident Polish nobles to protest against Russian occupation as well as policies of King Stanislaw Poniatowski.

1768–   War with Turkey, which led to penetration of Crimea but ended with
72   inconclusive armistice in July 1772.

1769   Advisory Council to Catherine II was created as wartime expedient, but continued to meet until end of reign.

Sep: Russian troops occupied Moldavia.

1772   *5 Aug*: First partition of Poland by which Russia received Byelo-Russia and part of Livonia comprising 92,000 sq. km. and 1,300,000 inhabitants.

1773–   Peasant rebellion led by Emilian Pugachev (who pretended to be
4   Peter III) which attracted widespread support from runaway serfs, Cossacks and displaced tribes. Pugachev was captured (Sep 1774) after dramatic successes and executed (Jan 1775).

1774   Grigory Potemkin made official favourite of Catherine II.

21 Jul: Treaty of Kutchuk-Kainardzhi with Turkey provided for independence of Crimea and Russian fortification of Azov; allowed Russian merchants to navigate Black Sea and to enjoy free passage through Dardanelles and Bosporus; and gave Russia vague right to protect Christian subjects of Turkish empire.

1775   *7 Nov*: Law on administration of provinces increased number of provinces, made local government directly responsible to Senate, segregated duties of local officials with elected representatives of nobles, burghers and state peasants.

Catherine abolished monopolies and allowed free establishment of industrial enterprises.

1780   Treaty with Austria against Turkey and for preservation of Polish constitution.

1780–   Gradual abolition of administrative colleges.
  6

1781   *27 Oct*: Catherine's policy of 'Russification' provided for division of Ukraine into three provinces and abolition of its autonomous institutions.

1783   *8 Apr*: Annexation of Crimea after forced abdication of last puppet ruler.

Ukraine made subject to poll tax.

1785   *21 Apr*: Charter of Nobility expanded aristocratic privilege by confirming nobles in hereditary tenure of estates and freedom from compulsory state service and set up local and regional corporations of nobles which chose officials subject to crown approval.

Charter of Towns, which divided urban population into six groups, each of which elected representatives to town assembly; actual business of urban government carried out by executive board of six, one from each group, but police powers were left to officials appointed by crown.

1787   *Aug*: Beginning of new war with Turkey, ended (9 Jan 1792) by Treaty of Jassy, which recognised Russian annexation of Crimea and conquest of Ochakov.

1788   *Jun*: Outbreak of war with Sweden, ended (14 Aug 1790) by Treaty of Verelä, which confirmed *status quo ante bellum*.

SPAIN

1648   *30 Jan*: Peace of Münster, by which Spain at last acknowledged independence of United Provinces; formalised by Treaty of Münster on 24 October.

Apr: Naples restored to Spanish rule after series of revolts.

1652 *13 Oct*: Don Juan of Austria recaptured Barcelona ending 12-year revolt of Catalonia.

1656 *Feb*: Declaration of war against Cromwell's England, followed by treaty of alliance with exiled Charles II.

1658 *15 Jun*: Loss of Dunkirk to Anglo-French force.

1659 *7 Nov*: Peace of Pyrenees ended war with France, which gained Artois and Rousillon; marriage arranged between Louis XIV and Philip IV's eldest daughter, Maria Theresa.

1660 *Jul*: Decree of King Philip IV against corruption in town councils, largely ineffectual.

1661 *26 Nov*: Death of Luis de Haro, principal minister of Spain since 1643. Philip IV appointed no successor, though Count of Castrillo and Duke of Medina de las Torres were influential advisers.

1665 *17 Sep*: Death of Philip IV. Succession of four-year-old Charles II, with Queen Mother Maria Ana as Regent and five-man Junta de Gobierno, which included Castrillo, Cristóbal Crespí, Marquis of Ayona, and Cardinal Pasqual de Aragón.

1666 *22 Sep*: Appointment by Queen Maria Ana of her Austrian Jesuit confessor and favourite, Johan Everard Nithard, as Grand Inquisitor, making him *ex officio* member of Junta de Gobierno and *de facto* prime minister.

1669 *25 Feb*: Fall of Nithard, whom Queen Maria Ana was forced to dismiss and send into exile; resumption of government by Junta in collaboration with Queen Mother.

1673 Emergence of Fernando Valenzuela as 'valido' or prime political confidant of Queen Mother.

1675 *6 Nov*: Retarded King Charles II judged to have reached his majority at age 14.

1676 Elevation of Valenzuela to position of Prime Minister.
Sep: Junta de Gobierno dissolved by Valenzuela, now given power to direct all councils of government, thus enraging nobility.
15 Dec: Manifesto of high Castilian nobility calling on King Charles II to remove Queen Mother from his presence, imprison Valenzuela, and call Don Juan of Austria to preside over government.

1677 *23 Jan*: Don Juan entered Madrid at head of 15,000 troops; followed by arrest and exile of Valenzuela to Philippines, banishment of Queen Mother to Toledo, and promotion to power of Don Juan.

1678 *10 Aug*: Peace of Nijmegen, whereby Spain regained Messina but was forced to cede Franche Comté to France.

1679 *17 Sep*: Death of Don Juan, effective ruler of Spain since 1677; followed by return to influence of Queen Mother.

1680   *21 Feb*: Duke of Medinaceli appointed Prime Minister by Charles II.

1684   *Jun*: Count of Oropesa appointed President of Council of Castile.

1685   *Apr*: Resignation of Duke of Medinaceli and appointment of Count of Oropesa as Prime Minister.

1689   *Feb*: Death of Queen Maria Luisa.

       15 Jun: Marriage of Charles II and Mariana of Neuburg, sister of Emperor Leopold of Austria.

1691   *25 Jun*: Resignation of Count of Oropesa after reversals in War of League of Augsburg; followed by rule of Queen Mariana in name of Charles II.

1693   Charles II persuaded to issue 'planta de gobierno' dividing government of Spanish regions among four members of nobility (later reduced to three).

1696   Queen Mariana demoted or dismissed remaining members of 'planta de gobierno', leaving Spain virtually without government.

1697   *10 Sep*: Treaty of Ryswick, ending War of League of Augsburg and restoring Spanish possessions in Netherlands and West Indies.

1698   *11 Oct*: First Partition Treaty, supposedly secret agreement by Great Powers to divide Spanish possessions on death of Charles II among three claimants – Prince Joseph Ferdinand of Bavaria (Spain, Spanish Netherlands and Spanish New World territories); Philip of Anjou (Naples, Sicily and Tuscan ports); and Archduke Charles of Austria (Duchy of Milan).

       Nov: Charles II, angered by news of Partition Treaty, signed will leaving all Spanish possessions to Joseph Ferdinand of Bavaria, who, however, died in Feb 1699.

1700   *2 Oct*: Charles II signed second will leaving all Spanish dominions to Philip of Anjou, grandson of Louis XIV.

       1 Nov: Death of Charles II followed by proclamation of Philip of Anjou as Philip V and creation of Junta de Gobierno.

1701   *18 Feb*: 17-year-old Philip V entered Madrid, inaugurating Spanish Bourbon dynasty. New king surrounded by pro-French ministers, including Cardinal Portocarrero who emerged as chief adviser.

       18 Jun: Louis XIV forced signing of alliance between Spain and Portugal, with Spain ceding claims north of Rio Plata in South America.

       22 Jun: Louis XIV dispatched Jean Orry to serve as financial adviser to Philip V. Subsequently produced report urging reform of royal revenues on French model.

       Sep–Oct: Philip installed as legal ruler of Aragon and Catalonia, which received promises of protection for traditional privileges and liberties.

       Dec Marriage of Philip V and Maria Luisa of Savoy, who was accompanied by Princess d'Orsini, guardian–adviser appointed by Louis XIV, who arranged match.

1702   *27 Apr*: Opening of last meeting of Aragonese Cortes.

1702–   *Apr–Jan*: Philip V's journey to Naples, Tuscany and Milan to
3   confirm Bourbon rule.

1703   *Mar*: Recall of Princess d'Orsini to Paris after quarrels with French ambassador.
        21 Apr: Defection of Portugal to Anglo-Austrian alliance in War of Spanish Succession.
        19 Sep: Archduke Charles of Austria, rival claimant of Spanish possessions, proclaimed King Charles III of Spain, at Vienna.
        Oct: Jean Orry recalled by Louis XIV to France.
        Nov: Piedmont–Savoy abandoned Spain, joining Grand Alliance.

1704   *24 Jul*: Gibraltar captured by British under Sir George Rooke.
        8 Nov: Royal decree imposing obligatory military service on all males of 20–50 years.

1705   *Mar*: Dismissal of Cardinal Portocarrero as royal adviser.
        Jul: José de Grimaldo appointed to fill new office of Secretary of War and Finance.
        Aug: Return to Madrid of Princess d'Orsini with mandate to choose Spanish ministers limited only by orders from Louis XIV; followed to Spain by Orry and by new French ambassador, Michel Amelot.
        22 Aug: Landing of 'Charles III' near Barcelona, sparking pro-Austrian rebellions in surrounding countryside.
        4 Oct: Archduke Charles recognised as King Charles III in Catalonia, Aragon, and Valencia.

1706   *May*: Marlborough and Allied forces conquered Spanish Netherlands.
        Jun: Archduke Charles proclaimed King Charles III of Spain in Madrid, Toledo and other cities temporarily occupied by Portugese forces.

1707   *14 Apr*: Defeat of British at Almanza.
        29 Jun: Abolition by Philip V of all traditional laws and privileges of Aragon and Valencia, substituting constitution of Castile.
        Aug: Austrian troops captured Naples and, subsequently, Sicily.
        Philip V created Junta of Incorporation to recover alienated crown lands (–1717).

1709   *Sep*: Recall of French ambassador Michel Amelot, who had become virtual prime minister of Spain; King's council turned over to Spanish noblemen led by Duke of Medinaceli.

1710   *Apr*: Medinaceli arrested on charge of treason.
        20 Aug: Spanish defeated by Allies at Saragossa.
        21 Sep: 'Charles III' entered Madrid but soon retired to Catalonia.

10 Dec: Franco-Spanish army defeated forces of 'Charles III' at Villa Viciosa, thus recapturing Aragon.

1711　*17 Apr*: Death of Habsburg Emperor Joseph I led to succession of Archduke Charles as Charles VI, causing Britain and other allies to consider recognition of Philip V as King of Spain.

1712　*15 Nov*: Philip V renounced claim to French throne and Dukes of Berry and Orleans gave up claims to Spanish throne.

1713　*16 Mar*: Spain agreed to cede Gibraltar and Minorca to Britain, and to grant Asiento for South American slave trade to Royal African Company.

31 Mar: Peace of Utrecht, by which Philip V was recognised as King of Spain, on provision that French and Spanish crowns could never be united: Spain forced to cede Netherlands to Austria and Sicily to Piedmont–Savoy.

10 Nov: Orry's proposals reorganising Councils of Castile, Indies, Finance and Inquisition imposed by Philip V.

1714　*11 Feb*: Death of Queen Maria Luisa.

11 Sep: Duke of Berwick, leading Franco-Spanish force, stormed Barcelona, last stronghold of Catalan supporters of 'Charles III'.

16 Sep: Marriage of Philip V and Elizabeth Farnese of Parma, who subsequently displaced Princess d'Orsini as chief influence on king; followed by rise to power of Giulio Alberoni.

30 Nov: Royal decree divided 'Despacho' – royal councils – into four ministries: of war; marine and Indies; justice, police and foreign affairs; and treasury.

1715　*6 Feb*: Second Peace of Utrecht ended war between Spain and Portugal.

Alberoni made Prime Minister; fall and expulsion of Princess d'Orsini.

3 Dec: Commercial treaty with Britain, amplified May 1716.

1716　*16 Jan*: New Plan re-established royal government in Catalonia, increasing power of crown; some privileges and Catalonian law retained.

1717　*12 Jul*: Giulio Alberoni made a cardinal.

22 Aug: Spain attacked Sardinia, capturing it in November.

1718　*Jun*: Spanish army sailed for Sicily, conquering it in July.

22 Jul: Quadruple Alliance formed by Britain, France, Austria and Holland to forestall Spanish aggression after seizure of Sicily; Alliance proposed exchange of Sicily for Sardinia by Savoy and succession in Tuscany and Parma to be secured for sons of Philip V and Elizabeth Farnese.

3 Aug: Admiral Byng crushed Spanish fleet off Cape Passaro after Philip's rejection of terms of Quadruple Alliance.

139

Nov: King of Sicily became King of Sardinia at command of Quadruple Alliance.

17 Dec: Britain declared war on Spain.

1719   *Apr*: French army overran Basque provinces and invaded Catalonia; subsequently British landed in Galicia, taking Vigo.

Oct: Spanish driven from Sicily by Austrians.

5 Dec: Cardinal Alberoni dismissed and banished by Philip V as condition of peace imposed by Quadruple Alliance.

1720   *26 Jan*: Treaty signed between Spain and Quadruple Alliance, whereby Emperor Charles VI renounced claims to Spain while Philip V gave up claims to Italy and France on condition that Charles VI recognise right of sons of Elizabeth Farnese to succeed to duchies of Parma–Piacenza and Tuscany. Sicily relinquished to Austria.

1721   *27 Mar*: Treaty of Madrid with France provided for mutual defence and double marriage alliance. French gave support to Spanish claims to Gibraltar and Italian duchies.

1723   *16 Nov*: Philip V recognised right of last of Medici line to succeed in Tuscany.

1724   *14 Jan*: Sudden abdication of Philip V in favour of his eldest son, Don Luis of Asturias, but Philip and Elizabeth Farnese continued to rule.

31 Aug: Death of Luis I from smallpox; resumption of Crown by Philip V on 7 Sep; followed by rise to power of Baron Jan Willem Ripperda, former Dutch ambassador.

24 Nov: Secret mission of Ripperda to Vienna to secure Austrian recognition of Spanish claims to Italian duchies.

1725   *Mar*: Breaking off of marriage engagement between Louis XV and Maria Ana, Spanish Infant, causing diplomatic rupture with France.

30 Apr–1 May: Treaty of Vienna negotiated by Ripperda, provided for reconciliation of Austria and Spain.

5 Nov: Secret treaty with Austria projected marriage alliances between daughters of Charles VI and sons of Philip V.

27 Dec: Ripperda given sole direction of Department of Foreign Affairs, making him Chief Minister.

1726   *14 May*: Dismissal of Ripperda from all offices following the failure of his diplomatic schemes. José Patiño made Minister of Marine and Indies and José de Grimaldo restored as Foreign Minister.

1727   *Feb*: Undeclared war began with Britain after Spain's attack on Gibraltar and threats against British shipping.

10 Jun: Queen Elizabeth Farnese assumed rule of Spain as Philip V retired due to nervous depression.

1728   *24 Feb*: Convention of Pardo ended Anglo-Spanish war.

Mar: Siege of Gibraltar abandoned.

1729   *29 Oct*: Treaty of Seville with England and France ended Spanish alliance with Austria, and provided for succession of Don Carlos to Tuscany and Parma.

1731   *10 Jan*: Death of Antonio Farnese, Duke of Parma; succession of Don Carlos, son of Philip V and Elizabeth Farnese; followed by seizure of Parma–Piacenza by Austria.

      11 Jul: War over Italian duchies averted by Treaty of Vienna, by which Spain was at last allowed by Charles VI to garrison Parma and Tuscany.

1733   *26 Sep*: League of Turin between France, Piedmont–Sardinia, and Spain, whereby Spain was to gain Naples and Sicily.

      7 Nov: First 'Family Compact' between Bourbons of France and Spain.

1734   *May*: Spanish army under Don Carlos captured Naples.

      Aug–Sep: Spanish reconquest of Sicily.

1735   *Jul*: Don Carlos crowned as King Charles III of Naples.

      3 Oct: Peace preliminaries at Vienna provided that Charles III was to retain Naples and Sicily, which could not be united under one crown with Spain; Charles VI to receive Parma and Duke of Lorraine to inherit Tuscany on death of last Medici Duke.

1736   *Now*: Death of José Patiño, Chief Minister.

      3 Jan: Convention of Pardo to settle Anglo-Spanish disputes over Asiento trade and quarrels over English smuggling in Spanish America.

      8 Oct: Britain declared war, accusing Spain of violating Convention of Pardo.

1741   *Mar*: José del Campillo appointed Financial Secretary, indicating his rise to power. By October, Campillo also controlled War, Navy and Indies departments.

1742   *18 Aug*: King Carlos of Naples/Sicily forced by British naval pressure to declare neutrality.

      25 Oct: Second Family Compact between France and Spain, which is promised Gibraltar; Milan, Parma and Piacenza to go to Don Phillip.

1743   *11 Apr*: Sudden death of José del Campillo and emergence of Marqués de Ensenada as Chief Minister.

1745   *19 Dec*: Franco-Spanish army entered Madrid, ending conquest of Lombardy.

1746   *16 Jul*: Spain defeated at Piacenza and are subsequently driven from Lombardy and Sardinia.

      9 Jul: Death of Philip V. Succession of King Ferdinand VI (–1759).

      Dec: José de Carvajal made Secretary of State.

1748   *20 Oct*: Spain signed treaty of Aix-la-Chapelle, by which Parma–Piacenza was settled on Don Phillip; Spain compelled to cede Britain Asiento privileges for four years.

1750   *24 Sep*: Britain gave up Asiento in return for confirmation of other trading rights with Spain.

1752   *14 Jun*: Treaty of Aranjuez between Spain and Empire provided for mutual guarantee of European possessions.

1753   *11 Jan*: New concordat signed between Spain and Vatican. (*See* Chapter 6: The Church.)

1754   *8 Apr*: Death of José de Carvajal.
       20 Jul: Fall of Marqués de Ensenada from power.

1759   *10 Aug*: Death of Ferdinand VI. Succession of Charles III, son of Philip V and Elizabeth Farnese, formerly Charles IV of Naples.

1761   *15 Aug*: Third Family Compact between France and Spain, which is to support France in Seven Years' War if no peace reached by May 1762.

1762   *4 Jan*: Britain declared war against Spain and Naples.

1763   *10 Feb*: Peace of Paris, ending Seven Years' War, by which Spain regained Cuba and Philippines (seized in 1762) from Britain, which in return received Florida. France was also forced to cede Louisiana to Spain.

1764   *Feb*: Geronimo Grimaldi made Minister of State (–1776).

1766   *Mar*: Extensive rioting in Madrid against Sicilian Finance Minister Esquilache; disturbances subsequently blamed on Jesuits.
       Apr: Count of Aranda appointed President of Council of Castile.

1767   *2 Apr*: Expulsion of Jesuits from Spain by Charles III, followed by confiscation of Jesuit property by state and introduction of secular education.

1776   *7 Nov*: Dismissal of Geronimo Grimaldi and appointment of José Moñino, Count of Floridablanca, as Minister of State.

1779   *16 Jun*: Spain declared war against Britain, recognising independence of American colonies and launching new siege of Gibraltar (–1783).

1781   *Jul*: Capture of Pensacola in Florida from Britain.

1782   *Jun*: Reconquest of Florida completed.

1783   *3 Sep*: Peace of Versailles, which confirmed Spanish possession of Florida and Minorca.

1786   Privileges of 'Mesta', powerful sheepowners' organisation, reduced.

1787   'Junta Suprema del Estado' or cabinet created by Floridablanca to reform central administration.

1788   *13 Dec*: Death of Charles III. Succession of King Charles IV.

SWEDEN–FINLAND

1648   *24 Oct*: Peace of Westphalia, by which Sweden received Western Pomerania and bishoprics of Bremen and Verden.

1650   Queen Christina secured unconditional designation of her cousin, Charles Gustavus, as heir to throne, over objections of nobility; but retreated from proposal of lower Estates to reclaim crown land alienated to nobles.

1651   Queen Christina confided to Council her intention to abdicate.

1654   *6 Jun*: Abdication of Queen Christina at Uppsala Riksdag in favour of Charles X.

      Death of Chancellor Axel Oxenstierna.

1655   Charles X secured one-quarter 'Reduktion' – restitution of crown lands alienated to nobility – from Riksdag.

      Jul: Charles X launched Swedish invasion of Poland.

      23 Aug: Charles X defeated John Casimir of Poland and, on 30 Aug, captured Warsaw.

      8 Oct: Cracow fell to Charles X, bringing whole of Poland under Swedish control.

1656   *Jan–Mar*: Poles rose against Swedish occupation.

      Jun: Russia invaded Ingria, Karelia and Finland.

      29–31 Jul: Charles X, now in alliance with Brandenburg, again defeated Poles under John Casimir at Warsaw.

1657   Denmark declared war against Sweden.

1658   *28 Feb*: Charles X forced Denmark to make Treaty of Roskilde, by which Sweden gained three Scanian and two Norwegian provinces.

      Aug–Sep: Charles X renewed war against Denmark with siege of Copenhagen.

      Dec: Sweden made alliance with Russia.

1659   Sweden driven from Western Pomerania and Poland by Brandenburg.

1660   *13 Feb*: Death of Charles X. Succession of four-year-old Charles XI and beginning of rule by Regency and Council of State, with Magnus de la Gardie as Chancellor; Gustavus Bonde later made Treasurer. Amendment to Form of Government of 1634, constituting victory of lesser Estates and lower nobility over higher nobility, provided that members of Regency and all great officers of state must be approved by Estates and that Riksdag must meet at least every three years.

      3 May: Treaty of Oliva ended war with Brandenburg and Poland.

      6 Jun: Treaty of Copenhagen provided for return of Norwegian provinces to Denmark.

1672   *14 Apr*: Treaty of Stockholm provided that Sweden should aid France against Dutch and German states in return for large subsidy.

Charles XI came of age, as Regency defeated attempt by Council of State (dominated by great nobles) to impose on king more restrictive charter than that Charles X granted in 1654.

1675   War breaks out with Brandenburg and Denmark.

28 Jun: Sweden defeated by Brandenburg at Fehrbellin, followed by loss of Western Pomerania and Bremen.

Sep: Attack of Estates on former Regents and Council of State, followed by Charles XI's approval of Estates' commission to investigate administration during his minority.

1676   *4 Dec*: Charles XI assumed command of Swedish army and defeated Danes at Lunden.

1679   *7 Feb*: Peace of Nijmegen ended war between Sweden and Empire; intervention of Louis XIV secured return of Swedish possessions.

23 Aug: Treaty of Fontainebleau, by which Denmark was forced to restore captured Swedish territories.

1680   *Oct*: Meeting of Riksdag where high nobility came under harsh attack from Estates, which proceeded to institute monarchical absolutism. Charles XI was declared not bound by Form of Government nor obliged to rule with advice of Council of State. Estates also passed 'Reduktion', restoring to crown many alienated estates held by higher nobility.

1682   Estates approved completion of 'Reduktion', allowing crown to resume all alienated lands.

9 Dec: Charles XI granted full legislative powers, including power to interpret and amend common law.

Councillors found guilty of maladministration during minority of Charles XI and fined heavily.

'Indelning' system instituted, whereby revenue from certain royal estates was set aside as payment to army officers and other government employees; and conscription was replaced by contracting with peasantry for military recruits.

1686   Charles XI informed Riksdag that in future debate of foreign policy was not necessary, that he would inform them of the foreign situation should he need supply.

Swedish church brought more closely under royal control. (*See* Chapter 6: The Church.)

1693   Charles XI informed diet that, thanks to Reduktion, no supply was required, but was still granted general permission to levy contributions and float loans under guarantee of Estates. This Riksdag also issued most extreme testament of Swedish absolutism – Declaration of Sovereignty, which proclaimed monarch to be 'an absolute, sovereign king, responsible to no one on earth, but with power and might at his command to rule and govern as a Christian monarch'.

1697   *5 Apr*: Death of Charles XI of stomach cancer. Succession of Charles

XII, 15 years old, on 17 June.

6 Nov: Charles XII, declared of age, accepted offer of absolute sovereignty from Riksdag.

1700– Great Northern War. (*See* Chapters 4 and 5: Defence and Warfare,
21 and Treaties and Diplomacy.)

1718 *11 Dec*: Charles XII killed at Frederikshall in Norway; followed by constitutional revolution – Charles's sister Ulrika Eleonora elected Queen by Riksdag and 'Royal Council' replaced by traditional 'Council of State'.

1719 *20 Nov*: First Treaty of Stockholm by which Sweden relinquished Bremen and Verden to Hanover.

1719– New Forms of Government instituted limited constitutional monar-
20 chy; Estates given power to nominate and dismiss members of Council and high officials; distinctions abolished within Estate of Nobles; legislation required approval of at least three Estates for passage; Councils and high offices still reserved for nobility.

1720 *1 Feb*: Second Treaty of Stockholm by which Sweden ceded Western Pomerania, including Stettin, to Brandenburg–Prussia.
29 Feb: Abdication of Queen Ulrika Eleonora and election of her husband Prince Frederick of Hesse–Cassel, as King Frederick I. Election of Count Arvid Horn as Landtmarskall by Estate of Nobles, followed by his appointment as Chancellor (–1738).

1721 *10 Sep*: Treaty of Nystad ended Russo-Swedish war; Sweden lost Ingria, Livonia, Estonia and East Karelia, but regained Finland.

1723 Riksdag Ordinance reinforcing supremacy of Estates in constitution, reducing monarch to titular head-of-state.

1724 Passage of 'Products Edict', providing that foreign ships could carry to Sweden imports from their own countries.

1726 Passage of Conventicle Edict, which enforced Lutheran orthodoxy and banned other religious sects. (*See* Chapter 6: The Church.)

1731 Swedish East India Company founded.

1734 New law code, replacing medieval national and town codes, approved by Riksdag, largely due to energies of Gustav Cronhjelm.

1738 Polarisation of Swedish politics into two distinct parties: 'Hats', opposing Chancellor Horn and advocating aggressive policy to recover Baltic provinces from Russia; and 'Caps', supporters of Horn and balanced, pacifistic foreign policy.
Oct: Meeting of Riksdag in which Hats commanded majority support; Chancellor Horn forced to resign and five 'Cap' members expelled from Council. 'Hat' Count Carl Gyllenborg made new Chancellor, subsequently renewing alliance with France.

1740 Hats obtained approval of Riksdag for new invasion of Russia over Cap opposition.

1741 *20 Jul*: Sweden declared war on Russia.

1742 *Jun*: Russians launched counter-attack against Finland, driving Swedish forces back to Helsinki.

24 Nov: Death of Queen Ulrika Eleonora.

1743 Peasants of Dalarna region marched on Stockholm in protest against Hat proposal to make Adolf Frederick of Holstein–Gottorp heir to Swedish throne.

17 Aug: Peace of Åbo, by which Russia withdrew from most of Finland in return for election of Adolf Frederick as heir to Swedish throne.

1746 *9 Dec*: Death of Count Gyllenborg; subsequently replaced as leader of Hat party by Count Karl Gustavus Tessin.

1748 British ambassador expelled and diplomatic relations with Great Britain broken off, not resumed until 1763.

1751 *25 Mar*: Death of King Frederick I. Succession of Adolf Frederick. Count Tessin dismissed as Chancellor, at instigation of Queen Louisa Ulrika, who was determined to restore royal power. However, Riksdag reacted by ending King's authority to appoint Chancellor.

1751– Growth of court party, centred around Adolf Frederick and Louisa
5   Ulrika, dedicated to recovery of royal prerogatives.

1756 Royalist plot to seize government detected and crushed; act drawn up providing for deportation of King and Queen should they attempt further intrigues; royal power to appoint military officials curtailed.

1757– Swedish participation in Seven Years' War as ally of France, Austria
62   and Russia limited to series of unsuccessful attacks on Prussia.

1762 Sweden made separate peace with Prussia, preserving *status quo*.

1765 Caps defeated Hats in elections to Rikstag, capturing control of all four estates. Chancellor and five Hat Councillors removed.

1766 Ordinance provided limited freedom of press.

1768– Constitutional crisis provoked by refusal of King and Hat-
9   dominated civil service to cooperate with execution of Cap policies.

1769 Hats secured control of Riksdag, having promised King partial restoration of royal powers – a promise not fulfilled.

1771 *12 Feb*: Death of King Adolf Frederick. Succession of Gustavus III.

1772 *25 Apr*: Cap party, having succeeded in imposing more stringent coronation oath, ousted Hat opponents from Council and threatened to eliminate remaining aristocratic privileges.

19 Aug: Gustavus directed military coup to restore power of crown, arresting senate and reconvening Riksdag.

21 Aug: Gustavus presented new constitution to Estates which they unanimously approved. King retrieved powers to summon and dismiss Riksdag, appoint ministers and propose legislation. Estates retained rights to pass and annul statutes, levy taxes and make aggressive war.

1774 Censorship of press re-established.

1776–
7
Scheme of currency stabilisation carried out by Johan Liljencrantz.

1778 *3 Sep*: Rikstag summoned for first time since 1772.

1780–
6
Gustavus III increasingly relied on advice of personal favourites, ignoring Council, thus encouraging opposition of nobles and other estates to King's despotic tendencies.

1786 New Rikstag summoned to meet economic crisis, but Estates defeated government proposals for state tobacco monopoly and financial reforms, grudgingly voting taxes for four years only.

1788 *Jun*: Gustavus III declared war on Russia, in contravention of constitution.

17 Jul: Russia repelled Swedish naval attack, inflicting heavy losses. This reversal followed by revolt of Finns, led by G. M. Sprengtporten.

Nov: Finnish revolt suppressed and leaders arrested.

1789 *26 Jan*: Riksdag met in Stockholm; Gustavus allied with clergy, burghers and peasants against nobility.

17 Feb: Beginning of second royal coup, whereby Gustavus summoned all four Estates to royal palace, upbraided nobles and selected representatives of other Estates to discuss new constitution. Noble opponents were then arrested.

20 Feb: Gustavus introduced Act of Union and Security, which was rapidly approved, receiving royal assent on 3 April. Act virtually restored royal absolutism, for Estates lost all legislative initiative and King gained authority to collect grants indefinitely and to make offensive war. Thereafter, all except highest offices opened to all classes.

1792 *22 Jan–24 Feb*: Gustavus III's last Riksdag met at Gävle.

16 Mar: Gustavus III mortally wounded at masked ball by Jakob Anckarström, former Guards officer hired by noble conspirators to assassinate King.

29 Mar: Death of Gustavus III.

SWITZERLAND

17th- and 18th-century Switzerland was a loose confederation of Protestant and Catholic cantons (with their dependent territories), each of which was autonomous and organised mainly along republican lines, ranging from the narrowly oligarchic to the broadly democratic.

1647   *19 Oct*: Emperor Ferdinand III of Austria explicitly recognised permanent separation of Swiss cantons from any dependence on Empire.

1648   *24 Oct*: Peace of Westphalia, which recognised total independence of Swiss cantons from Holy Roman Empire.

1653   *Apr–Jun*: Peasants' revolt in Lucerne, Bern, Basle, Zürich and other places under Leuenberger. Though rioting was suppressed, some reduction in taxation was subsequently introduced.

1655   Plan by Zürich for centralised Swiss state rejected by Catholic cantons.

1656   *24 Jan*: Protestant cantons of Zürich and Bern defeated at Villmergen by Catholic forces (First Villmergen War).

1663   Formal treaty of alliance with Louis XIV signed by Swiss cantons.

1668   *Defensionale* – confederate military organisation established to defend Swiss territory, providing for confederate council of war and commander-in-chief and specifying numbers of men and arms to be supplied by each canton in event of war.

1707   First limited democratic reforms adopted in Geneva under leadership of Fatio, who was later killed as 'traitor' by aristocracy.

1712   *25 Jul*: Battle of Villmergen between Protestant and Catholic cantons won by Protestant forces of Bern.
       11 Aug: Treaty of Arrau, ending Second Villmergen War, guaranteed real equality of religious rights and resulted in expanded influence of Zürich and Bern.

1723   Alliance with France renewed.

1738   *Règlement de Médiation*, new Genevan constitution, which conceded powers over taxation, war and peace, and legislation to citizens' assembly, introduced after popular rioting and intervention of Zürich, Bern and France.

1761   Helvetic Society founded by Isaac Iselin and Solomon Hirzel to break down barriers between inhabitants of various Swiss cantons and between adherents of different creeds.

1768   Edict granted burghers of Geneva right to elect one-half of members of town's Great Council annually.

1773   *May*: Swiss cantons, fearing Austrian aggression, confirmed alliance with France.

1782   France, Piedmont and Bern intervened to restore Genevan aristocracy to power after rioting had resulted in their overthrow.

3 THE ENLIGHTENMENT

GLOSSARY OF PEOPLE AND TERMS OF THE ENLIGHTENMENT

Addison, Joseph, 1672–1719. English essayist, poet, dramatist and statesman whose fame rests principally on his contributions to two seminal periodicals, the *Tatler* (published by Richard Steele, 1709–11), and the *Spectator* (published by Addison and Steele, 1711–12), both of which are crucially important as instruments for the reformation of manners and as popular disseminators of learning. In addition to providing a genre for men like David Hume and Lord Kames to exploit, these periodicals must be taken into account when tracing the origins of Scotland's intellectual revival. Addison also served in a number of government posts, finally becoming Secretary of State under George I from 1717 to 1718, and was the author of a successful tragedy, *Cato* (1713).

Alembert, Jean le Rond d', 1717–83. French mathematician, philosopher and writer. One of the leading figures in the French Enlightenment who elaborated a philosophy of science that established 'principles' making possible the interconnection of the various branches of science, he came to prominence as a mathematician, more particularly as the author of *Traité de dynamique* (1743). A rationalist thinker in the free-thinking tradition who believed, as did his fellow *philosophes*, that science was the only real source of knowledge and had to be popularised for the benefit of the people, he became associated with the *Encyclopédie* about 1746, being made editor of the mathematical and scientific articles. He introduced the first volume of the work in 1751 with his *Discourse préliminaire*, a brilliant short history of human accomplishment based on the theory that knowledge gained through observation and experience is responsible for all man's progress. He was Permanent Secretary of the French Academy from 1771, exerting considerable influence in that position until his death in 1783.

Aufklärung. The name given to the Enlightenment in Germany. Its representatives are known as Aufklärer.

Bacon, Francis, 1561–1626. An important forerunner of the 18th-century Enlightenment, he was the foremost populariser of scientific ideas in the early 17th century. His most celebrated work is *Novum Organum*, in which he presented his scientific method. A plan to reorganise the sciences is developed in *Instauratio Magna*, published together with the *Novum Organum* in 1620. The posthumously published *New Atlantis* (1627) provided a model for the scientific societies that appeared in the latter part of the century, especially the Royal Society of London. His determination to contemplate 'things as they are, without superstition or imposture, error or confusion', his concern with scientific method, and his representation of science as the handmaiden of technical progress gave a powerful impetus to the development of science in the 17th century.

Bahrdt, Karl Friedrich, 1741–92. German Protestant theologian and representative of rationalism who perceived the *Aufklärung* in terms of dramatic social change. He demanded 'absolute enlightenment' starting at the very roots of society and working upwards. Of a rather unstable character, his early, strict orthodoxy in religious matters was discarded by the late 1770s when all his efforts were directed to the propagation of a moral system which would replace supernatural Christianity.

Barbeyrac, Jean, 1674–1744. French jurist who moved to Switzerland after the revocation of the Edict of Nantes. He worked in Germany and the Netherlands, as well as Switzerland, to stress the moral aspects of international law, whose principles he reduced to those of the law of nature. In fundamental principles he followed Locke and Pufendorf, his fame resting chiefly on the preface and notes to his translation of the latter's treatise *De jure naturae et gentium*.

Basedow, Johann Bernard, 1723–90. German educational reformer. Influenced by the rationalist H. S. Reimarus, he abandoned theology in 1767 and devoted himself to educational reform, one of the most fruitful fields of action then available to progressive thinkers. He revealed himself to be strongly influenced by Rousseau's *Émile*, proposing his own ideas on educational reform in *Idea of a Humanitarian for Schools* (1768). He established an institute for education at Dessau called *Philanthropin*, a name which to him appeared the most expressive of his views, and the ideas incorporated here were so well received that similar institutes were soon established throughout the country.

Bayle, Pierre, 1647–1706. French philosopher who had a profound influence on the *philosophes* and encyclopedists of the 18th century, particularly through his *Dictionnaire historique et critique* (1685–97). He was an extreme freethinker for his day whose rationalism and ironic style were adopted by the *philosophes*, who incorporated into the *Encyclopédie* and other of their works many of his arguments against orthodoxy.

Beccaria, Cesare, 1738–94. Italian philosopher, criminologist and economist, he is the author of *Of Crime and Punishments* (1764), perhaps the most famous book of the Italian Enlightenment and the book which, above all others, interested the rest of Europe in the brilliance and originality of Italian enlightened thought. At the time of its publication and after, *Of Crime and Punishments* achieved considerable notice and popularity, helping to stimulate major changes in European criminal codes. Beccaria was also a noted economist, espousing a liberal economics that in some measure anticipated Adam Smith's *Wealth of Nations* (1776). His ideas were developed in *Il Caffé*, a periodical he helped found (in 1764) and edit, and in the posthumously published *Elements of Public Economy* (1804).

Bentham, Jeremy, 1748–1832. English philosopher, reformer and founder of the formal system of Utilitarianism, a term which he was first to introduce in 1781. Although a true child of the Enlightenment, developing the ideas of previous writers such as Beccaria, Helvétius and Hutcheson, he belongs more to the 19th century, when his writings had their major effect in the legal, constitutional and economic fields. His *Constitutional Code* (1830) and *The Rationale of Judicial Evidence* (1825) constitute exhaustive syntheses of his system of thought.

Bergman, Torbern Olof, 1735–84. Swedish chemist and naturalist. His most important chemical paper is his *Essay on Elective Attractions* (1775), a study of chemical affinity. His outlook was empirico-rationalist, and in methods of chemical analysis he effected many improvements, also making significant contributions to crystallography and to mineralogical and geological chemistry. He made observations on the transit of Venus in 1761, and in 1766 published a *Physical Description of the Earth*.

Berkeley, George, 1685–1753. Irish philosopher, economist, mathematician and bishop. In his greatest work, the *Treatise Concerning the Principles of Human Knowledge* (1710), he advanced a new theory of sense perception which discarded the traditional concept of material substance. Although he is regarded primarily as a pioneer of phenomenalism, his views were based on a rejection of that underlying scientific picture of the world which Locke took so for granted.

Bernouilli family. Originally from Antwerp, the Bernouilli family settled in the 17th century in Basel, where they ultimately obtained the highest distinction, representing the emergence of science and mathematics as powerful forces in society. In the course of a century eight of its members successfully cultivated various branches of mathematics and contributed greatly to the advance of the physical sciences. The most celebrated were Jakob, 1654–1705, whose pioneering work *Ars Conjectandi* (1713) contained his theory of permutations and combinations; Johann, 1667–1748, who exceeded his brother in the number of contributions he made to mathematics; and Daniel, 1700–82, an extraordinarily versatile scientist who was highly successful in clearly presenting the scientific principles of the day to an interested public.

Black, Joseph, 1728–99. Scottish chemist and physicist whose discoveries are among the outstanding achievements of the Scottish Enlightenment. He is best known for his work on alkaline substance and for defining specific heat and forming the concept of latent heat. These discoveries demonstrate the powerful effects which earlier improvements, such as those of William Cullen and Sir Isaac Newton in Black's case, had on Scottish intellectual life, and also demonstrate how specialisation had led chemistry to be regarded as a theoretical and utilitarian discipline in its own right, and not merely as an aid to medicine.

Blount, Charles, 1654–93. English author and a leading deist who contributed materially to the removal of restrictions on the freedom of the press with his pamphlets by 'Philopatris' in 1693, derived mainly from Milton's *Areopagitica*.

Bodmer, Johann Jakob, 1698–1773. Swiss literary critic who was influential in freeing German literature from the dominance of French classical forms. One of the leading *literati* of the Swiss Enlightenment, he published, along with the scholar Johann Jakob Breitinger, *Discourse on Painters* (1721–3), a critical journal.

Boháč, Jan Křtitel (Johann Tauffer Bohadsch), 1724–68. Bohemian academic and principal official of the Prague medical faculty who was one of the most distinguished microscopists of his time. He believed that the development of the arts, natural sciences and manufactures formed an inseparable unity, and he strongly defended the social function of scientific investigation against those who underrated its importance.

Bolingbroke, Henry St John, 1st Viscount, 1678–1751. English statesman and a political philosopher in touch with many of the trends of the European Enlightenment. The chief purpose of both his political and philosophic writings was to remove religion from politics. His philosophic works set forth a nonsectarian 'natural religion' called deism, but his most famous work, written after a brief visit to England in 1738 during which his hopes for a new opposition party revived, was the *Idea of a Patriot King* (1744; corrected version, 1749).

Bonnet, Charles, 1720–93. Swiss scientist and philosophical writer, he was a naturalist of the first rank and a founder of modern biology who turned in later life to philosophy. His major works are the *Essai de psychologie* (1754) and *Contemplation de la nature* (1764).

Born, Ignz Edler von, 1742–91. Austrian minerologist and metallurgist of note who edited (1775–86) the journal of the Private Learned Society, an organisation concerned with gaining and promulgating scientific knowledge of nature for practical use which he helped to found in 1774. Born rigorously defended open scientific communication and an organisation of scientific life on an international scale. He was also a determined reformer of Freemasonry, a critic of monasticism and a fighter for tolerance.

Boscovich, Ruggiero Giuseppe, 1711–87. Dalmatian mathematician and physicist who was one of the pioneers of geodesy and an important figure in the Roman Catholic Church. His reputation is based largely on his *Theoria philosophiae naturalis* (1758), a fundamental work on atomic physics which recombined the ideas of Lucretius and drew on Newton to advance understanding of the composition of matter.

Breitinger, Johann Jakob, 1701–76. Swiss member of the *literati* circle in Zurich, he is perhaps best known for his and J. J. Bodmer's assault on the Leipzig school of Gottsched which gave birth to modern German literature.

Buffon, Georges Louis Leclerc, Count de, 1707–88. French naturalist appointed in 1739 superintendent of the Jardin du Roi where he produced the fifteen volumes of his *Histoire naturelle générale et particulière* (1749–67), an attempt to synthesise all existing knowledge of natural history, geology and anthropology. It became one of the most widely read scientific works of the 18th century.

Campomanes, Pedro Rodriguez, Conde de, 1723–1802. Spanish statesman and writer. He is the author of the *Discourse on the Encouragement of Popular Industry* (1774) an official document which proposed the model of a society directed towards work and production, and one of the fundamental books of the Spanish Enlightenment.

Catherine II the Great, of Russia, 1729–96. Empress from 1762 to 1796, she declared herself to be a disciple of Voltaire and Diderot, but imposed the first formal censorship in Russia and was responsible for turning many thousands of peasants into bondage. Her celebrated *Nakaz, or Instructions to the Legislative Commission* (1767), was conceived as a grandiose reform of the Russian government, although the Charter of the Nobility (April 1785) had a more substantial effect on the empire's social and political structure.

Celsius, Anders 1701–44. Swedish astronomer and an important contributor to the progress of science in 18th-century Sweden who devised the centigrade (Celsius) thermometer in a paper read before the Swedish Academy of Sciences in 1742.

Chouet, Jean-Robert, 1642–1731. Swiss philosopher and liberal Protestant who as professor of philosophy at Saumar and at Geneva introduced the study of Cartesianism and helped create the intellectual freedom in which modern science and philosophy could flourish without ecclesiastical anathema.

Chydenius, Anders, 1729–1803. Finnish (Swedish) politician, reformer and priest. A fully fledged liberal economist before Adam Smith, he was the embodiment of libertarian ideas, demanding complete freedom in trade and commerce and freedom of the press. As a member of parliament for the ecclesiastical estate, he played a part in the overthrow of the 'Hats' by the 'Caps' in the *riksdag* of 1765–6.

Collins, Anthony, 1676–1729. English philosopher and deist whose writings are among the best examples of natural theology and freethinking deism. His *Essay Concerning the Use of Reason* (1707) challenged the idea that human reason was limited in its capacity to attain knowledge of God. His principal work is *A Discourse of Freethinking* (1713), a defence of deism which argued that free inquiry was the means of acquiring full knowledge of truth.

Comenius (or Komensky), Johann Amos, 1592–1670. Moravian educator and theologian sometimes called the 'grandfather of modern education'. The last bishop of the old church of the Moravian and Bohemian Brethren, he was driven into Poland by the 1621 Spanish invasion and persecution of the Protestants. As an educationist, he holds a prominent place in history, a key thinker during the transition from medieval to modern education, whose reforms were aimed at eliminating world tension by organising knowledge for universal consumption. His philosophy of universal education is known as pansophism. *Didactica magna* (1628–32) remains his great educational work.

Condillac, Étienne Bonnot de, 1715–80. French philosopher. He was alone among the Enlightenment *philosophers* in creating a systematic theory of knowledge. Instrumental in introducing Lockean psychological orientation into French 18th-century thought, he parted with Locke in his famous *Traité des sensations* (1754), where he claims that sensations alone dictate the workings of the mind and are the source of all knowledge.

Condorcet, Antoine Nicolas, 1743–94. French mathematician and philosopher best known as an exponent of Turgot's economics and Voltaire's humanitarianism. Born of aristocratic parents and raised by clerics, he became an ardent sceptic and an enemy of privilege, who rose to eminence as a mathematician but took an active political role during the Revolution, usually siding with the Girondists. His principal work, *Esquisse d'un tableau historique des progrès de l'esprit humain* (1794), written while in hiding from the authorities, is a major document in the history of the idea of progress which speaks of perfectability, or the capacity in man for earthly perfection.

Cook, James, 1728–79. English naval officer and one of history's greatest navigators. His explorations of the Pacific and Antarctic oceans provided much information of scientific and geographical value, but also fostered speculation about the earth, its evolution, as well as about its fauna, its flora, and the diversity of representatives of the human species.

Cramer, Gabriel, 1704–52. Swiss mathematician whose teaching at Geneva of Newtonian natural philosophy, Cartesian rationalism and Wolff's Platonism and rationalism helped to create an intellectual atmosphere that produced a host of distinguished scholars. His principal work is the *Introduction à l'analyse des courbes algébriques* (1750), one of the first treatises of analytical geometry.

Cullen, William, 1710–90. Scottish physician and medical teacher whose work, along with fellow Scotsman Joseph Black, contributed to chemistry being regarded as a science in its own right and not as simply an aid to medicine. He demonstrated the importance of chemistry to natural philosophy and to utilitarian matters, and in medicine he generalised the phenomena of disease.

Dalin, Olof von, 1708–63. Swedish poet, dramatist and historian who introduced Voltaire to Sweden and in 1733 started the weekly *Svenska*

Argus on the model of Addison's *Spectator*. In his 1746 history of Sweden, *Svea Rikes historia*, he used scientific findings to dispute patriotic Swedish historiography, which regarded Sweden as the cradle of all other cultures after the Flood.

Darwin, Erasmus, 1731–1802. English naturalist, physician and poet whose *Zoonomia* (1794–6) advanced theories on the evolution of species, anticipating some of the ideas later developed by Charles Darwin and Lamarck. His talent in poetry and his interest in science combined in *The Botanic Garden* (1791), where he described the classification system of Linnaeus.

Defoe, Daniel, 1660–1731. English novelist, pamphleteer and journalist whose fiction, including *Robinson Crusoe* (1719), *Moll Flanders* (1722), *Journal of the Plague Year* (1722) and *Roxana* (1724), presents a highly humane view of human life with great sympathy for those who have suffered isolation, poverty, hunger and the terror of death. He was regarded in his own day as a radical political thinker and a champion of social reforms.

Deism. A term usually applied to the theological and religious movement of the late 17th and the 18th centuries that espoused a concept of 'natural religion', or the acceptance of a certain body of religous knowledge in every person that is either innate or acquired by reason, as opposed to knowledge acquired through revelation or church teachings. It was an attempt of religion to come to grips with scientific advances, one of a series of efforts to liberate man from superstitious beliefs. Though the term is first used in 16th-century France, the high point of Deist thought occurred in England from about 1689 through 1742 when there was relative freedom of religious expression and when the educated person's view of the universe had experienced a radical change.

Descartes, René, 1596–1650. French philosopher and mathematician. First among the 17th-century precursors of the *Philosophes*, he had a profound effect upon the development of philosophy, mathematics and the natural sciences. He left Paris for the Netherlands in 1629 and spent most of his productive intellectual life in Holland. A complete sceptic, the foundation of his philosophy can be found in his statement, 'I think, therefore I am.' His philosophy was a great force undermining orthodoxy and fostering the spirit of free inquiry, and he did much to further the idea that science could be applied to ethics, political theory, law and the social sciences. Descartes's legacy was to present the ideas of mechanism and mathematical analysis and reason as the guide posts of scientific thought. His *Discours de la méthode* (1637) presented his new method, mathematical in nature. *Principia philosophiae* (1644) attempted a logical account of all natural phenomena in a single system of mechanical principles, and his ethical views were contained in his *Les passiones de l'âme* (1649).

Diderot, Denis, 1713–84. French encyclopedist, philosopher and man of letters. One of the most versatile and dynamic leaders of the Enlightenment, he wrote on philosophy, science, technology, theology and education, as well as being the author of plays, novels, essays and art and drama criticism. His most important achievement was as chief editor of the *Encyclopédie* (1751–72), an enterprise for which he enlisted nearly all of the important writers of his time and whose dual purpose was as a comprehensive work of reference and to bring about 'a revolution in men's minds'.

Dobner, Gelasius, 1719–90. Bohemian scholar who argued that rationalism and critical analysis were relevant to the scientific study of history. In 1761 he attacked a pro-feudal popular chronicle composed by Václav Hájek, thus inaugurating the first scholarly controversy in modern Czech historiography.

Dobrovský, Josef, 1753–1829. Bohemian philologist who represents the Czech Enlightenment at its best with his pioneering contribution in Slavonic philology and his persistent struggles against distortions of historical truth. His best-known works are *Scriptores rerum Bohemicarum* (1783) and *History of the Czech Language* (1818).

Empiricism. A system of epistomology which holds that all knowledge derives from the perceptions of the senses. The first Empiricists in Western philosophy were the Sophists. During the middle ages the empiric spirit was in abeyance, but it revived from the time of Francis Bacon and was systematised especially in John Locke's *Essay Concerning Human Understanding* (1690) and the works of Hume, Berkeley, the two Mills, Bentham and the associationist school generally.

Encyclopédie. The *Encyclopédie, ou dictionnaire raissoné des sciences, des arts et des metiers*, published between 1751 and 1772 in 28 volumes. This great work was intended not only as the repository of the latest information available, but to be itself an instrument of enlightenment, an agency through which to fight obscurantism. In the hands of Diderot and d'Alembert, the *Encyclopédie* developed into a storehouse of Enlightenment wisdom which typified the age, not only because its contributors included every great figure of the French Enlightenment, but because the encyclopaedic form itself embodied the intellectual preconceptions and aspirations of the age. Generally speaking, it preached the idea of progress through moderate change, was critical of existing institutions and exalted the arts, crafts and a liberal bourgeois society.

Encyclopedists. The name given to the group of men who wrote articles for the 28-volume French *Encyclopédie* (1751–72). There were more than 140 contributors, a diverse group of nobles, bourgeois and artisans, atheists and practising Christians, obscure and eminent authors. The latter included Voltaire, Rousseau and Montesquieu, as well as editors Diderot and d'Alembert.

Enlightenment. A movement of thought and belief centring around the efforts of certain European intellectuals of the late 17th and 18th centuries to use critical reason to liberate men's minds from prejudices, unexamined authority and oppression by church and state. The period is characterised by a challenging of tradition and a growing trend towards individualism, empiricism and scientific reasoning. What emerged from this intellectual activity were the terms 'nature', 'reason', 'man' and 'progress', which became a medium of exchange between thinking men and which were used to forge a scientific humanism. Its basic conviction was that through reason mankind could find knowledge and happiness. The Enlightenment has a peculiarly French caste, and only in France was there an organised movement, *le parti philosophique*, acutely aware of its goals.

Euler, Leonhard, 1707–83. Swiss mathematician. He was the most prolific mathematician of the 18th century, if not of all time, and made formative contributions to geometry, calculus and number theory, throwing new light, in the process, on nearly all parts of pure mathematics.

Felice, Fortunato Bartolomeo de, 1723–89. Italian lexicographer. The dominant philosophy of his 58-volume *Dictionnaire raisonné des connaissances humaines* (1770–80), based on Diderot's *Encyclopédie*, is Newtonian in science and Lockeian in psychology, allied with a form of natural religion opposed to modern atheism.

Ferguson, Adam, 1723–1816. Scottish historian, patriot and philosopher of the 'common sense' school. A central figure in the Scottish Enlightenment, he is remembered as a forerunner of modern sociology for his emphasis on individual and social interactions. A leader in the club life of Edinburgh, he was successor to David Hume as head of the Advocates' Library and a professor of natural philosophy (from 1759) and of mental and moral philosophy (1764–85) in the University of Edinburgh. His major works include *Essay on the History of Civil Society* (1767) and *Institutes of Moral Philosophy* (1769).

Filangieri, Gaetano, 1752–88. Italian jurist, publicist and reformer whose *The Science of Legislation* (1780–5) was an influential work on legislation advocating unlimited free trade and denouncing torture, secret government, entail and feudal rights, all of which were seen as impeding production and national well-being.

Fletcher, Andrew, 1655–1716. Scottish politician and patriot, sometimes called the ideological father of the Scottish Enlightenment. An opponent of arbitrary government, he is the author of *Two Discourses Concerning the Affairs of Scotland* (1698), which reviewed the country's present political discontents. He also contributed towards the English decision to pass the Act of Union (1707) with Scotland by his sponsorship in the 1703 Scottish Act of Security of a clause that might have led to civil war.

Florez de Setien y Huidobro, Enrique, 1702–73. Spanish historian and representative figure in the movement to reform education under Charles III. In 1754 he wrote the first of 29 volumes for his *Holy Spain*, a monument of 18th-century historiography that was completed by his successors.

Floridablanca, José Moñino y Redondo, Count, 1728–1818. Spanish statesman who, as chief minister of state (1776–92), established a number of agricultural societies and philanthropical institutions and gave encouragement to learning, science and the fine arts. He was much under the influence of French *philosophes* and economic writers.

Fontenelle, Bernard le Bovier de, 1657–1757. French scientist and man of letters who ranks as one of the major heralds of the Enlightenment in France. A prominent figure in the *salons* of Paris, he was one of the most influential authors of his time, popularising the Copernican and Cartesian systems of science. His vigorous attacks on dogma and superstition and the existence of an omnipotent God laid the way for the sceptical philosophers of the French Enlightenment. His anti-religious bias can be seen most notably in his *Histoire des oracles* (1687) and the satire *Relation de l'île de Borneo* (1686), but his most famous work was the *Entretiens sur la pluralité des mondes* (1688), which was extremely influential in securing acceptance of the Copernican system. He was permanent Secretary of the French Academy of Sciences from 1697 to 1739.

Forsskål, Peter, 1732–63. Swedish naturalist. In his *De libertate civili* (1759), Forsskål, a disciple of Linnaeus, demanded a series of liberties, including freedom of the press, in the spirit of the Enlightenment. *Dubia de principiis philosophiae recentioris*, published three years earlier (1756), tackled philosophical freedom, which was no less restricted than political liberty in Sweden.

Frederick II the Great, of Prussia, 1712–86. King of Prussia from 1740, he was a good example of Voltaire's ideal of government, the enlightened despot. Frederick II liberalised laws regarding religion, censorship and torture, although he governed as an absolute ruler.

Galiani, Ferdinando, 1728–87. Italian economist. During his service in Paris as secretary to the Neapolitan ambassador (1759–69), he found himself a favourite in the *salons* and at the center of the French argument over Enlightenment and the *Encyclopédie.* His correspondents included Voltaire, Diderot, Turgot and the abbé André Morellet, the spokesman of the Physiocrats. His *Dialogues sur le commerce des blés* (1770), an attack on the doctrine that free trade is a principle of universal application, was the first thesis on economics to make a distinction between backward and advanced countries and to discuss different conditions of society which effect the economy.

Gassendi, Pierre, 1592–1655. French mathematician, scientist and philosopher, he is an important forerunner of the Enlightenment whose scientific materialism can be seen as part of a trend later developed by the *philosophes.* He was the first to observe the transit of Mercury and one of the founders of meteorology. In his *Syntagma philosophicum,* published post-humously (1658), he defended a mechanistic explanation of nature and sensation.

Genovesi, Antonio, 1712–69. Italian economist and philosopher, he held the first chair of political economy ever created in Europe. An important figure in the Neapolitan Enlightenment, he proposed a series of reforms in Naples which combined humanist ideas with a radical Christian metaphysical system. Though he was, and always remained, a devout priest, he attacked the Pope, canon law and clerical privilege. To Genovesi goes the credit of having introduced the new order of ideas into Italy. His principal work is *Lessons of Commerce* (1765), the first complete and systematic work in Italian on economics.

Gibbon, Edward, 1737–94. English historian. His philosophical *History of the Decline and Fall of the Roman Empire* (1776–88) represented a new standard of scholarship and reflected the scientific ideal of the age in which it was written. He was one of several 18th-century historians responsible for putting forward two new concepts – the organic nature of society and the idea of progress – whose acceptance may be said to have created the historiographical revolution of the Enlightenment.

Gournay, C. M. V. de, 1712–59. French economist who, along with

François Quesnay, formed the philosophic sect of the *Economistes*, later called *Physiocrats*.

Grotius, Hugo, 1583–1645. Dutch jurist and scholar, often called the father of modern international law. His most influential work is *De jure belli ac pacis* (1625), in which he applied the doctrine of natural law to the conduct of nations, concluding that states, like individuals, are bound by universal, reasonable and unchangeable codes of duties and prohibitions.

Gustavus III, 1746–92. King of Sweden whose reign, 1771–92, is known as the Gustavian, or Swedish, Enlightenment. he saw himself in the role of 'enlightened despot' by patronising the arts and sciences and founding the Swedish Academy (1786). He was especially interested in drama and opera, collaborating with Johan Kellgren on the opera *Gustaf Wasa* (1786). Gustavus also introduced a number of enlightened reforms, including freedom of the press, amendment of the poor law, increased free trade and an ending of torture as a means of interrogation.

Haller, Albrecht von, 1708–77. Swiss scientist, the foremost biologist of the 18th century and the father of experimental physiology who made numerous contributions to anatomy, botany, embryology, physiology, poetry and scientific bibliography. His *Elementa physiologiae corporis humani* (1757–66) is regarded as a landmark in medical history. Though he made himself a willing apologist of Christian Revelation, Haller attacked superstitious faiths which attempted to silence reason, which he hailed as the true light to unprejudiced truth.

Helvétius, Claude-Adrien, 1715–71. French writer and philosopher whose *salon* was the rendezvous of *philosophes*. His most famous work, *De l'esprit* (1758), was a statement of materialist and utilitarian doctrine which attacked all forms of morality based on religion. Denounced by the Sorbonne, the book was ordered to be burnt in public. Helvétius's hedonistic philosophy is best summarised in his argument that society's aim should be 'the greatest possible pleasure and the greatest possible happiness of the greatest number of citizens'.

Herbert of Cherbury, Edward Herbert, 1st Baron, 1582–1648. English soldier, diplomat, historian, metaphysical post and philosopher. He is often called the 'Father of Deism'. *De veritate* (1624), his best-known work, attempted to establish reason as the safest guide in a search for truth. His writings attracted much attention abroad as well as in England.

Herder, Johann Gottfried von, 1744–1803. German literary critic, historian and theologian who played a major role in the 18th-century German literary revival. He was the principal figure of the *Sturm und Drang* literary movement and an important innovator in the philosophy of culture and history. His most celebrated work was the famous *Essay on the Origin of Language* (1772), which inaugurated the study of comparative philology.

Hobbes, Thomas, 1588–1679. English philosopher and scientist whose pessimistic assessment of human nature and absolutist solutions to political problems have earned him the title 'Father of Totalitarianism'. A classicist by training, Hobbes first exhibited his extreme royalist tendencies by publishing in 1629 a translation of Thucydides as a warning against the evils of democracy. Later he became convinced of the importance of mathematical solutions to questions of knowledge, making a thorough study of Euclid. Thus, while he held knowledge of the external world could only be derived through sense perception, he concluded that true understanding of the information so obtained must be gained by deduction from general principles. Subsequently, Hobbes arrived at a completely materialistic and deterministic view of the universe, denying free will and attributing all human actions to the dictates of appetite and aversion. His most celebrated work was *Leviathan* (1651), which traced the foundation of the state from an anarchistic state of nature, where life was 'hard, nasty, brutish and short' to a totalitarian regime established by means of a social contract among individuals, who thereupon sacrificed to the sovereign all political rights save that of self-protection.

Holbach, Paul Henri Dietrich, baron d', 1723–89. French encyclopedist and philosopher. He was the most celebrated exponent of atheism and materialism. D'Holbach was the author of many extremely radical and anti-religious books, all based upon a materialist philosophy that argued that the universe could come into being without the interposition of a creator. His most famous work is *Le système de la nature* (1770), a sensational statement of uncompromising atheistic materialism and the most complete exposition of his ideas. In *Le Christianisme dévoilé* (1761) he attacked Christianity as contrary to reason and nature.

Hontheim, Johann Nikolaus von, alias 'Justinus Febronius', 1701–90. German historian and theologian who founded Febronianism, a doctrine advocating the nationalisation of Catholicism, the restriction of papal authority and the reunion of Christian churches. He was a pioneer in modern historical methods and one of the most important members of the academic fraternity in Catholic Germany, where universities played a crucial role in the implementation of the Enlightenment. Under the pseudonym of Justinus Febronius he published *De statu ecclesiae et legitima potestate Romani pontificis* (1763), a book which exercised an immense influence on opinion within the Roman Catholic Church, whose rulers put into practice its principles in various countries during the late 18th and early 19th centuries.

Hooke, Robert, 1635–1703. English physicist and inventor best known for his formulation of Hooke's law of elasticity (1676). He was, in addition to being the most outstanding mechanic of the age, a prolific theorist and experimenter in such areas as optics, acoustics, microscopy and cosmology. His *Micrographia* (1665) described the microscope and introduced the term 'cell'.

Hume, David, 1711–76. Scottish philosopher, historian, political theorist, essayist, economist and a pivotal figure in the history of the Scottish Enlightenment. Conjoining British empiricism and French scepticism, Hume, in his economic, historical and political writings, set out to undermine legends about human society, while his religious writings aimed to destroy every form of superstition and fanaticism. In France, where he met most of the leading figures of the French Enlightenment, he composed his *Treatise of Human Nature* (1739). In his *An Enquiry Concerning Human Understanding* (1748), he laid the groundwork for a utilitarian ethic.

Hutcheson, Francis, 1694–1746. Scottish philosopher and major exponent of the moral-sense theory in ethics. He anticipated the Utilitarianism of Jeremy Bentham and was influential as a logician and theorist of human knowledge. His ethical theory was propounded in his *Inquiry into the Origin of our Ideas of Beauty and Virtue* (1725), *An Essay on the Nature and Conduct of the Passions and Affections* (1728) and in the posthumous *System of Moral Philosophy* (1755).

Hutton, James, 1726–97. Scottish physician and naturalist regarded as a founder of modern geology whose chief contribution to the science was the doctrine of uniformitarianism. In his *Theory of the Earth* (1795–7), he refuted the Biblical notion of the earth's age. A major *literatus* of the Enlightenment, he published an important work of moral philosophy entitled *An Investigation of the Principles of Knowledge and the Progress of Reason from Sense to Science and Philosophy* (1794).

Huygens, Christian, 1629–95. Dutch astronomer, mathematician and physicist who invented the pendulum clock and the manometer for ascertaining the elastic forces of gases, founded the wave theory of light, discovered the true shape of the rings of Saturn, and made original contributions to the science of dynamics. The theorems on the composition of forces in circular motion with which his greatest work *Horologium oscillatorium*

163

(1673) concluded, formed the true prelude to Newton's *Principia*. He was a founder member in 1666 of the Académie Royale des Sciences, Paris.

Joseph II, 1741–1790. Austrian emperor and 'enlightened despot' who introduced many reforms in an unsuccessful attempt to modernise the Austrian Habsburg domains. Thoroughly steeped in the French Enlightenment, Joseph II attempted to control and purge the Church of superstitious practices, to spread education throughout his domains and to free the serfs. Though well-intentioned, his 10-year-reign disturbed much of the older order without leaving lasting traces of his reforms.

Jovellanos, Gaspar Melchor de, 1744–1811. Spanish statesman and writer. One of the most significant figures of the 18th-century Spanish Enlightenment, he was a moderate reformer who opposed the Inquisition and favoured social, economic and political reforms in Spain. His most influential work, *Report on Agrarian Law* (1795), pleaded for agricultural reform on liberal economic principles.

Kames, Henry Home, Lord, 1696–1782. Scottish lawyer, agriculturalist and philosopher best known for his history of aesthetics, *Elements of Criticism* (1762), an important contribution to the Enlightenment which turned to the empirical method in an attempt to equate beauty with what is pleasant to the natural senses of sight and hearing, and for his *Essays on the Principles of Morality and Natural Religion* (1751), a title which points to one of the abiding interests of the Enlightenment: how to codify and structure the essential elements of moral knowledge and religious belief. This latter work, which in time became a cornerstone of Scottish common-sense philosophy, attempted to maintain the doctrine of innate ideas. Kames was also one of the founders of the Physical and Literary Society, later the Royal Society of Edinburgh.

Kant, Immanuel, 1724–1804. German philosopher. His comprehensive and systematic work in ethics, aesthetics and the theory of knowledge unites the Cartesian and Humean elements in 18th-century thought, and is at once the capstone of the Enlightenment and the forerunner of 19th-century philosophy. In the *Fundamental Principles of the Metaphysics of Morals* (1785) he sounds the keynote to the Enlightenment: the pre-eminence of reason in respect to the primacy of ethics. Other major works were the *Critique of Pure Reason* (1781), the *Critique of Practical Reason* (1788) and the *Critique of Judgment* (1790).

Kellgren, Johan Henrik, 1751–95. Swedish poet and critic, he was the dominant literary figure of the Gustavian Enlightenment. With Carl Lenngren, he founded in 1787 the *Stockholms Posten*, of which he became editor, and wrote a series of articles championing the rationalism of the European Enlightenment. Also in 1787 he created for his readers the imaginary society *Pro sensu communi*, which was to do battle with all forms of occultism and mysticism. His lyrics, often satirical and sensual, are reckoned among the most notable products of the Gustavian period in Swedish letters.

Kinský, Major-General Count František Josef, 1739–1805. Bohemian aristocrat, military officer, geologist and educational reformer who was instrumental in founding the National History Museum in 1775 and the Prague University Library in 1777. He argued the importance of the nobility having a knowledge of the natural and agricultural sciences in order to administer their domains. His progressive approach to education can be seen in his *An Account of a Significant Subject Matter* (1773), in which he argued, among other things, the cause of child psychology.

Klingenstierna, Samuel, 1698–1765. Swedish mathematician and physicist who was the first to repeat Newton's experiments with sufficient care to show his error in the field of optics regarding the possibility of correcting the dispersive properties of lenses. His experiments apparently paved the way for John Dolland's 1758 design of the achromatic lens.

Lambert, Johann Heinrich, 1728–77. Swiss-German astronomer, mathematician, physicist and philosopher who revealed in *Photometria* (1760) the results of his exact measurement of the strength of light by the use of his photometer, thus ensuring advances in all forms of visual research and enormous strides in astronomy. In 1774 he became editor of *Astronomical Yearbook*.

LeMettrie, Julien Offroy de, 1709–51. French physician and philosopher whose *L'Homme-machine* (1747), was the first systematic treatise on materialism. This controversial work also developed, with great originality, the author's atheistic views. LaMettrie's system of ethics was expressed principally in *L'art de jouir* (1751), in which he argued that self-love was the only basis of virtue and that sensual pleasure was the aim of life. His notorious remark that a nation of atheists would be the happiest of all was his extreme way of saying that morality is independent of religion.

Lavoisier, Antoine-Laurent, 1743–94. French scientist regarded as the father of modern chemistry. He is noted especially for his discovery of the role of oxygen in combustion. *Méthode de nomenclature chimique*, written in 1787, was an extremely influential book, but equally important was the *Traité élémentaire de chimie* (1789), which constitutes an introduction to the new chemistry.

Leibniz, Gottfried Wilhelm, 1646–1716. German philosopher, mathematician, physicist and historian. He was an important forerunner of the Enlightenment whose guiding idea was that of the cooperation of all nations in discovering the secrets of nature and in using this knowledge to enable all men to live peaceably and well. He saw the universe as composed of an infinite number of units of force called monads, a concept applied by 18th-century empiricists to material atoms. *Essais de Théodicée* (1710) is his only complete and systematic philosophical work.

Lessing, Gotthold Ephraim, 1729–81. German dramatist, critic and aesthetician who attempted to define the limits and relations of the several arts. One of the great seminal minds in German literature, his ideas make him one of the leading figures of the Enlightenment, and the leader of the Enlightenment in Germany. His play, *Miss Sarah Sampson*, first performed in 1755, marks the beginning of a new period in the history of German drama, being the first tragedy of common life, or *bürgerliches Trauerspiel*, in German. His *Laokoon* (1766) marks an epoch in the appreciation of Homer and Sophocles and of Greek literature generally. Lessing also gave a wholly new direction to religious philosophy with the publication of his *The Education of the Human Race* (1780), which argues that no dogmatic creed can be regarded as final.

Linnaeus, Carolus (Carl von Linné), 1707–78. Swedish naturalist and physician who ranks as the first to frame principles for defining genera and species of organisms and to create a uniform system of nomenclature. The contributions of Linnaeus were crucial in the botanical aspect of the development of natural science, which was still at the preliminary stage of organising and classifying nomenclature during the 18th century.

Locke, John, 1632–1704. English philosopher, psychologist and political scientist who laid the epistemological foundations of modern science. To the problem of knowledge he propounded the sensationalist view. As a political scientist, he argued against divine right in favour of social contract and consent, regarding man as naturally virtuous. His two most important works are *Essay Concerning Human Understanding* (1690) and *Two Treatises of Government* (1689), the former being an elaborate and influential presentation of empiricism. Along with Isaac Newton, Locke is the most significant forerunner of the Enlightenment.

Lomonosov, Mikhail Vasilievich, 1711–65. Russian scientist, poet, philologist and historian, he was a universal man of the Enlightenment, today hailed as the founder of Russian science. In 1774 he enunciated the principle of the conservation of matter, though his work was overlooked and it was left for Lavoisier to establish it as a fundamental principle in 1785. He was appointed councillor of Moscow State University, which he had helped plan in 1757. He was also the foremost theoretician of his language, and his poetry brought new forms of expression to Russian poetic composition.

Malebranche, Nicolas, 1638–1715. French metaphysician who may be regarded as the connecting link between Descartes and Spinoza. He is the major philosopher of Cartesianism, which he sought to synthesise with the thought of St Augustine and with Neoplatonism. His principal work is *De la recherche de la verité* (1674–8).

Mandeville, Bernard, de, 1670–1733. Dutch–English satirist and philosopher whose most famous work is a doggerel poem *The Grumbling Hive, or Knaves Turned Honest* (1705), republished anonymously in 1714 under its better-known title, *The Fable of the Bees; or, Private Vices, Publick Benefits*, which, in effect, denied the relevance of Christian virtue to 18th-century life.

Maupertuis, Pierre-Louis Moreau de, 1698–1759. French mathematician and astronomer who anticipated modern genetics by attributing primitve desire, aversion and memory to genetic particles. He became a member of the Académie des Sciences, Paris, in 1731, and in the following year he introduced into France the Newtonian doctrine of gravitation.

Mendelssohn, Moses, 1729–86. German Jewish philosopher who gave a strong impetus to the Haskalah, the Jewish Enlightenment movement. He stressed the idea of Enlightenment as not so much a mode of thought but a form of education. His philosophy is most fully developed in *Jerusalem* (1783), in which he calls for religious tolerance and the separation of church and state.

Montesquieu, Charles-Louis de Secondat, baron de la Brède et de, 1689–1755. French jurist and outstanding political philosopher of the 18th century. His *Lettres persanes* (1721), the first great critical work of the French Enlightenment, is a plea for liberty and toleration which details the arguments for natural religion and a virtue ethic, themes synonymous with the Enlightenment. His major work is *De l'espirit des lois* (1748), a seminal contribution to political theory which has as its premise that truth and justice, based on reason, are universal.

Muratori, Ludovico Antonio, 1672–1750. Italian scholar, historian and antiquary regarded as the 'Father of Italian History' due to his great 28-volume collection *Rerum Italicarum scriptores* (1723–51) and his 75 dissertations on medieval Italy, *Antiquitates Italicae Medii Aevi* (1738–42). As a priest, he fought against superstition and medieval scholasticism, as revived by the Jesuits, for moral and cultural reasons.

Newton, Sir Isaac, 1643–1727. English mathematician and physicist whose reputation in the 18th century was immense, as much because he was thought to exemplify the scientific method as because of the importance of his individual discoveries, including the composition of white light, the formulation of the three fundamental laws of mechanics leading to the law of gravitation, and the infinitesimal calculus. Newton's ideas and work inspired the philosophers' search for a simple, rational law of human nature and social life. His principal works were the *Opticks* (1704) and the *Principia Mathematica* (1687).

Nicolai, Christoph Friedrich, 1733–1811. German publisher and rationalistic writer. In Protestant Germany journals were the most important medium of the Enlightenment, serving as repositories of knowledge in addition to publishing ideas and manifestoes, and Nicolai founded some of the most distinguished of these. In association with Moses Mendelssohn he established in 1757 the *Library of Fine Arts*, and, in 1761, with Mendelssohn and Gotthold Ephraim Lessing, the famous *Letters on the Modern Literary Question*. From 1765 to 1792, he edited the *Universal German Library*, the organ of the 'popular philosophers' who frequently attacked authority in religion and 'extravagance' in literature.

Novikov, Nikolai Ivanovich, 1744–1818. Russian publisher, philanthropist and social critic. He served as a secretary in Catherine II's Legislative Commission and became one of the foremost promoters of the Enlightenment in Russia. Critical of serfdom and ignorance, he used the printing press to promote a reading public and public opinion in Russia. He occupies a signal place in Russian history as the founder of the book publishing trade in that country. Other activities included the founding of schools and libraries and the publication of several daring satirical periodicals, including *Drone* (1769–70), for which the model was Addison and Steele's *Spectator*. His work eventually antagonised Catherine II who had him arrested in 1792. Four years later he was released by Emperor Paul.

Order of the Illuminati. A secret society whose spread throughout Catholic Germany during the 1770s and 1780s illustrates the development of a popular *Aufklärung*, that is, one having no formal ties with the government. A short-lived movement of Republican freethought founded in Bavaria in 1776 by Adam Weishaupt, an ex-Jesuit and professor of Canon Law at Ingolstadt, it had branches throughout Catholic Germany and in most

European countries. The Illuminati aspired to project their moral principles into society and thereby to transform it, the goal being the universal brotherhood of man. Many literary men like Goethe and Herder were attracted to the Order, whose chosen title was *Perfektibilisten*, before its downfall in 1785, effected by an edict of the Bavarian government.

Pagano, Francesco Mario, 1748–99. Italian legal theorist, philosopher, historical scholar and social reformer. An important figure of the Neapolitan Enlightenment, his major work is *Political Essays* (1783–5), a vision of the development of civilisation which argued for an immediate breaking down of the major obstacles which stood in the way of the renewal of the country. It was partly due to his disappointment with the failure of reform which caused him to play a leading role in the Neapolitan Revolution of 1799.

Paine, Thomas, 1737–1809. Anglo-American pamphleteer and political scientist who, in his *Common Sense* (1776), issued the first public call for the American colonies to declare their independence from Britain. He later published a defence of the French Revolution, *The Rights of Man* (1791), becoming an international spokesman for political equality, natural rights and civil liberties. In *The Age of Reason* (1794), he applied to religion the principles of natural reason, developing a system of deism based on science and abstract morality.

Paoli, Pasquale, 1725–1807. Italian statesman and patriot responsible for ending Genoese rule of Corsica in 1755 and, under the principles of enlightened despotism, establishing important reforms. His enterprise ended in disaster following France's purchase of Corsica in 1768 and its invasion of the island and of the defeat of the nationalists in 1769.

Pelcl, František Martin, 1734–1801. Bohemian scholar who produced, in collaboration with Josef Dobrovský, the first modern edition of narrative sources in Czech history, *Scriptores rerum Boehmicarum* (1783–4). His principal aim was to strengthen the national consciousness of the intelligentsia, the aristocracy and the young.

Pestalozzi, Johann Heinrich, 1746–1827. Swiss educational reformer who shares with Rousseau the distinction of devising a method that remains the cornerstone of all sound theories of primary education. He founded an educational farm at Neuhof (1774–9) which laid the foundation of his later work. His popular didactic novel *Leonard and Gertrude* (1781–7) profoundly influenced the evolution of modern pedagogy, but his *How Gertrude Teaches Her Children* (1801) remains his most important elaboration of his principles of intellectual education. He tested and developed his theories with other progressive teachers at the teacher-training institute in Burgdorf (from 1799), which later moved to Münchenbuchsee (in 1804) and then to Yverdon (1805). Pestalozzi's reforms led to the gradual transfer of the school from church domination to a government-supported institution.

Peter I the Great, of Russia, 1672–1725. Russian emperor and czar of the Romanov dynasty who attempted to lift his country out of its technological and military backwardness. His programme of modernisation included the reform of the calendar; the establishment of a new tax system; publication of the first domestic newspaper; organisation of a network of technical schools; planning of the Academy of Sciences (founded 1725); etc. He also abolished the patriarchate of the Russian Orthodox Church and subjected the clergy to state control. His most far-reaching accomplishment was to draw Russia further into the European sphere.

Philosophes. The name given to a group of great 18th-century thinkers, writers and scientists who believed in the sovereignty of reason and nature as opposed to authority and revelation, and rebelled against old dogmas and institutions. Voltaire and Montesquieu dominated the early part of the century. In the second, more volatile half of the 18th century, Buffon, Condillac, Condorcet, Diderot, Rousseau and Turgot were among the *Philosophes* who contributed to the *Encyclopédie*, the great intellectual achievement of the Enlightenment.

Physiocrats. A group of 18th-century *philosophes* who formed a school of economic thought generally regarded as the first systematic school of political economy. They included Quesnay, their founder, Mirabeau and Gournay. Best understood as a reaction against mercantilist policies, the physiocratic school was concerned with problems of taxation, the development of trade, and the organisation of labour on the land. The term 'physiocracy' denotes the rule of nature, and the acceptance by the physiocrats of a more liberal policy on the part of the state, *laissez-faire*, reflected their belief that natural economic laws should prevail.

Price, Richard, 1723–91. English moral and political philosopher. An ardent supporter of both the American and French revolutions, he published the popular pamphlet *Observations on the Nature of Civil Liberty, the Principles of Government, and the Justice and Policy of the War with America* (1776) and later delivered the celebrated sermon *Discourse on the Love of Our Country* (1789). His philosophical importance rests entirely in the region of ethics, and his theory is contained in the *Review of the Principal Questions and Difficulties in Morals* (1758), which pleaded the cause of ethical intuitionism and rationalism, foreshadowing Kant's ethics.

Priestley, Joseph, 1733–1804. English political theorist, educator, scientist and clergyman best remembered as the discoverer of oxygen (1774–5). He was a prolific writer on many subjects, who represented the spirit of English dissent that produced important advances in liberal thought and experimental science during the Enlightenment. Representative of 18th-century liberal thought was his *Essays on the First Principles of Government, and on the Nature of Political, Civil and Religious Liberty* (1765), in which he emphasised individualism.

Prokopovich, Feofan, 1681–1736. Russian archbishop, theologian, statesman and reformer, and the first authentic voice in Russia of the early Enlightenment. Both a friend of piety and an implacable foe of ignorance and superstition, he was the chief ideologist of the Petrine state and the author of Peter's church reform, derived from a theory which combined concepts from the 17th-century English political philosopher Thomas Hobbes with Byzantine theocratic thought. As rector of the Academy of Kiev he entirely reformed the teaching of theology, substituting the historical method of the German theologians for the antiquated Orthodox scholastic system. His new constitution for Orthodoxy, the *Spiritual Regulations*, was drawn up in 1720.

Pufendorf, Samuel von, 1632–4. German jurist who constructed a system of universal law under the title of *Elementorum jurisprudentiae universalis libri duo* (1660). In 1672 he wrote his *De jure naturae et gentium*, a study of natural and public law that took up the theories of Grotius and sought to complete them by means of the doctrines of Hobbes and of his own ideas. In these works, natural law is based on man's existence as a social being. Pufendorf's influence as a philosopher, lawyer, economist, historian and statesman was considerable, and he left a profound influence on thought in Germany and elsewhere.

Quesnay, François, 1694–1774. French economist and intellectual leader of the physiocrats. He contributed articles to the *Encyclopédie* on economics (1756–7), and in his *Tableau économique* (1758), the first systematic portrayal of an entire economy whose methodology springs from an extreme form of the doctrine of natural law, he expounded his physiocratic theory. Other works included *Maximes* (1758) and *Physiocratie* (1768).

Radischev, Aleksandr Nikolayevich, 1749–1802. Russian jurist, philosopher and writer who founded the revolutionary tradition in Russian thought and literature. Under the impetus of such Enlightenment thinkers as Rousseau, he wrote *A Journal from St. Petersburg to Moscow* (1790), which, in addition to dealing at length with problems of Russian poetry and prosody, denounces serfdom, autocracy and censorship. The publication of the book, one year after the French Revolution, led to his forced exile in Siberia, where he remained until 1797.

Reid, Thomas, 1710–96. Scottish philosopher who, with Dugald Stewart, succeeded in reconciling the interests of science with those of religion and morality. He rejected the sceptical empiricism of Hume in favour of a 'philosophy of common sense', which was first put forward in his *An Inquiry into the Human Mind on the Principles of Common Sense* (1764). His *Essays on the Active Powers of Man* (1788) defended rationalistic ethics against a current of subjectivism.

Reimarus, Hermann Samuel, 1694–1768. German philosopher and man of letters best remembered for his Deism. In his major work, the posthumously published *Defence for the Rational Adorers of God* (1774–8), he argued that the human mind was capable of reaching a perfect religion without the aid of revealed principles.

Robertson, William, 1721–93. Scottish historian and a central figure in the Scottish Enlightenment because of his historical writings, principally the *History of Scotland* (1759), and for the leading part he played in some of the institutions of Scottish society crucial to the generation and expression of the Scottish Enlightenment. He was the leader of the moderate party from 1752 and Moderator of the General Assembly of the Church of Scotland between 1766 and 1780. From 1762 to 1793 he was Principal of Edinburgh University, which, under his leadership and administration, became a leading institution of higher education and a major contributor to the Scottish Enlightenment. He was also a founder of several learned societies, most notably the Select Society and the Royal Academy of Edinburgh.

Rosenstein, Nils von, 1752–1824. Swedish writer noted for his *Speech about the Enlightenment*, delivered to the Royal Swedish Academy of Sciences in 1789, which constituted a fervent defence of Enlightenment ideas and of the rationalistic endeavours of the century. The speech was published a year after the 1792 assassination of Gustavus III, at a time when the rationalistic attitude was being abandoned for mysticism, and when all remaining political and cultural freedoms were being suspended.

Rousseau, Jean-Jacques, 1712–78. French philosopher and political theorist who was one of the most original and certainly the most controversial of the *philosophes*. He made his mark in 1750 when he won a prize offered by the Academy of Dijon with his *Discours sur les sciences et les arts*, which attacked the sciences and arts as corrupting instruments that serve the rich.

172

This reputation was cemented by the *Discours sur l'inégalité* (1755), *La nouvelle héloïse* (1760), the *Contrat social* (1762) and *Emile* (1762). The basic idea in Rousseau's work is that society has corrupted the natural goodness of man, and only through a better society could man be improved. His central doctrine was that man, good by nature, could recover the benefits of the natural man without returning to the state of nature by transforming himself into a good citizen in a good society.

Salon. Literally, the drawing room or sitting room. It was an invention of the 17th century which, during the Enlightenment, was an important factor in the exchange and spread of new ideas. The *salons* of Paris and some of the provinces were, in the 18th century, captured by the purveyors of new and radical ideas, generally presided over by the great ladies of the day, e.g. the Duchesse de Maine, whose *salon* was frequented by freethinkers, the Marquise de Lambert, Mme de Tencier, Mme Geoffrin, Mme Necker, and, above all others, Mme du Deffand and Mlle de Lespinasse.

Saussure, Horace-Bénédict de, 1740–99. Swiss naturalist, physicist, inventor of the electrometer and first scientific explorer of the Alps. His descriptions of seven of his Alpine journeys, with scientific observations gathered *en route*, were published under the title *Voyage dans les Alpes* (1779–96), which introduced the word 'geology' into scientific nomenclature. Saussure studied geology in a manner never previously attempted, and his work on glaciers and the effects of erosion were important in the growth of geological interest in the study of mountains.

Scheele, Karl Wilhelm, 1742–86. Swedish chemist whose record as a discoverer of new substances, e.g. chlorine, barium oxide, glycerine, hydrogen sulphide, etc., is probably unequalled. He prepared oxygen in 1772, two years before Priestley, whose discovery of the gas was the culminating point of what may properly be called the pneumatic revolution of chemistry.

Schlözer, August Ludwig von, 1735–1809. German historian who helped to bring historical study into touch with political science and aroused much intelligent interest in universal history. He was also instrumental in laying the foundations of statistical science, as can be seen from several of his other works.

Shaftesbury, Anthony Ashley Cooper, 3rd Earl of, 1671–1713. English moral philosopher who concentrated on ethics and aesthetics. Freedom of thought and inquiry was central to his approach. He objected to revealed religion because, by resorting to the miraculous, it subverted the natural order and impugned the work of a benevolent Creator. His writings consist of a series of pamphlets and essays collected under the title of *Characteristicks of Men, Manners, Opinions, Times* (1711).

Smith, Adam, 1723–90. Scottish political economist and social philosopher, best known for his *An Inquiry into the Nature and Causes of the Wealth of Nations* (1776). In his materialist understanding of history and society, he stressed the primacy of economic and cultural variables in shaping men's ideas and generating social change. The prophet of the *laissez-faire* doctrine, he epitomised much of the character of Western liberal capitalism in *Wealth of Nations*, which became the bible of the new economic outlook.

Sonnenfels, Joseph von, 1733–1817. Austrian academic and jurist who attempted to commit the government of Maria Theresa to an irreversible course of enlightened reform. He was one of the first of those who drew practical political conclusions from the philosophy and culture of the Enlightenment, and his weekly journal was the first of the German periodicals in which political and social issues were directly raised. It was through his pressure that Maria Theresa's government abolished inquisitional torture. He was also one of the founders of the 'German Society', which presented German culture as a model for Austrian writers. He was, as well, the chief protagonist of bourgeois culture in Austria, a firm believer in the principle that a reformed German drama could play an important moral and educative role in society.

Spinoza, Baruch (Benedict de Spinoza), 1632–77. Dutch philosopher who emphasised the role of reason in metaphysics and ethics. He was an important forerunner of the Enlightenment, though his politics and biblical criticism were misconstrued by the *philosophes* as potential support of a materialist philosophy. Among his principal workers were the *Tractatus Theologico-Politicus* (1670), which advocated freedom of philosophising, and *Ethica* (1677).

Sporck, Count Franz Anton, 1662–1738. Bohemian publisher. During the first three decades of the 18th century he commissioned over 100 publications aimed at spreading Christian beliefs opposed to the fanaticism and intolerance enforced by Jesuits throughout the country. In 1732 Sporck was accused by the Jesuits of spreading heresy and was very heavily fined.

Steele, Sir Richard, 1672–1729. English essayist and dramatist, journalist and politician noted for his contributions, with Joseph Addison, to the *Tatler* (published by Steele, 1709–11) and the *Spectator* (published by Addison and Steele, 1711–12). The principal achievement of Steele and Addison was to set the pattern and establish the vogue for the periodical throughout the remainder of the 18th century.

Steuart, Sir James, 1712–80. Scottish economist. His *Inquiry into the Principles of Political Economy* (1767) was the most complete and systematic survey of that subject from the point of view of moderate mercantilism to be published in Britain, though the *Wealth of Nations*, published nine years later, greatly overshadowed his work.

Stewart, Dugald, 1753–1828. Scottish philosopher and principal exponent of the 'common-sense' school of philosophy founded by Thomas Reid. One of the late Enlightenment's most influential moralists, he elevated Reid's ideas to the status of an institution in Scottish philosophy. His most important work is *Elements of the Philosophy of the Human Mind* (1792–1827).

Sylvius, Franciscus (Franz de la Boe), 1614–72. Prussian physician, physiologist, anatomist and chemist regarded as the founder of the 17th-century iatrochemical school of medicine. His studies were crucial in shifting medical emphasis from mystical speculation to a rational application of universal laws of chemistry and physics. His collected *Opera medica* were first published in 1671.

Tanucci, Bernardo Marchese, 1698–1783. Italian statesman and jurist. He is the best example of the sort of 'enlightened' prime minister produced by most Italian states who strove to break exemptions and lessen the power of the church. He was professor of civil law from 1726 to 1735 at Pisa and Prime Minister of Tuscany from 1767 to 1776.

Tindal, Matthew, 1657–1733. English lawyer, pamphleteer and deist whose writings defended religious liberty and the freedom of the press. His major work is *Christianity as Old as the Creation* (1730), called the 'Deists' Bible', which reduced religion to a rationalistic belief in God and moral duties.

Toland, John, 1670–1722. Irish philosopher and deist whose *Christianity Not Mysterious* (1696) is the classic exposition of deism. Other controversial works included his *Life of Milton* (1698), which opened up the question of the history of the canon; *Letters to Serena* (1704), which railed against the imposition of custom and nature upon men's attitudes and ideas, and *Tetradymus* (1720), which offered a natural explanation of Gospel miracles.

Trembley, Abraham, 1710–84. Swiss naturalist whose studies drew attention to basic characteristics of plants and animals. His observations on regeneration were published in the extraordinary *Mémoires pour servir à l'histoire d'un genre de polypes d'eau douce à bras en forme de cornes* (1744), a model of controlled experiment and careful observation.

175

Turgot, Anne-Robert-Jacques, baron de l'Aulne, 1727–81. French economist, statesman and reformer. Acquainted with the *philosophes*, and himself a contributor to the *Encyclopédie*, Turgot was most at home with the physiocrats, whose interests in free trade he shared. After being appointed Controller-General in France in 1774 by Louis XVI, he attempted to reform the fiscal system, but was dismissed in 1776 due to opposition to his Six Edicts. As an economist he is best known for a physiocratic treatise composed in 1766, which decried government controls and excessive taxation.

Turrettin, Jean-Alphonse, 1671–1737. Swiss pastor and theologian appointed to the chair of theology at Geneva in 1669, a watershed in Swiss intellectual life. Along with Chouet, he was a significant factor in explaining the establishment of rationalism and, in due course, empiricism, in significant parts of the Swiss cantons. His liberal theology aimed at admitting the right of free critical enquiry and a rejection of intolerance.

Verri, Pietro, Conte, 1728–97. Italian political economist, philosopher, government official and journalist. From 1762 to 1764 he led a group of young Milanese intellectuals known as the 'Accademia dei pugni'. From 1764 to 1766 he directed the society's journal, *Il Caffé*, which became the focus of reforming ideas in Milan and had a considerable impact on contemporary Italian social consciousness. The periodical dealt with a wide range of topics, including medicine, music, philosophy, law, literature, etc., all expounding the need for social, economic and political reform. In his *Meditations on Political Economy* (1771), supporting liberalism and *laissez-faire*, Verri anticipated the modern concept of the shifting of taxes. In this and many other concepts, he presented in germ ideas which later became important in economic theory. For much of his life he held important posts in the Milanese government.

Vico, Giambattista, 1668–1744. Italian philosopher, legal theorist and historical scholar now recognised as the forerunner of anthropology and ethnology. His views were expressed in his *Principles of a New Science* (1725), a work of epochal importance in historical method because it demonstrated how the records of the past can be made to yield a rational history of the society that produced them.

Volta, Alessandro Giuseppe Antonio Anastasio, Count, 1745–1827. Italian physicist celebrated as a pioneer of electrical science after whom the 'volt' was named.

Voltaire (pseudonym of Jean François Arouet), 1694–1778. French author, philosopher, apostle of freethought and a leading *philosophe* now best known for his satirical novel *Candide* (1759), a satire on philosophical optimism. His prodigious output of pamphlets, plays, tracts and letters was characterised by his disrespect for authority, established tradition and the church. He was imprisoned in the Bastille for a time, and was also driven into exile in England, but in the end was able to retire to Paris. Voltaire has often been cited as the most representative personification of the Enlightenment.

Wieland, Christoph Martin, 1733–1813. German poet and man of letters. His translation of 22 of Shakespeare's plays into prose (1762–6) was the first attempt to present the English poet to the German in something approaching entirety. He also translated Horace, Cicero and Lucian, and in his novels and poetry, where, largely under French inspiration, he introduced remote and exotic settings, we have a good illustration of the Enlightenment in its rococo aspect.

Wolff, Christian, 1679–1754. German philosopher, mathematician and scientist. A leading figure of the German Enlightenment, he applied the principles of rationalist thinkers such as Leibniz in the development of his own philosophical system, the Wolffian philosophy, formed essentially of mathematical methodology and rationalism. His chief importance was as a systematiser and as a populariser of Enlightenment, and his efforts in various fields laid the groundwork for a distinctively German philosophy. However, his *Theologia naturalis* (1736–7) shows he had become increasingly orthodox with the years, using his philosophical method for the purpose of combating atheism and other forms of heresy and sectarianism.

CHRONOLOGY OF THE ENLIGHTENMENT

1649
René Descartes, *Les Passiones de l'âme.*

1650
Thomas Hobbes, *The Elements of Law, Moral and Political* (written 1640).

1651
William Harvey, *Exercitationes de generatione animalium* founded the study of embryology.
Thomas Hobbes, *Leviathan.*

1652
Naturae Curiosi, the German Scientific Academy, founded.

1653

Thomas Bartholin, Danish physician, described the lymphatic system.

1654

Duisburg University founded.

1655

John Wallis, *Arithmetica infinitorum*, treatise treating curves by the Cartesian method.

1656

Academia degli Arcadi founded, Rome.

James Harrington, *Commonwealth of Oceana*, expounded a system of republicanism and suggested educational reforms.

Christian Huygens invented the pendulum clock.

1657

Academia del Cimento, Florence, founded.

Durham College founded (dissolved 1660).

F. Le sieur Saunier, *L'encyclopédie des beaux esprits*, first reference book with 'encyclopédie' in its title.

1658

Pierre Gassendi, *Syntagma philosophicum*, defended a mechanistic explanation of nature and sensation.

Thomas Hobbes, *Elementorum Philosophiae*.

1659

Preussische Staats-bibliothek, Berlin, founded.

1660

Academy of Arts, Seville, founded.

Samuel von Pufendorf, *Elementorum jurisprudentiae universalis libri duo*, expounded a system of universal law.

1661

Robert Boyle, 'Sceptical Chemist', foundation of modern chemistry.

Christian Huygens invented manometer for ascertaining the elastic force of gases.

Franciscus Sylvius consolidated his iatrochemical medical theories into a systematic school.

1662

Academia Leopoldina, Vienna, founded.

Robert Boyle observed the elastic pressure of air in all directions (Boyle's Law).

Royal Society for the Improvement of Natural Knowledge, London, founded.

1663

Académie des Inscriptions, Paris, founded.

Gottfried Wilhelm Leibniz, *De principio individui*, a defence of nominalistic philosophy.

1664

René Descartes, *Traité de l'homme et de la formation du foetus.*

Thomas Willis, *Anatome Cerebri nervorumque descriptio et usus*, a study of the brain.

1665

Robert Hooke, *Micrographia*, described the microscope.

University of Kiel founded.

1666

Académie Royale des Sciences, Paris, founded.

Leibniz, *De arte combinatoria*, an arithmetical tract.

Isaac Newton discovered the infinitesimal calculus and postulated the laws of gravity.

University of Lund founded.

1667

College of Antiquities, Uppsala.

The National Observatory, Paris, founded.

1670

Baruch Spinoza, *Tractatus Theologico-Politicus.*

Leibniz, *Hypothesis Physica Nova.*

1671

Sylvius, *Opera medica.*

1672

Pufendorf, *De jure naturae et gentium libri octo*, placed international law on an ethical basis.

1673

Christian Huygens, *Horologium oscillatorium.*

1674
Nicolas Malebranche, *De la recherche de la vérité.*
Thomas Willis, *Pharmaceutice rationalis*, advanced diabetes research.

1675
Greenwich Observatory established under John Flamsteed as first Astronomer Royal.
Leibniz discovered the differential and integral calculus.

1676
Leibniz discovered the infinitesimal calculus.

1677
Academia Fisico-Mathematica, Rome, founded.
Descartes, *Le monde.*
Spinoza, *Ethica.*
University of Innsbruck founded.

1679
Théophile Bonet, *Sepulcretum*, founded the study of morbid anatomy.
Thomas Hobbes, *Behemoth.*

1680
Giovanni Borelli, *De motu animalium* (posthumously published), explained movements of animal body on mechanical principles and founded iatrophysical school.

1681
Academy of Sciences, Moscow, founded.
Jean Mabillon, *De re diplomatica*, standard work on diplomatics, laid foundation of modern historical criticism.

1682
Advocates Library (now National Library of Scotland), Edinburgh, founded (opened 1689).
Pierre Bayle, *Thoughts on the Comet of 1680*, used rationalism to oppose superstitions about comets.

1684
Leibniz, *Nova Methodus pro Maximis et Minimus.*

1685
Bayle, *Dictionnaire historique et critique* (–1697).
Slavo-Greco-Latin Academy, Moscow, founded.

1686

Collège de Saint-Cyr founded by Madame de Maintenon.

John Ray, *Historia Plantarum* (−1704).

Bernard le Bovier de Fontenelle, *Relation de l'île de Borneo*, a satire reflecting author's anti-religious bias.

1687

Fontenelle, *L'histoire des oracles*, attacked credulity and superstition.

Isaac Newton, *Philosophiae naturalis principia Mathematica*.

1688

Jean de la Bruyère, *Caractères*, attacked social injustice in France.

Fontenelle, *Entretiens sur la pluralité des mondes*.

1689

John Locke, *Two Treatises of Government* and *Letter Concerning Toleration* (the first; second, 1690; third, 1692).

Montaliche Erzählunger, periodical devoted to natural science, first issued.

1690

Academia dell'Arcadia, Rome, founded.

Huygens, *Traité de la lumiere*, theory of undulation of light (advanced in 1678).

John Locke, *An Essay Concerning Human Understanding*.

1691

Leibniz, *Protogaea*, a study of geology.

1693

Leibniz, *Codex juris gentium diplomaticus* (−1700), a treatise on positive law.

John Locke, *Thoughts Concerning Education*.

1694

Dictionnaire de l'Académie française, supplemented by *Dictionnaire des arts et des sciences*, prepared by Thomas Corneille.

Leibniz, *De primae philosophiae emendatione*.

University of Halle founded by Elector Frederick III.

1695

Bayle, *Dictionnaire historique et critique* (completed 1697).

Berlin University founded.

England's press censorship ended with expiration of Licensing Act.

Leibniz, *Systeme nouveau de la nature*.

1696

Academy of Arts, Berlin, founded.

Nicolas Antonio, *Bibliotheca Hispana vetus*, bibliography of all Spanish works from Augustus.

John Toland, *Christianity Not Mysterious*, classic exposition of deism.

1697

Daniel Defoe, *An Essay upon Projects*, urges higher education of women, the establishment of benefit societies, an income tax, etc.

1698

Andrew Fletcher, *Two Discourses Concerning the Affairs of Scotland.*

Algernon Sidney, *Discourses Concerning Government* (posthumously published), influential in encouraging liberal provisions in various constitutions.

1699

Lord Shaftesbury, *An Enquiry Concerning Virtue.*

1702

Daniel Defoe, *The Shortest Way with Dissenters.*

University of Breslau founded.

1703

Jean Le Clerc, *Bibliothèque choisie* (–1713).

Universal, Historical, Geographical, Chronological and Classical Dictionary, first English periodical of A–Z treatment of knowledge.

1704

John Harris, *Lexicon Technicum*, the first scientific encyclopaedia.

Leibniz, *Nouveaux essais sur l'entendement humain.*

Sir Isaac Newton, *Opticks*, defended emission theory of light.

Toland, *Letters to Serena.*

1705

Berlin Royal Observatory founded.

Moscow University founded by Peter the Great.

Shaftesbury, *The Sociable Enthusiast.*

1706

A Real-Schule founded at Halle by Christopher Semler for the study of mathematics and applied science.

O. Römer's catalogue of astronomic observation.

1707

Anthony Collins, *Essay Concerning the Use of Reason.*

1709

George Berkeley, *New Theory of Vision.*
Tatler began publication (–Jan 1711).

1710

George Berkeley, *A Treatise Concerning the Principles of Human Knowledge.*
Leibniz, *Essais de Théodicée.*

1711

Berlin Academy started under Presidency of Leibniz.
Royal Academy of Arts, London, founded.
Shaftesbury, *Characteristicks of Men, Manners, Opinions, Times.*
Spectator began publication (–1712).

1712

Académie des Sciences, Belles Lettres et Arts, Bordeaux, founded.
Biblioteca National, Madrid, founded.
Christian Wolff, *Rational Ideas.*

1713

Berkeley, *Dialogues between Hylas and Philonons.*
Arthur Collier, *Clavis Universalis; or A New Enquiry after Truth.*
Collins, *A Discourse of Freethinking.*

1714

Academia Española, Madrid, founded.
Leibniz, *La Monadologie.*
Mandeville, *The Fable of the Bees; or, Private Vices, Publick Benefits.*

1715

Brook Taylor, *Methodus Incrementorum Directa et Inversa*, expounded the
  calculus of finite differences.

1716

Rankens Society, Edinburgh, founded, which early espoused Berkeley's
  philosophy.
Shaftesbury, *Letters to a Student.*

1717

Imperial Library, St Petersburg, founded.

1718

Academia de Scienze, Lettere ed Arti, Palermo, founded.
London Society of Antiquaries founded.
Etienne Geoffroy presented *tables des rapports* to the French Academy.
Voltaire, *Edipe*.

1719

Leibniz, *Principes de la nature et de la grâce*.

1720

Giambattista Vico, *De uno universi juris principis*.
Feofan Prokopovich, *Spiritual Regulations*.
Toland, *Tetradymus*.
Wolff, *Rational Thoughts on God, the World and the Human Soul*.

1721

Johann Jakob Bodmer, *Discourse on Painters* (completed 1723; with Johann
   Jakob Breitinger).
Charles-Louis de Secondat Montesquieu, *Lettres persanes*.

1722

Parnassus Boicus, Munich, founded by A. E. Amort, to promote enlightened Catholic literature.
University of Dijon founded.

1723

M. A. Capeller, *Prodromus crystallographie*, the earliest treatise on crystal-
   lography.
Pietro Giannoni, *Civil History of the King of Naples*, first work of constitu-
   tional history proper.
Ludovico Antonio Muratori, *Rerum Italicarum scriptores* (-1751).
Voltaire, *Henriade*.

1724

Hermann Boerhaave, *Elementa chemicae*.
First Patriotic Society, Hamburg, founded (-1750, revived 1765), became
   'a model of an active and purposeful enlightened society'.

1725

Francis Hutcheson, *Inquiry into the Origin of our Ideas of Beauty and Virtue*.
St Petersburg Academy of Science founded.
Vico, *Principi d'una scienza nuova intorno alla natura* (revised 1730,
1744).

1726

Académie des Sciences, Belles Lettres et Arts, Marseilles, founded.
Real Academia Española, Madrid, founded.

1727

University of Camerino founded.

1728

James Bradley discovers the aberration of light from fixed stars.
Ephraim Chambers, *Cyclopaedia; or An Universal Dictionary of Arts and Sciences.*
Hutcheson, *An Essay on the Nature and Conduct of the Passions and the Affections.*

1729

Academia de Beunas Letras, Barcelona, founded.

1730

De Moivre propounded theorems of trigonometry concerning imaginary quantities.
Matthew Tindal, *Christianity as Old as the Creation, or Republication of the Religion of Nature* ('The Deists' Bible').

1731

Medical Society of Edinburgh, later the Philosophical Society, founded by Alexander Monro.

1732

Berkeley, *Alciphron; or the Minute Philosopher.*
Boerhaave, *Elements of Chemistry*, pioneer study of organic chemistry.
J. J. Moser, *Foundations of International Law.*
Voltaire, *Zaïre.*
Johann Heinrich Zedler, *Universal-Lexicon* (−1750).

1733

Stephen Hales, *Haemostaticks*, on blood circulation.
Alexander Pope, *Essay on Man.*
Society of Dilettanti, London, founded to encourage the study of antiquities.
Svenska Argus founded by Olof von Dalin.

1734

Montesquieu, *Considerations sur les causes de la grandeur des Romains et de leur decadence.*

Spanish Academy of Medicine founded.
Voltaire, *Lettres sur les Anglais.*

1735
Carolus Linnaeus, *Systema Naturae.*
University of Rennes founded.

1736
Leonhard Euler founded study of analytical mechanics.
Wolff, *Theologia naturalis* (−1737).

1737
Göttingen University founded by George II.
Philosophical Society, Edinburgh, founded.
René Réaumur, *History of Insects.*

1738
Viscount Bolingbroke, *Letters on the Study and Use of History.*
Muratori, *Antiquitates Italicae Medii Aevi* (−1742).
Voltaire, *Discours sur l'homme* introduced Newtonian ideas to France.
Wolff, *Philosophia practica universalis* (−1739).

1739
Diccionario, vol. 1, published by Real Academia Española, Madrid.
David Hume, *A Treatise on Human Nature* (−1740), pioneered modern empiricism.
Bernard de Montfaucon, *Bibliotheca bibliothecarum,* a catalogue of manuscripts in European libraries.
Muratori, *Novus thesaurus inscriptionum* (−1743).
Royal Swedish Academy of Sciences founded.

1740
Pierre Bouguer experimented on earth's gravity.
Frederick II the Great, *Anti-Machiavel*; and founded the Berlin Academy of Science.

1741
David Hume, *Essays Moral and Political* (−1742).
Royal Academy of Sciences, Stockholm, founded.

1742
Anders Celsius invented the centigrade thermometer.
Royal Society of Denmark, Copenhagen, founded.

1743

University of Erlangen founded.
Political Economy Club, Glasgow, founded.

1744

Berkeley, *Siris*.
Euler, *Theoria motuum planetarum*.
Muratori, *Annali d'Italia* (–1749).
Abraham Trembley, *Mémoires pour servir à l'histoire d'un genre de polypes d'eau douce à bras en forme de cornes.*

1745

Charles Bonnet, *Traite d'insectologie*.
Julien Offroy de La Mettrie, *L'Histoire naturelle de l'âme* published and burnt in France.
Maupertuis, *Venus physique*, challenged the pre-existence theory of genetics advanced by Jan Swammerdam in 1699.
LaMettrie, *Histoire naturelle de l'Âme*.

1746

Étienne Bonnot de Condillac, *Essai sur l'origine des connaissances humaines*.
Diderot, *Les pensées philosophiques*.
Societas eruditorum incognitorum in terris austriacis, earliest scientific society in the Habsburg Empire, founded at Olomouc, former capital of Moravia, by Joseph von Petrasch.

1747

D'Alembert, *Réflexion sur la cause générale des vents*.
Biblioteca Nazionale, Florence, founded.
Dalin, *Svea Rikets historia* (–1762).
LaMettrie, *L'Homme-machine*.
National Library, Warsaw, opened.
Oekonomisch-Mathematische Realschule, Berlin, founded.
Voltaire, *Zadig*.

1748

Euler, *Analysis infinitorum*, an introduction to pure analytical mathematics.
Hume, *An Enquiry Concerning Human Understanding* (–1735).
Montesquieu, *De l'Esprit des lois*.
John T. Needham, *Observations upon the Generation, Composition and Decomposition of Animal and Vegetable Substances*, gave 'proof' of spontaneous combustion.

1749

Buffon, *Histoire naturelle générale et particulière* (–1767).

Condillac, *Traité des systèmes*.

Diderot, *Lettre sur les aveugles à l'usage de cieux qui voient*, expounded the doctrine of relativity, for which he is imprisoned.

David Hartley, *Observation on Man*.

1750

Academy of Sciences and Observatory, Stockholm, founded.

Linnaeus, *Philosophia botanica*.

Maupertuis, *Essai sur la philosophie morale*.

Rousseau, *Discours sur les sciences et les arts*.

Wolff, *Philosophia moralis* (–1753).

1751

Diderot and d'Alembert published first volume of *Dictionnaire Raisonné des sciences, des arts et des métiers, par une société de gens de lettres* (known as *Encyclopédie*) (–1772).

Göttingen Society of Sciences founded.

Hume, *Enquiry Concerning the Principles of Morals*.

Lord Kames, *Essays on the Principles of Morality and Natural Religion*.

Maupertuis, *Systéme de la nature*.

Real Academia Sevillana de Beunos Letras founded.

Voltaire, *Siècle de Louis XIV*.

1752

Hume, *Political Discourses*.

Voltaire, *Micromégas*.

1753

Buffon, *Discours sur le style*.

Euler, *Theoria Motus Lunae*.

Linnaeus, *Species planatarum*.

Voltaire, *Essai sur les moeurs*.

1754

Charles Bonnet, *Essai de psychologie*.

Condillac, Traité des sensations.

Danish Academy of Arts, Copenhagen, founded.

E. Flórez, *Sacred Spain*.

Hume, *History of Great Britain* (–1757).

Rousseau, *Discours sur l'origine et les fondements de l'inégalité parmis les hommes* (–1755).

The Select Society, Edinburgh, founded (–1746).

1755

Joseph Black, *Experiments upon Magnesia, Quicklime and other Alkaline Substances*, gave impetus to the study of chemistry.

Cantillon, *Essai sur la nature du commerce en général*, founded Physiocratic School of French economists.

Hutcheson, *A System of Moral Philosophy*.

Immanuel Kant, *The True Measure of Forces*.

Moscow University founded.

Rousseau, *Discours sur l'inequalité*.

1756

Arcadia Ulysisponense, Lisbon, founded.

Edmund Burke, *A Vindication of Natural Society*.

Peter Forsskål, *Dubia de principiis philosophiae recentioris*.

Vienna Imperial Observatory founded.

Royal Society of Naples founded.

1757

Ruggiero Boscovich, *Theoria philosophiae naturalis redacta ad unicam legem virium in natura existentium*, propounded an atomic theory.

Diderot, *Entretiens sur Le Fils naturel*.

Albrecht von Haller, *Elementa physiologiae corporis humani* (–1766).

Hume, *The Natural History of Religion; Four Dissertations*.

C. F. Nicolai, *Bibliothek der schönen Wissenschaften*.

1758

Aberdeen Philosophical Society (The Wise Club) founded.

Claude-Adrien Helvétius, *De l'esprit*, published and publicly burned in Paris.

Richard Price, *Review of the Principal Questions and Difficulties in Morals*.

François Quesnay, *Maximes: tableau économique*.

1759

Academy of Science, Munich, founded.

Alembert, *Eléments de philosophie*.

British Museum opened.

Forsskål, *De Libertate civili*.

Lessing, *Die Litteraturbriefe* (–1765).

William Robertson, *History of Scotland during the Reigns of Queen Mary and James VI*.

Adam Smith, *The Theory of Moral Sentiments*.

189

Voltaire, *Candide*.
Wolff, *Theoria generationis*, observed the development of growing plants.

1760
J. H. Lambert, *Photometria*.
Norwegian Royal Society of Sciences founded.

1761
Holbach, *Le Christianisme dévoilé*.
Lord Kames, *An Introduction to the Art of Thinking*.
Rousseau, *Julie ou la nouvelle Héloïse*.

1762
Bibliothèque de l'Université de France, Paris, founded.
El Pansador, rationalist periodical, Madrid.
Kames, *Elements of Criticism*.
Rousseau, *Du contrat social; ou principes du droit politique* and *Emile*.

1763
Justinus Febronius (Montheim), *De statu ecclesiae et legitima potestate Romani pontificis*.
Frederick II the Great established village schools in Prussia.
Voltaire, *Treatise on Tolerance*.

1764
Cesare Beccaria, *Of Crimes and Punishments*.
Il Caffé published in Milan.
Kant, *An Inquiry into the Distinctness of the Fundamental Principles of Natural Theology and Morals*.
Thomas Reid's *An Inquiry into the Human Mind on the Principles of Common Sense* founded the philosophical school of natural realism.
University of Cagliari founded.
Voltaire, *Dictionnaire philosophique*.
J. G. Zimmermann, *On Discovery in Medicine*.

1765
Antonio Genovesi, *On the Lessons of Commerce*.
A. R. J. Turgot, *Reflections on the Formation and Distribution of Wealth*.
Universal German Library, an organ for popular philosophy, edited by C. F. Nicolai, began publication (–1792).

1766
Diderot, *Essai sur la peinture*.
Lessing, *Laokoon*.

1767

Catherine II the Great of Russia, *Nakaz* (1767).
Adam Ferguson, *Essay on the History of Civil Society.*
Moses Mendelssohn, *Phaedon.*
Joseph Priestley, *History of Electricity.*
Société des Economistes, Paris, founded.
Sir James Steuart, *Inquiry into the Principles of Political Economy.*

1768

J. B. Basedow, *Idea of a Humanitarian for Schools.*
Holbach, *Theologie portative.*
Priestley, *Essay on the First Principles of Government.*
François Quesnay, *Physiocratie.*
Royal Academy of Arts, London, founded.

1769

Bonnet, *Palingénésie philosophique* (–1770).
Adam Ferguson, *Institutes of Moral Philosophy.*

1770

Euler, *Introduction to Algebra.*
Fortunato Bartolomeo de Felice, *Dictionnaire raisonné des connaissances humaines* (–1780).
Holbach, *Le système de la nature ou des lois du monde physique et du monde moral,* first blunt denial of any divine plan in nature.
Kant, *De mundi sensibilis et intelligibilis forma et principiis.*
Voltaire, *Questions sur l'Encyclopédie* (–1772).

1771

Encyclopaedia Britannica, first edition.
Pietro Verri, *Meditations on Political Economy.*

1772

Euler, *Lettres à une princesse d'Allemagne,* expounded principles of mechanics, optics, acoustics and astronomy.
J. G. von Herder, *Essay on the Origin of Language,* began the study of comparative philology.
Norske Selskab, Copenhagen, founded.
Priestley, *History of Optics.*
Daniel Rutherford discovered nitrogen.

1773

Lord Monboddo, *Origin of Language* (–1792).

1774

Astronomischer Jahrbuch, Berlin, founded by J. E. Bode.

Pedro Campomanes, *Discourse on the Encouragement of Popular Industry.*

A. L. Lavoisier, *Opuscules physiques et chemiques.*

Philanthropinum, Dessau, founded.

Priestley discovered oxygen, ammonia gas.

Private Learned Society, Prague, founded, later (1784) the Bohemian Society of Sciences and then (1790) the Royal Bohemian Society of Sciences.

Scheele discovered chlorine.

1775

Bohemian Natural History Museum founded by F. J. Kinsky.

J. C. Fabricius, *Systeme entomologiae,* classification of insects.

Hohe Karlsschule, Stuttgart, founded.

Scheele, *Air and Fire.*

A. G. Warner inaugurated modern study of geology.

1776

Jeremy Bentham, *A Fragment on Government.*

Edward Gibbon, *The Decline and Fall of the Roman Empire* (–1788).

The Sect of Illuminati formed in Bavaria; suppressed 1785.

Paine, *Common Sense.*

Richard Price, *Observations on the Nature of Civil Liberty, the Principles of Government, and the Justice and Policy of the War with America.*

Adam Smith, *An Inquiry into the Nature and Causes of the Wealth of Nations.*

University of Zagreb founded.

1777

Priestley, *Disquisitions Relating to Matter and Spirit.*

Scheele prepared hydrogen sulphide.

K. F. Wenzel's work on atomic theory.

1778

Buffon, *Époques de la nature.*

The Newtonian Club, Edinburgh, founded.

1779

C. A. Coulomb investigated laws of friction.

Royal Academy of Sciences, Lisbon, founded.

Horace-Bénédict de Saussure, *Voyage dans les Alpes* (–1796).

1780
Gaetano Filangieri, *Science of Legislation* (–1785).

1781
William Herschel discovered the planet Uranus.
Kant, *Critique of Pure Reason*.
Mendelssohn, *On the Civil Amelioration of the Condition of the Jews*.
J. H. Pestalozzi expounded his educational theory in *Leonard and Gertrude* (–1787).

1782
Royal Irish Academy, Dublin, founded.

1783
Josef Dobrovský, *Scriptores rerum Bohemicarum*.
Herschel, *Motion of the Solar System in Space*.
Kant, *Prolegomena to any Possible Metaphysic*, answered attack on *Critique of Pure Reason*.
Mendelssohn, *Jerusalem*, a plea for freedom of conscience.
F. M. Pagano, *Political Essays* (–1785).
F. M. Pelcl, *Scriptores rerum Bohemicarum* (–1784).
Royal Academy of Edinburgh founded.

1784
Herder, *Ideas towards a Philosophy of History* (–1791).
Kant, *Notion of a Universal History in a Cosmopolitan Sense*.
University of Lwow founded.

1785
Kant, *Fundamental Principles of the Metaphysics of Morals*.
Reid, *Essays on the Intellectual Powers of Man*.

1786
Buffon, *Histoire naturelle des oiseaux*.
Swedish Academy of Arts and Sciences, Stockholm, founded by Gustavus III.
University of Bonn founded.

1787
Lavoisier, *et al., Méthode de nomenclature chimique*.

Torbern Bergman, *Traité des affinities chymiques, ou attractions electives.*

1788
Frederick II the Great, *Oeuvres Posthumes.*
James Hutton, *New Theory of the Earth.*
Kant, *Critique of Practical Reason.*
Joseph-Louis Lagrange, *Mechanique Analitique*, a strictly analytical treatment of mechanics.
Pierre Laplace published his laws of the planetary system.
Reid, *Essays on the Active Powers of Man.*

1789
Bentham, *Introduction to the Principles of Morals and Legislation.*
Antoine Jussieu, *Genera Plantarum*, a modern classification of plants.
Lavoisier, *Traité élémentaire de chimie*, first modern chemical textbook.
Nils von Rosenstein, *Speech about the Enlightenment.*

1790
Burke, *Reflections on the Revolution in France.*
Kant, *Critique of Judgment.*
A. N. Radischev, *A Journey from St. Petersburg to Moscow.*

1791
Darwin, *The Botanic Garden.*
Aloisio Galvani, *De Viribus electricitatis in motu musculari.*
Paine, *The Rights of Man* (–1792).

1792
Stewart, *Elements of the Philosophy of the Human Mind* (–1827)
Mary Wollstonecraft, *Vindication of the Rights of Women.*

1793
Jacques Hébert edited *Père Duchesne*, which advocated atheism.
Kant, *Religion within the Boundaries of Reason.*

1794
Condorcet, *Esquisse d'un tableau historique des progrès de l'esprit humain.*
Darwin, *Zoonomia, or the Laws of Organic Life* (–1796).
Hutton, *An Investigation of the Principles of Knowledge and the Progress of Reason from Sense to Science and Philosophy.*
Paine, *The Age of Reason* (–1795).

1795

Hutton, *Theory of the Earth* (–1797).

G. M. de Jovellanos, *Report on Agrarian Law* pleaded for agricultural reform on liberal economic principles.

4 DEFENCE AND WARFARE

PRINCIPAL EUROPEAN ARMED CONFLICTS

Venetian–Turkish Wars, 1645–70

The Ottoman Sultans had long held the belief that control of the Eastern Mediterranean was incomplete so long as the Venetians held Crete. Thus, when Maltese corsairs based in Venetian ports in Crete captured the wives of Ibrahim I, a Turkish expedition of 50,000 men captured Canea (Aug 1645) and Retino (1646). Siege was laid to Candia in 1645, but the town held out until 1669. Ibrahim was overthrown and killed in 1648, succeeded by his 7-year-old son Mohammed IV. In the same year the Venetians blockaded the Dardanelles, maintaining this blockade in the naval battles of 1649 and 1656, when they briefly threatened Constantinople itself. This led to a major rebuilding of the Turkish navy (1656–7) and the reorganisation of the civilian and military sides of the Ottoman government under the Grand Vizier, Mohammed Koprulu. In the third naval battle of the Dardanelles (1657), the Turks were victorious, regaining control of the Aegean in 1658. Turkish efforts intensified on Crete in 1666. The French sent a force of 7000 men to Candia in 1669 but withdrew in the same year, and Venetian General Francesco Morosini was forced to surrender (27 Sep). In the subsequent treaty, Venice lost much of Dalmatia to Turkey, as well as most of its Aegean islands, and all of Crete excepting three small seaports.

Second Civil War, 1648–52

(a) England, 1648–9

The second Civil War started in March 1648 when dissident Welsh Parliamentarians proclaimed allegiance to Charles I. In July, Cromwell captured their Pembroke Castle stronghold, while Fairfax suppressed simultaneous revolts in Kent and Essex. On 8 Jul the Scots, under James, the Duke of Hamilton, invaded England, only to be defeated by Cromwell at the Battle of Preston (17–19 Aug). On 1 Dec Charles was seized by the army, which intended to bring the king to trial. When Parliament defied the military, Colonel Thomas Pride, by order of the Council of Affairs, forcibly excluded 96 Presbyterian members from the Parliament (Pride's Purge, 6 and 7 Dec) and those permitted to sit (the Rump Parliament) instituted a High Court which tried the king for treason. After a summary trial (20 and 27 Jan) the king was sentenced to death and beheaded at Whitehall (30 Jan). The crown was abolished and a Commonwealth established under military control.

(b) Ireland, 1649–51

On 5 Feb 1649 the Scottish Presbyterians proclaimed Charles II King of Great Britain and the Irish rose in his favour in August under Ormond, and on the 15th of that month Cromwell went to Ireland, subsequently suppressing the rebellion and capturing the principal Catholic-Royalist strongholds at Drogheda (11 Sep), Wexford (11 Oct) and Conmel (9 May 1650). Cromwell then returned to London leaving Ireton to complete his work. Two years later (May 1652) the last Royalist stronghold at Galway surrendered to the English Parliamentary army, ending the Royalist resistance in Ireland.

(c) Scotland, 1650–1

In Scotland, Montrose arrived in 1650 with a Royalist mercenary force from France, but was defeated by the Scots at Carbiesdale (27 Apr 1650) and executed (21 May). On 23 Jun Charles II landed in Scotland (and was crowned on 1 Jan 1651). Cromwell, having been installed as commander-in-chief, defeated the Scots under David Leslie at the Battle of Dunbar (3 Sep 1650), and on 2 Aug 1651 took Perth, then pursued the king and completely defeated the royal army at the Battle of Worcester (3 Sep 1651). Charles, in disguise, escaped to France, and the Civil Wars were ended.

The Fronde, 1648–53

Resentment of the people and nobles against royal power and taxation under Richelieu and Mazarin led to full-scale revolt immediately the Thirty Years' War was over. The Frondes of 1648–9 and 1650–3 constituted the most serious revolt against the central government during the *ancien regime*. The first or parlementaire Fronde began on 15 Jan 1648. Six months later, on 12 Jul, demands of the Paris parlement were rejected by Anne and Mazarin. From then until December there was unrest and rioting in Paris. On 15 Jan 1649, as Mazarin prepared to repudiate his concessions made at a conference between royal and parlementaire representatives (25 Sep to 4 Oct 1648), civil war broke out with many nobles on the rebel side. The Great Condé encircled the capital, captured the fortress of Charenton, and laid seige to the city (Jan–Feb 1649). Renewed threats of a Spanish invasion and an unsuccessful royal siege brought the two sides to terms, embodied in the Peace of Rueil (11 Mar 1649). Parlement dismissed its troops, Mazarin was

197

reinstated and the queen declared a general amnesty. Following the court's return to Paris in Aug 1649, the uneasy alliance between Condé and Mazarin broke down, leading to the Fronde of the princes. Condé was imprisoned on 18 Jan 1650, and Turenne took over the military leadership of the Fronde. A planned invasion of France by a joint Spanish-Frondist army was unsuccessful and Turenne was finally defeated at the Battle of Champ Blanc (15 Oct 1650). On 15 Feb 1651, the princes were released from prison and in Sep 1651 the civil war was renewed. Mazarin returned to Paris from Germany in Dec 1651, but the rival armies under Condé and Turenne brought chaos to the capital. The rebellion finally collapsed after Turenne outmanoeuvred superior forces of the Frondeurs, Spanish and Lorrainers. This was followed by Louis XIV's re-entry into Paris on 21 Oct followed by Mazarin on 3 Feb 1653. Condé had now joined the Spaniards, and with the remnants of aristocratic opposition in Bordeaux overwhelmed by the reassertion of royal authority (Jul–Aug 1653), the Fronde was over.

Polish-Cossack War, 1648–54

The reign of John II Casimir (1648–68) was marked by grave internal disturbances, e.g. the uprising of the Ukranian Cossacks led by Bogdan Chmielnicki which devastated and depopulated the Ukraine. After Cossack victories at the Battles of Zolte Wody, Korsun and Piławce in 1648–9, Poland was on the defensive. A temporary peace in 1649 at Zborów was ended at the Battle of Beresteczko (28–30 Jun 1651) at which 34,000 Poles under Casimir decisively defeated 200,000 Cossacks, Lithuanians and Tartars under Chmielnicki. Though the Cossacks made peace at the Treaty of Biala Cerkew (Jun 1651), Chmielnicki, with a few followers, continued the war. Under the Treaty of Pereiaslavl in May 1654, the Cossacks placed the Ukraine under the protection of Tsar Alexis, thus precipitating a prolonged conflict between Russia and Poland for possession of the Ukraine.

First Anglo-Dutch War, 1652–4

The First Anglo-Dutch War was essentially a naval conflict which arose primarily from maritime competition, particularly in respect to the East Indies trade. War broke out (8 Jul 1652) as a result of the First Navigation Act (9 Oct 1651), which helped the British merchant navy to gain supremacy over the Dutch. The British commanders were Blake and Monck: The Dutch, Tromp and Ruyter. The British had already defeated the Dutch off The Downs (28 Jul 1652) and, later, off Portland (18 Feb 1653), North Foreland (2–3 Jun 1653), and, most significantly, Texel (31 Jul 1653). The peace Treaty of Westminster (5 Apr 1654) ended the First Anglo-Dutch War with the Dutch agreeing to recognise the Navigation Acts.

Franco-Spanish War, 1653–9

Although the Peace of Westphalia ended the war between France and the Empire, it did not terminate the struggle between France and Spain. In 1653 Condé, now a Spanish generalissimo, invaded France and threatened Paris, which was saved by the strategy of Turenne. In a war of manoeuvre and siege in northern France, Turenne won a victory at Arras (25 Aug 1654), but was defeated at Lalenciennes (16 Jul 1656). The following year Britain and France concluded a treaty of alliance (Treaty of Paris, 23 Mar 1647) whereby their forces were to attack jointly the coast towns of Graveline (where the Spanish were defeated 24 Aug 1658), Dunkirk (lost by Spain on 25 Jun 1658 following the Anglo-French victory at the Battle of the Dunes, 13 Jun 1658) and Mardyke (captured by the French under Turenne on 3 Oct 1657). On 7 Nov 1659, the Peace of the Pyrenees was signed, ending the final phase of the Thirty Years' War and marking the end of Spanish hegemony in Europe.

Russo-Polish Wars, 1654–67

(a) 1654–6

Fought for the possession of the Ukraine after the Cossack leader, Bogdan Chmielnicki, offered to surrender the Ukraine to Tsar Alexis. Smolensk was captured by Alexis after a three-month siege (2 Jul–26 Sep 1654), and a smaller Russian force simultaneously invaded the Ukraine and occupied Kiev. The Polish staged a successful counter-offensive in Jan 1655, at the Battle of Okhmativ, but Russia soon resumed offensives in Lithuania (May 1655), facilitated by Swedish attacks on Poland from Livonia. By October 1655 Russo-Cossack forces reoccupied most of the Ukraine, but after the defeat and capture of Chmielnicki at Zolozce (Nov 1655) by Poland's ally, Crimean Khan Mahmet Girei, the Russians withdrew to the north. The war was terminated by a three-year truce and an anti-Swedish alliance between Russia and Poland at the Treaty of Vilna (3 Nov 1656).

(b) 1658–67

Russia resumed hostilities with the expiration of the Russo-Polish truce of Nimieza. The Russian Prince Trubetskoi invaded the Ukraine, but was severely beaten by the Ukrainian John Wykowski at the Battle of Konotop (8 Jul 1659). In the following year the Poles, freed by the peace with Sweden, liberated Lithuania and scored further victories at the Battle of Lubar, with the assistance of the Tartars, and at the Battle of Slobodyszcze. Several years of sporadic frontier fighting followed (1661–7), and, on 20 Jan 1667, the Treaty of Andruszov (Andrusovo) was signed, ending the Thirteen Years' War, whereby Poland ceded Smolensk and Kiev to Russia.

First Northern War, 1655-60

In an attempt to extend Sweden's possessions on the southern Baltic coast, Charles X declared war on Poland in Jul 1655. His pretext was the failure of John Casimir to recognise his own special status of 'Protector of Poland'. In fact, Charles was encouraged in his declaration of war by the internal divisions and weakness of Poland and by Russia's invasion of Poland and the capture of Smolensk in Sep 1654. Charles defeated Casimir (23 Aug 1655) who fled to Silesia, took Warsaw (30 Aug) and, later, Cracow (8 Oct). The Swedes, allied with the Elector of Brandenburg (Treaty of Königsberg, 17 Jan 1656, and Treaty of Marienberg, 25 Jun 1656), invaded Poland and won a great battle at Warsaw (29-31 Jul 1656), whereupon Russia (3 Nov 1656), the Empire (1 Dec 1656) and Denmark (1 Jun 1657) came to the aid of Poland. On 19 Sep 1657, Poland renounced sovereignty of Prussia on behalf of Brandenburg under the Treaty of Wehlau and by the Treaty of Bromberg (6 Nov 1657), Brandenburg allied with Poland against Sweden. In the spring of 1657, the Swedes withdrew from Poland. In Jul, Charles invaded mainland Denmark and in Jan 1658, Denmark sued for peace. The Treaty of Roskilde was signed on 8 Mar 1658 between the two countries, but war was resumed in June when Charles invaded Denmark for a second time. The siege of Copenhagen commenced on 11 Aug 1658, but a national patriotic movement helped the city withstand the Swedish assault, aided by the intervention of a Dutch fleet (11 Oct 1659) which caused Charles to withdraw. The Danes defeated the Swedes at the Battle of Nyborg (Nov 1659) and the death of Charles (13 Feb 1660) facilitated the Treaty of Oliva (3 May 1660), ending war between Brandenburg, Poland, Austria and Sweden. By its terms, John Casimir abandoned his claims to the Swedish throne and ceded Livonia to Sweden. By the Treaty of Copenhagen (6 Jun 1660), the war was ended between Sweden and Denmark and the Baltic was opened to foreign warships. The Treaty of Kardis (21 Jun 1661) confirmed the *status quo ante bellum* between Sweden, Poland and Austria and ended the Northern War.

Second Anglo-Dutch War, 1665-7

The Second Anglo-Dutch War was again the result of commercial competition exacerbated by the British attack (Oct 1663) on the source of the Dutch slave trade, the West African ports, and the seizure of New Amsterdam, surrendered on 7 Sep 1664. War was declared on 4 Mar 1665, following the Dutch recapture of the African ports and Michael de Ruyter's attack on Barbados. On 3 Jun 1665, the Dutch were defeated by the British fleet off Lowestoft.

As a result of the Battle of Bergen (13 Aug 1665), during which the Danes repulsed Edward Montagu, in pursuit of a Dutch merchant convoy, Britain declared war on Denmark. France entered the war against Britain on 26 Jan

1666. Monck was beaten by de Ruyter and De Witt off the North Foreland (1–4 Jun 1666), but the Dutch were later defeated at the same place (25 Jul 1666). However, the Dutch rallied, burnt Sheerness, and entered the Medway (13 Jun 1667), causing Britain to seek peace in earnest. The terms of the treaty of Breda (21 Jul 1667) between England, Holland, France and Denmark was a standoff, slightly in favour of the Dutch, who did, however, acknowledge British possession of New Amsterdam.

War of Devolution, 1667–8

After the death of his father-in-law, Philip IV of Spain, Louis XIV demanded the inheritance right of devolution, or succession, and laid claim to the whole of the Spanish Netherlands. Spain refused, and Turenne invaded the Spanish Netherlands (24 May 1667), conquering a part of Flanders and Hainault. Alarmed by these successes, the Dutch joined Britain in an alliance (23 Jan 1668), to which Sweden acceded (2 May 1668), to form the Triple Alliance. At about the same time, Louis signed a secret treaty with the Emperor Leopold I for the future partition of the Spanish Empire in the event of the death of Charles II without heirs (19 Jan 1668). This prospect induced Louis, after Condé, leading French troops, invaded Franche-Comté (13 Feb 1668), to sign the Treaty of Aix-la-Chapelle (2 May 1668), restoring Franche–Comté to Spain and retaining the frontier fortresses.

Polish–Turkish War, 1671–6

As a result of Polish efforts to suppress the Cossack revolt, Turkey demanded cession of the Ukraine. When Poland refused, Sultan Mohammed IV declared war (9 Dec 1671). In the summer of 1672 Grand Vizier Ahmed invaded Poland, besieging Kamieniec (Aug 1672) and taking Lublin (Sep 1672), which led to the Treaty of Buczácz (18 Oct 1672), whereby the Polish king, Michael Wiśniowiecki, ceded Podolia and the western Ukraine. The Polish *diet* refused to ratify the treaty and the Poles resumed the struggle under the leadership of John Sobieski, who rallied Poland and was victorious against the Turks at Chocim (11 Nov 1673) and Lwów (24 Aug 1675). Following the inconclusive Battle of Zurawno (Sep–Oct 1676), the Treaty of Zurawno was signed (27 Oct) whereby the Turks agreed to the return of the western Ukraine to Poland and the division of Podolia.

Third Anglo-Dutch War, 1672–4

This was a deliberately provoked war of aggression by Britain and France which followed the Treaty of Dover (1 Jun 1670), in which Charles II agreed to join Louis XIV in an attack on Holland. Britain declared war on 17 Mar, France on 28 Mar. A naval victory was scored by Britain at Southwold Bay (28 May 1672), at which Lord Sandwich was killed, followed by a lull in naval actions and a successful counter-attack by de Ruyter against the

British under Prince Rupert at the Battle of Schoonveldt Channel (28 May 1673). De Ruyter frustrated allied plans for a seaborne invasion at the Battle of Texel (11 Aug 1673) and the British made peace with Holland at the Treaty of Westminster (19 Feb 1674). Louis then withdrew from Holland to concentrate on the Spanish Netherlands and Franche-Comté, and to protect Alsace from the Germans, as the Elector of Brandenburg and a number of other princes had entered the war against France in 1674. The Treaty of Nijmegen (10 Aug 1679) brought peace between France and Holland.

Franco-Dutch War, 1672–8
Determined to isolate Holland from her allies, Louis XIV secured the disruption of the Triple Alliance by the secret Treaty of Dover with Charles II of England (1 Jun 1670). A similar treaty was concluded with Sweden (14 Apr 1672), as well as treaties with Cologne and Münster. The conquest of southern Holland was quickly accomplished (May–Jun, 1672). Although the French advance threatened Amsterdam, the sluices were opened in Holland to save that city from the French (15 Jun 1672). Shortly after, an alliance was signed between Brandenburg and Emperor Leopold I to prevent extension of French power (23 Jun 1672). Frederick William of Brandenburg later concluded the separate peace of Vossem with France (6 Jun 1673) whereby the Great Elector promised not to support any enemies of Louis XIV. In Jan 1674, Denmark joined the coalition against France. By the Treaty of Westminster (19 Feb 1674) Brandenburg withdrew from the war and made peace with the allies. Louis then withdrew from Holland so as to concentrate on the Spanish Netherlands and Franche-Comté, conquering the latter in May–Jun 1674. Turenne was given the mission of protecting Alsace (14 Jun 1674–27 Jul 1675), but fell at Sasbach, in Baden (27 Jul 1675). There were naval successes in the Mediterranean against the Dutch and Spanish in 1676 and a successful assault on besieged Valenciennes in 1677 (17 Mar). The French capture of Ghent (Mar 1678) and Ypres (Mar 1678) led to the treaties of Nijmegen, between France and Holland (10 Aug 1678) whereby Holland pledged its neutrality for the return of its territories, between France and Spain (17 Sep 1678) whereby Spain ceded Franche-Comté and sixteen Flemish towns and France restored Charleroi, and between France and the Empire (5 Feb 1679) whereby Louis obtained Freiburg and Breisach, but restored Philipsburg. At the Peace of Fontaine-bleau (2 Sep 1679) between Denmark and Sweden, Denmark restored all her conquests. Formal peace was signed by the Treaty of Lund (26 Sep 1679). Louis XIV also forced the Elector of Brandenburg to conclude the Treaty of St Germain-en-Laye (29 Jun 1679), whereby the Elector surrendered nearly all his conquests in Pomerania to Sweden.

Habsburg–Ottoman Wars, 1682–99

During most of the 17th century, Hungary was the main battleground in the occasional but continuing struggle between the Habsburg and Ottoman Empires. In 1682, the leaders of an anti-Habsburg Hungarian nationalist movement, Nicholas Zrinyi and Count Imre Thököly, sought Ottoman assistance in return for promises to accept the sultan's suzerainty. Kara Mustafa proceeded to conquer all of upper Hungary during the late summer of 1682 and recognised Thököly as king of Hungary in December of the same year. The Emperor formed a new European coalition to resist the threat, his most important ally being John Sobieski of Poland. The Ottoman advance on Vienna began in later Jun 1683, and the Habsburg capital was put under siege on 17 Jul. Heavy fortifications and the last-minute arrival of Sobieski (Aug 1683) compelled the Turks to retire on 12 Sep 1683. Sobieski pursued the Turks, liberating Gran in Oct 1683 and much of northwest Hungary. Kara Mustafa was dismissed and executed at Belgrade (15 Dec 1683). Ottoman morale and organisation was now shattered. Pest and most of northern Hungary fell during the summers of 1684 and 1685, followed by Buda on 2 Sep 1686. During the summer of 1688, the Habsburgs crossed the Danube and took Belgrade (6 Sep 1688). In an astonishing turnabout during the winter of 1689–90, the Ottomans drove the Habsburgs back across the Danube. Between Aug and Oct 1690, Serbia was reconquered, but after the Battle of Szalánkemen (19 Aug 1691) and the defeat of Thököly and the new Turkish Grand Vizier, Mustafa Koprulu, Transylvania was firmly in Habsburg hands. Inconclusive frontier campaigns were fought for the next five years, but at the Battle of Zenta in 1697, Prince Eugene of Savoy attacked and practically annihilated the Turkish army. At the Peace of Karlowitz (26 Jan 1699), Austria received all of Hungary and Transylvania except the Banat. Poland recovered Podolia, Venice obtained the Peloponnesus and much of Dalmatia, and Turkey retained Belgrade.

Glorious Revolution, 1685–9

James II, a Catholic, succeeded to the throne on 6 Feb 1685. On 6 Jul 1685, the Duke of Monmouth lead a Protestant revolt as pretender to the English throne at Sedgemoor but was repulsed, captured and beheaded. English Protestants resented James's attempts to restore Catholicism to equality (1685–8). An invitation by seven Tory and Anglican leaders was dispatched to William of Orange, Stadholder of the Netherlands and married to Mary, daughter of James II, to save England from Catholic tyranny. William accepted the invitation, his real purpose being to bring England into the struggle against Louis XIV begun by the League of Augsburg, and landed at Torbay (5 Nov 1688). James fled to France (25 Dec 1688) and William and Mary were proclaimed joint sovereigns of England (12 Feb 1689).

War of the League of Augsburg, 1688–97

The League of Augsburg was a defensive alliance signed on 9 Jul 1686 by the Emperor Leopold I, the kings of Sweden and Spain and the Electors of Bavaria, Saxony and the Palatinate. William III was instrumental in forming this league, provoked by the *réunion* policy of Louis XIV. Savoy, in 1687, along with England and the United Provinces (12 May 1689), later joined the league, thus forming the Grand Alliance of 1689. This alliance opposed France in the War of the League of Augsburg, which began (24 Sep 1688) when Louis XIV invaded the Rhenish Palatinate (24 Sep 1688) to enforce a questionable claim to that district. The parallel conflict in the American colonies was called King William's War (1689–99), which had great colonial and commercial implications. The War of the League of Augsburg was the first major conflict in modern times in which sea power was a decisive factor. Although the French navy at first successfully challenged English and Dutch control of the Channel, its expedition to Ireland to aid James II proved disastrous, as William III defeated the Jacobite forces in the Battle of the Boyne (1 Jul 1690). The English and Dutch decisively defeated a French fleet at La Hague (19 May 1692), but the English under William III were defeated by French troops led by the Duke of Luxembourg at Steenkerke (3 Aug 1692) and at Neerwinden (29 Jul 1693). Elsewhere, Marshal Catinat conquered Savoy (Aug–Sep 1690) and Nice (Mar 1691) and Vendôme took Barcelona (Aug 1697), but English naval power prevented Louis from exploiting his land victories in that area. The Duke of Savoy reached an accord with Louis on 29 Jul 1696, and French conquests were restored to Savoy. By the Treaty of Ryswick (20 Sep–30 Oct 1697) Louis XIV accepted William III as king of England; France, Spain, England, Holland and the German principalities agreed to restore all territories taken since the Treaty of Nijmegen (1678).

War of the English Succession, 1689–91

This is the British phase of the continental War of the League of Augsburg (1688–97). It resulted from James II's attempt to regain the English throne from William III, and from Louis XIV's attempt to divert William from operations in Flanders, as well as by Irish support for James II. James landed in Ireland on 12 Mar 1689, besieged the Protestant town of Londonderry (20 Apr–30 Jul 1689), which was finally relieved by Kirke. In Scotland, Claverhouse defeated the Whig general Mackay at the Battle of Killiecrankie (17 Jul 1689), but fell on the field. In Mar 1690, William went to Ireland and defeated James at the Battle of the Boyne (1 Jul 1690). James fled to France, while his army continued the war for another year. At the Battle of Aughrim (12 Jul 1691), Godert de Ginkel led a Williamite army against an Irish–French force. The allied effort collapsed, and the defeat ended James's Irish aspirations, as well as the war – excepting for the continuing siege of Limerick. The liberal terms of the surrender of Limerick (3 Oct 1691), though ratified by the English Parliament, were rejected by the predominantly Protestant Irish assembly, who enacted a harshly anti-Catholic penal code.

Great Northern War, 1700–21

This was caused by the common opposition of Peter I of Russia, Augustus II of Poland (also Elector of Saxony) and Frederick IV of Denmark to Swedish supremacy in the Baltic. The Treaty of Preobrazhenskoe was signed between the three sovereigns in the autumn of 1699 (22 Nov), and in the next year the war opened with an invasion of Schleswig by the Danes (Apr 1700) and of Livonia by Augustus's Saxon troops (Jun 1700). Charles replied by landing near Copenhagen (4 Aug 1700) with British and Dutch naval support and driving the Danes out of the war (Treaty of Travendal, 18 Aug 1700). He then defeated the Russians at Narva (20 Nov 1700) and in the following year expelled the Saxons from Livonia (Battle of Riga, 17 Jun 1701) and annexed and occupied Courland following the Battle of Dunamunde (9 Jul 1701). In 1702 Charles seized Cracow (Battle of Kliszów, 2 Jul 1702) and spent the next several years attempting to defeat Augustus II, who was at last compelled to sign the Treaty of Altranstädt (24 Sep 1706). The second phase of the war opened with Charles's invasion of Russia (1 Jan 1708). At the Battle of Poltava, the Russian army completely defeated the Swedes (8 Jul 1709) and Charles fled to Turkey. Two years later he induced the Porte to declare war against Peter, who quickly met their demands at the peace of the Pruth (21 Jul 1711). Charles, indignant at this treaty, remained in Turkey for a further three years. When he returned to Sweden in 1714 the situation had deteriorated past retrieving and he fell at Fredrikshall on 11 Dec 1718. Sweden then tried to make peace with her other enemies at Russia's expense (Treaty of Stockholm with Hanover, 20 Nov 1719; Treaty of Stockholm with Prussia, 1 Feb 1720; Treaty of Frederiksborg with Denmark, 3 Jul 1720), but received no effective help, forcing her to accept the Treaty of Nystad (10 Sep 1721). By the cession of Livonia, Estonia, Ingria and part of Finland, Sweden acknowledged her displacement as a great power. The other main result of the war was Russia's emergence as a great European power.

War of the Spanish Succession, 1701–14

The origins of the war are to be found in the rival claimants disputing the inheritance of the childless Charles II, last of the Spanish Habsburg line, who died on 1 Nov 1700. The leaders of the two European coalitions, Louis XIV and William III, attempted to prevent a war by negotiating the Partition treaties of 11 Oct 1698 and 25 Mar 1700. But by accepting the last will of Charles II, which bequeathed the entire Empire to Philip of Anjou, grandson of Louis XIV, the latter aroused the hostility of William III. Only the Habsburg Emperor, Leopold I, whose son Archduke Charles was a rival claimant, refused to recognise Philip V as King of Spain. But by a series of blunders Louis caused the formation of the Grand Alliance at the Treaty of the Hague (7 Sep 1701), by which Britain, Holland and the Emperor allied against France. This coalition was extended in 1703 to include Portugal (16 May 1703) and Savoy (4 Nov 1703). Its objectives were the destruction of French hegemony and the expulsion of Philip from Spain. In the end, the coalition succeeded only in its first objective. The war commenced in Feb 1701 when Philip of Anjou entered Madrid as Philip V of Spain while French troops also occupied Southern Spanish Netherlands. For the first few years, the war was waged almost exclusively in Italy, Flanders and the Americas (Queen Anne's War, 1702-13). In May 1704 Archduke Charles entered Lisbon with British and Dutch troops and was there proclaimed King of Spain; Portugal declared herself to be an ally and entered the war alongside the enemies of France. On 13 Aug 1704, Marlborough and Prince Eugène defeated the French and Bavarians at Blenheim. In the following year the British navy took Barcelona (4 Oct) and Charles III was recognised in Catalonia, Valencia and Aragon. Thenceforward the Peninsula was the centre of the war, which continued until 1714 with great vicissitudes for the cause of Philip V, whose French and Spanish troops were victorious at Almanza (14 Apr 1707), Brihuega (9 Dec 1710) and Villa Viciosa (10 Dec 1710), but were routed at Almenara (27 Jul 1710) and Saragossa (20 Aug 1710). By the end of 1710, the Bourbon forces held all of Spain, save Catalonia. The allies had been generally victorious in the broader European struggle, but all participants were exhausted and increasingly interested in a solution to the conflict. On 12 Jan 1712, a Peace Congress opened at Utrecht. In the following year, France and Britain, the United Provinces, Savoy, Portugal and Prussia signed the Peace of Utrecht (31 Mar), which divided the Spanish inheritance somewhat along the lines of the prewar parition agreements. This was followed up by peace treaties between Britain and Spain (13 Jun 1713), the latter ceding Gibraltar and Minorca, and, on 26 Jun 1714, Spain and the United Provinces, which was to be recognised as a 'most favoured nation' for trade, apart from the Assiento, and Spain and Portugal on 6 Feb 1715.

Austro-Turkish War, 1716-18

This began on 13 Apr 1716, when the Austrian Emperor Charles VI renewed his alliance with Venice, already at war with Turkey since 9 Dec 1714. When Charles VI demanded their evacuation of the Balkans, the Turks reacted by declaring war on Austria. Prince Eugene inflicted a crushing defeat upon the Turks at the Battle of Peterwardein (5 Aug 1716), then captured Temesvár, the last Turkish stronghold in Hungary (13 Oct

1716) and relieved the whole of southeastern Hungary. On 16 Aug 1717, Prince Eugene defeated the Turks at Belgrade, which he subsequently occupied. The war ended with the Treaty of Passarowitz (21 Jul 1718), whereby Austria retained Belgrade, thus completing the possession of Hungary, and kept the Banat of Temesvár and part of Serbia. Venice relinquished the Morea, but was given new coastal strongholds in Albania and Dalmatia.

War of the Quadruple Alliance, 1718–20

The Quadruple Alliance was signed between France, Austria, Britain and the United Provinces (in name only) on 2 Aug 1718 to counteract the attempts of Philip V of Spain to overturn the peace settlements of Utrecht (11 Apr 1713) and Rastatt (7 Mar 1714). Philip, grandson of Louis XIV, hoped to gain the crown of France. These ambitions were encouraged by his powerful Italian minister Cardinal Alberoni, whose plans – which finally came to nothing – included an alliance with Russia, Sweden and Turkey against Austria, and the removal of Philip of Orleans as Regent of France. War was declared on 17 Dec 1718. Spain had suffered a severe defeat at the naval battle of Cape Passaro (31 Jul 1718), and the British fleet later landed an Austrian force in Sicily, capturing Messina (Oct 1719), while the French invaded the Basque country and Catalonia (Apr 1719). In Dec 1719, Alberoni was dismissed, and the war was concluded by the Treaty of the Hague (17 Feb 1720) whereby Philip abandoned his claims to the French throne, to Sardinia and Sicily, and to his former possessions in Italy, though the dukedoms of Parma, Piacenza and Tuscany were later allowed to revert to his son (later Charles III of Spain).

War of the Polish Succession, 1733–8

This European conflict was the result of rival claimants to the Polish throne, which became vacant on the death of Augustus II (1 Feb 1733). Stanislas Leszczynski, Louis XV's father-in-law, was supported by France, Spain and Savoy–Sardinia. Frederick Augustus II, Elector of Saxony and son of the late king, was supported by Russia and Austria. The first engagement of the war took place when an army of 30,000 Russians, later joined by 10,000 Saxons, besieged and took Danzig (Oct 1733–30 Jun 1734). The principal theatre of conflict then shifted to Italy, where the Austrians were defeated at Parma (29 Jun 1734), and throughout Italy (1734–5), losing everything except Milan. There was also some action on the Upper Rhine, where Prince Eugene was unsuccessful in preventing the French from taking Philipsburg (Jun–Jul 1734). Though the fighting largely ceased by 1735, several years of negotiations followed before the signing of the Treaty of Vienna (18 Nov 1738), which gave the Polish throne to Augustus III.

207

Austro–Russian–Turkish War, 1736–9

This grew out of the War of the Polish Succession (1733–8) when France urged Turkey to enter the war of the Ottoman Empire's traditional enemies, Austria and Russia. Turkey remained out of the conflict until she had concluded an ongoing war against Persia. By this time the War of the Polish Succession was also over, and a new war resulted when Russia, learning of Turkish intentions and anxious to gain revenge for the Treaty of Pruth (21 Jul 1711), attacked Turkey, with the support of the Emperor Charles VI, in order to regain Azov, which succumbed on 1 Jul 1736. Operations were conducted in Moldavia, the Balkans and the Ukraine, with the Russians gaining the upper hand. Alarmed by Russia's success, the Austrians concluded with Turkey the Treaty of Belgrade (18 Sep 1739), giving up Serbia and Belgrade. The Russians, deserted by Austria, made peace with the Treaty of Nissa (3 Oct 1739), agreeing to raze the fortifications of Azov and not to build a fleet on the Black Sea.

War of the Austrian Succession, 1740–8

When, on the death of Emperor Charles VI (20 Oct 1740), Maria Theresa inherited the Habsburg Empire in accordance with the Pragmatic Sanction (19 Apr 1713), Frederick II of Prussia entered into an alliance with Bavaria and France. The basis of this coalition was the French desire for the Austrian Netherlands, the prospect of the imperial title for the Bavarian Elector, Charles Albert, and the Austrian province of Silesia for Prussia. However, the war was not confined to these states. Britain supported Maria Theresa as it opposed French expansion in the Netherlands (Britain and France again collided in King George's War, 1744–8, the North American version of the War of the Austrian Succession) and was at war with Spain over economic and imperial matters (the War of Jenkins' Ear, 1739–43, which became absorbed into the larger conflict). Spain also joined France in hope of regaining some of her lost position in Italy. In addition, Saxony and Sardinia joined the opponents of Austria, while the United Provinces allied with Maria Theresa and Britain. Frederick was initially successful in Silesia, invaded on 16 Dec 1740 and secured in 1742 under the terms of the Peace of Berlin (28 Jul 1742), which ended the first Silesian War and, temporarily, Frederick's participation in the War of the Austrian Succession. But after operations in Bohemia and South Germany, in the course of which Maria Theresa and her allies were successful against the French and Bavarians at the battles of Braunau (9 May 1743) and Dettingen (27 Jun 1743), the French officially entered the conflict, declaring war on Maria Theresa on 26 Apr 1744. Frederick, in alliance with France, now rejoined the war. Thus began the second Silesian War, which opened with Frederick's invasion of Saxony (15 Aug 1744). On 28 Dec 1744, at Warsaw, the day after Bamberg, Austria, Saxony, Britain and the United Provinces united themselves against France, Bavaria and Prussia in the Quadruple Alliance. Peace

208

between Austria and Bavaria was later made at the Treaty of Füssen (22 Apr 1745), when Maximilian Joseph succeeded Charles VII as Elector of Bavaria and renounced his claim to the Austrian throne. In return, Maria Theresa restored all the young Elector's possessions which the Austrians had seized. Frederick, in the north, was now completely isolated from his only allies, the French, in the south. The latter scored successes in Flanders, overrunning the entire country following the Battle of Fontenoy (10 May 1745), while Frederick scored successes at the battles of Hohenfriedberg (4 Jun 1745), Sohr (30 Sep 1745), Hennersdorf (23–4 Nov 1745) and Görlitz (25 Nov 1745), forcing Maria Theresa to make peace (the Treaty of Dresden, 25 Dec 1745), recognising Frederick's conquest of Silesia while he in turn recognised the election of her husband, Francis Stephen, as Emperor. The war continued, inconclusively, for three years, with campaigns in the Netherlands (1746–8), Italy (1741–8), and at sea, when the British gained the more important victories, as against a combined Franco-Spanish fleet at the Battle of Toulon (11 Feb 1744). The war was closed by the Treaty of Aix-la-Chapelle (7 Oct 1748). Silesia was definitely confirmed to Frederick, and Francis of Lorraine became Emperor. The French evacuated the Austrian Netherlands, recognised George II as King of Great Britain and transferred Madras to Britain in exchange for Louisburg (Cape Breton Island).

Jacobite Rebellion, 1745–6

A rebellion in Scotland inspired by the Young Pretender, Prince Charles Edward Stuart, against the Hanoverian rule in Scotland and England. On 3 Aug 1745, 'Bonnie Prince Charles' arrived, with only seven companions and a few thousand weapons, in the Hebrides. After some hesitation the Cameron and MacDonald clans joined him and he marched on Edinburgh (Aug–Sep 1745), capturing the city on 11 Sep 1745, and driving back a government army under Sir John Cope at Prestonpans (21 Sep 1745). Hoping for a rising of English Stuart supporters and direct aid from France, Charles and Lord George Murray invaded England (Nov–Dec 1745), but was disappointed on both counts, despite capturing Carlisle (9–15 Sep 1745) and marching triumphant into Manchester (28 Nov 1745) and on to Derby (4 Dec 1745). Charles retreated north, but in January had gathered sufficient Highland reinforcements to defeat a government army at Falkirk (17 Jan 1746). However, the Duke of Cumberland pursued him through the Highlands and on 16 Apr 1746, inflicted the terrible defeat of Culloden. Charles finally returned to France (20 Sep 1746) while the English undertook a savage pacification of the Highlands.

Seven Years' War, 1756–63

Also called the Third Silesian War, this was a general European conflict which grew out of the struggle for supremacy in Germany between Prussia under Frederick II the Great and Austria under Maria Theresa, and the undeclared worldwide struggle between France and Britain for control of North America (the French and Indian Wars, 1754–63) and India (Bengal Wars, 1756–63). Open hostilities were preceded by the Treaty of Westminster between Britain and Prussia (16 Jan 1756) by which Frederick II guaranteed the neutrality of Hanover, and, on 1 May 1756, by the Alliance of Versailles between Austria and France, which constitutes the Diplomatic Revolution (later joined by Russia, Sweden, Saxony, and, in 1761, Spain). The immediate cause of the war was Frederick's invasion of Saxony (29 Aug 1756) on the pretext of having learnt of the Franco-Austrian alliance. In a war fought mainly in East Europe, the allies were ultimately defeated and the *status quo ante* was restored. At the start of the war, Frederick capitalised on the advantage of seizing the initiative, defeating the Austrians at the Battle of Lobositz (1 Oct 1756), but the far superior numbers of his enemies forced him to withdraw from Bohemia following the Battle of Kolin (18 Jun 1757). Frederick's outstanding generalship enabled him to defeat the French at Rossbach (5 Nov 1757), the Austrians at Leuthen (5 Dec 1757) and the Russians at Zorndorf (25 Aug 1758). But setbacks followed at Hochkirch (14 Oct 1758) and Kunersdorf (12 Aug 1759). During the last years of the war, the Prussians were on the defensive. Victories at Liegnitz (15 Aug 1760) and Torgau (3 Nov 1760) were more than offset by such coalition successes as the Russian burning of Berlin (9 Oct 1760) and their serious incursions into Prussian territory. When all seemed lost, Elizabeth of Russia died (5 Jan 1762), and Peter III, her successor, immediately began peace negotiations. He was assassinated on 17 Jul 1762, and was succeeded by Catherine II, and although she broke off the alliance with Prussia she did not renew the war. Inconclusive fighting preceded the armistice agreements of late 1762, which were followed by the peace treaties of 1763. The overseas campaigns between Britain and France, aided by Spain, were ended by the Peace of Paris (10 Feb 1763), which dealt primarily with colonial affairs and made Britain the pre-eminent colonial power. Maria Theresa of Austria concluded peace terms with Prussia at Hubertusburg (15 Feb 1763), which confirmed Prussia as a major European force and restored the prewar *status quo*.

Russo-Turkish Wars, 1768–74, 1787–92
These wars resulted from a desire by Russia to dominate the Balkans for strategic, commercial and ideological reasons. War was first declared on 4 Oct 1768 by Sultan Mustapha when the Russians invaded Bessarabia in pursuit of fugitive Poles and destroyed the Turkish town of Balta. The generals of Catherine the Great overran Moldavia and Wallachia in 1769 and sent agents to Greece to raise a revolt in 1770 which was officered by Russians. At the Battle of Chesme (6 Jul 1770) a Russian fleet, officered by

Britain, defeated a Turkish fleet. In June of the following year, the Russians conquered the Crimea. Alarmed by Russian successes, Frederick the Great offered mediation and arranged the first partition of Poland (5 Aug 1772), but the war continued until the Russians were diverted by the great revolt of the Pretender, Pugachev, in southeast Russia (16 Oct 1773), which checked the Russian advance in Turkey. At the Treaty of Kutchuk-Kainardzhi (21 Jul 1774), Turkey ceded to Russia the Crimea and the mouth of River Dnieper, granting her full navigation for trade in Turkish waters and promising to protect Christians in Constantinople. The war of 1787–92, declared by Turkey on 10 Aug 1787, resulted from Turkish intrigues with the Crimean Tartars. The Austrians, who signed a defensive treaty with Catherine II in Jan 1787, joined the Russians on 9 Feb 1788. The combined armies were ultimately successful on land after forcing the Turks, following the battles at Focsani (31 Jul 1789) and Rimnitz (22 Sep 1789), to withdraw to the Danube. At sea, where the American John Paul Jones fought with the Russian fleet at Kinburn (17 May 1787), and Liman (17 Jun 1788), the Russians gained the upper hand. Turkish operations were hampered by a revolt in Morea, Greece, in 1790, and the war ended on 9 Jan 1792, with the Treaty of Jassy, wherein Jassy and Moldavia were returned to Turkey, while Russia retained all conquered territories east of the Dniester.

American Revolution, 1775–83

With the collapse of the French empire in North America following the French and Indian War (1754–63), the dependence of the thirteen British North American colonies on their mother country was reduced. Although the colonials still valued their membership of the British empire, British efforts to reinvigorate the Old Colonial System – the Proclamation Line of 1763; the Sugar Act of 1764; the Stamp Act of 1765; the Declaratory Act of 1766 – aroused vigorous opposition. American resentment was further intensified following the Townshend Duties of 1767, the 1768 posting of British troops in Boston, the Boston Massacre of 1770 and, three years later, the Boston Tea Party. After the failure of North's Conciliatory Plan in Feb 1775, the first pitched battles ensued between colonial militia and the British regulars on 19 Apr 1775 at Lexington and Concord. In the following year, on 4 Jul, the American patriots declared their independence, an act which, along with the American victory at Saratoga (7 Oct 1777), gained the allegiance of France (1778). The entry of Spain in 1779 and the Netherlands in 1780 completed British isolation in a world conflict. Against the tenacious resistance of General George Washington's Continental troops, Britain steadily dissipated its strength until, on 19 Oct 1781 at Yorktown, General Lord Cornwallis surrendered, thus effectively ending the war. In the Treaty of Paris signed on 3 Sep 1783, Britain acknowledged the independence of the United States of America.

211

PRINCIPAL LAND BATTLES

Land Battles (War)	Date	Combatants	Numbers Engaged	Casualties	Commanders
Almanza (Spanish Succession)	25 Apr 1707	French	33,000	6000	Berwick
		British, Portuguese, Dutch	33,000	10,500	Galway; das Minas
Arcot (Carnatic War)	1 Sep–Nov 1751	British, Sepoys	500	180	Clive
		Indians, French	10,150	400	Chunda Sahib; De Saussey
Arras (Franco-Spanish)	24–5 Aug 1654	French	30,000	3000	Turenne
		Spanish	30,000	3000	Condé
Aughrim (English Succession)	12 Jul 1691	English	35,000	700	de Ginkel
		French, Irish	25,000	7000	St-Ruth; Lucan
Barcelona (Spanish Succession)	14 Oct 1705	British, Dutch	6500	–	Peterborough; Shovell
		French, Catalans	3600	600	Prince George; Prince Lichtenstein
Belgrade (Austro-Turkish)	16 Aug 1717	Austrians	155,000	5128	Eugène of Savoy
		Turkish	174,000	23,000	Hatschi Hali
Bennington (American Revolution)	16 Aug 1777	British, Germans	1442	907	Baum; Breymann
		Americans	2330	70	Stark; Warner
Beresteczko (Polish-Cossack)	28–30 Jun 1651	Polish	100,000	2615	John II Casimir
		Cossacks, Lithuanians, Ukraine Tartars	200,000	'enormous loss'	Bogdan Chmielnicki
Bergen (Seven Years' War)	13 Apr 1759	French, Saxons	70,000	2615	Duc de Broglie
		Prussians, Brunswickers, British	35,000	3400	Duc de Brunswick

Bergen-op-Zoom (Austrian Succession)	15 Jul–18 Sep 1747	French British, Dutch	25,000 4500	22,000 4000	von Löwendahl Cronstrom
Bitonto (Polish Succession)	25 May 1734	Spanish Austrians and allies	12,000 9000	3000 8000	Count of Montemar; Infante Don Carlos von Traun
Blenheim (Spanish Succession)	13 Aug 1704	British, Austrians French, Bavarians	52,000 60,000	12,000 38,600	Marlborough, Prince Eugène Marsin, Maximilian II
The Boyne (English Succession)	1 Jul 1690	English Irish, French	36,000 25,000	500 1500	William III; von Schomberg James II; Lauzun
Brandywine Creek (American Revolution)	11 Sep 1777	British Americans	18,000 8000	590 1200	Howe Washington
Braunau (Austrian Succession)	9 May 1743	Austrians Bavarians, French	50,000 30,000	1500 4000	Charles of Lorraine; Prince Lokkowitz Count von Seckendorf
Breslau (Seven Years' War)	22 Nov 1757	Austrians Prussians	70,000 20,000	8000 8600	Charles of Lorraine Wilhelm von Brunswick– Bevern
Brihuega (Spanish Succession)	9 Dec 1710	British French, Spanish	2536 1700	2536 2700	Stanhope Vendôme
Bunker Hill (American Revolution)	17 Jun 1775	British Americans	2800 1600	1050 370	Gage Prescott
Calcutta (Seven Years' War)	16–20 Jun 1756	Bengalis, Fench British	50,200 515	7000 167	Siraj-ud-Daula Minchin; Drake

213

Land Battles (War)	Date	Combatants	Numbers Engaged	Casualties	Commanders
Camden (American Revolution)	16 Aug 1780	British / Americans	2240 / 5000	324 / 1800	Cornwallis / Gates; de Kalb
Campo-Santo (American Revolution)	8 Feb 1743	Spanish / Austrians, Pietmontese	12,400 / 10,600	3976 / 1703	Gages / Traun
Carbiesdale (Third Civil War)	27 Apr 1650	Royalists / Parliament	1500 / 2100	796 / 2	Montrose / Strachan
Cassano (Spanish Succession)	16 Aug 1705	French, Spanish / Austrians	36,000 / 20,000	5000 / 4000	Vendôme / Prince Eugène
Chiari (Spanish Succession)	1 Sep 1701	Austrians / French, Spanish	28,000 / 40,000	117 / 3000	Prince Eugène / Villeroi
Chotusitz (Austrian Succession)	17 May 1742	Austrians / Prussians	30,000 / 30,000	6500 / 4800	Prince Charles of Lorraine / Frederick II; Prince Leopold of Anhalt-Dessau
Concord (American Revolution)	19 Apr 1775	British / Americans	700 / 4000	287 / 75	Lawrence Heath; Buttrick
Crefeld (Seven Years' War)	23 Jun 1758	Hanoverians, Hessians, Brunswickers / French	33,000 / 47,000	1700 / 8200	Duke of Brunswick / Condé
Cremona (Spanish Succession)	1 Feb 1702	French / Austrians	15,000 / 10,000	1600 / 811	Villeroi / Prince Eugène

Battle (War)	Date	Opposing sides	Numbers	Casualties	Commanders
Culloden (Jacobite Rebellion)	16 Apr 1746	Royalists / Jacobites	10,000 / 9000	309 / 1700	Duke of Cumberland / Prince Charles Edward Stuart
Caneo (Coni) (Austrian Succession)	30 Sep–22 Oct 1744	Austrians, Sardinians / French, Spanish	40,000 / 40,000	5000 / 8000	Charles Emmanuel I; Prince Lokkowitz / Prince Louis de Conti; Philip, Infante of Spain
Czaslau (Austrian Succession)	17 May 1742	Prussians / Austrians	28,200 / 30,600	4204 / 6191	Frederick II / Charles of Lorraine
Denain (Spanish Succession)	24 Jul 1712	Dutch, Prussians, Austrians / French	10,500 / 24,000	8000 / 500	Prince Eugène / Villars
Dettingen (Austrian Succession)	27 Jun 1743	British, Hanoverians, Austrians / French	35,000 / 28,000	2500 / 5000	King George II / Duc de Noailles
Donauwörth (Spanish Succession)	2 Jul 1704	British, Austrians, Dutch / French, Bavarians	50,000 / 12,000	5374 / 5400	Louis de Bade; Duke of Marlborough / Count D'Arco
Drogheda (English Civil War)	11 Sep 1649	Parliamentary Army / Royalists	10,000 / 2500	– / 4000	Oliver Cromwell / Ormonde
Dunbar (English Civil War)	3 Sep 1650	Parliamentary Army / Royalists	11,000 / 22,000	30 / 13,000	Oliver Cromwell / Leslie
Dunes (Anglo-Spanish War)	13 Jun 1658	Spanish / British, French	14,000 / 14,000	1000 / 4000	Don John of Austria; Condé / Turenne

Land Battles (War)	Date	Combatants	Numbers Engaged	Casualties	Commanders
Eckeren (Spanish Succession)	30 Jun 1703	French Dutch, Germans	19,000 11,000	1300 3135	Boufflers Obdam
Enzheim (Second Dutch War)	4 Oct 1674	French Germans	22,000 38,000	3500 3000	Turenne Bournonville
Eutaw Springs (American Revolution)	8 Sep 1781	British Americans	2000 2200	866 522	Stewart Greene
Falkirk (Jacobite Rebellion)	17 Jan 1746	Jacobites Royalists	8000 9000	120 1300	Prince Charles Hawley
Fehrbellin (Swedish–German War)	28 Jun 1675	Swedish Brandenburgers	11,000 6500	6500 1000	Wrangel Elector Frederick William
Fleurus (League of Augsburg)	1 Jul 1690	French Germans, Dutch, English, Spanish	39,500 37,800	4000 14,000	Duc de Luxembourg Prince of Waldeck
Focsani (Russo-Turkish)	31 Jul 1789	Turks Russians, Austrians	55,000 40,000	4000 800	Yusuf Pasha Count Suvorov; Prince Friedrich Josias of Saxe-Coburg
Fontenoy (Spanish Succession)	10 May 1745	British, Dutch, Austrians, Hanoverians French	50,000 56,000	9000 5257	Duke of Cumberland Comte de Saxe
Fort Frontenac (Kingston) (Seven Years' War)	27 Aug 1758	British, Colonials French, Canadians	3000 150	2 2	Bradstreet de Noyan

Battle (War)	Date	Combatants	Strength	Casualties	Commander
Fort Ticonderoga (Seven Years' War)	8 Jul 1758	French, Canadians, Indians	3600	377	Montcalm
		British, Colonials	12,000	1964	Abercromby; Amherst
Fort William Henry (Seven Years' War)	4 Aug 1757	British, Colonials	2300	1850	Monro
		French, Canadians, Indians	6600	20	Montcalm
Friedlingen (Spanish Succession)	14 Oct 1702	French	18,000	1429	Villars
		Austrians	25,000	3900	Prince Louis of Baden
Germantown (American Revolution)	4 Oct 1777	Americans	11,000	1075	Washington
		British	9000	540	Howe
Gross-Jägerndorf (Seven Years' War)	30 Aug 1757	Prussians	28,000	3000	von Lehwald
		Russians	85,000	9000	Apraxin
Guildford Courthouse (American Revolution)	15 Mar 1781	British	1900	548	Cornwallis
		Americans	4300	261	Greene
Hastenbeck (Seven Years' War)	26 Jul 1757	Hanoverians, Hessians, Brunswickers	36,000	1480	Duke of Cumberland
		French	74,000	2331	d'Estrées
Hennersdorf (Austrian Succession)	23–4 Nov 1745	Prussians	60,000	1000	Rochow
		Saxons	40,000	10,000	Buchner
Hochkirch (Seven Years' War)	14 Oct 1758	Prussians	42,000	9097	Frederick II
		Austrians	90,000	5939	von Daun
Hoechstaedt (Spanish Succession)	13 Aug 1704	Germans, English	56,000	11,000	Prince Eugène; Marlborough
		Bavarians, French	60,000	29,000	Elector Maximilian; Tallard

217

Land Battles (War)	Date	Combatants	Numbers Engaged	Casualties	Commanders
Hohenfriedberg (Austrian Succession)	4 Jun 1745	Austrians, Saxons	76,414	15,221	Duke of Weisenfels; Charles of Lorraine
		Prussians	76,975	4743	Frederick II
Inverkeithing (Third Civil War)	20 Jul 1651	English	4500	–	Lambert
		Scots	4000	3500	Brown
Kesselsdorf (Second Silesian War)	15 Dec 1745	Saxons, Austrians	26,300	6500	Rutowsky; Grune
		Prussians	34,670	5072	Prince of Dessau
Killiecrankie (Jacobite Rising)	27 Jul 1689	Royalists	3400	2500	Mackay
		Jacobites	2500	900	Dundee
Kliszów (Great Northern War)	2 Jul 1702	Swedish	12,000	1100	Charles XII
		Polish, Saxons	24,000	2000	Augustus II
Kolin (Seven Years' War)	18 Jun 1757	Prussians	34,000	13,773	Frederick II
		Austrians	53,790	8114	von Daun
Künersdorf (Seven Years' War)	12 Aug 1759	Prussians	43,000	18,495	Frederick II
		Austrians, Russians	88,000	14,673	von Futak; von Laudon; Soltikow
Landshut (Seven Years' War)	23 Jun 1760	Prussians	10,400	10,400	Fouqué
		Austrians	38,000	5000	von Laudon
Lauffeld (Austrian Succession)	2 Jul 1747	British, Dutch, Hanoverians, Austrians	90,000	6000	Duke of Cumberland; von Daun
		French	42,000	14,000	Comte de Saxe

Battle (War)	Date	Combatants	Numbers	Casualties	Commanders
Lens (Thirty Years' War)	20 Aug 1648	French / Austrians, Spanish	14,000 / 15,000	200 / 10,000	Condé / Archduke Leopold William
Leuthen (Seven Years' War)	5 Dec 1757	Prussians / Austrians	30,000 / 80,000	6000 / 26,750	Frederick II / Charles of Lorraine
Lexington (American Revolution)	19 Apr 1755	British / Americans	200 / 70	1 / 18	Pitcairn / Parker
Liegnitz (Seven Years' War)	15 Aug 1760	Prussians / Austrians	30,000 / 90,000	3516 / 9791	Frederick II / von Daun
Lille (Spanish Succession)	13 Aug–10 Dec 1708	Austrians, British / French	120,000 / 16,000	3632 / 7000	Prince Eugène; Marlborough / Vendôme; Duc de Boufflers
Lobositz (Seven Years' War)	1 Oct 1756	Prussians, Hanoverians / Austrians	30,000 / 33,354	3308 / 2863	Frederick II / Count von Browne
Londonderry (English Succession)	19 Apr 1689	Ulster Protestants / British	7000 / –	3000 / 5000	Baker / Kirke
Lutternberg (Seven Years' War)	10 Oct 1758	Hanoverians, Prussians, Hessians / French	23,500 / 40,000	1200 / 600	D'Oberg / Prince of Soubise
Luzzara (Spanish Succession)	15 Aug 1702	French, Spanish / Austrians	35,000 / 25,000	4000 / 5000	Duc d'Anjou; Vendôme / Prince Eugène
Maastricht (Austrian Succession)	7 May 1757	French / Hanoverians, Austrians, Dutch, British	40,000 / 70,000	4000 / 5000	Comte de Saxe / Prince of Orange and Prince William Augustus

Land Battles (War)	Date	Combatants	Numbers Engaged	Casualties	Commanders
Madras (Seven Years' War)	13–17 Feb 1759	French British	7300 3950	700 1180	Lally-Tollendal Lawrence
Malplaquet (Spanish Succession)	11 Sep 1709	British, Dutch, Prussians, Hanoverians, Danish, Austrians French, Bavarians	100,000 90,000	18,250 14,000	Duke of Marlborough; Prince Eugène de Villars; Boufflers
Maxen (Seven Years' War)	21 Nov 1759	Austrians Prussians	36,500 13,500	300 12,300	von Daun von Finck
Minden (Seven Years' War)	1 Aug 1759	French, Saxons Hanoverians, British, Prussians	51,400 36,920	7086 2822	Marquis de Contades Duke of Brunswick
Mollwitz (First Silesian War)	10 Apr 1741	Prussians Austrians	22,600 19,400	4613 4410	Frederick II Count von Neipperg
Monongahela River (Seven Years' War)	9 Jul 1755	French, Indians British, Colonials	1200 1300	44 877	de Beaujeu Braddock
Narva (Great Northern War)	20 Nov 1700	Swedish Russians	9000 60,000	2000 18,000	Charles XII Duke of Croy
Neerwinden (English Succession/ League of Augsburg	29 Jul 1693	British, Bavarians French	50,000 80,000	18,000 7500	William III Duc de Luxembourg
Newport (American Revolution)	29 Jul–31 Aug 1778	British French, Americans	3000 10,000	250 210	Pigot Sullivan; Comte d'Estaing

Battle (War)	Date	Combatants	Numbers	Casualties	Commanders
Olmütz (Seven Years' War)	May–1 Jul 1758	Prussians Austrians	40,000 36,000	4500 400	Frederick II von Daun
Oswego (Seven Years' War)	11 Aug 1756	British, Colonials French, Canadians	10,000 5000	1550 40	Earl of Loudon Montcalm
Oudenarde (Spanish Succession)	11 Jul 1708	British, Prussians, Dutch, Hanoverians, Danish French	85,000 85,000	6000 13,000	Marlborough; Prince Eugène Duc de Burgogne; Vendôme
Parma (Polish Succession)	29 Jun 1734	French, Pietmontese Austrians	30,000 30,000	6000 6300	de Coigny de Mercy
Peterwardein (Austro-Turkish Wars)	5 Aug 1716	Austrians Turks	80,000 110,000	5000 20,000	Prince Eugène Darnad Ali Pasha
Plains of Abraham (Seven Years' War)	13 Sep 1759	British French	4500 4500	600 1400	Wolfe Montcalm
Plassey (Seven Years' War; Bengal Wars)	23 Jun 1757	British, Indians Bengali, French	53,025 50,000	63 500	Clive Siraj-ud-Daula
Poltava (Great Northern War)	8 Jul 1709	Sweden Russia	17,000 80,000	10,000 1300	Charles XII Peter the Great
Prague (Seven Years' War)	6 May 1757	Prussians Austrians	64,000 60,600	12,520 13,300	Frederick II Charles of Lorraine
Preston (English Civil War)	17–19 Aug 1648	Royalists, Scots Parliamentarians, Roundheads	4000 8500	5000 180	Langdale; Hamilton Cromwell

Land Battles (War)	Date	Combatants	Numbers Engaged	Casualties	Commanders
Preston (Jacobite Rebellion)	12–14 Nov 1715	Jacobites Royalists	1700 2000	1542 200	Forster Wills; Carpenter
Prestonpans (Gladsmuir) (Jacobite Rebellion)	21 Sep 1745	Royalists Jacobites	2300 2500	2300 140	Cope Murray
Princeton (American Revolution)	3 Jan 1777	Americans British	1600 1200	40 400	Washington Mawhood
Pultava (Great Northern War)	8 Jul 1709	Sweden Russia	17,000 80,000	10,000 1300	Charles XII Peter the Great
Pultusk (Great Northern War)	21 Apr 1703	Swedish Saxons	10,000 10,000	30 1600	Charles XII von Stenau
Quebec (Seven Years' War/French and Indian Wars)	27 Jun–18 Sep 1759	British French	8000 12,000	1160 1400	Wolfe Montcalm
Quebec (Seven Years' War)	27 Apr–17 May 1760	French, Indians, Canadians British	8500 4000	1000 1300	Duc de Levis Murray
Quiberon Bay (Belleisle) (Seven Years' War)	7 Apr–8 Jun 1761	British French	8000 3000	700 60	Keppel; Hodgson Saint Croix
Ramillies (Spanish Succession)	23 May 1706	British, Austrians French	62,000 62,000	3635 13,000	Marlborough; Prince Eugène Villeroi; Vendôme
Rathmines (English Civil War)	2 Aug 1649	Royalists Roundheads	10,200 7700	6517 100	Ormonde Jones

222

Battle	Date	Combatants	Numbers engaged	Casualties	Commanders
Raucoux (Austrian Succession)	11 Oct 1746	French / Austrians, Dutch, British, Hessians, Bavarians	111,000 / 74,700	3000 / 4558	Comte de Saxe / Charles of Lorraine
Reichenberg (Seven Years' War)	21 Apr 1757	Prussians / Austrians	15,000 / 20,000	1000 / 1000	Duke of Bévern / Count of Koenigseck
Rimnitz (Russo-Turkish Wars)	22 Sep 1789	Austrians, Russians / Turks	25,000 / 60,000	– / 60,000	Prince of Saxe-Coburg; Count Suvorov / Hasan Pasha
Rossbach (Seven Years' War)	5 Nov 1757	French, Austrians / Prussians	63,600 / 22,000	8000 / 541	Prince de Soubise; Prince Joseph of Saxe-Hildburghausen / Frederick II
Rottofredo (Austrian Succession)	Jul–12 Aug 1746	Austrians / French	30,000 / 26,000	4000 / 8000	Prince Wenzel von Lichtenstein / Marquis de Maillebois
Sandershausen (Seven Years' War)	23 Jul 1758	French / Hessians	6800 / 4000	2000 / 1000	Duc de Broglie / Prince d'Isembourg
Saratoga (Stillwater) (American Revolution)	5 Oct 1777	British / Americans	6000 / 7000	4689 / 150	Burgoyne / Gates
Savannah (American Revolution)	16 Sep–9 Oct 1779	French, Americans / British	6000 / 3200	920 / 60	Comte d'Estaing; Lincoln / Prevost
Sedgemoor (Glorious Revolution)	6 Jul 1685	Royalists / Rebels	2500 / 3700	– / 3700	Earl of Faversham / Duke of Monmouth

Land Battles (War)	Date	Combatants	Numbers Engaged	Casualties	Commanders
Seneffe (Franco-Dutch War)	11 Aug 1674	French / Flemings, Spanish	45,000 / 50,000	10,000 / 30,000	Condé / William III of Orange
Sheriffmuir (Jacobite Rebellion)	13 Nov 1715	Royalists / Jacobites	3300 / 8000	500 / 500	Duke of Argyle / Earl of Mar
Sinsheim (Franco-Dutch War)	16 Jun 1674	French / Austrians	8900 / 9000	1900 / 2500	Marshal Turenne / Duke of Lorraine
Sohr (Austrian Succession)	30 Sep 1745	Prussians / Austrians	22,925 / 32,478	3519 / 7447	Frederick II / Charles of Lorraine
Steenkerke (League of Augsburg)	3 Aug 1692	British / French	15,000 / 15,000	8000 / 3000	William III / de Luxembourg
Stralsund (Great Northern War)	19 Jul–Dec 1715	Prussians, Danes / Swedish	36,000 / 9000	– / 9000	Frederick William III of Prussia; Frederick IV of Danmark / Charles XII
Torgau (Seven Years' War)	3 Nov 1760	Prussians / Austrians	46,000 / 60,000	14,000 / 11,000	Frederick II / von Daun
Turin (Spanish Succession)	7 Sep 1706	Saxons, Austrians, Prussians / French	35,000 / 44,000	3346 / 8465	Prince Eugène / Duc d'Orleans; Duc de la Feuillade
Valenciennes (Franco-Spanish)	16 Jul 1656	Spanish / French	20,000 / 20,000	4300 / 4400	Condé / Turenne; La Ferté

Battle (War)	Date	Combatants	Numbers engaged	Casualties	Commanders
Velletri (Austrian Succession)	11 Aug 1744	Austrians / Spanish, Neopolitans	6000 / 6000	500 / 2600	Prince Lokkowitz; Count von Browne / King Charles IV; de Gages
Vienna (Habsburg–Ottoman Wars)	12 Sep 1683	Turks / Habsburgs	138,000 / 76,000	'enormous loss' / –	Kara Mustapha Pasha / John Sobieski III; Charles V
Wandiwash (Seven Years' War)	22 Jan 1760	British / French	5330 / 3550	187 / 560	Coote / Lally de Tollendal
Warburg (Seven Years' War)	31 Jul 1760	French / British, Hanoverians, Hessians	21,500 / 24,000	3700 / 1230	Chevalier du Muy / Prince of Brunswick-Lunebourg
Worcester (Second Civil War)	3 Sep 1651	Royalists / Parliamentary Army	12,000 / 28,000	11,000 / –	Charles II / Cromwell
Yorktown (American Revolution)	30 Sep–19 Oct 1781	British, Hessians / Americans, French	9750 / 20,000	8677 / 341	Cornwallis / Washington; Comte de Rochambeau
Zenta (Habsburg–Ottoman Wars)	11 Sep 1697	Austrians / Turks	70,000 / 150,000	2018 / 10,000	Prince Eugène / Sultan Mustafa II
Zorndorf (Seven Years' War)	25 Aug 1758	Prussians / Russians	32,760 / 52,000	12,385 / 21,531	Frederick II / Fermor
Zullichau (Seven Years' War)	23 Jul 1759	Russians / Prussians	72,000 / 27,380	4791 / 8148	Soltikow / Wedell

PRINCIPAL SEA BATTLES

Sea Battles (War)	Date	Combatants	Ships Engaged	Ships Lost	Casualties	Commanders
Beachy Head (League of Augsburg)	30 Jul–10 Jul 1690	English Dutch	56 68	9 0	– –	Torrington Tourville
Cape Finisterre (Austrian Succession)	3 May 1747	British French	14 9	0 9	– 3000	Anson de la Jonquiere
Cape Finisterre (Austrian Succession)	2 Oct 1747	British French	14 8	0 6	598 4340	Hawke de l'Etenduère
Cesme (Russo–Turkish Wars)	7–8 Jul 1770	Russian, British Turkish	9 14	1 13	– –	Orlov; Elphinston Hassan Bey
Cuddalore (Second Mysore War/ American Revolution)	13 Jun 1783	British French, Mysoreans	18 15	0 0	1532 1000	Stuart; Tipu Sultan; Hughes Bussy-Castelnau; de Suffren
Dogger Bank (Anglo–Dutch War/ American Revolution)	5 Aug 1781	British Dutch	7 8	0 1	471 545	Parker Zoutman
Dominica (Battle of The Saints) (American Revolution)	12 Apr 1782	British French	35 36	0 9	1059 2700	Rodney Comte de Grasse
Dover (First Anglo–Dutch War)	19 Nov 1652	Dutch British	95 40	2 8	– –	Van Tromp Blake

Battle (War)	Date	Combatants				Commanders
Gabbard Bank (First Anglo-Dutch War)	2–3 Jun 1653	British / Dutch	110 / 104	0 / 20	— / —	Monk / Van Tromp
Gibraltar (Spanish Succession)	23–4 Jul 1704	British, Dutch / Spanish	22 / 0	8 / 0	288 / —	Rooke / de Salinas
Grenada (American Revolution)	6 Jul 1779	British / French	20 / 24	0 / 0	529 / 949	Byron / d'Estaing
Havana (Seven Years' War)	5 Jun 1762	British / Spanish	26 / 15	2 / 14	351 / 2109	Keppel / de Prado
Kentish Knock (First Anglo-Dutch War)	28 Sep 1652	Dutch / English	62 / 60	3 / 2	— / —	De Will / Blake
Lagos Bay (League of Augsburg)	27–8 Jun 1693	British, Dutch, Germans / French	23 / 71	3 / 0	— / —	Rooke; van der Goes / de Cotentin; de Tourville
La Hogue (Barfleur) (League of Augsburg)	29 May–3 Jun 1692	Dutch, English / French	99 / 44	10 / 18	— / —	Russell; Ashley; van Almonde / de Tourville
Louisbourg (Seven Years' War)	30 May–27 Jul 1758	British, Colonials / French, Canadians	23 / 5	6 / 5	— / 6837	Lord Amherst; Wolfe; Boscawen / Chevalier de Drucour
Lowestoft (Second Anglo-Dutch War)	13 Jun 1665	English / Dutch	150 / 150	2 / 32	790 / 6000	Duke of York / Opdam
Malaga (Spanish Succession)	13 Aug 1704	British, Dutch / French, Spanish	51 / 52	0 / 0	2346 / 3239	Rooke / de Toulouse
Martinique (American Revolution)	17 Apr 1780	British / French	21 / 23	0 / 0	474 / 759	Rodney / Comte de Guichen

227

Sea Battles (War)	Date	Combatants	Ships Engaged	Ships Lost	Casualties	Commanders
Minorca (Seven Years' War)	20 May 1756	British / French	12 / 12	0 / 0	207 / 162	Blakeney; Byng / Richelieu; Galissonière
North Foreland (Second Anglo-Dutch War)	25–6 Jul 1666	British / French	99 / 118	3 / 20	300 / 7000	Duke of Albemarle; Prince Rupert / Van Tromp; de Ruijter
Portland (First Anglo-Dutch War)	18–20 Feb 1653	British / Dutch	70 / 80	50 / 51	2000 / 2200	Blake; Deane; Monck / Van Tromp; de Ruijter
Quiberon Bay (Seven Years' War)	20–2 Nov 1759	British / French	23 / 21	2 / 14	270 / 2000	Hawke / Conflans
Scheveningen (First Anglo-Dutch War)	31 Jul 1653	Dutch / English	100 / 100	30 / 15	1600 / 700	Van Tromp / Monck
Southwold Bay (Solebay) (Third Anglo-Dutch War)	28 May 1672	British, French / Dutch	101 / 75	4 / 5	2500 / 350	Duke of York / de Ruijter
Texel (First Anglo-Dutch War)	30 Jul–1 Aug 1653	British / Dutch	105 / 100	20 / 17	363 / 1300	Monck; Blake / Van Tromp
Texel (Third Anglo-Dutch War)	11 Aug 1673	British, French / Dutch	54 / 42	0 / 0	– / –	Prince Rupert of Germany; Comte d'Estrées / de Ruijter
Toulon (Austrian Succession)	19–22 Feb 1744	British / French, Spanish	27 / 27	0 / 1	274 / 200	Mathews / de la Brujère de Court; Navarro
Vigo Bay (Spanish Succession)	12 Oct 1702	British, Dutch / French, Spanish	36 / 32	2 / 21	122 / 790	Rooke; Ormonde / Sorel; Chateau-Renaud

5 TREATIES AND DIPLOMACY

1648

30 Jan   Peace between Spain and the United Provinces, later incorporated in the Peace of Westphalia.

24 Oct   Peace of Westphalia at Münster and Osnabrück between the Empire, France and Sweden ends Thirty Years' War.

1649

11 Mar   Treaty of Rueil ends First Fronde.

1650

26 Jun   Exchange of peace treaties between the Empire and Sweden amplifies the Peace of Westphalia.

1651

Mar   Formation of Catholic and Protestant Leagues in German states to carry out terms of Peace of Westphalia.

Jun   The Cossacks make a treaty with Tsar Alexis.

1652

Feb   Alliance of Hildesheim between Sweden and North German Protestants.

1653

10 Mar   Commercial treaty between Britain and Portugal.

1654

5 Apr   Treaty of Westminster between Britain and United Provinces which recognised Navigation Acts and ended the First Anglo-Dutch War.

11 Apr   Commercial treaty between Britain and Sweden.

May   Treaty of Pereiaslavl concluded whereby the Cossacks placed the Ukraine under the protection of Tsar Alexis.

10 Jul   Treaty between Britain and Portugal, granting concessions to British merchants.

14 Sep   Commercial treaty between Britain and Denmark.

1655

27 Jul   Defensive treaty between Brandenburg and United Provinces.

24 Oct   Commercial treaty between Britain and France.

1656

17 Jan   Alliance between Britain and Sweden at Königsberg; East Prussia becomes Swedish fief.

24 Feb   Alliance of Brandenburg and France.

Apr   Treaty between Philip IV and the exiled Charles II.

25 Jun   Treaty of Marienberg, a secret partition of Poland agreed upon by Brandenburg and Sweden.

Jun   Commercial treaty between Britain and Sweden.

5 Sep   Treaty of friendship between Britain and France.

3 Nov   Treaty of Vilna between Russia and Poland.

20 Nov   Treaty of Labiau between Brandenburg and Sweden; Sweden renounced sovereignty over Prussia.

1 Dec   Alliance between Empire and Poland.

1657

23 Mar   Treaty of Paris between Britain and France against Spain.

19 Sep   Treaty of Wehlau: Poland renounced sovereignty of Prussia on behalf of Brandenburg.

6 Nov   Brandenburg allied with Poland against Sweden at Bromberg.

10 Nov   Offensive alliance between Brandenburg and Denmark.

1658

8 Mar   Treaty of Roskilde between Sweden and Denmark.

15 Aug   Rhenish League founded under French Protectorate.

1659

21 May   Treaty of the Hague between Britain, France and United Provinces to force Denmark and Sweden to make peace.

7 Nov   Peace of the Pyrenees between France and Spain; Spain ceded much of Flanders and other frontier regions.

1660

3 May   Peace of Oliva ends First Northern War between Brandenburg, Poland, Austria and Sweden.

6 Jun   Peace of Copenhagen between Sweden and Denmark.

1661

21 Jun   Peace of Kardis between Sweden and Russia confirmed the *status quo ante bellum.*

6 Aug   Treaty between United Provinces and Portugal by British mediation; the Dutch retain Ceylon, the Portugese Brazil.

1662

6 Feb   Treaty of Montmartre: Lorraine ceded to France.

27 Apr   French Alliance with United Provinces.

1664

6 Mar   French alliance with Brandenburg.

6 Apr   French alliance with Saxony.

10 Aug   Peace of Eisenburg between Turkey and the Empire.

1666

2 Feb   Alliance between Denmark and United Provinces.

16 Feb   Alliance between Brandenburg and United Provinces.

25 Oct   Quadruple Alliance between United Provinces, Brandenburg, Brunswick and Denmark.

Dec   Treaty of Cleves between the Great Elector and the Duke of Neuburg for the partition of Jülich-Cleves.

1667

20 Jan   Truce of Andruszov between Russia and Poland ended the Thirteen Years' War; Poland ceded Smolensk and Kiev.

31 Mar   Secret treaty between Charles II and Louis XIV.

21 Jul   Peace of Breda between Britain and United Provinces.

Aug   Rhenish Confederation of 1658 dissolved.

1668

19 Jan   Treaty of Partition between Louis XIV and Emperor Leopold I for the future partition of the Spanish Empire.

13 Jan   The Triple Alliance of Britain, United Provinces and, subsequently (April 1668), Sweden, against France; signed at The Hague.

13 Feb   Treaty of Lisbon: Spain recognised independence of Portugal.

2 May   Peace of Aix-la-Chapelle; France obtained 12 Flemish fortresses.

1669

31 Dec   Secret treaty of alliance between Brandenburg and France.

1670

17 Feb   Defensive alliance between France and Bavaria.

May   Alliance between France and Sweden for three years.

1 Jun   Secret Treaty of Dover between Britain and France: France given free hand in United Provinces and Spain; Britain received subsidies from France (made public 31 Dec).

1671

Feb   Treaty of assistance between Brandenburg and United Provinces; effective 6 May 1672.

Jul–   Louis XIV makes series of treaties with Hanover, Osnabrück,
Dec   Brunswick and the Palatinate.

1 Nov   Treaty of Neutrality between France and the Empire.

17 Dec   Treaty between Spain and United Provinces.

1672

14 Apr   Alliance between France and Sweden.

2 May   Alliance between Elector Frederick William of Brandenburg and United Provinces.

23 Jun   Alliance between Brandenburg and Emperor Leopold I.

25 Jul   Alliance between Emperor and United Provinces.

18 Oct   Treaty of Buczácz: Poland ceded Podolia to Turkey.

27 Oct   Alliance between Emperor and United Provinces.

1673

6 Jun   Peace of Vossem between Brandenburg and France; Great Elector promised not to support any enemies of Louis XIV.

1 Jul   Defensive alliance between William of Orange and Denmark.

30 Aug   Alliance of Emperor with United Provinces, which is joined by Spain and the Duke of Lorraine, against France.

1674

9 Feb   Treaty of Westminster: Britain withdrew from war against United Provinces.

1 Jul   Triple Alliance of Emperor, Dutch and Spanish against French formally concluded; later joined by the Pope and the Elector of Brandenburg.

1675

11 Jun   Alliance between France and Poland.

1676

17 Feb   Secret alliance between Charles II and Louis XIV.

16 Oct   Peace of Zurawno between Turkey and Poland, who divide Podolia.

1677

Apr   Treaty between Empire and Poland.

1678

10 Aug   Peace of Nijmegen between France and United Provinces; *status quo.*

17 Sep   Peace of Nijmegen between France and Spain which ceded Franche–Comté and 16 Flemish towns.

1679

5 Feb   Treaty of Nijmegen between France and the Empire which ceded Freiburg and Breisach.

29 Jun   Peace of St Germain-en-Laye between Brandenburg and Sweden; Britain loses all her conquests.

2 Sep   Peace of Fontainebleau between Denmark and Sweden; Denmark restored all her conquests. Formal peace signed by Treaty of Lund, 26 Sep 1679.

1680

29 Dec   Alliance between Bishop of Münster and France.

1681

8 Jan   Treaty of Radzin: the Turks abandoned most of Ukraine to Russia.

11 Jan   Defensive alliance between Brandenburg and France.

Apr   Defensive alliance between Brandenburg and Sweden formed by the Treaty of Finsterwalde.

1682

Feb   Alliance between Brandenburg and Denmark.

1683

Feb   Association of The Hague against France.

31 Mar   Alliance between Poland and the Emperor against Turkey.

1684

5 Mar   Holy League of Linz between Empire, Poland and Venice against Turkey.

15 Aug   Truce of Ratisbon between Empire and France for 20 years.

1685

18 Oct   Edict of Fontainebleau: Louis XIV revoked Edict of Nantes.

1686

1 Apr   Alliance between Emperor and Great Elector of Brandenburg, who obtained Schweibus and renounced claims to Silesia.

9 Jul   League of Augsburg between Emperor, Spain, Sweden, Saxony, Palatinate and Brandenburg against Louis XIV.

1688

22 Oct   Magdeburg Convention against Louis XIV.

1689

12 May   Britain and United Provinces joined League of Augsburg.

1690

20 Oct   Savoy joined Grand Alliance.

1696

6 Oct   Treaty of Turin between France and Savoy; Savoy withdrew from Great Alliance, recovered Pinerolo.

1697

20 Sep   Treaty of Ryswick between France, Britain, United Provinces and Spain ended the War of the Grand Alliance; France recognised William III as king and Anne as his heir presumptive.

30 Oct   Peace of Ryswick between France and Austria; France restored right bank of Rhine, and is bought off as regards her claim to Palatinate.

1698

19 Jul   Alliance between France and Sweden.

11 Oct   First Partition treaty for division of Spanish possessions involving Electoral Prince of Bavaria, Dauphin and Archduke Charles.

1699

26 Jan   Treaty of Karlowitz between Austria–Hungary, Poland, Venice and Turkey ends war between Turks and Habsburgs.

24 Aug   Defence convention signed by Denmark and Russia.

25 Sep   Alliance between Denmark, Germany and Poland against Sweden.

22 Nov   Treaty of Preobrazhenskoe between Denmark, Russia, Saxony and Poland for the partition of Swedish empire.

1700

2 Feb   Alliance between Brandenburg and Poland.

25 Mar Second Partition treaty ratified (First signed in June 1699).
6 Apr Alliance between Brandenburg and Denmark.
23 Jun Truce between Russia and Turkey which ceded Azov and Kuban.
18 Aug Peace of Traventhal enforced on Denmark by Charles XII.
16 Nov Crown treaty between Emperor and Elector of Brandenburg.

1701

9 Mar Electors of Bavaria and Cologne signed treaties of alliance with France.
4 Apr Treaty between France and Savoy.
4 Jan Alliance between Denmark, the Empire and United Provinces.
7 Sep Coalition treaty of The Hague, known as the New Grand Alliance, signed. Britain, United Provinces and Empire ally against France and Spain.

1703

16 May Methuen Treaty between Britain and Portugal. Portugal joined Grand Alliance.
4 Nov Savoy joined the Grand Alliance.

1704

7 Oct Convention of Ilbersheim placed lands of the Elector of Bavaria under control of the Emperor.

1706

24 Sep Peace of Altrandstädt between Sweden and Saxony; Augustus renounced Polish throne.

1707

13 Mar Convention of Milan concluded by Emperor and France whereby French troops are to leave northern Italy.
1 May Union between England and Scotland under name of Great Britain.
Aug 'Perpetual' Alliance between Prussia and Sweden.

1709

29 Oct First Dutch Barrier Treaty negotiated by Charles Townshend.

1710

31 Mar Alliance of The Hague established neutrality of Swedish possessions in Germany.

1711

1 May Peace of Szatmár ended Hungarian rebellion against Austrian control over their country.

21 Jul   Peace settlement of the Pruth ended war between Russia and Ottoman Empire.

1712

12 Jan   Peace Congress opened at Utrecht.

11 Aug   Treaty of Aarau ended Second Villmergen War in Switzerland.

1713

30 Jan   Second Dutch Barrier Treaty.

21 Mar   Asiento Treaty between Spain and Britain granted Britain slave trading privileges.

31 Mar   Peace of Utrecht between France and Britain, United Provinces, Savoy, Portugal; and between France and Prussia.

19 Apr   Pragmatic Sanction issued by Charles VI.

13 Jun   Peace of Utrecht between Britain and Spain.

27 Jul   Peace of Adrianople between Turkey and Russia.

1714

7 Mar   Peace of Rastatt between France and the Empire.

26 Jun   Peace of Utrecht between Spain and United Provinces.

7 Sep   Peace of Baden between France and the Empire.

1715

6 Feb   Peace of Madrid between Spain and Portugal.

3 Apr   Treaty between France and Sweden.

1 May   Alliance between Prussia, Denmark, Hanover, Saxony and Poland against Sweden completed.

15 Nov   Barrier Treaty between Austria and United Province.

1716

26 Jan   Commercial treaty between Britain and United Provinces renewed former treaties of alliance and commerce.

15 May   Commercial treaty between Britain and Spain amplified earlier treaty of 3 Dec 1715.

25 May   Treaty of Westminster between Britain and Austria for mutual defence.

28 Sep   Treaty of Hanover between Britain and France formed basis of Triple Alliance of December.

26 Dec   Triple Alliance between Britain, France and United Provinces.

1717

17 Aug   Convention of Amsterdam between France, Russia and Prussia to maintain treaties of Utrecht and Baden.

236

1718

21 Jul   Treaty of Passarowitz between Austria and Turkey.

2 Aug   Quadruple Alliance between France, the Emperor, Britain and United Provinces.

1719

5 Jan   Alliance of Vienna between the Emperor, Saxony–Poland and Britain–Hanover against Russia and Prussia.

1720

1 Feb   Treaty of Stockholm between Sweden and Prussia, which obtained Pomerania.

17 Feb   Peace between Quadruple Alliance and Spain.

3 Jul   Treaty of Frederiksborg between Sweden and Denmark, which is exempted from Sund duties.

1721

21 Jun   Defensive Alliance between Britain, Spain and France.

30 Aug   Treaty of Nystad between Sweden and Russia, which obtained Livonia, Estonia, Ingria and Eastern Karelia.

1723

12 Oct   Treaty of Charlottenburg between Britain and Prussia.

1724

22 Feb   Treaty of Assistance between Sweden and Russia at Stockholm.

23 Jun   Treaty of Constantinople between Russia and Turkey against Persia.

1725

1 May   First Treaty of Vienna between Austria and Spain reconciled the two powers.

23 Sep   Treaty of Herrenhausen between Britain, France and Prussia to counteract Spanish alliance with the Emperor.

1726

Aug   Austria and Palatinate agreed by treaty on succession of Elector to Jülich and Berg.

6 Aug   Treaty between Russia and Austria against Turkey.

12 Oct   Treaty of Wusterhausen between Austria and Prussia.

1727

12 Nov   Secret Treaty of 1714 between France and Bavaria renewed.

1728

5 Mar   Convention of the Pardo ends war between Britain and Spain.

23 Dec   Treaty of Berlin between Emperor Charles VI and Frederick William of Prussia.

1729

9 Nov   Treaty of Seville between Britain and Spain joined by France and United Provinces ends Austro-Spanish alliance.

1731

22 Jul   Treaty of Vienna between Britain, United Provinces, Spain and Austria.

1732

21 Jan   Treaty of Riascha: Russia gave up claim to certain Prussian territories.

1733

26 Sep   League of Turin signed between France, Spain and Sardinia against the Emperor.

7 Nov   Treaty of the Escorial between France and Spain against Britain (First 'Family Compact').

15 Nov   Treaty between France and Bavaria.

1734

2 Dec   Anglo-Russian treaty of commerce (–1786).

1735

3 Oct   Peace of Vienna ended War of the Polish Succession (confirmed by the definitive Treaty of Vienna, 18 Nov 1738).

1736

18 May   Spain acceded to Treaty of Vienna.

1738

Oct   Alliance between France and Sweden.

18 Nov   Definitive peace treaty of Vienna: France recognised Pragmatic Sanction.

1739

Jan   Secret treaty between Austria and France to guarantee Wittelsbach claim to Jülich–Berg.

14 Jan	Convention of the Pardo to settle Anglo-Spanish disputes over Asiento trade and maritime quarrels.
5 Apr	Secret treaty between Prussia and France to divide Jülich–Berg.
18 Sep	Peace of Belgrade between Austria and Turkey.
3 Oct	Treaty of Belgrade between Russia and Turkey.

1741

8 May	Treaty of Nymphenburg between France and Bavaria.
28 May	Treaty between Spain and Bavaria to partition Habsburg lands.
5 Jun	Treaty of Breslau between France and Prussia against Austria.
9 Oct	Secret armistice of Klein Schnellendorf between Austria and Prussia (broken 1 Nov 1741).
1 Nov	Agreement between Austria and Saxony and Bavaria for partition of Empire.

1742

15 Mar	Alliance between France and Denmark.
11 Jun	Preliminary Peace of Breslau resulted in Peace of Breslau (28 Jul) between Austria and Prussia ending First Silesian War.
29 Nov	Anglo-Prussian defensive alliance aimed at France.

1743

17 Aug	Peace of Abö between Russia and Sweden which ceded South Finland and ended Russo-Swedish War (1741–3).
13 Sep	Treaty of Worms between Austria, Britain and Sardinia.
25 Oct	Offensive and defensive alliance of Fontainebleau (Second 'Family Compact').

1744

| 5 Jun | Alliance between France and Prussia against Maria Theresa guaranteed the Union of Frankfurt. |

1745

8 Jan	Quadruple Alliance of Maritime Powers with Austria and Saxony.
22 Apr	Peace of Füssen between Austria and Bavaria, which renounced its claim to the Empire.
25 Dec	Peace of Dresden: Prussia kept Silesia, recognised Pragmatic Sanction.

1746

| 21 Apr | Treaty between France and Saxony. |
| 2 Jun | Austro-Russian alliance against Prussia. |

1747
29 May Prusso-Swedish Alliance of Stockholm.
9 Dec   Convention of St Petersburg between Britain, United Provinces and Russia, whose troops were allowed to pass through Germany.

1748
30 Apr Preliminary Peace of Aix-la-Chapelle between France and Maritime Powers.
Jun   Treaty of neutrality between Turkey and Russia.
18 Oct Peace of Aix-la-Chapelle: general recognition of Pragmatic Sanction and conquest of Silesia.

1749
5 Oct   Treaty of Aquisgran between Britain and Spain.

1750
5 Oct   Treaty between Spain and Britain: British renounced Asiento trade.

1751
13 Sep Britain joined Austro-Russian alliance of June 1746.

1752
14 Jun Treaty of Aranjuez between Spain and Austria provided mutual guarantees for their European possessions.

1753
11 Jan Spanish Concordat enhanced rights of crown over clergy.

1755
19 Aug Britain ended alliance with Austria.

1756
16 Jan Treaty of Westminster between Britain and Prussia.
1 May   Alliance of Versailles between France and Austria reversed French policy.

1757
2 Feb   Alliance between Russia and Austria.
1 May   Second Treaty of Versailles between France and Austria by which Prussia to be partitioned.

1758

11 Apr   London Convention: Britain granted annual subsidy to Prussia.

31 Dec   Secret Treaty of Paris between France and Austria.

1760

1 Apr   Treaty between Austria and Russia against Prussia.

27 Sep   Secret treaty between English East India Co. and Mir Kassem, who became Nawab of Bengal.

1761

15 Aug   Alliance between France and Spain (Third 'Family Compact').

1762

5 May   Peace between Prussia and Russia by Treaty of St Petersburg.

22 May   Peace between Sweden and Prussia by Treaty of Hamburg.

3 Nov   Peace preliminaries of Fontainebleau between France, Spain and Britain (confirmed by Peace of Paris, 10 Feb 1763).

24 Nov   Truce between Austria, Prussia and Saxony.

1763

10 Feb   Peace of Paris between Britain and Spain ends Seven Years' War.

15 Feb   Peace of Hubertusburg between Austria and Prussia which definitely ceded Silesia.

1764

11 Apr   Treaty between Russia and Poland to control Poland (revised April 1767).

1768

15 May   Treaty of Versailles: France ceded Corsica to Genoa.

1771

6 Jul   Alliance between Austria and Turkey.

1772

5 Aug   First partition of Poland.

1773

Feb   Alliance between France and Sweden renewed.

1774

21 Jul   Peace of Kutchuk-Kainardzhi between Russia and Turkey which ceded mouth of Dnieper and Crimea.

241

12 Aug   Russia signed secret treaty with Denmark.

1775
19 Mar   Prusso-Polish commercial treaty.

1776
4 Jul   American declaration of independence.

1777
28 May   Defensive alliance between France and Switzerland.

1778
3 Jan   Convention between Austria and Palatinate on partition of Bavaria.
6 Feb   France and American colonists signed offensive and defensive alliance and a commercial treaty.
4 Sep   Treaty of Amity and Commerce between United Provinces and American colonies.

1779
12 Apr   Franco-Spanish alliance of Aranjuez against Britain.
13 May   Peace of Teschen ended War of Bavarian Succession.

1780
10 Mar   Russian declaration of Armed Neutrality in American Revolution later confirmed by France, Spain, Austria, Prussia, Denmark, Sweden and Sicily.

1781
Feb   Austro-Russian treaty.
19 May   Prussia joined League of Armed Neutrality.

1782
Apr   Joseph II abrogated Barrier Treaty of 1715.
17 May   Treaty of Salbai ended Mahratta war.
Jul   Portugal joined League of Armed Neutrality.

1783
3 Sep   Peace of Paris between Britain, France, Spain and the United States: Britain recognised American Independence.

1784
6 Jan   Treaty of Constantinople between Russia and Turkey.

| 11 Mar | Britain signed peace treaty of Mangalore with Tipu Sahib. |
| 20 Mar | Peace of Versailles between United Provinces and Britain. |

1785

23 Jul	League of German Princes formed by Frederick the Great.
10 Sep	Commercial treaty between United States and Prussia.
8 Nov	Treaty of Fontainebleau abrogated Barrier Treaty of 1715.
10 Nov	Alliance between France and United Provinces.

1786

| 26 Sep | Anglo-French commercial treaty. |

1788

15 Apr	Anglo-Dutch alliance.
13 Aug	Prussia joined Anglo-Dutch alliance to form Triple Alliance for preserving peace in Europe.
6 Nov	Convention of Uddevalla provided for evacuation of Danish troops from Sweden.

1789

| 13 Dec | Austrian Netherlands declared its independence under name of Belgium. |

6 THE CHURCH

DENMARK–NORWAY

The Danish Church Order of 1537 established a Lutheran state church for both Denmark and Norway. Bishops became royal officers who administered the church for the king, who became *summus episcopus*. Between 1539 and 1555 the crown seized all monastic properties and the last of the Norwegian monks disappeared in 1562. The Reformation was extended to Iceland by force in 1539, and, after a revolt briefly restored Catholicism in 1549–50, the island finally acquiesced to Lutheranism in 1551 after Danish troops crushed the rising.

In the 17th and 18th centuries, Lutheranism was the religion of the overwhelming majority of Danes and Norwegians. This was just as well, since there was, except for the brief period 1770–2, no religious toleration at all for native Protestant dissenters or Roman Catholics. Conversion of a Dane to Catholicism meant confiscation of property and exile.

In both Norway and Denmark, the Danish crown had at its disposal the revenues of the church, which were often diverted to military purposes. The Danish church suffered physical and subsequently spiritual decline in the 18th century due to royal mismanagement of ecclesiastical affairs. During the reign of the evidently pious Frederick IV, the crown sold 620 Lutheran churches to the highest bidder. Some went to their congregations but a majority were bought by private investors eager to acquire church land and income. A proportion of such income was supposed to be spent on maintenance, but in fact churches were neglected and many fell into disrepair.

1624
Law prohibited residence of Catholic priests in Denmark on pain of death.

1629
27 Mar: Ordinance 'Regarding the Office of the Church and its Authority Over the Impenitent' prescribed pillory for cursing, swearing and drunkenness – enforced by rectors and lay assistants chosen by congregations.

1682
Grant of freedom of worship for foreigners in garrison city of Fredericia.

1685
Introduction of revised ritual in Danish church.

1688
Introduction of new ritual in Norwegian church.

1689
Appearance of new hymnbook by psalmist-Bishop Thomas Kingo of Fyen.

1730–46
Reign of Christian VI, heavily influenced by German Pietism (which he misinterpreted), who introduced era of religiosity and moral stringency in Denmark–Norway.

1735
Publication of Sabbath Ordinance which prescribed fines or even pillory for people absent from Sunday worship without valid reason.

1736
Lutheran catechism and confirmation for all youth prescribed by law.

1739
System of compulsory education established for children aged 7–12 years: teaching based on Luther's Catechism, Pontoppidan's *Explanation*, the Bible, and Bishop Bratt's Hymnbook; in 1741, because of public opposition to costs involved, provision of instruction by congregations made voluntary.

1770–2
Rule of Struensee, when a decree of toleration gave religious freedom to all Protestant dissenters and Roman Catholics as part of wider libertarian reforms; annulled at his overthrow in 1772.

FRANCE

Roman Catholicism was the official religion of France and a large majority of the population was Catholic. However, there was a sizeable body of Protestants – the Huguenots – whose rights to freedom of worship was protected by the Edict of Nantes, issued by Henry IV in 1598. To a greater extent than any other national church, the Gallican church had a tradition of independence from Rome and subordination to the crown – characteristics embedded in the historic concordat of 1516. Even so, the lengthy personal rule of Louis XIV (1661–1715) was to be a period of dispute with the papacy as the French king further encroached on remaining papal powers. Furthermore, bent on the establishment of 'one faith' in his dominions, Louis XIV progressively restricted the toleration granted to Huguenots, eventually resorting to brutal persecution and ultimately to the proscription of the Protestant religion. Louis was also implacably opposed to the Jansenists, followers of the Dutch bishop Cornelius Jansen, who advocated a more ascetic and mystical variety of Catholicism. However, although hounded by the king and condemned by the papacy, Jansenism survived the reign of Louis XIV and furnished a focus of controversy in France for much of the 18th century.

The size of the French clergy before 1700 is uncertain, but in the 18th century the ecclesiastical population of France totalled some 130,000 persons. Of these, approximately 65,000 were priests, 25–27,000 were monks, and 38–40,000 were nuns. Some 8000 were members of the 'upper clergy', that is they were bishops, abbots, abbesses, cathedral canons, etc., with incomes of 10,000 livres or more. The French episcopacy was composed (after 1689) of 139 bishops, whose dioceses ranged in size from a few parishes in the Midi to 600–800 parishes in the north and east, and whose annual revenue ranged from 10,000 livres for small sees to the 200,000 livres p.a. which went to the Archbishop of Strasbourg. *All* bishops in 17th- and 18th-century France were of aristocratic birth – largely recruited from the older 'nobility of blood'.

The wealth of the French church was based on a number of sources, the most important of which was land. Ecclesiastical estates accounted for some 10% of the national territory, ranging from no more than 4% in some southern provinces to more than 30% in Picardy and Cambresis. Estimates of church income vary from 60 million livres a year to more than three times that amount.

1643

8 Jul: Issuance, on death of Louis XIII, of declaration guaranteeing 'free and unrestricted' exercise of religion to French Protestants, the Huguenots.

1644

Synod of Charenton – Huguenots swore absolute fidelity to French crown, a loyalty given proof by their abstention from the Fronde and their public adherence to Louis XIV.

1654

Blaise Pascal retired to Jansenist convent of Port-Royal.

1658

Catholic Societé des Missions Étrangéres founded in Paris.

246

1659
Synod of Loudun reaffirmed Huguenot fidelity to Louis XIV.

1660–1
Assembly of French clergy successfully demanded that commissions be sent to all provinces to scrutinise administration of Edict of Nantes and report all infractions – thus launching long campaign of harassment and suppression of Protestants.

1662
20 Aug: Palazzo Farnese, French embassy in Rome, attacked by papal troops after heated row over diplomatic immunities.

1663
26 Jul: French declared Venaissin united with France and seized Avignon after dispute with papacy.

1664
Armand de Rancé founded Trappist Order of Monks at La Trappe in Normandy.
   12 Feb: French pressure compelled Pope Alexander VII to sign humiliating Treaty of Pisa, granting concessions to Louis XIV.

1666
Edict of Louis XIV decreed that all Protestant churches built since 1598 be demolished and all privileges not expressly stated in Edict of Nantes revoked. Edict also set forth ways Huguenots could be persecuted, excluded Protestants from *all* grades of government, and offered economic inducements to those who converted to Catholicism.
   Companie de Saint-Sacrement, founded in 1627, suppressed by Louis XIV because of government fears of company's secret ways and influence among high-ranking laymen.

1669
'Peace of the Church': agreement reached between four French Jansenist bishops together with nuns of Port-Royal and the papacy, in which the former signed a document condemning five allegedly Jansenist propositions, thus allowing nuns to be readmitted to communion.

1671
Bishop Bossuet published *Exposition de la Foi Catholique*.

1673
Louis XIV revoked Edict of 1666, but persecution of Huguenots continued

and actually made worse by deliberate billeting of troops on Protestant homes.

Louis XIV issued edict which extended '*régale temporelle*' – that is, royal rights to revenues of certain sees during vacancy – to whole of France; king also made new claim to '*régale spirituelle*' – the right to nominate during vacancy to certain convents and benefices.

1675

New royal edict reinforced claim to '*régale*'; crown's claims opposed by two French Jansenist bishops – Nicolas Pavillon of Alet and François de Caulet of Pamiers – who appealed to pope.

1676

Establishment of '*Caisse des Conversions*' (Conversion Fund) with revenues drawn from vacant abbeys and a share of income from '*régale*' under directorship of convert Paul Pellisson.

1679

Louis XIV ordered seizure of Bishop Caulet's temporalities in see of Pamiers; Pope Innocent XI finally intervened directly by sending critical briefs to French king and setting up special congregation to consider '*régale*'.

1681

French clergy in convocation agreed to extend '*régale*' to all French dominions.

Institution by Marillac, intendent of Poitou, of the notorious plan by which dragoons were forcibly quartered on Huguenot households.

1682

Louis XIV convoked General Assembly of Clergy, which approved the Four Articles formulated by French bishops, which declare:
1. Pope has no power in temporal affairs;
2. General Councils are superior to pope in spiritual authority;
3. generally accepted laws of French church are inviolable;
4. in matters of faith, pope's views become dogma only when ratified by General Council.

In reaction to Four Gallican Articles, Pope Innocent XI refused bulls of institution to bishops participating in General Assembly, so that by 1688, 35 sees were vacant.

1683-6

The 'Dragonnades': measures against Huguenots increased in numbers and severity. Facilities for public worship of Huguenots drastically curtailed;

their taxes sharply raised; their ministers limited in numbers and mobility; funds from Protestant charities seized; Huguenot schools, colleges and hospitals closed; their churches destroyed in great numbers; their members barred from learned professions; their children abducted and forcibly indoctrinated in Roman Catholicism. And then the 'Dragonnades' proper: extension of forcible quartering of soldiers on Huguenot homes to all provinces; soldiers allowed a latitude which made ruin, death or flight the only alternatives to conversion. Many Huguenots consequently made verbal acquiescence to Catholicism, while thousands more fled abroad, causing loss of commercial and industrial expertise and wealth.

1685
18 Oct: Revocation of Edict of Nantes – Louis XIV issued Edict of Nantes, arguing that conversion of overwhelming majority of Huguenots made original edict unnecessary. All Protestant churches ordered to be destroyed, all Protestant worship, public and private, proscribed, 'unrepentent' ministers expelled within fifteen days, and adult laymen prohibited to emigrate. Over 200,000 Huguenots fled abroad to England, United Provinces, Brandenburg, Switzerland, North America and South Africa as a result of Revocation.

1686
Pierre Bayle wrote *Commentaire Philosophique sur les Paroles de Jesus-Christ*.

1687
Lavardin, French ambassador to Vatican, provoked new quartering dispute in Rome; French national church, San Luigi dei Francesi, placed under interdict by Innocent XI, who secretly threatened Louis XIV with excommunication.

1688
16 Sep: Louis XIV once again seized Avignon, threatened to invade Papal States, and virtually cut off contact between French clergy and Rome.

1690
Louis XIV restored Avignon to papacy, death of Innocent XI the previous year having reduced tensions.

1692
Compromise between Louis XIV and Pope Innocent XII: pope agreed to confirm bishops who had *not* taken part in 1682 Assembly of Clergy, while Louis withdrew order that Gallican articles be generally taught.

1693

Innocent XII confirmed French bishops who *had* participated in 1682 Assembly; issue over *'régale'* sidestepped rather than solved, with Louis XIV enjoying a practical victory.

1695

P. Quesnel published *Moral Reflections on the New Testament*.

1702-11

War of the Camisards: Camisards, French Protestants of Cévennes valleys of Languedoc, rebel under Jean Cavalier; full-scale hostilities continue until 1711 when rebellion finally quelled.

1709

Remaining inmates of Jansenist convent of Port-Royal forcibly removed and the buildings destroyed.

1713

8 Sep: Publication of *Unigenitus* – bull of Pope Clement XI which condemned the *Moral Reflections* of P. Quesnel as Jansenist and proscribed *Augustinus*, chief work of Jansen himself. Bull became litmus test for both religious and political convictions in 18th-century France, with those opposing it sympathetic to Jansenism and the attempts of the Parlement of Paris to establish itself as a check on royal absolutism, and those supporting it upholding Roman orthodoxy and prerogatives of French crown.

1714

15 Feb: Louis XIV compelled Parlement of Paris to register bull *Unigenitus*; Archbishop of Paris declined to accept bull and was condemned by Pope Clement XI on 28 Mar.

1715

8 Mar: Louis XIV announced that he had ended the practice of the Protestant religion in France.

21 Aug: First 'Synod of the Desert' – Huguenots under Antoine Court met secretly at Monoblet in Languedoc to renew struggle for freedom of worship and to re-establish ravaged Protestant church in France.

1715-63

Period of the Desert for Huguenots when French Protestants were imprisoned and sent to galleys and yet still managed to increase number of clandestine congregations.

1749

Amortisation law passed to prevent further acquisition of property by church in France.

1753

Louis XV supported Archbishop of Paris in dispute over ecclesiastical causes and exiled Parlement of Paris, which in 1752 had seized archbishop's temporal possessions.

1756

Papal encyclical ended affair of confession tickets in France.

1762

Parlement of Paris ordered suppression of Jesuit order.

1763

Voltaire published *Treatise on Toleration*.

1766

French clergy again required to observe the Gallican Articles of 1682, limiting papal authority in France.

1767

May: Jesuit order expelled from France.

1778

'Commission des Réguliers' appointed to reform French religious houses, which leads to edict limiting number of admissions and size of monasteries.

1787

Nov: Edict of Versailles restored religious toleration and most civil rights to Huguenots.

1789

2 Nov: Nationalisation of all church property in France.

GERMANY

The Peace of Westphalia of 1648 determined the ecclesiastical map of Germany for the next two centuries. Although Sweden, Brandenburg and

France gained additional territories, generally a political amnesty returned affairs to the conditions that had prevailed in 1618. However, 1 January 1624 was chosen as the date for determining proprietorship of ecclesiastical lands and religious practice. The *jus reformandi*, the right of the territorial rulers to determine the religion of their subjects (first laid down in the Peace of Augsburg of 1555), was retained in a greatly modified form. After 1648, rulers were to possess the authority to regulate religious life in their territories but not the right to impose a new faith on their subjects – provisions which were shamelessly dishonoured in some states. In addition, the Peace of Westphalia extended a degree of religious toleration by providing that such freedoms which had existed in 1624 were to be inalienable and by distinguishing between the public and private practice of religion, which extended protection for private and domestic worship to minorities. Moreover, Calvinists were accorded equal status with Lutherans and Roman Catholics, although no provision was made for lesser sects. At the insistence of Catholic princes, rulers were allowed five years to expel religious dissidents from their lands. The degree to which the 300-plus German principalities observed the agreements of Westphalia varied widely from one state to another and among successive rulers of particular states. In the main, although there were some multi-denominational states, the confessional boundaries laid down in 1648 had a tendency to harden, thus fixing the religious geography of Germany.

1 *Bavaria*

In the 16th century, Protestantism spread to Bavaria fairly late but subsequently made considerable headway in the towns and among the nobility. However, due to the firm opposition of the Wittelsbach dynasty, which gave strong encouragement to the Jesuits and expelled troublesome Lutheran burghers, Protestantism was almost wholly suppressed. In the 17th century, the Bavarian Catholic church grew richer and more powerful, so that, although a decree of 1704 forbade further accumulation of ecclesiastical property, the church had already amassed some 30–40% of the electorate's land by that date. Bavarian territory was subject to 18 bishops and archbishops, all of whom lived outside the electorate. Unlike the hierarchies of ecclesiastical territories, the Bavarian prelacy between 1648 and 1789 was dominated by civil servants (30%) and burghers (30%); nobles constituted only 7% of the total, and peasants 6.5%.

The Wittelsbach dynasty had long since controlled most episcopal electtions, but in the 18th century there was a further movement towards the subordination of the church to an absolute secular authority. Between 1747 and 1777, Elector Maximilian III Joseph, inspired by his advisers J. A. von

Ickstatt and Peter von Osterwald, restricted the financial privileges of the church, curtailed ecclesiastical censorship, suppressed the Jesuit order, and imposed the placet (approval by ruler of papal decrees or appointments). His successor, Karl Theodor, although failing to realign diocesan boundaries to coincide with political ones, made an alliance with the papacy and established a papal nunciature in Munich to combat the growth of episcopal autonomy advocated by Bishop J. N. von Hontheim. By 1789, Rome had agreed to the establishment of a court diocese in Munich, exempt from ties with the Bishop of Freising and the Archbishop of Salzburg, which was the first step in the reorganisation of the Bavarian episcopate along political lines.

1672, 1704, 1730
Decrees issued which limited ability of church to amass land.

1747–77
Electorate of Maximilian III Joseph whose policies of 'enlightened absolutism' restricted financial, educational and political powers of church.

1764
13 Oct: Amortisation law passed to forbid further accumulation of land by church.

1768
Reorganisation of Ecclesiastical Council which restored influence of laity to status prior to concordat of 1583.

29 Sep: First monastic mandate demanded precise details about houses and extent of endowment.

9 Dec: Founding of religious brotherhoods made more difficult; existing confraternities required to reveal assets, statutes and activities.

20 Dec: Foreigners and all non-natives excluded from Bavarian benefices.

1769
16 Feb: Institution of state book censorship, independent of church censors.

Mandate for reform of religious orders prohibited taking of vows before the age of 21, limited penal authority of superiors, and abolished monastic incarceration.

30 Dec: Following prohibition of visitations and electoral supervision by non-resident prelates, law passed to divorce Bavarian monastic orders from foreign superiors and provinces; only one-sixth of Bavarian regular clergy could be foreigners; Bavarian commissioners to supervise elections in Freising, Regensburg, Passau and Chiemsee.

1769–70

Bavarian clergy made subject to taxation.

1770

3 Apr: Electoral placet, occasionally imposed previously, prescribed for all church regulations.

1774

Conciliatory agreement reached between government and ecclesiastical hierarchy concerning election of prelates.

1777

Accession of Elector Karl Theodor of Palatinate branch of Wittelsbach family; incorporation of largely-Protestant Palatinate into Bavaria.

1782

Meeting between Elector Karl Theodor and Pope Pius VI in Munich.

1785

Permanent establishment in Munich of papal nunciature with jurisdiction corresponding to political boundaries of Bavaria.

1786

Jul–Aug: Conference of representatives of four German archbishops formulated Punctation of Ems which attacked papal nunciatures.

1789

In papal brief *Convenit provide*, Pius VI agreed to establishment of court diocese free of control of Bishop of Freising and archbishop of Salzburg: first step in reorganisation of Bavarian episcopate along political lines.

2 Brandenburg–Prussia

All of the scattered possessions of the Hohenzollern dynasty had embraced Protestantism in the 16th century. Prussia and Brandenburg were thoroughly Lutheran while the territories of Cleves and Mark were decidely Calvinist. In all of these areas, most church lands had been secularised and church government had been subordinated to the state. The conversion of Elector John Sigismund to Calvinism led to the official toleration of both the reformed and Lutheran churches in all Hohenzollern territories in 1614. However, in East Prussia, Calvinists were slowly tolerated if at all and excluded from most important offices, while in Cleves Lutherans had to be protected from the Calvinist majority. Between 1640 and 1789, all the rulers of Brandenburg–Prussia exhibited a preference for religious toleration which was only partly obstructed by the entrenched prejudices of the nobility and the churches themselves. Frederick William, the 'Great Elector', attempted to increase the degree of religious freedom within his own lands and offered refuge to Huguenots and other persecuted foreign Protestants. King Frederick I, himself a devout Calvinist, was instrumental in removing such 'popish' remnants as private confession, exorcism, crucifixes and vestments from the Lutheran church. He continued the consistorial government of the churches and founded a number of 'union churches' on whose altars the Lutheran and Reformed catechisms lay side by side. However, like the Great Elector before him, Frederick I was unable to secure a union between the two denominations.

As was the case in other German Protestant states, Roman Catholicism had no legal status in Prussia, although private worship was tolerated. An advance was made during the reign of King Frederick William I (1713–1740), when Catholic chaplains were allowed in the Prussian army, mainly for foreign recruits. There were, in fact, few Catholics under Prussian rule until the conquest of Silesia in 1740 by Frederick II and the subsequent annexations in Poland. Frederick II, whose own sceptical rationalism made him largely indifferent to questions of religious doctrine, saw the churches as extensions of state administration, and was determined to subjugate the Catholic as well as Protestant hierarchies to secular authority. However, his policy of toleration led Frederick to guarantee the religious *status quo* in Silesia and to aid in the construction of a Catholic cathedral in Berlin itself. Even Frederick William II's Religious Edict of 1788 did not grant true equality to Catholics. Although free to worship and build churches, they were still for some time discriminated against in the army and civil service.

1613
Elector John Sigismund abandoned Lutheranism and embraced Calvinism.

1614
Confessio Sigismundi – issued after failure of John Sigismund to convert Lutheran clergymen or nobility to Calvinism – granted freedom of worship to both confessions in Hohenzollern territories, which after 1618 included East Prussia.

1648
Elector Frederick William used influence to secure equal protection for Calvinists in Peace of Westphalia.

1662

Conference of Lutheran and Calvinist ministers at Berlin summoned by Frederick William to discuss religious reunion. Failed because of obduracy of representatives of both faiths.

Toleration edict issued to reinforce *Confessio Sigismundi*; Frederick William compelled to use pressure to secure office for Calvinists in East Prussia.

1664

Further edict of toleration. Practice of abusing opponents by name from pulpit and public criticism of other confessions forbidden. Ministers refusing to submit in writing to be subject to ejection.

1666

Flight to Saxony of intolerant Lutheran preacher and hymnist, Paul Gebhardt, where he made his famous avowal: 'I cannot regard Calvinists as Christians.'

1685

Edict of Potsdam promised refuge to French Huguenots fleeing persecutions of Louis XIV. These religious exiles subsequently injected economic, intellectual and spiritual vigour into Brandenburg.

1688–1713

Reign of Elector Frederick III (King Frederick I after 1701): Lutheran churches purged of 'popish' practices and vestments. 'Union churches' where Lutheran and Calvinist catechisms were both employed founded to encourage religious reunion.

1694

Foundation of University of Halle, which became centre of religious and intellectual influence spreading beyond Prussia and considered the cradle of Lutheran Pietism. Orphanage at Halle, under direction of August Hermann Franke, became model of Pietist system of education and exerted great influence over Junker nobility and civil service.

1713–40

Reign of King Frederick William I. Roman Catholic chaplains allowed in Prussian army, chiefly for foreign recruits.

1742

Treaty of Breslau: Frederick II, after conquering largely Catholic Silesia, agreed to maintain religious *status quo*. Religious freedom was in fact

256

extended, but Catholic hierarchy brought under state control and Catholics excluded from many offices. However, church lands were not secularised, nor were Jesuits expelled.

1773

Completion in Berlin of Catholic St Hedwig's cathedral with assistance of Frederick II. First legal place of public worship for Roman Catholics in Brandenburg since Reformation.

1788

9 Jul: Religious Edict issued by King Frederick William II to combat religious scepticism encouraged by Frederick II and to 'restore Christianty'. Edict officially placed Lutheranism, Calvinism and Catholicism on equal footing, and recognised Jews, Mennonites, Moravian Brethren and Bohemian Brethren as 'tolerated sects'. All other sects prohibited as 'pernicious'. All proselytising banned. Schedule of errors and heresies attached to edict which decreed that any clergyman or teacher holding such views was to be dismissed. Repealed in 1797.

18 Dec: Censorship law promulgated to secure religious orthodoxy of all published writings. Repealed in 1797.

1794

Land Law officially established civil equality of Roman Catholics with Protestants, but discrimination against Catholics continued, especially in army and civil service.

3 Catholic Ecclesiastical Principalities

The Peace of Westphalia restored both the religious and the political rights of bishops in the Roman Catholic ecclesiastical principalities. There were 65 ruling archbishops, bishops, abbots and priors, who between them controlled some 14% of the land and 12% of the population of Germany. Ecclesiastical territories had approximately three-and-a-half million subjects, so that the 'Reichskirche' was the second largest form of government in the Empire after the dynastic princes. The principal ecclesiastical states were the archbishoprics of Cologne, Mainz and Trier; the bishoprics of Augsburg, Bamberg, Constance, Frieising, Hildersheim, Münster, Paderborn, Regensburg, Speyer, Worms and Würzburg; and the abbeys of Corvey, Berchtesgaden, Fulda, Ellwangen and Weissenburg. Osnabrück had the peculiar fortune to be ruled alternately by Catholic and Protestant bishops.

Although the ecclesiastical territories were independent states, the intimate ties of kinship between their rulers and the dynastic families and the nobility greatly limited the nature of episcopal autonomy. Between 1583 and 1761, the archbishopric of Cologne was governed by a succession of Wittelsbach (Bavarian) princes, and the bishoprics of Liege, Münster, Paderborn and Hildersheim were during much of this time in the hands of the Wittelsbach archbishops of Cologne. Furthermore, the bishoprics of Regensburg and Freising also took their rulers from the Bavarian dynasty. The Franconian territories preferred to elect their bishops from the ranks of the nobility whose members formed their chapters. The Schönborn family was especially prominent, providing bishops for Mainz, Worms, Würzburg, Bamberg and Trier between 1650 and 1750.

The ambivalent nature of the German ecclesiastical princes significantly influenced their relations with Rome. After 1648, resentment against the papal nunciatures in Cologne, Vienna and Lucerne against the Roman Curia, and against the claims of the papacy itself grew steadily. The concept of 'episcopalism' which emerged in the late 17th and 18th centuries was the German ecclesiastical equivalent of Gallicanism. The German bishops were perfectly willing to defer to the pope in matters of faith and morals but increasingly unwilling to accede in the areas of discipline, finance and elections. The publication in 1763 of *De statu ecclesiae* by Bishop Johann Nikolaus von Hontheim under the pseudonym 'Justinus Febronius' was only the culmination of a long development of episcopalist thinking. Hontheim represented the view of many German bishops when he wrote that church affairs should be kept as far as possible in episcopal and civil hands.

1648

Peace of Westphalia restored both religious and political rights of bishops in ecclesiastical principalities.

1657

Coronation Tractate solved dispute between archbishops of Mainz and Cologne concerning right to crown Holy Roman Emperor.

1661

Unsuccessful Protestant-led insurrection in Münster against militarist and would-be absolitist Bishop Christof Bernhard von Galen.

Ernest Augustus of Brunswick-Lüneburg elected Protestant bishop of Osnabrück, which alternated between Catholic and Protestant rule.

1665

Imperial Diet and Supreme Court meeting in Speyer unequivocally opposed practice of appeals to Pope and nuncios in trials concerning temporal matters.

1673

Gravamina contra Curiam Romanum, drawn up by archbishop–electors of Cologne, Mainz and Trier, protesting papal violations of Vienna Concordat of 1448 and demanding that German church be accorded equal treatment with French and Spanish churches.

1683

Johannes Schilter, Protestant canonist, wrote *De Libertate Ecclesiarum Germaniae*, one year after French church declared Gallican liberties. Helped sow seeds of German episcopalism. Urged reunification of Catholics and Protestants by reducing powers of popes and curia and abandonment of doctrine of papal infallibility.

1695

Pope Innocent XII, in order to limit powers of dynastic and noble families in selection of German bishops, forbade all 'capitulations of elections'.

1700

Zeger-Bernhard van Espen published pioneering *Jus Ecclesiasticum* in which episcopal, erastian and Jansensist ideas were assimilated into German church.

1746

Georg Christoph Neller published *Principia Juris Ecclesiastici ad Statum Germaniae Accommodata*, compiled substantially from French Gallican authors and attacking Jesuit government.

1763

Johann Nikolaus von Hontheim published, under pseudonym Justinus Febronius, *De statu ecclesiae et legitima potestate Romani pontificis*. Recognised Pope as supervisor of church administration and, subject to a general council, of faith and morals, but attacked claims of papal supremacy and urged that church affairs be kept as far as possible in hands of bishops and secular rulers.

1764

De statu ecclesiae placed on Index of banned works.

1769

Archbishop of Mainz, Cologne and Trier gave general support to Gravamina of Coblenz, 31 objections to papal authority over German church.

1778
Hontheim made formal retraction of *De statu ecclesiae*, but indicated little real change of view.

1786
Jul–Aug: Punctation of Ems, 22-point reform programme for church of Empire formulated by representatives of archbishops of Cologne, Mainz, Trier and Salzburg. Punctation advocated independence of German bishops from Roman authority, cancellation of exemptions and quinquinnial faculties, complete abolition of nunciatures, right of bishops to dispose of charitable contributions, episcopal 'placet' for papal bulls and briefs, and convocation of a church council at national level to redress these grievances.

4 *Hanover*
(Brunswick–Lüneburg–Celle–Kalenberg–Grubenhagen)

The population of the territories which eventually became the electorate of Hanover was overwhelmingly Lutheran.

1645
Beginning of Syncretist Dispute between Georg Calixtus, theologian at Brunswick University of Helmstedt who advocated religious reunion, and orthodox Lutherans.

1651
Conversion to Catholicism of John Frederick of Brunswick–Lüneburg; forced to live abroad until 1665.

1665
John Frederick became Duke of Kalenberg–Göttengen–Grubenhagen so that Catholic services in Hanover had to be allowed according to Peace of Westphalia.

1679
Duke John Frederick died; succeeded by younger brother Ernest Augustus, Lutheran bishop of Osnabrück, made Elector of Brunswick in 1692. His wife Sophia was sympathetic to reunionist principles of Calixtus.

1714
Elector George of Hanover succeeded as King George I of Great Britain. Anglicanism of British Hanoverian rulers had no influence in Lutheran Hanover.

5 *Hesse–Cassel*

1567
Permanent separation of Hesse–Cassel and Hesse–Darmstadt.

1605
Landgrave Maurice of Hesse–Cassel converted from Lutheranism to Calvinism and attempted to impose it in all his territories. He met strong resistance, especially among Lutheran nobility and among populace of Upper Hesse. After this, population was mixed Lutheran and Calvinist with gradual Calvinist predominance. Hesse–Darmstadt remained strongly Lutheran.

1648
Lutherans in Upper Hesse granted limited official toleration.

1652
Conversion from Calvinism to Catholicism of Landgrave Ernest of principality of Hesse–Rheinfels, with his wife; conversion subsequently cost Landgrave Ernest his sovereignty.

1657
Calvinist Church Order promulgated in Hesse–Cassel by Landgrave Wilhelm VI despite protests from Lutherans and many Reformed ministers.

6 *Rhenish Palatinate*

1648–80
Reign of Calvinist Elector Karl Ludwig. Majority Calvinist, large minority Lutheran but degree of toleration extended to Roman Catholics, especially in refounded Mannheim where full freedom was given to all three faiths and a church built dedicated to Holy Unity, in which alternate Calvinist, Lutheran and Catholic services were held.

1649
Consistory re-established to govern Calvinist church in Palatinate.

1685
Death of Karl II, last Protestant Elector. Succession of Roman Catholic Philip Wilhelm of Neuburg, who continued to extend toleration to Protestants.

261

1690

Death of Philip Wilhelm. Succession of Elector Johann Wilhelm.

1697

Peace of Ryswick: withdrawal of Louis XIV in return for sum of money and understanding with Elector Johann Wilhelm that Roman Catholicism would be reimposed in Palatinate. Johann Wilhelm, with aid of Jesuits, launched intense campaign of persecution and conversion, depriving Protestants of civil rights and severely restricting freedom of worship.

1703

Intervention of Prussia and Brunswick brought some redress, but persecution of both Lutherans and Calvinists resumed, so that large numbers were forced to emigrate during 18th century. Despite persecution, Protestantism remained religion of majority. As late as 1789, there were 140,000 Calvinists and 50,000 Lutherans as opposed to 90,000 Catholics.

1777

Elector Karl Theodor became Elector of Bavaria on extinction of main branch of Wittelsbach family, thus reuniting Bavaria and Palatinate and putting Palatinate Protestants in minority in electorate as a whole.

7 *Saxe–Weimar*

Overwhelmingly Lutheran.

8 *Saxe–Gotha*

Under Duke Ernest the Pious (died 1675), great stress was placed on religious education and practice. The state put its full powers of coercion behind the reimposition of Lutheran church discipline. The politico-religious ideas of Duke Ernest were reflected in the *Christian State* by his longtime councillor Veit Ludwig von Seckendorf, published in 1685, which endorsed princely supremacy in religion (as in all else) but exhorted Christian rulers to promote religion and education actively.

9 *Saxony*

The population of Saxony was almost entirely Lutheran in the 17th and 18th centuries.

1539

Lutheran Reformation introduced into Saxony by Duke Henry, strongly influenced by his wife, Catherine of Mecklenburg.

1580

Lutheran consistory established to administer Saxon church.

1589

Consistory and Lutheran oath abolished under Christian I by Calvinist sympathiser Chancellor Nicolaus Crell.

1591

Chancellor Crell removed by Lutheran opponents at death of Christian I.

1601

Crell executed.

1606

Consistory and strict Lutheran church government restored at request of estates.

1620

Saxony supported Catholic and Habsburg forces against Calvinist Elector Palatine and Protestant states in Thirty Years' War.

1631

Elector John George forced by events, not inclination, to switch Saxon support to Swedish and Protestant side. In 1635, Saxony made peace with Emperor, deserting other Protestants in return for territory of Lusatia.

1647

Elector John George bitterly opposed recognition of Calvinists as co-equals of Lutherans and Catholics in Germany.

1697

Elector Frederick Augustus I (Augustus the Strong) announced conversion to Roman Catholicism in order to secure election to Polish throne (on 27 June) after death of King John III Sobieski.

1717

Revelation of Frederick Augustus's son's conversion to Rome incites anti-Catholic feeling in Saxon Estates and populace.

263

1718

Saxon Estates renewed pledge of loyalty to Augsburg confession; banned Catholics from membership in Estates.

1722-7

Moravian Brethren allowed by Lutheran Pietist Count Zinzendorf to build settlement at Herrnhut.

10 *Württemberg*

1535

Duke Ulrich introduced Lutheran Reformation with concessions towards Swiss Reformed faith, seized church lands, and used ecclesiastical revenues for his own benefit.

1547

Duke Ulrich forced to restore lands to monasteries and reinstate Catholic prelates; few concessions granted to Protestants.

1552

Defeat of Emperor Charles V by Maurice of Saxony allowed re-emergence of Protestantism in Württemberg. Monastic lands gradually passed to Protestant prelates.

1630-48

Imperial troops restored monasteries to Catholic church and reinstalled religious orders.

1648

Monasteries reverted to Protestant prelates at Peace of Westphalia.

1733

Accession of Catholic convert, Duke Charles Alexander. Lutheran estates insisted that episcopal prerogative be exercised by privy councillors. Charles Alexander, determined to disestablish Lutheran church, still pursued pro-Catholic policy.

1737

Death of Charles Alexander, followed by arrests of non-Lutheran favourites and advisers.

1744

Duke Charles Eugene, also Roman Catholic, came of age and assumed direction of Württemberg government. Although an absolutist, Charles Eugene made no attempt to dispossess Protestantism.

GREAT BRITAIN AND IRELAND

1 *England*

The Protestant Reformation in England had been accomplished in stages over a span of some 30 years in the middle of the 16th century. Only in 1559, in the first year of Queen Elizabeth's reign, had Anglicanism in its definitive form been made the established religion of England. Despite the moderate nature of the church settlement, Elizabeth I, James I and Charles I had to struggle for the next 80 years to achieve a true uniformity of faith. However, both the small remnant of Roman Catholics and the much larger number of Protestant dissenters defied all attempts to impose conformity. It was Puritan opposition which provided the strongest challenge to Elizabeth, and, after a period of relative quiescence under James I, Puritan sentiment gained new ground during the reign of Charles I – provoked in large part by the rise to ascendancy of Archbishop William Laud and his faction of Arminians. Laud's rejection of predestination, his emphasis on the role of the priest and sacraments, and above all his authoritarian attempts to impose his own rigid views in every parish, alienated not only the commercial elements in the towns but – much more importantly – a large sector of the gentry and aristocracy.

Indeed, religious grievances against Laud in particular and bishops in general were among the principal causes for the civil war which erupted in 1642. After Charles I's defeat by parliament, the episcopacy was abolished in 1646 and replaced, more in theory than in practice, by a Presbyterian system of church government. However, the 1640s saw a great flowering of more extreme Protestant sects, and after 1648 congregationalism in various guises became the norm. In fact, there was a great deal of continuity in the parishes with some two-thirds of the surviving Anglican clergy at least outwardly conforming in order to retain their livings. Although the Book of Common Prayer was banned, Anglican services were secretly held throughout the Commonwealth and Protectorate, with officials making little effort to suppress them. Furthermore, although the number of Anglican bishops steadily dwindled, a kind of underground hierarchy was preserved.

Thus, with the restoration of Charles II, there was little doubt that episcopacy would be restored, especially since the English elite had learned to their cost that James I's dictum – 'No Bishop, no King' – was all too true. In fact, shortly after his return, the king began restoring the Anglican episcopal hierarchy on the strength of the royal prerogative. However, for both political and temperamental reasons (not ones of conscience), Charles II favoured the comprehension of moderate dissenters, especially Presbyterians, within the framework of the established church and the toleration of other loyal Protestant sects and Roman Catholics. He was to be foiled in this by the restored bishops led by Gilbert Sheldon and the Cavalier parliament which met in 1661. The Act of Uniformity of 1662 excluded some 1000 ministers who could not conform to its provisions, thus abandoning a century-long attempt to achieve uniformity of faith in England. Although Charles II for many years tried to extend a modicum of toleration to religious nonconformists, parliament passed a series of draconian statutes in the period 1664–70 and forced the king to withdraw a Declaration of Indulgence issued in 1672. Consequently the period 1662–85 was one of religious persecution unparalleled since the days of Mary Tudor. Nor was James II to secure better results. His confessed Catholicism rendered his two Declarations of Indulgence all the more suspect and his absolutist policies ended in his overthrow in 1688.

The Revolution of 1688–9 which brought William and Mary to the throne brought relief for Protestant dissenters at last, as they were allowed to worship publicly and build chapels by the Act of Toleration of 1689, although they remained excluded from public offices, the army, navy and universities by the Test Acts. Roman Catholics and Unitarians were given no relief.

The 18th century saw a gradual diminution of the religious passions and prejudices which had so marked the previous 200 years. After 1715, largely for political reasons, the Whig party gradually eased restrictions on Protestant nonconformists and the suppression of Roman Catholics was progressively lessened. In the late 1770s, there came the first of the Catholic relief acts which would lead eventually to Catholic Emancipation in 1829.

Once the established church was firmly secured, the Anglican hierarchy and clergy entered a period of comfortable complacency. Both the church and older nonconformist groups failed to reach large sectors of the population, especially among the masses which crowded into the burgeoning cities. It was thus the Methodists, led by John Wesley and George Whitefield, who attempted to minister to the neglected multitudes. Beginning in the 1740s, a wave of evangelicalism swept England and Wales which led eventually to the establishment of the independent Methodist connections in the later years of the century.

In the 17th and 18th centuries England and Wales had in the vicinity of 9000 parishes. There were two metropolitan provinces – Canterbury and

York – and 23 dioceses. At the beginning of the 18th century there were perhaps 11,000 Anglican clergy, over 9000 of whom were beneficed, and Anglican clerical numbers grew to some 14,500 by 1800. In addition, there were approximately 3000 nonconforming ministers of various denominations. Clerical salaries varied enormously. The income of bishops ranged from £7000 for Canterbury and £6000 for Durham to £1000 for Llandaff. In 1700, over 5500 ordinary livings paid less than £50 a year and 1200 less than £20, with some as tiny as £3–5 p.a. There is little to suggest that these figures rose substantially in the course of the 18th century.

During the whole period, more than 90% of the population of England and Wales were nominally Anglican. There were probably from 75,000 to 100,000 Roman Catholics and perhaps 500,000 Protestant dissenters at most. Despite the evangelical revival, religious observance declined markedly after 1700, with attendance at Anglican services falling most steeply. By 1800, no more than 10% of the total population was present at Easter communion. The numbers of Methodists, of course, rose sharply after 1750: in 1767 there were 22,410 Wesleyan Methodists and in 1791 56,605.

Archbishops of Canterbury		Archbishops of York	
William Laud	1633–45	Richard Neile	1632–40
William Juxton	1660–3	John Williams	1641–50
Gilbert Sheldon	1663–7	Accepted Frewen	1660–4
William Sancroft	1678–90	Richsrd Sterne	1664–83
John Tillotson	1691–4	John Dolben	1683–6
Thomas Tenison	1695–1715	Thomas Lamplugh	1688–91
William Wake	1716–37	John Sharp	1691–1714
John Potter	1737–47	Sir William Dawes	1714–24
Thomas Herring	1747–57	Lancelot Blackburn	1724–43
Matthew Hutton	1757–8	Thomas Herring	1743–7
Thomas Secker	1758–68	Matthew Hutton	1747–57
Frederick Cornwallis	1768–83	John Gilbert	1757–61
John Moore	1783–1805	Robert Hay Drummond	1761–76
		William Markham	1777–1807

1645

4 Jan: Ordinance abolishing Book of Common Prayer (containing the liturgy of the Anglican church as established in 1559) and putting into execution the Directory for the Public Worship of God, compiled by Westminster Assembly of Divines – the first major step in establishing Presbyterianism.

10 Jan: Archbishop William Laud executed.

1647

1 Apr: Roman Catholics excluded from London and Westminster.

9 Oct: Ordinance abolishing bishops and archbishops and all episcopal courts; episcopal lands and possessions settled on trustees for use of Commonwealth.

1648

29 Jan: Ordinance settling counties into classical Presbyterian and Congregational elderships.

29 Aug: Ordinance establishing church government for England and Ireland, erecting a fully Presbyterian system.

1649

30 Apr: Act abolishing deans, canons, prebends, chapters; church lands settled on trustees for benefit of Commonwealth.

1650

27 Sep: Repeal of laws imposing penalties for not attending church.

1653

16 Dec: Instrument of government proposed toleration for all but 'prelatists and papists', thus hesitantly endorsing toleration for all but Anglicans and Catholics.

1654

20 Mar: Commissioners for the Approbation of Public Preachers, or 'Triers', appointed.

22 Aug: Commissioners for ejecting scandalous, ignorant and insufficient ministers, or 'Ejectors' appointed.

1655

Jews readmitted to England.

1660

4 Apr: In Declaration of Breda, Charles II promised to consent to any legislation which offered a measure of religious toleration to 'tender consciences'.

13 Sep: Act for settling and restoring ministers, readmitting ejected Anglican ministers to their livings and expelling 695 intruded clergy.

25 Oct: Charles II's Worcester House Declaration which promised a degree of compromise to Presbyterians; resulted in summoning of Savoy Conference.

1661

Apr–Jul: Savoy Conference, officially convoked to provide comprehension for moderate Presbyterians, dominated by 'Laudian' bishops who refused to compromise on matters of ritual and discipline.

30 Jun: Bishops restored to House of Lords.

Nov: Corporation Act excluded from town government all who refused to take oaths of allegiance and supremacy, to receive Anglican communion, or to abjure the Solemn League and Covenant.

1662

Act against those who refused to take oaths, aimed against Quakers.

19 May: Act of Uniformity authorised use of revised Book of Common Prayer and excluded all clergymen not accepting the established liturgy and discipline of the Anglican church.

Aug: Some 1000 ministers ejected for refusal to comply with Act of Uniformity (in addition to those deprived between 1660 and 1662).

25 Dec: Royal declaration in favour of toleration; Charles II proposed, if Parliament agreed, to exercise his dispensing power on behalf of Protestant dissenters and Roman Catholics.

1663

Feb: The House of Commons angrily refused to allow Charles II to dispense with the provisions of the Act of Uniformity and instead initiated attempts to strengthen the laws against Roman Catholics.

Aug–Oct: 'Yorkshire' plot to overturn monarchy and abolish episcopacy, in which several former Cromwellian officers were implicated, was foiled, scores arrested and 20 executed for treason.

1664

May: Parliament passed Conventicle Act which forbade meetings of five or more people not of the same household for the purpose of holding non-Anglican services.

1665

Oct: Passage of Five Mile Act, which forbade dissenting ministers to come within five miles of any corporate town or of any parish where they had formerly preached.

1668

First Conventicle Act expired; nonconformist meetings continued to flourish.

1670

11 Apr: Passage of second Conventicle Act which renewed harsh penalties on Protestant dissenters attending nonconformist services.

May: Secret Treaty of Dover between Charles II and Louis XIV. To the knowledge of only Duke of York, Earl of Arlington and Lord Clifford, Charles II promised to reimpose Roman Catholicism with aid of French troops if necessary. The sincerity of Charles II's pledge is in doubt and the clause was never acted on.

1672

15 Mar: In partial fulfilment of Secret Treaty of Dover, Charles II issued a Declaration of Indulgence suspending the penal laws against both Roman Catholics and Protestant dissenters. Catholics were allowed to worship privately, while dissenters were allowed to register to teach, preach and establish meeting-houses.

1673

8 Mar: Parliament forced Charles II to retract Declaration of Indulgence by withholding supply. The information provided by the register of nonconformists was used to enforce renewed persecution.

29 Mar: Parliament passed first Test Act barring from all public office those who refused to deny transubstantiation and take the oaths of supremacy and allegiance. James, Duke of York, a Catholic, forced to resign offices.

1676

Archbishop Sancroft, in alliance with Lord Treasurer Danby, instructed Anglican priests to undertake a religious census in every parish to prove that Anglicans comprised overwhelming majority of English population.

1678-9

Popish Plot: A plot to murder Charles II, put James on the throne, and forcibly reimpose Roman Catholicism was revealed (Sep 1678) by Titus Oates and others. Shortly afterwards Sir Edmund Berry Godfrey, the magistrate before whom Oates had deposed his evidence, was murdered; and Coleman, the Duke of York's secretary, was found in possession of treasonous correspondence with continental Jesuits. Panic ensued which resulted in the arrest and execution of many innocent Catholics, including Lord Stafford. Furthermore, the parliamentary opposition exploited the anti-Catholic fear to oust the Earl of Danby as chief minister and to launch a campaign to exclude the Duke of York from the succession to the throne.

1678

John Bunyan published *The Pilgrim's Progress*, Part I.

Nov: Second Test Act, passed during frenzy of Popish Plot revelations, imposed strict oath on members of both Lords and Commons, thus barring Catholics from sitting in parliament until 1829.

1679

Whig majority in House of Commons passed first Exclusion Bill to exclude Duke of York from throne; bill stopped by Charles II's dissolution of parliament.

Bishop Gilbert Burnet published *History of the Reformation of the Church of England.*

1680

Nov: Second Exclusion Bill passed by House of Commons but defeated in House of Lords. Attempts to ease statutory penalties against Protestant dissenters prevented by dissolution of parliament.

1681

Mar: Third Exclusion Bill foiled by swift dissolution of Charles II's last parliament.

1681–5

Renewed persecution of both Protestant dissenters and Roman Catholic recusants.

1683

Rye House Plot, allegedly intended to murder Charles II and Duke of York and put Duke of Monmouth on throne, intensified fears of Protestant dissenters, identifying them with sedition.

1684

John Bunyan published *The Pilgrim's Progress*, Part II.

1685

6 Feb: Death of Charles II and accession of his Catholic brother, James II.

Jun: Rebellion led by Duke of Monmouth, the 'Protestant Champion', crushed by James II's army.

Pope Innocent XI appointed John Leyburne Bishop of Andrumentum to supervise the Roman Catholic clergy in England, but without the powers of an ordinary.

James II extended to England the practice of dispensing with the Test Act for army officers, a practice already existing in Ireland.

1686

Roman Catholics appointed to commissions of peace, lieutenancies, and other positions in county government after James II had dispensed with the Test Act in their cases.

Aug: Court of Ecclesiastical High Commission established illegally by James II to exert tighter control on Anglican church, which was baulking at king's pro-Catholic policy. Archbishop Sancroft refused to serve on court.

Godden vs Hales: Collusive court case which sanctioned James II's power to dispense with the laws in individual cases, thus encouraging the king's evasion of the Test Act in favour of Catholics.

1687

Roman Catholics appointed to central government offices by dispensation of James II.

Fellows of Magdalen College, Oxford, expelled and replaced by Catholics after refusal to elect a Catholic as president.

4 Apr: James II's first Declaration of Indulgence, which suspended operation of penal laws and church courts for both Protestant dissenters and Roman Catholics.

3 Jul: Papal Nuncio received by James in London.

1688

England and Wales divided into four provinces for administration of Catholic clergy; three vicars apostolic, in addition to Bishop of Andrumentum, appointed.

25 Apr: James II's second Declaration of Indulgence repeating terms of first.

4 May: James ordered bishops to have Declaration read from every pulpit. Seven bishops, including Archbishop Sancroft, refused and petitioned to king against illegality of his use of suspending power.

8 Jun: Seven bishops summoned before privy council, charged with publishing seditious libel, and committed to Tower of London.

10 Jun: Birth of a son to James's wife, Queen Mary of Modena – more of a threat than a blessing since it provided a prospective Catholic heir and alarmed Protestants.

29 Jun: Trial of seven bishops; all found not guilty of conspiring to diminish royal power – another blow to king's authority.

Oct: Fearing for his crown and as part of wholesale reversals, James II restored president and fellows of Magdalen College, Oxford.

3 Oct: Archbishop Sancroft and five other bishops presented James with set of 10 propositions for reform of Church of England. James belatedly complied with some, refused others.

5 Nov: William of Orange landed in England at head of 15,000 troops; there followed Protestant risings in his favour all over England.

25 Dec: James fled to France.

1689

12 Feb: William and Mary declared joint monarchs.

Feb–Dec: Bill of Rights limited royal powers of suspension and dispensation, outlawed prerogative courts, and barred Roman Catholics from the throne.

24 May: Toleration Act allowed freedom of worship to all Protestant dissenters but continued to exclude Catholics and Unitarians. Test and Corporation Acts remained in force.

1 Aug: Nine English bishops suspended for refusing to swear allegiance to William III, protesting that James II was still king *de jure*.

1695

John Locke published *The Reasonableness of Christianity*.

1698

Society for the Promotion of Christian Knowledge founded.

1700

Act 'for preventing growth of popery' required Roman Catholics to abjure their religion in order to inherit or buy land.

1701

12 Jun: Act of Settlement excluded Catholics from English succession and provided that only Anglicans could hold throne.

Foundation of Society for the Propagation of the Gospel in Foreign Parts.

1711

15 Dec: Occasional Conformity Act passed by Tory majority in parliament; required frequent communion for all office-holders in England.

1714

Schism Act forbade anyone to keep a private school unless a member of the Anglican church and licensed by a bishop (not enforced by Whigs after death of Queen Anne).

1718

Act for quieting and establishing corporations passed by Whig majority: dissenters could retain town office without taking Anglican communion if not challenged within six months.

1719
7 Jan: Repeal of Schism Act and Occasional Conformity Act by Whigs.

1723
Regium donum of royal bounty for ministers' widows. Levy of £100,000 on Roman Catholic recusants.

1727
Annual Indemnity Act passed, enabling Protestant dissenters to take Anglican communion after, not before, elections.

Ministers of Presbyterian, Independent and Baptist congregations formed General Body of Protestant Dissenting Ministers.

1729
John Wesley (1703–91), junior fellow of Lincoln College, Oxford, became leader of strict religious society formed by brother Charles Wesley (1707–88) and nicknamed 'Methodists'.

Dr Williams's Library founded in London in memory of nonconformist minister, Daniel Williams, for students of religion and philosophy.

Matthew Atkinson, Roman Catholic priest, died in Hurst Castle after thirty years' imprisonment.

1730
Circulating schools started by Griffith Jones (1683–1761) in Wales.

1735
John Wesley started his *Journals* – kept until 1790 – and went to Savannah, Georgia, as Anglican minister.

1738
24 May: John Wesley's 'heart-warming experience' at Moravians' meeting in Aldersgate Street, London.

1739
George Whitefield (1714–79) started open-air preaching at Hanham Mount, Rose Green, Kingswood, Bristol.

Methodist Society met in Old Foundry, Moorfields, London.

1740
John Wesley, a believer in free will (Arminian), and Whitefield, a believer in predestination (Calvinist), agreed to differ.

1744

5–6 Jan: George Whitefield's meeting at Wadford, Glamorgan, at which the Welsh Calvinist Methodists formed the first Methodist Association.

1746

SPCK published first Bible and Book of Common Prayer in Welsh.

1747

Methodist societies grouped into circuits. First of John Wesley's 42 visits to Ireland.

1760

Methodist lay preachers at Norwich administer holy communion.

1771

Francis Asbury (1745–1816) sailed for America as Wesleyan missionary; became first Methodist bishop in America.

1778

28 May: Sir George Savile's Act passed, permitting Roman Catholics to worship and buy and inherit land, but also imposed new loyalty oath.

1779

David Hume published *Dialogues of Natural Religion.*

1780

2–8 Jun: Savage week of rioting called Gordon Riots occurred in London after Lord George Gordon led procession to present to parliament petition calling for repeal of 1778 Catholic Relief Act. Roman Catholics attacked and their chapels pillaged and burned.

1781

Lady Huntingdon's Connection (Calvinist Methodist) separated from Anglican church.

1784

John Wesley signed Deed of Declaration, the beginning of modern Methodism (Arminian). Conference control over ministers and churches throughout connection.

Thomas Coke (1747–1814) ordained by John Wesley as 'superintendent' of Methodist Society in America. Bishops of Methodist Episcopal church in America derived their authority from Coke.

1785
London Society for the Establishment of Sunday schools founded.

1787–90
Bills for repeal of Test and Corporation Acts defeated in House of Commons.

1791
Second Catholic Relief Act.

2 Mar: Death of John Wesley at Methodist chapel house, City Road, London.

2 *Ireland*

Roman Catholicism was the religion of the overwhelming majority of the people of Ireland in the 17th and 18th centuries. All attempts by English monarchs to impose Protestantism in Ireland failed, with the exception of the six northern counties of Ulster, where a Protestant ascendancy was established through the plantation of Scottish settlers during the reign of James I. In the remainder of the country, the Church of Ireland, little more than a branch of the Anglican church, commanded the loyalty of a very thin but extremely wealthy veneer of Anglo-Irish landowners. At the start of the English Civil Wars, Irish Catholics had rebelled against English authority, massacring Protestants in Ulster in 1641. Consequently, when, after the execution of Charles I, Cromwell reconquered Ireland for the Common-wealth in 1650, Catholics were savagely treated. Thousands were slaugh-tered and most Catholics were stripped of their lands. Until 1660, there was no toleration for Roman Catholics: all Roman Catholic clergy were declared enemies of the state and the saying of mass was forbidden. After the Restoration Charles II's sympathy towards Roman Catholics allowed an unofficial policy of toleration, so that chapels were built and priests carried out their usual functions. Furthermore, the Act of Explanation enabled some, though far from all, Irish Catholics to regain a portion of their lands. Catholics enjoyed a brief interlude of freedom and even patronage under James II and it was thus from Ireland that James attempted to regain his throne from William III in 1690. However, James and his Catholic forces were crushed by William's Protestant army at the Battle of the Boyne. Thereafter, for many years, Irish Roman Catholics were severely restricted: they were legally excluded from the professions, education, civil and military office, juries, and the rights to vote and keep arms; all regular clergy and prelates were excluded and secular clergy were restricted to one per parish. However, as the 18th century progressed, the enforcement of the penal laws was gradually relaxed in purely religious matters. By 1745, priests were no longer imprisoned and in the 1770s and 1780s economic and religious restrictions were largely lifted. It was only after 1789, however, that political restraints on Catholics were gradually removed.

Religious Division of Irish Population in 1800

Roman Catholic	3,150,000
Presbyterian	900,000
Church of Ireland (Anglican)	450,000

1641
Massacre of Ulster Protestants by Catholics.

1650
Massacre of thousands of Catholic troops, civilians and clergy at Drogheda and other Irish towns by Oliver Cromwell at the head of English army.

1650–8
Catholicism outlawed; Catholic clergy exiled or proscribed; most Catholics stripped of lands.

1660
Restoration of Charles II ushered in era of unofficial toleration, although Catholics still excluded from office and parliament.

1665
Act of Explanation restored a small percentage of expropriated lands to Catholic landowners.

1681
1 Jul: Execution of St Oliver Plunkett, Archbishop of Armagh, for implication in Popish Plot against Charles II. (Plunkett was canonised 12 Oct 1975.)

1685–8
Reign of James II, a Catholic, briefly halted persecution of Irish Catholics.

1690
1 Jul: Protestant forces under William III defeated James II and his Irish Catholic supporters at Battle of the Boyne.

1691

Treaty of Limerick: William III allowed Catholic landowners who pledged loyalty to English throne to retain lands but extended provisions of English Test and Corporation Acts to Ireland and excluded Catholic secular clergy and prelates.

1703

Act determining conditions of Catholic worship; priests required to register name and parish in order to celebrate mass, or face imprisonment or execution. 1080 priests registered.

1709

Oath of Abjuration, requiring denunciation of title of Stuart pretender, refused by 1000 Irish Catholic priests, although sworn by Anglicans and Presbyterians.

1727

Roman Catholics deprived of right to vote.

1747

John Wesley's first of 42 visits to Ireland; first Methodist church established in Whitefriar's Street, Dublin.

1750

Roman Catholics admitted to lower grades of army.

1771

Bogland Act enabled Roman Catholics to take lease for 61 years of not more than 50 acres of unprofitable land, free of taxes for seven years.

1774

Act denying the pope had any civil or temporal authority in Ireland, following declaration by Münster bishops, accepted by Roman Catholics.

1778

Act passed to allow Roman Catholics to inherit land and take leases on simple oath.

1779

Irish Protestant dissenters relieved from provisions of Test Act.

1782

Catholics allowed to purchase land freely and to establish their own schools.

1793

Act by Irish parliament conferred franchise on Roman Catholics on same terms as Protestants and allowed them to receive degrees and hold fellowships at Dublin University; however, Catholics were still barred from parliament and most offices.

1800

Church of Ireland officially united with Church of England.

3 *Scotland*

The church in Scotland had been far more thoroughly reformed in the 16th century than had the English church. John Knox and his disciples had taken the church of Calvin in Geneva as their model and rigorously imposed its Presbyterian discipline in the whole of Lowland Scotland. The wilder reaches of the Highlands resisted, however, and clung fast to Catholicism. In the early 17th century, James I and VI, despite (or perhaps because of) his own strict upbringing at the hands of zealous Presbyterian divines, managed to graft bishops onto Knox's system of church government, but he wisely made no attempt to alter the Scottish liturgy or to wrest the real discipline of the church from elders and presbyters. This was precisely the error of Charles I, who, at the insistence of Archbishop Laud of Canterbury, attempted in 1637 to impose the Anglican Book of Common Prayer, thus igniting rebellion in Scotland. Between 1638 and 1653, it was to be the General Assembly of the Presbyterian church which exercised much of the country's political as well as the moral leadership, so that Scotland approached the condition of a Calvinist theocracy in this period.

Although Scotland had in 1650 been subdued by Cromwell because of its adherence to Charles II, the General Assembly had continued to meet, though greatly weakened in authority. In 1653, however, Cromwell dispersed the Assembly by military force and forbade it to convene. Nevertheless, the English army did not intefere with the meetings of Kirk sessions, presbyteries and synods; nor was the established worship often disturbed. On the whole, the zeal of the occupying force accorded well with the stringent piety of the Presbyterian clergy.

The church in Scotland was to be far more sorely tried during the reign of Charles II, whom it had once seen as its defender. Despite promises to protect the Presbyterian system, the king soon proceeded to induce a pliable Scottish parliament to reimpose government by bishops and archbishops, although there was, shrewdly, no attempt to impose the Anglican Prayer Book. Nevertheless, although a majority of ministers conformed, more than 300 did not, so that mass field conventicles were soon held in many parishes where the established church was practically deserted. Such defiance led to savage military suppression.

The ferocity of persecution was eased by the accession of James II and VII in 1685. But James's suspension of the religious penal laws in 1687 was viewed in Scotland as an attempt to set up popery rather than a genuine toleration for Presbyterians. Thus, except in the Catholic Highlands, James's expulsion in 1688 was welcomed in Scotland. And with good reason, for in 1690 the episcopal system was dismantled and the Presbyterian church re-established.

The course of religious history was far more tranquil in the 18th century, with a lengthy dispute over ecclesiastical patronage providing the most serious source of friction. Toleration was extended to the Episcopalian minority in 1712 but was retracted in 1746 after the involvement of Episcopalians in the Jacobite rising of the previous year. Roman Catholics continued to be persecuted until the 1780s and George I authorised a royal bounty for the conversion of the Highlanders.

In the 17th and 18th centuries there were approximately 900 parishes and about 1200–1400 clergymen. Perhaps the apogee of clerical numbers occurred in the period 1662–88 when, in addition to the established clergy, there were 300 ejected Presbyterian ministers. Clerical (and indeed episcopal) salaries were very modest, and, after the abolition of bishops, the income of dissenting Episcopalian clergymen was extremely meagre. During the 1662–88 period, Scotland had been divided into 13 dioceses.

1643

Solemn League and Covenant adopted by General Assembly of Presbyterian church and Convention of Estates in Scotland; accepted (22 Sep) by English parliament and Westminster Assembly of Divines. Subscribers bound themselves to labour for the preservation of reformed (that is, Presbyterian) church in Scotland and the reformation of religious practice, doctrine and discipline along Presbyterian lines in England.

1645

3 Feb: Directory for the Public Worship of God, drawn up by Westminster Assembly of Divines, sanctioned by General Assembly of Scottish church and ordered to be observed by all ministers. It was shortly afterwards ratified by Scottish parliament.

1647

Charles I, imprisoned in Carisbrook Castle, agreed to accept Solemn League and Covenant and establish Presbyterianism in England for three years in return for Scottish support.

1648

17 Aug: Scottish 'Engagers Army' defeated by English New Model Army at Preston.

1649

Charles II proclaimed King of Scotland by Estates on execution of Charles I.

1650

Charles II landed in Scotland, took Solemn League and Covenant, and promised to establish Presbyterianism in England and practise that religion with his family.

   3 Sep: Cromwell defeated Scottish Covenanters' army at Dunbar.

1651

1 Jan: Charles II crowned King of Scotland at Scone.

   3 Sep: Subjugation of Scottish forces at Worcester; Charles II forced to flee to continent.

1653

Jul: General Assembly forcibly dispersed and ordered to cease meeting by English army of occupation.

1660

May: Restoration of Charles II.

   3 Sep: Letter of Charles II to Presbytery of Edinburgh promising to protect government of church of Scotland as established by law and to countenance all dutiful ministers.

1661

Compliant Scottish parliament forbade Covenant to be renewed and passed Rescissory Act which, among other things, repealed Presbyterian polity and allowed former episcopal laws to return to force. However, Charles II promised to settle church in Scotland in a way 'most complying with the public peace and quiet of the Kingdom', and in the meantime allowed the existing administration by presbyteries and synods to continue.

   5 Sep: Declaration by Charles II announced his decision to restore church government by bishops in Scotland as it had existed prior to 1638.

1662

8 May: Act re-established government of church of Scotland by bishops and archbishops and rescinding all laws sanctioning Presbyterian polity. Some 300 ministers forfeited their livings rather than conform. Act did not attempt to reimpose Anglican liturgy.

1663

5 Jun: Act passed prohibiting religious conventicles. Act enforced with troops by Sir James Turner.

1668

11 Jul: attempted assassination of Archbishop Sharp of St Andrews in Edinburgh.

1669

7 Jun: Indulgence granted 42 Presbyterian ministers.

10 Nov: Assertory Act passed by Scottish parliament declaring that the king and his heirs possessed the supreme authority in ecclesiastical matters and might order church government as they thought fit.

1670

Act passed prescribing death penalty to anyone who preached at field conventicles.

1679

3 May: Archbishop Sharp of St Andrews assassinated.

Jun: Duke of Monmouth crushed Covenanters' Rebellion at Battle of Bothwell Bridge.

1681

Aug: Succession Act passed by Scottish parliament asserting that kings' right of ascent was ordained by God and that no differences of religion or statute could alter royal succession.

Aug: Test Act which required all officeholders to swear allegiance to the Protestant religion as explained in the Confession of 1567, acknowledge the king to be supreme in all causes ecclesiastical and civil, and pledge never to attempt any alteration in government. Largely used against Presbyterians (1681–8).

1687

James II and VII suspended all penal laws against Scottish Catholics, allowing them free exercise of religion and making them eligible for public office, and by proclamation authorised Presbyterians and other non-Episcopalian Protestants to worship in public or private provided they did not preach disloyalty, or assemble in the open air.

1688

Dec: Expulsion of James II and VII from throne followed by sacking of royal chapel of Holyrood Palace and anti-Catholic riots in Edinburgh.

1690

Episcopal church in Scotland disestablished and disendowed. Presbyterianism re-established, although Episcopalians retained strong support in east and north-east. Selection of ministers removed from patrons and given to congregations and presbyteries.

16 Nov: General Assembly met for first time since 1653.

1694

General Assembly accepted Episcopalian ministers who agreed to accept Westminster Confession and recognise Presbyterian government of Church of Scotland. 165 Episcopal ministers conformed and retained livings.

1696

Law established Scottish parochial school system: heritors of every parish to found school and furnish salary and house of schoolmaster. General Assembly then enjoined presbyteries to see that law was obeyed.

1707

Treaty of Union reiterated that government by presbyteries, synods and general assemblies should be the only government of the Church of Scotland.

1712

Toleration Act gave freedom of religious observance to Scottish Episcopalians.

22 Apr: Act restored right of nominating ministers to traditional landed patrons, unless Roman Catholics, thus depriving Kirk sessions of right to elect ministers, an essential of Presbyterian system.

1725

Royal 'Holy Bounty' to Protestantise Highlands, where majority of inhabitants remained Roman Catholic.

1732

Secession from Church of Scotland, led by Ebenezer Erskine (1680–1756), in protest against patronage, growth of toleration, and abolition of penal statues against witches.

1746

Complicity of Episcopalian clergy and laymen in Jacobite Rebellion of 1745 led to passage of penal statute against them: illegal for Episcopalians to have churches or chapels; public services banned; clergy not allowed to minister to above five persons at a time; infractions punishable by imprisonment or banishment.

1747
Secession church split into Burghers (led by Erskine) and anti-Burghers.

1752
Compromise on patronage: each presbytery could satisfy itself on life, learning and doctrine of patron's nominee; but friction continued into 19th century.

1779
No-Popery riots in Edinburgh following first Catholic Relief Act.

1784
Scottish Episcopal church gave episcopate to American church by consecration in Aberdeen of Samuel Seabury (1729–96), first Bishop of Connecticut.

HABSBURG EMPIRE

This section includes Austria and the other Habsburg hereditary lands, Hungary, and the so-called 'Triune Kingdom', that is, the Slavic possessions of the Habsburg Emperor. The Italian possessions and the Southern Netherlands are dealt with separately.

1 *Austria and the Hereditary Lands (Bohemia, Moravia, Silesia)*

The Reformation had made a profound impact on the Habsburg territories. Lutheranism had gained a strong footing in all the Austrian provinces except the Tyrol. Similarly, in both Bohemia and Moravia, receptive to heterodox currents since the advent of Jan Huss in the 15th century, a large proportion of the population had become Lutheran or United Brethren. Consequently, these lands became prime targets for the Counter-Reformation, which was carried out with thoroughness and vigour by successive Habsburg rulers in alliance with the Catholic clergy. The Peace of Westphalia confirmed the ascendancy of Roman Catholicism in these territories, and thereafter Protestantism was suppressed with renewed determination. Nevertheless, despite mass migrations after 1648 and constant persecution, there remained a considerable number of crypto-Protestants in the Hereditary Lands. Some 14,000 people in Upper Carinthia admitted that they were Protestants, while Bohemia continued to be a centre of undergound Protestantism. Until

284

the reign of Joseph II, however, Roman Catholicism was the only tolerated religion, and by 1700 the overwhelming majority of the population had been reclaimed by the Catholic church.

Although the restoration and preservation of Catholicism was an essential policy of the Habsburg dynasty, Austrian rulers were never instruments in the hands of the papacy. In fact, monarchs from Ferdinand I to Maria Theresa, even while pursuing the goals of the Counter-Reformation, gradually imposed greater controls over the church in their possessions. Ferdinand III (1637–57) proscribed the visitation of monasteries by foreign superiors, while Leopold I (1658–1705) and Charles VI (1711–40) drastically limited appeals to Rome, among other actions. Maria Theresa (1740–80), herself a devout Catholic, nevertheless approved extensive controls over the financial administration of the church and important educational reforms. However, it was Joseph II (1780–90) who was most radical in his attempts to subordinate the church to his dream of a truly enlightened absolute state. Monasteries were dissolved and their lands appropriated, church administration was carefully scrutinised, papal authority was severely curtailed, and even the liturgy and ritual were reformed.

In 1700 there were only 12 dioceses in the Habsburg Hereditary Lands, and, until Vienna was raised to metropolitan status in 1717, Prague (created 1073) was the only archbishopric. By 1800, the number of bishoprics had risen to 15, but there were still more than 800,000 inhabitants per diocese. Both the episcopacy and the canonry were monopolised by the aristocracy. All other candidates were mercilessly excluded from the ranks of the high secular clergy, which numbered about 200 in all. The high regular clergy – abbots and priors – were recruited in a slightly more democratic manner. However, the heads of the great monastic foundations – about 50 in all – displayed attitudes typical of feudal lords because of the importance of the property they administered.

The higher clergy was both politically and economically powerful before 1780. Ecclesiastics were the first estate in each of the Hereditary Lands, and prelates were well represented in imperial diets and administration. The political strength of the Austrian and Bohemian clergy was based on landed wealth. In Bohemia, the church owned 12.3% of all cultivated land, while the abbeys and bishops of Lower Austria owned vast estates. In addition, the church benefited from the feudal *robot*, which compelled the peasantry to supply free labour and which in Lower Austria was often replaced by a cash payment.

1637

Reign of Frederick III: Emperor banned visitation of monasteries by foreign heads of orders.

1658–1705
Reign of Leopold I: Emperor introduced principle of reviewing judgments of church courts by secular ones; also prohibited sale of secular estates to church.

1681
Leopold I imposed placet in Habsburg territories (*placet*: assent by crown to papal appointments or pronouncements).

1711–40
Reign of Charles VI: Emperor ruled that appeals in ecclesiastical matters in which secular power took primary interest should go from consistories to state courts and not to Holy See.

1740–80
Reign of Maria Theresa: Severe persecution of Jews and Protestants; Catholic church subjected to reforms of administration, discipline and religious emphasis – inspired by chief minister, Count Wenzel Anton von Kaunitz.

1742
Queen Maria Theresa announced that it was harmful to allow Austrian church to accumulate more wealth and that church's financial administration needed reform.

1749
After this date, monastic orders had to agree to pay taxes for ten-year period and could no longer discuss amount to be paid.

1750
Maria Theresa charged imperial commission with supervision of all ecclesiastical institutions.

1752
Reforms of Gerhard van Swieten: New curriculum for philosophers and theologians, new administration of religious education, both designed to produce well-educated and committed clergy.
  10 May: Decree restricting right of church asylum.

1753
Royal ordinance further restricted civil rights of Jews, who were not allowed to own land or employ Christian servants (other ordinances in 1747, 1764 and 1768).

286

Maria Theresa informed bishops that only authorised university religious studies would be allowed and diocesan and monastic teaching establishments were to be abolished.

1754
24 feastdays reduced to half feastdays.

1760
Jesuits expelled from Austrian territories.

1768
Property of priesthood taxed.
   Excommunication without official permission forbidden; public penances outlawed.

1769
Processions and pilgrimages limited.

1770
Monastic orders required to make annual reports of landed income.

1771
Amortisation law radically restricted assets of mortmain.
   Heads of orders forbidden to send money to Rome and their communications with papacy could go only through state chancery.
   Religious confraternities restricted: no new ones allowed without official permission and existing bodies investigated.
   Monastic prisons abolished.
   Regular clergy forbidden to draw up wills or to act as witnesses.

1772
Standardised catechism imposed in Austria.

c. 1773
Candidates not allowed to take monastic vows before the age of 24; dowry of novices limited to 1500 gulden.

1775
Patent further restricted ecclesiastical asylum – equivalent to abolition of traditional privileges.
   Heads of orders forbidden to dispose of convents' assets and forbidden to make agreements concerning annuities.

1776

The 'Dritter Orden' forbidden to take on new members.

1777

Ordinance of Maria Theresa forbade known Jews to remain in Vienna without written permission.

Introduction of 'enlightened' catechism, which reduced emphasis on Virgin Mary and saints, and encouraged study of selected Biblical texts.

1780–90

Reign of Joseph II: Emperor through numerous edicts attempted to transform Catholic church into instrument of state and granted toleration to religious minorities.

1781

4 May: Emperor ordered suppression of papal bulls *In Coena domini* of 1362 (condemning heretics) and *Unigenitus* of 1713 (attacking Jansenists). Bishops compelled to swear oath of allegiance and loyalty to secular authorities.

13 Oct: Patent of Toleration gave Protestants and Greek Orthodox right to worship in private meeting-houses and allowed non-Catholics to own houses and land, run schools, enter the professions and hold military and political offices. In five years, numbers of Protestants more than doubled in number, from 74,000 to 157,000.

29 Nov: Decree initiated the abolition of all monastic orders not engaged in preaching, teaching or charity, and the appropriation of their wealth; subsequently extended to non-contemplative orders. 738 monastic establishments (out of a total of 2163) were suppressed, leaving 1065 monasteries and 360 convents. 27,000 monks and nuns remained of the original 65,000 inmates. Confiscated property (eventually amounting to c. 60 million gulden) used to endow Religious Fund, which supported schools, charitable institutions, pensions and salaries of parish priests. Ex-monastics either given pensions or made state teachers. Unsuppressed monasteries lost ancient right to inherit property and were ordered to reduce number of inmates by one-third. Monastic administration was taken from abbots and given to laymen or secular clergy. Eventually, all ecclesiastical possessions, suppressed or not, were registered by the government, and a law was passed forbidding their alienation, sale or exchange.

Reform of censorship: All provincial censorship abolished and commission in Vienna made sole arbiter. Works judged obscene or anti-Christian were still banned. All ecclesiastical publications, including announcements, placed under secular jurisdiction.

1782

Jan: First toleration edict for Jews. Separate patents issued for Austrian, Bohemian, Moravian and Silesian Jews. Patent for Galician Jews not granted until 1789.

28 Feb: Formation of Religious Fund from proceeds of abolished monastic houses for charitable and educational purposes (see under 29 Nov 1781).

1 Mar: Hermits disendowed.

17 May: All orders made by provincial officials to be read out in pulpit by parish priests. Subject of sermons circumscribed.

1783

Abolition of religious confraternities (642 in Austria, 121 in Vienna alone).

4 Feb: Priests forbidden to criticise persons of other religions or imperial decrees regarding church. Priests had to retain written copy of sermon to be submitted upon request.

25 Feb: First reform of liturgy and rituals (others promulgated on 18 Mar 1784 and 12 Oct 1785). Unnecessary 'decorations' (images, etc.) thrown out; 'superstitious' observances such as kissing of relics prohibited; length and number of divine services rigorously regulated; altar ceremonies, music and litanies simplified.

30 Mar: Replacement of old diocesan seminaries with four general theological seminaries at Vienna, Pest, Louvain and Pavia, together with subsidiary affiliated institutions at Graz, Prague, Olmütz, Innsbruck, Freiburg and Luxemburg.

28 Aug: Further restriction of processions and pilgrimages, which were forbidden unless approved by secular authorities.

24 Oct: Reorganisation of parishes, intended to increase number of parishes and improve pastoral care.

1784

German litanies introduced in Austrian churches.

1786

Archbishop of Salzburg forced to give up diocesan rights in Styria and Carinthia.

1787

Diocesan boundaries in Bohemia, Moravia and Galicia realigned.

2 *Hungary and Serbia-Croatia*

Hungary, like Austria, had been significantly affected by the Protestant Reformation. However, for much of the 16th and 17th centuries, Hungary was under Turkish domination, during which time all Christian denominations suffered persecution. Only after 1687 did the Habsburgs begin to re-establish their authority.

At the close of the 17th century, Hungary was still very much a multi-denominational country: 48% of the people were Roman Catholic, 17% Orthodox, 15.3% Calvinist, 10.3% Eastern Catholic (Uniate), 7.7% Lutheran, 1.4% Jewish and 0.3% Unitarian. Transylvania had in 1568 proclaimed toleration for all religious practices and other Hungarian territories not under Turkish sway were also relatively lenient. In 1690, Leopold I had recognised the religious freedom of Transylvania because he dared not risk alienating the territory. In the rest of Hungary, a far more tenuous toleration was preserved for Protestants, who were limited to two places of worship in each county and placed under the supervision of Catholic bishops. Once the Habsburgs had managed to consolidate their hold over Hungary and its associated lands, and were no longer dependent on Protestant aid against the Turks, toleration was progressively dismantled. Charles VI outlawed mixed marriages unless performed by a Catholic priest, made conversion to Protestantism a crime, and imposed an oath intended to exclude Protestants from office. Maria Theresa issued a whole series of decrees extending the intolerant measures of her predecessors. Yet Protestantism survived and took a new lease on life from the reforms of Joseph II after 1780.

Union rather than persecution was the policy of the Roman Catholics towards the Orthodox churches. The Ruthenes were the first to accept union in 1689, followed by the Transylvanian Orthodox in 1697. The Uniate Catholics retained their own rites but accepted the supremacy of the pope and were integrated into the structure of Roman Catholic discipline. The Orthodox of Serbia and Croatia were more resistant to Roman blandishments. Since their religious identity and nationality were closely intermingled, they retained 11 Orthodox dioceses of their own.

After the devastation of the Turkish period, the Roman Catholic church was rebuilt with Counter-Reformation zeal in the 18th century. There were 2 archdioceses and 11 dioceses in 1700, increased to 15 by 1781. The senior member of the hierarchy was the Archbishop of Estergom, who was usually a cardinal and was made a prince of the Holy Roman Empire in 1715.

An extensive monastic system had also sprung back to life by the mid-18th century. In Hungary and Serbia–Croatia there were 152 monasteries with 3234 inmates; of these, 84 foundations were Black Franciscan while 25 were Jesuit, 24 Piarist, and 11 Capuchin. 12 convents housed 274 nuns and 116 lay sisters.

1550

Legislative diet of Transylvania passed first of series of laws making first

Lutheranism and then Calvinism established religions equal to Roman Catholicism.

1568
Diet of Torda proclaimed toleration for all religious practices.

1689
Ruthene Orthodox accepted union with Roman Catholic Church.

1690
Leopold I upheld principle of religious freedom in Transylvania.

1691
Explanatio Leopoldina restricted toleration in remainder of Hungary: Protestants limited to two specific places of worship in each county and subjected to supervision of Catholic bishops.

1692
Diploma Leopoldinium placed Ruthene Uniate parishes under jurisdiction of Catholic Bishop of Eger.

1697
Transylvanian Orthodox accepted union with Roman Catholics at synod of Alba Iulia.

1701
Romanian Uniate parishes placed under jurisdiction of Catholic Archbishop of Estergom.

29 Apr: Leopold I claimed title of Apostolic King of Hungary, title bestowed on St Stephen by Pope Sylvester II which carried with it right of investiture and headship of Hungarian church.

1731
Carolina resolutio extended control of Catholic bishops over Protestant churches, banned mixed marriages unless performed by Catholic priest, ruled conversion to Protestantism a crime punishable by lay courts, and forced official oaths to be sworn in decretal form to exclude Protestants from public office.

1742
Maria Theresa reaffirmed *Carolina resolutio* and launched new series of anti-Protestant decrees: Protestant publications banned, clergy who chal-

lenged Catholic doctrine could be deported, strict enforcement of decretal laws, etc.

1758

19 Aug: Pope Clement XIII recognised title of Apostolic ruler of Hungary for Maria Theresa and her successors.

1763

Archbishop of Estergom codified Hungarian anti-Protestant laws and edicts at behest of Maria Theresa.

1780–90

Joseph II dispensed with title of Apostolic King of Hungary, claiming to rule church as state absolutely, answerable only to God. Issued 6000 decrees relating to Hungarian church, introducing many of same reforms as in other Habsburg territories (*see* Austria). Result was transformation of Hungarian church into state department and virtual separation from Rome.

HOLLAND (UNITED PROVINCES)

The Protestant Reformation was not imposed by princes or armies in the Netherlands, although the hatred of the Dutch towards their Catholic rulers in Spain doubtless influenced their desire to break with Rome. By 1609 the northern provinces had established their independence, but still there was no attempt to impose the Protestant religion by force on the very large minority of the population which remained Catholic. Lutheranism had held very little appeal in the Low Countries, so that the Dutch Reformed church of the 17th and 18th centuries was Calvinist both in doctrine and polity. Like other Calvinist denominations, the Reformed church strongly resisted attempts by the state to subject it to secular authority. However, in this it was to be unsuccessful. For after the celebrated Synod of Dort [Dordrecht] when Calvinists drew on political support to subdue the advocates of free will (the Arminians or Remonstrants), the church found itself very nearly approaching the position of official establishment with all the political restrictions that accompanied it.

The Netherlands acquired a reputation for tolerance in the 17th century which has perhaps been somewhat exaggerated. The relatively high degree of religious freedom in no way reflected the principles of the Reformed church and seems to have been preserved more by failing to put the law into execution than by altering it. Thus the Arminians (Remonstrants) were proscribed by the Synod of Dort but strongly supported by the Regent class and thus widely tolerated. In Amsterdam and Rotterdam, several Protestant sects were allowed to worship publicly and Jews were permitted to build synagogues.

The position of Roman Catholics was much more complicated. In the first place, they were surprisingly numerous, comprising as much as 45% of the Dutch population in 1650. Moreover, they were especially strong in the eastern provinces and the powerful merchant class of Amsterdam. Catholics had no legal right to worship and were in theory excluded from political offices, magistracies and guilds. However, judicial officers in nearly every town allowed Catholics to hold religious services in homes and barns in return for the payment of fines or bribes. Similarly, many wealthy Catholics managed to secure public office despite the official ban. Nevertheless, it is undeniable that the pressure to conform to the Protestant order was compelling and had a deleterious effect on Catholicism in the Netherlands. It is true that the state resisted pressure from the Reformed church to expel Catholic priests, and in the 17th century there were some 400–500 priests in the country. However, early in the 18th century, the Estates of Holland forbade the appointment of a Vicar Apostolic and new bishops. This not only left Dutch Catholics without a legitimate leader but also meant that churches were not consecrated and confirmation was not administered. As a result of these conditions, the number of Catholics declined to about 35% of the population.

1618–19
Synod of Dort (Dordrecht): Convened to deal with Arminian controversy, the synod was essentially a gathering of Dutch theologians, though Scottish, Swiss, English and other delegates attended. From 13 November 1618 to 9 May 1619 there were 154 formal sessions, but Remonstrants (followers of theologian Arminius who rejected predestination and embraced doctrine of free will) were not given equal hearing but treated as men on trial. Decisions, as much political as religious, were a foregone conclusion.

23 Apr 1619: Synod confirmed (1) unconditional election, (2) limited atonement, (3) total depravity of man, (4) irreversibility of grace, and (5) the final perseverance of saints.

9 May 1619: Synod drew up 93 canonical rules and confirmed the authority of Belgic Confession and Heidelberg Confession – both of which upheld predestination.

1655
Synod of Reformed church proposed 'free and public residence' of Roman Catholic priests and other clerics should be forbidden and forcibly prevented. Firmly rejected by States General.

1656

South Holland Synod resolved that Cartesian ideas be prohibited. States General responded by imposing oath on professors of philosophy and theology that they would cease propagation of Cartesianism.

1662

Friesland forbade Quakers, Socinians and Immersers to enter province.

1665-6

Dispute between orthodox Voetius and Cartesian Coccejus, resulting in toleration of Cartesian methodology in theological writings.

1670

Philosopher Spinoza published his *Tractatus Theologico-Politicus* in which he attested and defended the right of secular authorities to regulate religious matters, pronounce on morals, determine the basic doctrines of the church and select its servants, and care for poor. Banned by authorities in province of Holland because of theological implications of work and despite their approval of Spinoza's interpretation of secular powers.

1691

Publication by Balthasar Bekker of *Betoverde Wereld (Bewitched World)*, which attacked superstition and denied that the devil or evil spirits play a role in human life. Condemned by South Holland Synod of Reformed church and opposed by William III, though never actually banned.

1730

21 Sep: Oath of the Placet by which the much reduced Dutch Catholic hierarchy rejected extreme claims of papal jurisdiction over church life and government in Netherlands, swore to instruct communicants to obey civil authorities, and prohibited payment of money to foreign monasteries and institutions.

1796

5 Aug: Decree of Batavian National Assembly ended close union of state and Reformed church, gave religious freedom to Roman Catholics, and allowed them to become magistrates.

HUNGARY: *See under* Habsburg Empire

ITALY

Although virtually the whole of Italy was nominally Roman Catholic in the 17th and 18th centuries, the country remained politically fragmented. Consequently, there was not one Italian church, but rather a number of Italian churches, each with its own character and specific relationship with its secular authority and with the papacy. There were, however, a number of common characteristics. All over Italy, the ecclesiastical population reached its peak in the first half of the 18th century and declined after 1750. Everywhere the church was gradually losing its monolithic hold over the populace, both rural and urban, despite concentrated efforts to emphasise popular religion – the veneration of saints and relics, festivals, processions and elaborate rituals. Thus, in 18th-century Italy, there also arose a widespread domestic missionary movement stressing personal piety and penance. Finally, except in the Papal States, church–state conflicts like those which appeared in other Catholic countries resulted in the strengthening of secular authority over the church and the loosening of ties with Rome.

1 *Lombardy*

Lombardy was almost wholly Catholic in the 17th and 18th centuries. The Roman Catholic church owned some 23% of the land, an increase from the 18% recorded in 1550. In 1750, the number of monastic houses reached a peak of 291 and thereafter fell sharply to 200 by 1790 as a result of government reforms. Restrictions imposed by the state also led to a decline in the numbers of priests in the last quarter of the 18th century.

Lombardy was ruled by Spain during the period 1648–1714 and thereafter by Austria. Consequently, the condition of the Lombard church and its relation to the papacy depended largely on decisions reached in Madrid or, later, Vienna. In fact, though wealthy, the church lacked the influence in political matters in Lombardy which it often wielded elsewhere in Italy. Even so, as late as 1757 the church was able to preserve a portion of its tax exemptions in the concordat concluded in that year. Thereafter, however, Lombardy was to be used as a testing ground for the policies which the Austrian chief minister Kaunitz and the future Joseph II wished to introduce in Austria itself. Under Count Karl von Firmian a Junta of Stewardship advised Vienna on all church matters, publication of papal utterances was made subject to government approval, a series of decrees was issued against mortmain and other economic privileges of the church, and censorship was transferred to state control.

On the death of Maria Theresa in 1780, Joseph II launched a direct offensive against the Roman church practically identical to those waged in his other territories. Supported by the influential Jansenist community at the University of Pavia, Joseph denounced the concordat of 1757 and issued an edict of toleration. Thereafter, the remaining financial privileges of the church were abolished, numerous monasteries were suppressed, and charity was brought under state control. In short, by the death of Joseph II in 1790, the church in Lombardy, like that in Austria, had become a department of the Habsburg government.

1757
New concordat preserved part of ecclesiastical tax exemptions. Junta of Stewardship created to advise government on church affairs.

1762
Publication of papal letters and decrees made subject to royal approval.

1765
Giunta Economale established in Milan as highest authority in ecclesiastical matters.

1767
Publication of violently anti-clerical and socially radical *Of Reform in Italy* by Carlantonio Pilati, which advocated reduction in size of clergy, wealth of church and subjugation of ecclesiastical to secular authority.

1768–9
Censorship brought under state control, mortmain prohibited.

1781
Concordat of 1757 denounced by Joseph II. Edict of toleration issued in Lombardy.

Bull *Unigenitus* prohibited, meeting approval of Jansenists.

Giunta Economale replaced by Ecclesiastical Commission with three departments responsible for the secular clergy, regular clergy, and public education and charity.

1782
Suppression of monasteries begun; numbers reduced from 291 to 200 by 1790; those allowed to survive separated from mother houses.

1784
Concordat gave state greater control over rights of appointment to bishoprics of Milan and Mantua, hitherto exercised by Holy See.

1786

General Seminary at which all Lombard priests were to be trained established at Pavia under control of Jansenists.

Religious confraternities abolished and all charity brought under state control in new Company of Charity Towards One's Neighbour.

2 *Modena*

In Modena, as in other Italian states, the population was almost entirely Roman Catholic. In the 18th century, the church owned 20–5% of the duchy's land, and there were some 10,000 clergy.

Church–state relations were conservative and largely untroubled until after 1750, when the enlightened writings of the great Lodovico Muratori began to exert an influence in Modena. The suppression of some convents and charitable institutions developed quickly, and in the 1760s the Great Hospice for the Poor was established along Muratorian lines to help solve the problem of pauperism. In the 1770s, the number of religious feasts was reduced and a junta of stewardship, based on the Lombard model, was created to administer vacant benefices. Between 1780 and 1790, under Duke Ercole III and directed by the reforming minister Ludovico Ricci, further attacks were made against church power. The Holy Office was suppressed, censorship at Reggio Emilia was placed under the anti-clerical Agostino Paradisi, and Ricci further secularised the administration of charity.

1750

Death of Lodovico Muratori (born 1672) whose writings helped shape the future of church–state relations in Modena.

1764–8

Great Hospice for the Poor constructed, after dissolution of some religious charities.

1774

Number of religious feast days reduced.

1780–90

Holy Office suppressed; censorship at Reggio Emilia placed under anti-clerical Agostino Paradisi.

1787

Publication of Ludovico Ricci's *Reform of the Charitable Institutions of the City of Modena*, proposing transformation of almshouses into workshops controlled by guilds.

3 Naples–Sicily

The population of the Kingdom of Naples, which included the lower third of the Italian peninsula and the island of Sicily, was entirely Catholic. The church was immensely wealthy, owning over 50% of the land in some areas and perhaps as much as 40% over all. There were 130 dioceses in the kingdom. Some 30% of bishops were members of the aristocracy and many of the heads of the numerous religious houses were younger sons of the nobility. The clerical population grew throughout most of the 17th and 18th centuries, reaching a peak of 48,174 in 1773. Thereafter, largely for political reasons, the religious population began to decline, falling to 46,216 in 1780 and plummetting to 36,125 by 1801.

Relations with the papacy were largely amicable in the 17th century, but the crisis of the Spanish succession embittered relations, resurrecting ancient conflicts in the process. Since the Middle Ages the secular authority had possessed enormous powers over the church in the kingdom. Based on a grant by Pope Urban II to Count Roger in 1098, the rulers of the Kingdom of Naples claimed extensive legative powers termed Monarchia Sicula, which included rights of visitation, of decision in election of church superiors, and of excommunication and absolution. Indeed, in 1579 Philip II had established the Tribunal of the Monarchy to act as the highest ecclesiastical court, whose decisions could not be over-ruled by the pope. Latent conflict over this matter erupted during the papacy of Clement XI. Compelled by armed force to recognise the Austrian Charles III as King of Spain and thus of Naples, the pope incurred the wrath of the occupant of the Spanish throne, Philip V. After a series of bitter exchanges, Clement XI annulled Monarchia Sicula in 1715, thus producing a virtual schism which the transfer of Sicily to Austria in 1718 did little to remedy. Only very gradually were relations mended, and even the partial restoration of Monarchia Sicula in 1728 did not end the dispute. In fact, the return of Naples and Sicily to Spain in 1735 exacerbated matters, so that even the concordat of 1741, in which Benedict XIV made numerous concessions, did little to settle relations. Moreover, the conflict grew far worse during the long ministry of Bernardo Tanucci, 1759–76, a virulent anti-clericalist. The terms of the concordat were ignored and the secular authorities assumed greater powers over ecclesiastical appointments and jurisdiction. Although without the 'enlightened' motivation of Joseph II, rulers of Naples also transformed the church in their territories into an arm of an absolutist state.

298

1712

12 Jun: Pope Clement XI nullified absolutions to excommunicated persons granted by Tribunal of the Monarchy (see above) and reconfirmed excommunications. Sicilian viceroy responded by declaring all papal edicts null and void. More excommunications followed, countered in Sicily by more absolutions by Tribunal, suspension of temporalities, and expulsions of bishops of Catania, Girgenti and archbishop of Messina.

1715

20 Feb: Clement XI annulled Monarchia Sicula in bull *Pontifex Romanus.*

1725

Return of territory of Comacchio to Papal States by Austria, thus opening door to compromise on Monarchia Sicula.

1728

Bull *Fideli* gave King of Naples right to appoint highest judicial official with jurisdiction over ecclesiastical cases, thus largely restoring Monarchia Sicula.

1741

2 Jun: Concordat, concluded after lengthy negotiations, failed to improve relations with Rome, despite papal concessions. Agreement reached concerning high ecclesiastical court – 'Tribunal of Monarchia' – by which three clerics and two laymen were appointed to execute church jurisdiction. Rome also made concessions regarding personnel, immunities (right of sanctuary limited); clergy and church lands to be taxed; foreigners excluded from benefices; few smaller bishoprics abolished. In exchange, 'placet' was eliminated and 'Recursus ad Principe' (recourse to ruler about church abuses) modified.

1767

20 Nov: Jesuit order expelled by order of prime minister, Bernardo Tanucci.

1768–76

Series of anti-papal laws promulgated by Tanucci: some convents suppressed, tithes abolished, mortmain forbidden and royal permission required for all ecclesiastical decrees.

1776

Upon refusal of Pope Pius VI to make Archbishop Filangieri of Naples a cardinal, Tanucci suspended *Chinea*, symbolic feudal payment to Rome, thus rejecting papal suzerainty.

Fall of Tanucci in this year failed to ease relations with Rome.

1778

All communications between Rome and Sicilian and Neapolitan monasteries forbidden; ban soon extended to rest of church. Royal claim of presentation to bishoprics – rejected by Pius VI – led to 30 vacant sees by 1784 and 60 vacant sees by 1798.

1782

Jansenist Giovanni Andrea Serrao, appointed bishop of Potenza; Serrao later convoked synod which readily accepted royal authority and rejected papal claims.

1787

Naples–Sicily formally refused papal feudal rights over kingdom, intensifying dispute with Pius VI.

4 *The Papacy and the Papal States*

The period 1648–1789 saw a steady waning of the influence of the papacy over international politics and diplomacy, and a considerable erosion of papal powers within the Catholic church itself. The Peace of Westphalia of 1648, which fixed the religious configuration of Europe, also meant a turning point in the position of the papacy. The vehement protests of Pope Innocent X were not heeded. In future, the papacy was to be assigned a peripheral role in diplomatic negotiations and often excluded altogether. As far as the Catholic powers were concerned, the papacy became a pawn of their politics: one pope after another was caught in the conflict between France and the Habsburgs. Even papal elections turned into power plays, with blocks of cardinals being manipulated and bullied by the great Catholic powers, each of which possessed what amounted to a veto. Consequently, lengthy conclaves resulted which often produced compromise candidates whose election would have been impossible without massive political interference.

The position of the papacy in the field of dogma and church discipline was damaged by the protracted disputes of Gallicanism and Jansenism which stretched well into the 18th century. The refusal of the papacy to recognise any good in the rationalism of the Enlightenment also diminished confidence in the intellectual and moral authority of the pope and even the church.

The general development of European countries into modern states was not shared by the Papal States, partially because they lacked dynastic continuity. In the first half of the 18th century, the Papal States proved too weak to enforce their often-proclaimed neutrality or to defend themselves against invasion. In fact, rather than ensuring the strength and independence of the papacy, the Papal States became a liability – a ready-made and easily-seized hostage. Internally, the Papal States remained largely backward, dominated by great landowners who resisted all attempts by various popes to initiate economic and social reforms.

Pope Innocent X (Giovanni Battista Pamphili) 1644–55

1644

15 Sep: Election of Cardinal Pamphili against opposition of Cardinal Mazarin and Barberini relatives of papal predecessor Urban VIII.

1646

17 Jan: Cardinal Francesco and Taddeo Barberini fled Rome, threatened with prosecution for corruption during pontificate of their uncle, Urban VIII.

29 Apr: Violent affray between Frenchmen and Spaniards in Piazza Gesu, Rome.

10 May: French, angered over election of Innocent X, expulsion of Barberini, and alleged papal favouritism towards Spain, attacked Papal States.

17 Sep: Innocent X pardoned the Barberini under French pressure.

1646–7

Widespread damage caused in Papal States by flooding of Tiber.

1647

Innocent X refused demand by Venice that vacant bishoprics in its territories be filled by consistory of Venetian cardinals.

1648

Severe famine in Papal States due to crop failures.

Nov: Innocent issued stern private protest to Catholic powers against Peace of Westphalia.

1649

Capture of Farnese town of Castro from Parma and its annexation to Papal States.

1649–51

Reform of Italian monastic orders begun by Innocent X and carried out by special congregation.

301

1650

20 Aug: *Zelo Domus Dei*, protest against Peace of Westphalia retrodated to 26 November 1648, ordered by Innocent X to be published as simple brief, not as solemn bull as originally intended.

1652

Innocent X refused Philip IV of Spain right of nomination in vacant bishoprics in Catalonia.

15 Oct: Papal bull suppressed Italian monasteries too small to carry out functions intended by founders and transferred properties to bishoprics to be used for pious purposes.

1653

9 Jun: Five propositions in *Augustinus* of Cornelius Jansen condemned by Innocent X in bull *Cum Occasione*.

Pope Alexander VII (Fabio Chigi) 1655–67

1655

7 Apr: Election of Alexander VII over objections of Cardinal Mazarin – after 80-day conclave.

Dec: Arrival in Rome of ex-Queen Christina of Sweden after her celebrated conversion to Roman Catholicism.

1657

28 Aug: Laying of cornerstone of St Peter's Square, with monumental colonnade designed by Bernini. Alexander VII also commissioned Bernini to execute the great cathedra and tabernacle in St Peter's.

1662

20 Aug: Attack, after quartering dispute, by papal troops on French embassy in Rome; despite apologies by Alexander VII, Louis XIV occupied Avignon and used incident to extract concessions.

1664

12 Feb: Treaty of Pisa concluded; Alexander VII forced to erect memorial pyramid admitting guilt in quartering incident of 1662 and to comply with Louis XIV's wishes about appointment of bishops in newer French territories.

1665

Alexander VII issued bull *Regiminis Apostolici*, requiring Jansenists to sign formulary.

Pope Clement IX (Giulio Rospigliosi) 1667–9
1667
20 Jun: Election of Clement IX with support of Spain, France and 'Squadrone Volante' (block of supposedly independent cardinals) after conclave of only 18 days.

1668
2 May: Papal mediation helped secure Peace of Aachen ending War of Devolution.

31 May: Clement secured removal of humiliating pyramid imposed by France at Pisa in 1664.

1669
6 Sep: Loss of Candia by Venice despite Clement IX's securing of French aid against Turks.

9 Dec: Death of Clement IX.

Pope Clement X (Emilio Altieri) 1670–6
1670
29 Apr: Election of 80-year-old Cardinal Albieri after France and Spain blocked four leading contenders. Advanced age of pope meant that Cardinal-Nephew Paluzzi-Altieri gained importance at expense of secretary of state, predictably enriching himself despite personal thriftiness of Clement X.

1672
Deceptive assurances of Louis XIV led Clement to bless rapacious French invasion of United Provinces as 'holy cause'.

1673
11 Nov: King John Sobieski's defeat of Turks at Chocim, helped by pope's financial aid to Poland.

1675
Disabused of French sincerity, Clement X sent nuncios to Vienna, Madrid and Paris to instigate peace process. Papal representative for the first time empowered to negotiate directly with Protestant states.

Publication in Rome of *Guia Espirituel* by Spanish priest Miguel Molinos – placed emphasis on contemplative prayer and efficacy of grace to the diminution of personal deeds. In 1685, Molinos was arrested by Inquisition and 1687 was condemned to life in prison, where he died in 1696.

Pope Innocent XI (Benedetto Odescalchi) 1676–89

1676

21 Sep: Election of Innocent XI with French support, after Louis XIV was persuaded to withdraw his veto.

1678

Mar: Brief by Innocent XI reproving Louis XIV for extension of right of 'régale' in France – issued after appeal from French bishops Pavillon of Alet and Caulet of Pamiers (see France). Second similar brief dispatched in January 1679.

1679

Venice relinquished extensive quartering rights in Rome after lengthy dispute with papacy.

1680

Mar: Third brief concerning 'régale' warning of heavenly wrath unless Louis XIV retracted his extension of royal powers of ecclesiastical appointment.

1681

13 Jan: Sharp condemnation of France by Innocent after French Assembly of Clergy had sided with Louis XIV.

1682

11 Apr: Innocent XI condemned Gallican Articles adopted by French Assembly of Clergy which upheld powers of crown over church in France.

Spain followed Venice in surrendering excessive quartering rights in Rome.

1687

Innocent refused to receive new French ambassador unless France conceded quartering rights.

Dec: Innocent placed French national church in Rome under interdict after French ambassador-designate, de Lavardin, received sacraments there on Christmas Eve.

1688

Clement von Wittelsbach of Bavaria, candidate of Emperor Leopold I, appointed bishop co-adjutor of Cologne by Innocent, sparking off War of League of Augsburg.

1689

12 Aug: Death of Innocent XI, shortly afterwards venerated by Romans but not actually canonised until 1956 – by Pius XII.

Pope Alexander VIII (Pietro Ottoboni) 1689–91
1689
6 Oct: Election of 80-year-old Cardinal Ottoboni after assurances were given to French that canonical investiture would be conferred on bishops who had taken part in 1681–2 Assembly of Clergy (a promise not fulfilled).

1691
30 Jan: Alexander VIII issued decree originally prepared by Innocent XI nullifying Gallican Articles of 1682, after French refused to make concessions on this point.

1 Feb: Death of Alexander VIII after pontificate of only 16 months, during which he had restored nepotism, abolished by Innocent XI, and enriched numerous relatives.

Pope Innocent XII (Antonio Pignatelli) 1691–1700
1691
12 Jul: Election of 75-year-old ascetic Cardinal Pignatelli, native of southern Italy.

1692
22 Jun: Innocent XII issued bull against nepotism, which forbade popes to enrich relatives in any way and limited salary of relatives appointed on merit to 12,000 scudi p.a. Promulgation of this bull decreased nepotism dramatically.

1693
Compromise between Innocent XII and Louis XIV which allowed canonical investiture of French hierarchy. Louis revoked decree prescribing Gallican Articles as dogma but retained right of 'régale' despite Innocent XII's protestations.

1700
27 Sep: Death of Innocent XII.

Pope Clement XI (Gian Francesco Albani) 1700–21
1700
23 Nov: Election, after protracted manipulations, of Cardinal Albani, then 51 years old. First half of pontificate dominated by War of Spanish Succession, during which both Austria and France violated neutrality of Papal States.

305

1703

San Michele, penal institution for juveniles, pioneering reform in emergence of modern prison system, established in Rome by Clement XI.

1707

May: Pope forced to grant free passage through Papal States to Naples for Austrian troops.

Parma and Piacenza, contrary to papal claims, taxed as imperial (Austrian) liens. Bull of 27 July against these abuses achieved nothing.

1708

Apr: Charles III, Austrian pretender to Spanish throne, froze church revenues in Lombardy and Naples because Clement XI continued to recognise Philip V as King of Spain.

Imperial forces invaded Papal States without declaration of war and occupied papal territory of Comacchio.

1709

15 Jan: Clement XI forced to disarm papal troops and recognise Charles III as King of Spain. Recognition definitively confirmed on 10 October.

Philip V of Spain, in retaliation for papal recognition of Charles III, broke off relations with Rome, expelled papal nuncio from Madrid, and suspended ecclesiastical immunity and jurisdiction.

1711

Clement XI sent official papal nuncio to Charles III, resident in Barcelona.

11 Oct: Pope declared all Spanish decrees against church immunities and jurisdiction null and void and refused to grant canonical investiture to bishops nominated by Philip V.

1713

8 Sep: Clement signed bull *Unigenitus Dei Filius*, which condemned 101 theses from *Reflexions morales sur le Nouveau Testament* by Jansensist leader Pasquier Quesnel.

1714

After recognition of Philip V at Utrecht, relations with Spain restored and canonical investitute extended to Spanish bishops.

1718

Traditional feudal rights of Holy See disregarded in Parma–Piacenza after succession of Don Carlos, son of Philip V and Elizabeth Farnese.

1721
19 Mar: Death of Clement XI.

Pope Innocent XIII (Michel Angelo de'Conti) 1721–4
1721
8 May: Unanimous election of Cardinal de'Conti. Brief papacy beset by continual illness. Only pope in modern times not to have monument in St Peter's, although buried there.

1724
7 Mar: Death of Innocent XIII.

Pope Benedict XIII (Vincenzo Maria Orsini) 1724–30
1724
29 May: Election of Dominican Cardinal Orsini, who accepted papacy only after strenuous resistance. An ascetic mainly concerned with needs of faithful in diocese of Rome, Benedict XIII ignored needs of wider church for leadership.

1725
Niccolò Coscia of Benevento made cardinal and given control of papal administration. Coscia's corrupt management isolated Benedict XIII, reduced financial affairs of Papal States to disorder, and diminished diplomatic standing of papacy.

1726
12 Jun: Niccoló Maria Lercari, protégé of Coscia, appointed Secretary of State.

1727
Concordat with Savoy-Piedmont recognised royal title of Victor Amadeus II and his right to present bishops in Sardinia. King also granted right of episcopal appointment for virtually whole of territory. Concordat undoubtedly secured by Piedmont's bribery of Coscia and other Vatican officials.

Pope Clement XII (Lorenzo Corsini) 1730–40
1730
12 Jul: Election of 78-year-old Cardinal Corsini of Florence. Infirmity weakened pontificate. Blind after 1732, Clement XII left administration to advisers.

1731
Piedmontese concordat of 1727 ruled invalid by Clement XII.

1733

Niccoló Coscia found guilty of corruption and sentenced to 10 years' imprisonment in Castel Sant'Angelo.

1736

Spain occupied some of Papal States after riot in Rome against Spainish recruitment of troops.

May: Spain, followed by Kingdom of Naples, broke off relations with Rome. To restore them, Clement XII forced to make concessions in new concordat with Spain.

1738

Pope condemned Free Masons for first time in bull *In Eminenti.*

1740

6 Feb: Death of Clement XII, during whose papacy administration and fiscal stability of Papal States had been greatly improved by Cardinal Alberoni.

Pope Benedict XIV (Prospero Lambertini) 1740–58
1740

17 Aug: Election of Cardinal Lambertini, Archbishop of Bologna, after conclave of six months, longest since Great Schism.

1740–8

Wars of Austrian Succession, during which Spanish and Austrian troops ignored neutrality of Papal States, interrupting administration and reducing revenues.

1741

2 Jun: Benedict approved new concordat with Kingdom of Naples, which conceded establishment of mixed law court, including laymen, to judge ecclesiastical issues and persons, and which implicitly granted the placet.

1742

Treaty of Breslau guaranteed religious *status quo* in Silesia, but, after initial resistance, Benedict XIV appointed Frederick II's candidate as Bishop of Breslau.

1747

Henry Stuart, 'Duke of York', brother of Stuart pretender to British throne, made cardinal by Benedict XIV.

1748-58
Period of cultural activity and reform: many Roman churches 'restored', sometimes violating traditional character; Index made less draconian, allowing Catholic authors to vindicate their writings and 'improve' their works; Vatican Library expanded by acquisition of private book collections.

1753
Benedict XIV concluded new concordat with Spain, granting far-reaching concessions: royal control over clerical appointments vastly increased.

1758
Cardinal Saldanha, relative of powerful minister Pombal, made visitor of Jesuit order in Portugal, thus sealing its doom in that country and its overseas possessions.
  3 May: Death of Benedict XIV.

Pope Clement XIII (Carlo de la Torre de Rezzonico) 1758-69
1758
6 Jul: Election of Venetian Cardinal Rezzonico, Bishop of Padua since 1743. Papacy dominated by issue of Jesuits, who were successively expelled from Portugal, France and Spain.

1763-4
Years of famine and high prices in Papal States; reform of finances blocked by great landowners.

1765
7 Jan: Clement unequivocally condemned expulsion of Jesuits and rejected pressure to abolish order in bull *Apostolicum pascendi*.

1768
30 Jan: Pope declared anti-clerical actions in Parma–Piacenza null and void; Clement's refusal to retract monitory led to French and Spanish occupation of papal enclaves of Benevento, Pontecorvo, Avignon and Venaissin.

1769
2 Feb: Death of Clement XIII.

Pope Clement XIV (Lorenzo Ganganelli) 1769-74
1769
19 May: Election of Cardinal Ganganelli.

Clement XIV restored relations with Portugal, severed since 1759. Bishoprics could thus be filled, but only with nominees of Pombal.

Sep: Clement promised to abolish Jesuit order in letter to Louis XV of France, but did not set firm date.

1773

Revocation of celebrated bull *In coena Domini*.

Return of Benevento and other papal territories seized by Bourbon powers in 1768.

22 Sep: Death of Clement XIV.

Pope Pius VI (Giovanni Angelo Braschi) 1775–99
1775
15 Feb: Election of Cardinal Braschi after conclave of 134 days.

1777
Abolition of internal customs duties in Papal States (except for Bologna).

1778
1 Nov: Recantation of Johann Nikolaus von Hontheim, suffragan Bishop of Trier, author (under pseudonym of Justinus Febronius) of 'heretical' book *De statu ecclesiae*, which had upheld the authority of secular authorities and bishops against the pope and supported the theory of conciliae supremacy in church government.

1782
Mar–Apr: Pius VI's journey to Vienna to attempt, unsuccessfully, to dissuade Emperor Joseph II to abandon radical ecclesiastical reforms.

1782–3
Dec–Jan: Joseph II's return visit to Pius VI in Rome.

1782
28 Dec: Pius gave up right of presentation of Milanese bishops to Joseph as 'Duke of Milan'.

1785
Pius VI prompted revision of penal code in Papal States.

1786
Attempts of Pius VI to establish nunciature in Munich at request of Bavarian Elector provoked German bishops to draw up Punctation of Ems, which upheld episcopal against papal authority.

18 Sep: Synod of Pistoia, assembly of Tuscan and other Italian clergy under leadership of Bishop Scipione de'Ricci, published decrees hostile to papal authority. On 3 June 1791, Pius VI finally forced Ricci to quit see of Pistoia and in 1794 condemned him and theses of Pistoia in bull *Auctorem fidei*.

1788

Kingdom of Naples broke off relations with Rome after lengthy dispute with Pius VI over papacy's claims of feudal suzerainty over Naples and Sicily.

1789

Pius VI admitted that 9th-century decretals of Isidore, on which much papal authority was based, were forged, but nevertheless refuted Ems articles of August 1786.

1791

10 Mar: Pius VI condemned French Civil Constitution of the Clergy.

5 *Parma–Piacenza*

The duchies of Parma and Piacenza, almost wholly Catholic territories where the church owned some 20% of the land, had been papal possessions before they passed into the hands of the Farnese family in 1545. Thus, even afterwards, the papacy continued to claim feudal overlordship over the territories – a claim which would greatly irritate Parma's relations with Rome in the 17th and 18th centuries. In 1731, when the Farnese line died out, the duchies passed to Don Carlos of Bourbon, son of Philip V of Spain and Elizabeth Farnese, with the feudal claims of the papacy being ignored – as they were again in 1748. With this history of diplomatic friction as a backdrop, in the 1760s Parma found itself at the centre of the wider conflict between secular authorities and the papacy. Although its reforms were no more extreme – and in some cases more moderate – than those of Piedmont, Lombardy, and Tuscany, Parma was singled out because of its small size as a state where Rome could stem the establishmentarian tide. Yet the duchy's ties with other Bourbon states not only encouraged the chief minister, Guglielmo du Tillot, to resist papal pressure, but actually to extend secular controls over the church. However, the personal piety of the new Duke Ferdinand and popular hostility led to the fall of du Tillot in 1771, after which the minister's successor reverted to a more moderate course, while retaining the essence of his reforms.

1644

31 May: Peace of Ferrara ended first War of Castro between Parma and Pope Urban VIII.

1649

Second War of Castro, which saw recapture of this Farnese town by papacy under Pope Innocent XI.

1731

Papal feudal overlordship ignored by Parma–Piacenza at passage of duchies to Don Carlos of Bourbon.

1748

Papal suzerainty again ignored.

1764

Guglielmo du Tillot, chief minister, abolished mortmain.

1765

Church lands subjected to taxation.

1765–67

Royal Junta of Jurisdiction established to supervise church; placet and exequator imposed to regulate relations with Rome; church courts restricted in authority; and small convents suppressed.

1768

30 Jan: Duke of Parma–Piacenza excommunicated by Pope Clement XIII. Jesuits expelled.

1771

Fall of du Tillot, signalling reversion to moderate course in ecclesiastical policy and relations with papacy.

6 *Piedmont–Savoy–Sardinia*

Well over 90% of the population was Roman Catholic. However, there was a small minority of Piedmontese Protestants – the Waldensians – who were subjected to severe persecution during most of the 17th century and indeed were driven from their homes into the inaccessible valleys of the Alps. Victor Amadeus allowed the Waldensians to return home in 1694 and extended a limited toleration which lasted until 1741, when a policy of religious uniformity was again imposed.

The Catholic church was less powerful and wealthy in Piedmont than in other Italian states. The clergy numbered no more than 20,000 in the 18th century, and the church owned less than 15% of cultivated land. Between 1717 and 1731, an establishmentarian policy greatly increased the secular authority over the church and thus diminished the influence of the papacy. Indeed, the concordats of 1727 and 1742 largely confirmed the subjugation of the church to the crown. Thus, after 1742, there was little need to further limit the church. Bishops were unable to take any step without royal approval, and the king was in actuality the head of the church in his territories, exercising wide powers of appointment and excluding unwelcome papal pronouncements.

1648–94
Waldensians – Piedmontese Protestants – severely persecuted and hounded from homes in lower Alpine valleys.

1655
Massacre of Waldensians in Savoy.

1694
Waldensians allowed to return home and granted limited toleration by Victor Amadeus.

1717–31
Establishmentarian reforms asserted monarch's control over church and broke ecclesiastical monopoly in education.

1726–7
New concordats obtained through corrupt machinations of papal favourite, Coscia. Pope recognised royal title of Victor Amadeus II, right of presentation to Sardinian bishoprics, and right of episcopal appointment for whole territory. Also Inquisition was suppressed and foreign clerics excluded from church hierarchy.

1729
University of Turin reformed and given monopoly of higher education; provincial colleges offering scholarships founded to train new bureaucracy.

1742
Condordat largely confirmed earlier agreements.

1770–1

Right of *Recursus ad Principem* (recourse to ruler from church abuses) expanded.

7 Tuscany

The church in Tuscany had long been closely tied to the papacy by the Medici family and thus there was no anti-curialist tradition as in Naples. However, when the Medici dynasty came to an end in 1737, with the accession of the Duke of Lorraine and Tuscany's subsequent attachment to the Habsburg Empire, the position of the church was transformed. Giorgio Rucellai, the grand-duchy's chief administrator, took it upon himself to 'emancipate' the Tuscan church from Rome. Consequently, censorship was removed from church control, ecclesiastical immunities were limited, gifts of land to the church were outlawed, and a number of monasteries were closed. After 1769, Grand Duke Leopold went further towards subjugating the church to secular authority in Tuscany: the right of sanctuary was further restricted, more monasteries were suppressed, and publication of papal decrees made subject to government approval. In the 1770s and 1780s there was an active encouragement of Jansenism as a means to combat papal influence and in 1786 the famous Synod of Pistoia was convened by the Jansenist Bishop de'Ricci to manifest clerical support for the grand-duke's establishmentarian policies. However, the government's and de' Ricci's extremism led to a reaction among the Tuscan clergy, proving that the old ties with Rome were stronger than imagined.

1737

Extinction of the Medici dynasty and accession of Grand Duke Francis of Lorraine.

1743

State control asserted over censorship and sale of books.

1745

Personal immunities of clergy and number of ecclesiastical sanctuaries limited.

1751

Further gifts or legacies of land to church prohibited.

1754

Inquisition strictly limited in powers and restructured.

314

1769
Mortmain outlawed; ecclesiastical rights of refuge further restricted.

1771
Powers of church courts limited.

1773
Suppression of numerous monasteries and appropriation of monastic properties: numbers of houses reduced from 345 to 215; regular clergy reduced by 43% (from 5848 to 3182).
  Superstition attacked and penitential processions banned.

1778 (and 1783)
Begging limited.

1780
Scipione de' Ricci made bishop of Pistoia and Prato by Grand Duke Leopold I (1765–90). Ricci introduced radical reforms in ecclesiastical discipline, studies, administration and liturgy in his diocese. Also caused Jansenist literature to be widely disseminated.

1782
Holy Office abolished.

1784
Ecclesiastical jurisdictions suppressed.

1785
Confraternities dissolved and replaced by single company of charity in each parish.

1786
Sep: Synod of Pistoia, convened by Bishop Ricci with encouragement of Grand Duke Leopold; this assembly of Tuscan and other Italian clergy approved 57 propositions epitomising ascetic and anti-papal reforms advocated by Ricci.

1787
National assembly called to create autonomous Tuscan church. Extremity of measures provoked strong reaction among Tuscan bishops and clergy: Ricci's policies disavowed. Leopold abandoned attempt to govern church through Ricci and other bishops and reverted to traditional policy of asserting royal control.

1788

Closure of papal nuncio's tribunal and separation of religious orders from foreign superiors.

1791

Papal, clerical and public hostility to Bishop Ricci forced his resignation from see of Pistoia and Prato.

1794

Pope Pius VI condemned Ricci and theses of Synod of Pistoia in bull, *Auctorem fidei.*

8 *Venice*

The Republic of Venice was a pioneer in reducing the power of the pope and the Catholic church in its territories. Between 1595 and 1605, the Venetian oligarchy imposed secular censorship, granted a modest religious toleration to *foreign* residents, assumed the right of jurisdiction in criminal cases involving clerics, and prohibited the further donation of secular property to the church. The Servite friar Paolo Sarpi was a vigorous and eloquent defender of the erastian policies of Venice against the condemnations of Pope Paul V and the Roman Curia. In 1605 Paul V placed Venice under interdict and excommunicated the city's rulers, whereupon the Doge – on Sarpi's advice – expelled the Jesuits in 1606. In the following year, Paul V lifted the interdict when he saw it had failed. As a consequence, Venice throughout the 17th and 18th centuries retained more power over the temporal affairs of the church than any other state in Italy and most other Catholic countries. Even after 1650, when popes repeatedly ceded generous grants and negotiated alliances to aid Venice in its protracted struggle against the Turks, the city continued to retain its extensive powers over ecclesiastical matters and occasionally to expand them.

The Venetian church although wealthy was less so than in many states. The church owned some 10% of the plains and 7% of the hilly land. In the 18th century there was a maximum of 40,000 clergy in the Venetian territories, with between 6000 and 7000 priests, monks and nuns resident in the city proper.

1657

Jesuit order (banished in 1606) readmitted to Venetian lands, but their influence over education strictly limited.

1684

Venice adhered to Holy League against Turks under persuasion of crusading Pope Innocent XI.

1754

Republic required government permission for lay and ecclesiatical communications with Rome as well as for execution of papal bulls and decrees. Mortmain was forbidden, some monasteries were closed, and religious orders placed under authority of bishops, who could not leave their dioceses without official leave.

1767–72

Number of clergy limited by law; legacies to convents and religious institutions forbidden; most tax exemptions on church property abolished; census of religious inmates and assessment of church wealth and income required; 127 convents suppressed and land converted to lay uses.

1773

Jesuits expelled, but not until dissolution of order by Pope Clement XIV.

1787

Number of feastdays reduced to combat idleness.

POLAND–LITHUANIA

The denominational make-up of the Polish–Lithuanian state was a complex one. By 1596 the Union of Brest-Litovsk had brought about the merger of the country's Roman Catholic and Orthodox churches, so that in the 17th and 18th centuries the Catholic church represented a large majority of the population but was divided into two nearly equal halves – the Orthodox, Greek or Uniate and the Roman or Latin. There were five to six million Roman Catholics who were almost exclusively ethnic Poles or Lithuanians. There were some four-and-a-half million Uniate or Greek Catholics who were in the main ethnic Russians or Ukranians. Protestantism had been an important force in 16th-century Poland but had been much diminished by the onslaught of the Counter-Reformation. At the beginning of the 17th century, several Protestant groups returned (partially by compulsion) to Catholicism, but there remained a considerable number which did not. There were about 500,000 Protestants, mainly Lutherans, living for the most part in the north and north-east. There was also a very significant

317

Jewish community in Poland of some 750,000, 500,000 of whom lived in towns – many of which had a Jewish majority.

In the 16th and early 17th centuries, a remarkable degree of religious toleration had prevailed in Poland which had attracted religious exiles from all over Europe. However, the Counter-Reformation totally transformed the religious atmosphere. Protestant peasants were forcibly reconverted by their Catholic landlords, and vehement anti-Protestant upheavals took place in many towns – Cracow in 1591, Poznan in 1616, and Lublin in 1627 – bringing the destruction of many Protestant churches. Discriminatory practices by towns and guilds led to a rapid diminution of Protestant numbers. Yet in spite of such measures, a modicum of toleration survived. During the Thirty Years' War, Lutheran and Bohemian Brethren refugees found protection on the lands of some Polish aristocrats and it was on these and similar lands that Protestantism survived. Thus, it was the privileges of the aristocracy, a considerable number of whom remained Protestant, which lay at the root of the attenuated religious toleration which was preserved in Poland in the period 1648–1789. Even so, the rights of Protestants were progressively curtailed, culminating in their exclusion from all offices in 1732. In addition, anti-Semitism, always a potent force in Poland, was exacerbated by the Catholic church in the 18th century, so that even the boldest of reformers drew back from proposing equality for Jews.

There were two metropolitan provinces in Poland – Gniezno and Lwow – and the country was further divided into 18 dioceses. From the 15th century, the Archbishop of Gniezo held the title of primate of Poland and was perhaps the most important person in the country after the monarch. For centuries the very numerous Polish nobility (which comprised about 10% of the whole population) reserved for itself the most important and lucrative church posts – that is, all bishoprics and cathedral canonries. It also exercised the right of patronage over a majority of parish appointments. During the 17th and 18th centuries, both the secular and regular clergy were mainly recruited from the towns and lesser nobility, with peasants finding great difficulty in entering the priesthood. Among Latin-rite clergy, the seculars numbered some 10,000 in the period, while the regulars grew from some 7500 in 1650 to about 14,500 in 1772. The number of Uniate clergy was around 10,000, with regulars probably outnumbering seculars.

The monastic orders played an extremely important role in Polish life – a role which expanded in the 18th century. There had probably been no more than 500 Latin-rite houses in 1650, whereas by 1772 there were 884. Regulars often assisted or replaced the secular clergy in pastoral duties and almost exercised a monopoly in education, with Jesuits and Piarists dominating in Latin areas, and Bisilians in Uniate dioceses. The number of secondary schools or colleges maintained by the orders grew from about 60 in 1700 to some 115 in 1772. In the same period, the number of students enrolled rose from 10,000 to 30–35,000. The Enlightenment had some influence on Polish education in the 1740s and 1750s, notably in the reform of Piarist colleges under the direction of the writer Stanislav Konarski, whose most important achievement was the establishment in Warsaw of the Collegium Nobilium, a model school with a reformed curriculum designed to educate the nation's elite.

Economic factors were not of primary importance in maintaining the strength of the Polish church. In 1772 only 9% of land belonged to the church as opposed to the 13% owned by the crown and a preponderant 78% by the nobility. The expansion of ecclesiastical holdings had been halted in 1635 when the Polish parliament (Sejm) passed the Amortisation Degree forbidding the transfer of property to the church, a law which was im-plemented throughout the period 1648–1772. However, the orders owned extensive urban property which was exempt from municipal taxes, and, in the 18th century the church was wealthy enough to cause resentment among the aristocracy. Consequently, parliament imposed taxes on the clergy for military purposes, placed restrictions on bequests to the church, and lowered fees for religious services, regulated tithes, etc. There was for similar reasons friction between the Polish commonwealth and the papacy, which only concessions by Rome finally diminished.

1635
Amortisation Decree of Polish parliament (Sejm) forbade bequest of land to church.

1647
Edict forbade Polish Brethren (Protestant) to maintain schools or printing offices.

1658
Arians banished from Poland.

1668
Abandonment of Catholic faith made capital offence.

1686
Treaty placed remaining members of Orthodox faith in Poland–Lithuania under protection of Russia.

1717
First coronation of celebrated Black Virgin of Czestochowa.

1719

Parliament imposed taxes on clergy for military purposes, placed further restrictions on bequests to church, lowered fees for religious services, lowered interest rates on debts on landed estates owed to church, curtailed clergy's right to keep and sell spirits, regulated tithes, and limited competence of ecclesiastical courts.

1724

Violent clash between students of Jesuit school and Protestant burghers of Torún – a town with Protestant majority – resulting in beheading of mayor and nine burghers.

1726

Parliament demanded that papal nuncio be recalled.

1732

Parliament barred Protestant dissenters from all offices, membership in parliament, and function of deputy in local tribunals.

1736

Ten-year dispute between Poland and Rome resolved by concordat which restricted authority of papal nuncio's court in Warsaw, gave Polish hierarchy greater power over appointments, and limited bequests to Rome.

1740

Foundation of Collegium Nobilium in Warsaw by Stanislav Konarski for education of elite.

PORTUGAL

Roman Catholicism was the official religion of Portugal, and virtually all Portuguese were actually or nominally Catholic. Relations between church and state within Portugal were intimate, although there were lengthy periods of hostility between the papacy and the Portuguese crown. Largely due to Spanish pressure, Rome was unable to recognise John IV as King of Portugal after his successful re-establishment of the country's independence in 1640, an issue which disrupted the Portuguese church for nearly forty years. After a lengthy interlude of peaceful relations, another violent confrontation between Lisbon and Rome arose during the ministry of the anti-clerical Pombal in the middle of the 18th century.

One of the most ferocious aspects of the Portuguese church was the

Inquisition, which had become a state within a state. Throughout the 17th century and the first half of the 18th, the Inquisition persecuted 'heretics' (that is, Protestants), Jews and the 'cristãos novos' – the so-called New Christians who were mainly wealthy urban business, mercantile and artisan families whose forebears had been converted from Judaism or Islam in the previous 200 years. The four centres of the Portuguese Inquisition were Lisbon, Evora, Coimbra and Goa in Portuguese India. Between 1543 and 1684, the total number of persons condemned by the Inquisition was 19,247, of which 1379 were burned at the stake. Between 1684 and 1747 a further 4672 were sentenced and 146 burnt, with hundreds more dying in prison where they were kept indefinitely without trial.

Estimates for the size of the clergy in 17th- and 18th-century Portugal cannot be easily made, although it is clear that the ecclesiastical population reached nowhere near the staggering heights of 200,000–300,000 suggested by various critical foreigners. It is likely that the size of the clergy reached its peak in the late 17th century and then began a decline which became much more pronounced after 1750. A population estimate of 1765 listed a total of 42,200 regular clergy – 30,772 monks and 11,428 nuns. No figure was given for priests, but it was quite possibly a figure as large or larger than the numbers of regulars. There were three provinces, 16 dioceses and 4099 parishes in 18th century Portugal, and in 1765 there were 493 religious houses. Unlike that of neighbouring Spain, the episcopal hierarchy in Portugal was completely dominated by the aristocracy. Of the 156 bishops in Portugal between 1668 and 1820, more than four-fifths were noblemen.

By the 18th century, the wealth of the Portuguese church was proportionately greater than that of the Spanish or French. It is probable that the church owned nearly one-third of the arable land in Portugal, and although it is true that the church was almost entirely responsible for charity, it did not use its resources for educational or cultural purposes to the same extent as did the Spanish church.

1640–56
Reign of John of Braganza – John IV: In 1645, John sent the Prior of Sodofeita to Rome to promote his claim to nominate bishops to consolidate his hold on Portugal. When Innocent X refused due to Spanish pressure and instead appointed bishops to the vacant sees of Guarda, Miranda and Viseu, John in retaliation appointed bishops to three other vacant sees, thus shutting the door on compromise. By 1649, there was only one bishop of undoubted validity in Portugal.

1656
John IV excommunicated posthumously by his implacable enemy, the Portuguese Inquisition.

1669

Resolution of deadlock with Rome (made possible by peace with Spain in 1668): pope recognised legitimacy of Portuguese dynasty and crown's right of future nomination, making it possible to fill vacant sees canonically.

1716

Archbishop of Lisbon made Patriarch of Portugal.

1728–30

Major rift with papacy over King John V's attempts to subjugate Portuguese church.

1737

Quarrel with Rome settled by new concordat: in response to John V's generous contributions, papacy recognised right of royal *padroado*, or investiture, to all Portuguese sees; further, papal nuncio to crown as well as Patriarch of Lisbon raised to rank of cardinal.

1750–77

Chief ministry of Sebastião José de Carvalho e Melo, created Marquis of Pombal in 1770: period of intense anticlericalism during which power of Catholic church in Portugal was greatly reduced.

1751

Pombal drastically restricted influence of both Inquisition and Jesuits.

1759

1 Jun: Pombal secured the dissolution of the Jesuit order in Portugal, the expulsion of its members, and the confiscation of its property.

1760

Expulsion of papal nuncio from Lisbon, disrupting relations with papacy for ten years, during which time Pombal restored the right of *beneplacito regio*, by which the crown could censor church decisions and proclamations.

1768

Public *autos-da-fé* ended and death penalty for religious offences repealed.

1769

Pope Clement XIV achieved restoration of relations with Portugal, allowing vacant sees to be filled with Pombal's nominees.

Pombal achieved destruction of Inquisition by converting it into a royal tribunal entirely dependent on the secular government.

1773
All statutes enforcing discrimination based on blood repealed, thus abolishing distinctions between Old Christians and New Christians.

SOUTHERN NETHERLANDS (BELGIUM)

The Reformation made little impact in the southern provinces of the Netherlands where the overwhelming majority of the inhabitants remained Roman Catholic throughout the period 1648–1789. The Southern Netherlands revolted against Spain in the 16th century but failed to win their independence along with Holland and the other northern provinces. Thus, under Spanish rule until 1715 and under Austrian control thereafter, Roman Catholicism was the established religion and all other denominations were suppressed.

Religious controversy was confined to the Catholic church itself and largely centred on the problem of Jansenism. Cornelius Jansen, himself a Netherlander, was professor of theology at Louvain for 19 years and bishop of Ypres for two years before his death in 1638. Jansen's teachings were strongly supported by the bishops of Mechelen and Ghent who were suspended by the pope and refused to submit until 1653. During the latter half of the 17th century Jansenism numbered fervent adherents among Louvain professors, bishops, clergy and educated laymen. However, Jansenism was largely subdued in the 18th century thanks to successive archbishops of Mechelen and some professors at Louvain. After 1780, Emperor Joseph II introduced the same schedule of religious reforms in the Southern Netherlands as in his other dominions (see Austria), provoking resistence from the Catholic hierarchy and clergy and resentment by the populace. Indeed, popular and clerical indignation at the emperor's high-handed meddling in religious affairs played no small part in provoking the rebellion which in 1789 led to the temporary collapse of Austrian authority in the Southern Netherlands.

1638
6 May: Death of Cornelius Jansen.

1640
Sep: Publication of *Augustinus* by followers of Jansen, containing the whole of that theologian's teachings.

1643

Jean Bolland, a Jesuit, began to publish *Acta Sanctorum*, critical lives of the saints.

1715

Southern Netherlands passed from Spanish to Austrian rule.

1781

Joseph II's Edict of Toleration eased restrictions on small group of Netherlandish Protestants.

1782

Joseph suppressed contemplative monastic orders and confiscated property of 2600 contemplative monks. Parishes reorganised and liturgy revised.

1786

Seminarians in Southern Netherlands required to study at college of philosophy founded at Louvain – staffed with professors who supported religious changes of Joseph II.

RUSSIA

Although in large measure integrated into the state apparatus, the Russian Orthodox church preserved its institutional identity and some semblance of autonomy until the end of the 17th century. The church was an entity different from the state, with its patriarch and episcopal hierarchy, its administrative, judicial and fiscal offices, and its properties whose inhabitants it taxed and judged. In the mid-17th century, ecclesiastical administration had been brought more tightly under secular control, but it was only in the reign of Peter the Great that the church became a mere department of state, its patriarchy abolished and its hierarchy subordinated to the tsarist bureaucracy.

Like the Eastern Orthodox churches with which it was in communion, the Russian church stressed liturgy, ritual, icons and music. Preaching was a rarity, and indeed the clergy was largely ignorant even of the scriptures. Priests were allowed to marry although monastics were not. It was largely from the latter group that the ecclesiastical hierarchy was chosen. Both higher and lower clergy were mainly peasant in social origin, as the Russian aristocracy spurned church office.

The Russian church was immensely wealthy until its properties were eventually secularised in the 18th century. Over the centuries, the aristocracy had made generous bequests in their wills, so that at the accession of Peter the Great the church was the landlord of some 750,000 peasants out of a total of about 13 million.

As the state religion, Orthodoxy was the official faith of all who lived under Russian rule. There were virtually no Roman Catholics or Protestants except among foreigners living mainly in Moscow and later St Petersburg. However, in the 17th century, the Russian church was itself beset by schism. A significant minority, objecting to the grecophile innovations in the liturgy and ritual introduced by Patriarch Nikon in the 1650s, seceded (or were expelled) from the church and became the schismatic group known as the Old Believers. Expecting the apocalypse, many schismatics fled to the forests or lay down in coffins. Threatened with death unless they conformed, some 20,000 Old Believers rushed to accept martyrdom. Those who survived fled into the remoter regions of northern Russia or to Siberia and themselves split into two sects – the priestly and the non-priestly. Although still excluded from the mainstream of Russian life, the Old Believers were granted a modicum of toleration by Peter, which was much extended by Catherine the Great.

The Russian Orthodox Church in 1738

	Actual numbers	No. per 100,000 inhabitants
Churches	16,901	106
Secular clergy	124,923	781
Monks, nuns and novices	14,282	89
Monasteries and convents	948	6

1551
Council of a Hundred Chapters: Traditional Russian translations of Greek liturgy and Russian ritual practice upheld against 'reforms' of Greek scholar Maximus.

1589
Russian church gained formal independence from Greek Orthodox Church; Moscow made a patriarchy.

1649
New law code subjected monastic lands to secular administrative control and placed clergy under jurisdiction of lay courts; diocese of Novgorod exempted by Tsar Alexis in making Nikon metropolitan there.

1652

Nikon installed as Patriarch of Moscow after Tsar and boyars (nobles) had sworn to obey him in matters of dogma, doctrine and morals.

Foreigners (mainly western Europeans) refusing to embrace Orthodoxy forced to move to separate suburb of Moscow (later famous as the 'German Suburb').

1652-6

Patriarch Nikon's controversial reform of Russian liturgy and ritual according to Greek Orthodox observance. Denounced by zealous traditionalists known as 'Old Believers'.

1656

Nikon's reforms upheld by church council. Publication of *Book of Faith* in which Old Believers denounced revisions of Patriarch Nikon and predicted apocalypse in 1666.

1658

Jul: Patriarch Nikon entered Monastery of New Jerusalem following dispute with Tsar Alexis and boyars over relative powers of church and state.

1659

Tsar Alexis began transferring control of church administration to state officials.

1663

Nikon placed under arrest at Monastery of New Jerusalem.

1666

Church council upheld reforms of liturgy and ritual and condemned Old Believers as heretics.

1667

Final anathema pronounced on Old Believers, who realised reconciliation and compromise were now impossible.

1672

Council of Jerusalem: Eastern patriarchs accepted confession prepared by Metropolitan of Kiev as defining the beliefs of the Orthodox faith.

1684

Tsarina Sophia issued decree threatening all impenitent Old Believers with death by fire; 20,000 or more chose immolation.

1696

Tsar Peter I limited rights of parish and monastic clergy to dispose freely of their income.

1700

On death of Patriarch Adrian, Peter left patriarchate vacant, placing nominal leadership in hands of *locum tenens*. Authority over church properties, income and secular responsibilities placed under monastery *prikaz*, charged with administering, judging and taxing inhabitants of ecclesiastical lands.

1701

Principle established that monasteries forward all revenues to state treasury in return for fixed salaries.

1721

Peter the Great's Ecclesiastical Regulation: Formal abolition of office of patriarch, replaced by Ecclesiastical College (later called Most Holy All-Ruling Synod). Head of college or synod usually layman. Church lost distinct institutional existence and formally merged with state apparatus.

1762

Formal appropriation of church holdings: Peter III ordered all ecclesiastical lands incorporated into state properties.

1764

Catherine II confirmed 1762 edict and closed 569 of 954 active monasteries. Of 385 monasteries remaining, only 161 placed on state establishment; 224 others disendowed and left to fend for themselves. Secular clergy placed on government salary, so that of several million rubles of former church income, only some 400,000 was returned to clergy.

1771

Group of Old Believers allowed by Catherine II to establish themselves in Moscow.

1784

Pejorative term 'schismatic' abandoned; double taxation of religious dissenters removed.

SPAIN

Roman Catholicism was the official religion of Spain. The overwhelming majority of Spaniards were Catholic, and religious dissenters were persecuted to virtual extinction by the Inquisition. Although church and state were closely linked throughout the period, power over ecclesiastical affairs gradually shifted to the secular authority in the 18th century. From the reign of Philip II, the Catholic kings exercised the power to nominate, and thus to appoint, archbishops, bishops and abbots through a chamber of the Council of Castile. However, until 1753, the crown had surprisingly few patronage powers except in Spanish America. Relations with the Vatican were often poor, but during considerable periods Spain was able to exert strong pressure on the papacy because of its position of political and military power on the Italian peninsula and in Sicily.

The population of the Spanish clergy rose steeply from a total of c. 85,000 in 1600 to some 150,000 in 1700. During the 18th century clerical numbers remained fairly stable, with a slight decline after 1775. The census of 1797 counted 70,840 priests, 58,098 monks, and 24,471 nuns: a total of 153,409 or approximately 1.5% of the general population. The number of bishoprics rose from 56 in 1648 to 60 in the 18th century, while the number of parishes was c. 19,000. The episcopacy was not dominated in Spain by the aristocracy as it was in France and Germany, although a number of the lesser, poorer nobility sought profitable preferment in the church. Except in Catalonia, where the middle classes were more developed, the great majority of the clergy came from the peasantry.

As yet, the wealth of the church in Spain has not been precisely determined, although it is certain that it received lucrative revenue from tithes, rents from urban and rural property, mass stipends, and income from investments. In Castile, the church possessed one-seventh of the region's agricultural and pastoral lands and produced one-quarter of agrarian income. In wealthier Catalonia, the percentage of land owned by the church rose to one-fourth; while in the impoverished south ecclesiastical holdings were less extensive.

1621–65
Reign of Philip IV: Early attempts to restrict wealth and power of church (prohibition of further increase of property in mortmain and extension of certain taxes to clergy) not pursued after 1643 when the king came under the strong influence of Sor Maria de Ágreda.

1665–9
Rise to political power by Queen Maria Ana's confessor, the Austrian Jesuit Johan Nithard, which marked the resurgence of clerical domination in the highest councils of the Spanish government.

1675
Publication by Miguel Molinos of *Guía Espiritual*, advocating quietism and

contemplative prayer. Molinos was arrested in 1685 by Papal Inquisition and in 1687 sentenced to life in prison.

1677
Ministers of the retarded Charles II persuaded the king to (1) limit the foundation of new religious houses; (2) outlaw excommunication in matters exclusively concerned with laymen or temporal possessions; and (3) slightly curtail the excessive jurisdiction of the Inquisition. Nothing done to curb the mounting power of the Jesuits.

1682
Compromise reached with Holy See over quartering rights and immunity from police supervision in Rome.

1700–46
Reign of first Spanish Bourbon monarch, Philip V, who opposed the powers of the popes over the Spanish church.

1709
Bishop Francisco de Solis, with encouragement of Philip V, attacked papal centralism and slavery to Roman Curia in *Dictamen sobre los abusos de la*

Corte Romana....
25 Feb: Philip V, reacting violenty to forced papal recognition of Habsburg Archduke Charles as King of Spain, founded Junta Magna, which ordered nuncio expelled and nunciature closed, Spolia and revenues of vacant bishoprics sequestered, and all relations between Spanish clerics and Rome forbidden.

1713
Communications between Holy See and Spanish clergy restored by Peace of Utrecht.

1717
New concordat with Rome provisionally concluded.

1718
Concordat broken and papal nuncio expelled again.

1720
Nuncio allowed to return to Madrid, but apostolic council and Spanish nunciature continued to come under attack over rates for marriage dispensations, administration of vacant sees, etc.

1736

Following a riot in Rome against Spanish recruitment of troops, Spain occupied parts of the Papal States, and in May broke off relations with the Vatican.

1753

Concordat concluded between Spain and Pope Benedict XIV: resolved most of the points at issue in Spain's favour, greatly extending the royal patronage. Afterwards, bishops who resisted royal policies faced harassment and even dismissal.

1759–88

Reign of Charles III, formerly King of Naples, strong opponent of papal centralism who accelerated restrictions on Catholic church in Spain.

1767

27 Feb: Royal decree, giving no reasons, banished the Jesuits from Spain and confiscated their possessions. Charles III acted only after death of Jesuits' protectress, Elizabeth Farnese, the queen mother, and at the instigation of his reputedly Deist chief minister, Conde de Aranda.

SWEDEN–FINLAND

Sweden, like other northern countries, had been swept by the Protestant Reformation in the 16th century. Yet King Gustavus Vasa, like Henry VIII of England, had been motivated to break with Rome more for political and economic than theological reasons. Consequently, the Lutheran character which the Swedish church assumed was only gradually shaped in the course of the century. In fact, the church in Sweden became a very individual institution, one strict in Lutheran doctrine and yet in many ways traditional in its rituals and trappings. Furthermore, for many years the church retained a relationship with the state perhaps unique in a Protestant country. As early as the 15th century the clergy had been recognised as one of the four estates in the nation, and in 1617 Gustavus Adolphus's *riksdagsordnung* had regularised ecclesiastical representation in a separate house of the Swedish parliament. Thus, there was in the 17th century at least partial admission of the church's existence as a discrete sphere where the clergy were entitled to regulate their own affairs. Of course, there was conflict between church and crown – as in Catholic countries – on appointments to livings, election of bishops, the crown's right of *régale*, and the right to make regulations, to ensure good order in the church. Yet unlike their Lutheran colleagues in

Germany, the Swedish church resisted relegation to a department of state, although it is true that the clergy functioned as an adjunct of the civil service, performing tasks such as tax collection and recruiting. In the period 1620–50, they thwarted successive proposals to entrust church government to a General Consistory, which would have placed ecclesiastical discipline in lay hands. However, despite the steady support the clergy had offered the crown, in the 1680s Charles XI was able to subject the church, as all other aspects of Swedish life, to the absolutist state he was erecting. And, even after the revolution of 1719–20 had ended royal absolutism, the church found itself largely in the regulatory clutches of a lay parliament.

The discipline and observance of the Swedish church retained many elements from the Catholic past. The church was governed by an episcopal hierarchy which believed that it had preserved the apostolic succession; Swedish cathedrals still had chapters; ceremony and vestments were traditional; Latin canticles were allowed; crucifixes and images were displayed; and there were a score of saints' days and festal days.

As in most countries there was something of a split between upper and lower clergy along economic and social lines. For a Protestant country, Sweden possessed a rather numerous lower clergy: there were as many as 12,000 ministers who earned comfortable but modest stipends. The far smaller hierarchy, on the other hand, could acquire lands with the same immunities enjoyed by the aristocracy. Moreover, although bishops could not themselves be ennobled, their sons could be and often were. Private endowments such as land grants were necessary to remunerate the clerical hierarchy because the Swedish church no longer possessed large enough resources within itself. Before the Reformation, the church had owned one-fifth of the land in the country, but most of this had been appropriated by the crown. However, the church had been left with some lucrative farmland and could claim exemption from certain taxes.

There was very little religious toleration in 17th- and 18th-century Sweden. Only Lutherans could hold office and teach. There was no attempt to persecute Protestant dissenters on matters of personal conscience, but they were forbidden to hold public or even private services. When Pietism swept into Sweden in the early 18th century, fierce statutes against conventicles were passed. There was no toleration at all for Catholics: even to hold Roman beliefs was a crime. Even the liberalisation under Gustav III in the 1770s applied to non-Lutheran foreigners only. As far as native Swedes were concerned, the state church managed to maintain its monopoly right down to 1860.

1611

All except Lutherans excluded from holding office and teaching.

331

1617
Statute of Orebo: ordered all Catholics to leave Sweden within three months; all who remained or who converted to Rome in future deprived of civil rights.

1634
Form of Government laid down that provincial governors were to support episcopal authority; subsequently constables accompanied bishops on visitations.

1650
Queen Christina granted bishops right to be consulted about presentation of livings in crown's gift; clerical revenues placed on a firm legal basis; church control of education strengthened.

1655
Statute enacted punishing those holding heretical services (though not prayer meetings) or who imported heretical teachers.

1665
Statute condemning misuse of God's name, profanation of holy days, and absence from church.

1671
Rights of foreign embassies further restricted; admission of Jesuits to Sweden forbidden in all circumstances.

1686
Church law: Revision of Church Ordinance, ending lengthy controversy by providing that Lutheran Formula of Concord was to be accepted as a symbolic book; establishment of absolute uniformity in church services; loss of church judicial powers, with ecclesiastical cases tried in lay courts.

1687
Instructions for provincial governors: Governors enjoined to 'maintain religion and the proper form of worship, so that the word of God be preached with truth, purity and zeal and no delusive, heretical doctrines be disseminated, openly or secretly among our subjects'.

1688
New catechism formulated by Archbishop Olof Svebelius, authorised to be used throughout the country.

1693

New Handbook of Worship promulgated (which enjoined sign of cross in baptism).

1698

New national hymnbook introduced.

1703

Swedish version of Bible known as 'Charles XII's Bible' prescribed.

1710–25

Spread of Pietism in Sweden.

1726

Conventicle Act forbade all prayer meetings in private houses not confined to members of resident family; not repealed until 1860.

1778–81

Gustav III allowed freedom of worship to foreign non-Lutherans. Swedes not given toleration until after 1860.

1782

Jews allowed to settle in some large towns subject to certain restrictions.

SWITZERLAND

The population of Switzerland in the 17th and 18th centuries was roughly three-fifths Protestant and two-fifths Roman Catholic. The moderate reformer Ulrich Zwingli early succeeded in persuading Zurich and Bern to adopt Protestantism but was thwarted in his later attempts to spread the Reformation by force of arms. In the 1540s and afterwards, Jean Calvin made Geneva the centre of the Reformed faith. However, neither the Zwinglians or the Calvinists were able to subdue or convert the Catholic cantons, led by Lucerne and Fribourg, and in the period 1648–1789 the Swiss confederation existed only in the loosest form. Indeed, basically due to the split along religious lines, there was no meeting of the diet between 1663 and 1776.

1655

Proposals put forward by Protestant Zurich for more centralised Swiss state thwarted by Catholic cantons.

1656

First Villmergen War: Protestant Bern and Zurich pitted against Catholic cantons. Protestants defeated at Villmergen (24 Jan) and thus complete control of religious affairs had to be left to individual members of Swiss confederation.

1693

Protestant cantons, incensed by Louis XIV's use of mercenaries against the Dutch, agreed to supply soldiers to Holland and later England. Catholic cantons subsequently sent men to fight for Spain. Consequently, in War of Spanish Succession, thousands of Protestant and Catholic Swiss soldiers fought on opposing sides.

1712

Second Villmergen War: Last armed conflict between Protestant and Catholic cantons, this time resulting in Protestant triumph (25 Jul) – again at Villmergen. Victory firmly established Protestant dominance, with Catholic cantons losing control over important dependent territories.

7 POPULATION

DENMARK–NORWAY

DENMARK (*National totals*)
1769	798,000
1787	842,000
1801	929,000

Copenhagen
1709	66,000
1800	101,000

NORWAY (*National totals*)
1650	450,000
1700	550,000
1735	616,000
1755	671,000
1775	741,000
1795	843,000

Oslo
1750	6,800
1800	10,000

FRANCE

National totals
1650	19,000,000
1700	19,300,000
1750	22,000,000
1789	27,000,000

Cities

Paris	
1650	450,000
1700	550,000
1750	550,000
1789	600,000

Lyon	
1726	90,000
1760	120,000
1789	139,000

Marseilles	
1720	90,000*
1760	90,000
1789	76,000
1800	111,000

Rouen	
1726	80,000
1745	92,000
1789	65,000
1800	86,000

Bordeaux	
1726	40,000
1745	62,500
1789	82,500

Nantes	
1726	20,000
1745	38,500
1789	65,000

Lille	
1688	52,500
1726	51,000
1745	52,500
1789	63,000

Toulouse	
1695	38,000
1790	53,000

Nîmes	
1726	29,500
1745	50,000
1789	48,500

Metz	
1726	23,000
1745	40,000
1789	46,500

Strasbourg	
1726	43,000
1745	46,000
1789	41,500

Amiens	
1726	35,000
1745	43,500
1789	43,342

Orleans	
1726	20,000
1760	38,000
1789	43,000

Nancy	
1726	8,000
1745	28,500
1789	33,500

Tours	
1726	26,500
1789	32,000

---

* 40,000 inhabitants of Marseilles died in plague of that year.

Cities

Caen			*Angers*	
1726	36,000		1726	30,000
1745	32,000		1760	36,000
1789	32,000		1789	28,000

Reims			*Grenoble*	
1726	22,500		1726	6,500
1748	23,000		1745	24,500
1789	30,500		1789	25,000

Rennes			*Dijon*	
1726	18,500		1726	13,500
1745	35,500		1745	20,500
1789	29,500		1789	22,000

GERMANY

GERMANY
(*National totals*)

1650	11,500,000
1700	13,500,000
1750	15,700,000
1800	18,500,000

Bavaria

1750	2,900,000
1800	3,400,000

Brandenburg – Prussia

1650	1,400,000
1700	1,600,000
1740	2,250,000
1750	3,480,000
(including Silesia)	
1775	4,910,000
1800	6,221,000

Hesse – Cassel

1750	340,000
1800	390,000

Saxony

1650	1,800,000
1700	2,000,000
1750	1,700,000
1800	1,900,000

Württemberg

1650	250,000
1700	400,000
1750	467,000
1800	650,000

Cities

Berlin

1648	6,000
1680	10,000
1709	56,000
1730	72,387
1750	113,289
1786	147,338
1800	172,132

Hamburg

1650	60,000
1764	92,000
1787	100,000

Breslau (Wrocław)

1675	28,000
1710	40,000
1750	47,861
1790	55,747
1800	64,520

Dresden

1700	c. 20,000
1800	61,794

Königsberg

1723	39,475
1755	55,000
1770	52,196
1802	54,535

Danzig (Gdańsk)

1650	77,000
1675	53,200
1705	50,400
1745	47,600
1793	36,231
1800	48,000

München

1650	c. 17,000
1700	c. 24,000
1722	29,097
1781	37,840
1796	46,000

Köln (Cologne)

1650–1750	c. 40,000
1794	44,512

Mainz

1650	c. 25,000
1771	26,753
1780	32,482
(including garrison)	

Leipzig

1650	14,000
1700	c. 20,000
1800	32,146

Brunswick

1671	15,600
1773	23,385
1783	27,063
1793	27,301
1800	30,525

Bremen

1650	c. 20,000
1774	c. 28,000
1790	c. 30,000

Nuremberg

1620	c. 40,000
1650	c. 20,000
1789	c. 25,000

Cities

Aachen	
1656	c. 25,000
1730	c. 15–20,000
1780	c. 20,000
1795	23,413

Lübeck	
1650	31,068
1700	23,596
1750	18,772
1790	18,693
1800	22,550

Würzburg	
1621	9,782
1687	18,070
1800	c. 22,000

Augsburg	
1645	19,960
1789	c. 21,000

Düsseldorf	
1630	c. 5,000
1700	8,578
1738	c. 8,800
1750	c. 9,100
1792	18,794

Cassel	
1626	6,329
1723	12,289
1750	18,720
1789	18,450

Stuttgart	
1631	8,327
1648	c. 4,500
1700	13,000
1750	17,000
1790	18,012

Stettin	
1631	10,000
1709	10,900
1750	12,966
1790	16,249

Bamberg	
1620	c. 11,000
1650	c. 7,000
1700	c. 10,000
1750	c. 12,000
1795	c. 16,000

Hannover (Hanover)	
1650	c. 6,000
1766	11,874
1790	c. 13,000

Ulm	
1600	c. 21,000
1650	c. 13,500
1750	c. 15,000
1795	c. 13,000

Bonn	
1650	c. 6,000
1750	c. 8–9,000
1784	12,644

Heidelberg	
1618	c. 6,500
1766	9,828
1784	10,754

Koblenz	
1663	1,409
1787	7,475
1799	10,035

Cities

Freiburg		*Mannheim*	
1630	c. 9,000	1618	c. 1,200
1650	c. 3,500	1660	c. 3,000
1700	c. 5,500	1688	c. 11,000
1789	7,916	1710	c. 5,000
1800	9,050		

GREAT BRITAIN AND IRELAND

GREAT BRITAIN AND IRELAND (*Total*)

1650	8,250,000
1700	8,940,000
1725	9,785,000
1750	10,475,000
1775	12,575,000
1800	15,960,000

England and Wales		**Scotland**	
1650	5,500,000	1650	1,000,000
1700	5,400,000	1700	1,040,000
1725	5,835,000	1725	1,100,000
1750	6,225,000	1750	1,250,000
1775	7,200,000	1775	1,375,000
1800	9,210,000	1800	1,500,000

Ireland	
1650	1,750,000
1687	2,167,000
1700	2,500,000
1725	2,750,000
1750	3,000,000
1754	3,191,000
1775	4,000,000
1791	4,753,000
1800	5,250,000

English cities

Cities	1650	1700	1750	1801
London	400,000	550,000	675,000	818,129
Liverpool	1,500	5,500	22,000	88,358[1]
Manchester	4,500	8,000	18,000	88,134[2]
Birmingham	3,500	7,000	23,500	73,670[2]
Bristol	15,000	20,000	40,000	64,000
Plymouth	5,000	7,000	14,000	43,194[3]
Norwich	20,000	30,000	36,000	36,832
Sheffield	2,500	3,500	12,000	35,344[4]
Bath	1,000	2,500	6,500	34,160
Portsmouth	3,000	5,000	10,000	33,226[5]
Leeds	4,000	6,000	11,000	30,669[6]
Nottingham	5,000	7,000	12,000	28,860
Newcastle	12,000	15,000	25,000	28,366
Hull	3,500	6,000	11,000	27,609
Sunderland	3,000	5,000	9,000	24,500
Leicester	3,500	5,500	9,000	16,933
Exeter	12,000	14,000	15,000	16,827
York	10,000	10,500	12,000	16,145
Coventry	7,000	7,000	12,000	16,034
Chester	7,500	9,000	11,000	15,052
Yarmouth	10,000	11,000	12,000	14,845
Oxford	8,500	9,000	10,000	11,694
Worcester	8,000	8,500	9,500	11,532
Colchester	9,500	10,000	9,500	11,520
Cambridge	8,500	9,000	9,500	10,087
Canterbury	7,000	7,500	8,000	9,071
Salisbury	7,000	7,000	7,000	7,668

[1] Including suburbs and seamen in port.
[2] Including suburbs.
[3] Including dock.
[4] Including Brightside.
[5] Including Portsea.
[6] 53,162 with suburbs.

Scottish cities

Edinburgh

1650	25,000
1700	35,000
1755	57,000
1801	81,600

Glasgow

1700	12,000
1750	25,000
1801	83,700

HOLLAND (UNITED PROVINCES)

National totals

1650	1,900,000
1700	1,900,000
1750	1,950,000
1800	2,078,000

Cities

Amsterdam

1650	150,000
1700	200,000
1750	200,000
1795	217,000

Utrecht

1600	35,000
1700	30,000
1795	35,000

Rotterdam

1650	35,000
1700	50,000
1750	45,000
1795	53,000

Leiden

1622	45,000
1660	60,000
1750	35,000
1795	31,000

The Hague

1650	19,000
1680	23,000
1730	30,000
1795	38,500

Haarlem

1622	39,500
1707	32,500
1748	27,000
1795	21,000

Population of some other Dutch cities in 1795

Gronigen:	23,500
Middelbourg:	20,000
Dordrecht:	18,000
Maastricht:	18,000
Leeuwarden:	15,500
Delft:	15,500

ITALY*

National totals (calculated for a post-1945 land area of c. 301,000 sq. km.)

1650	11,000,000
1700	13,000,000
1750	15,500,000
1770	17,000,000
1790	18,500,000

Republic of Genoa

1620 (including Corsica)	630,000
1750 (minus Corsica)	500,000
1797	603,000

Corsica		*Ajaccio*	
1741	120,000	1741	4,500
1801	164,000	1801	6,000

Genoa (city)

1681	65,000
1750	70,000
1788	77,500

Lombardy (Duchy of Milan)

1650	1,250,000
1750	1,152,000 (Austrian)
	143,000 (Piedmontese)
	—————
	1,295,000
1744	1,110,000 (Austrian)
	535,000 (Piedmontese)
	—————
	1,645,000

Cities

Milan		*Cremona*	
1658	100,000	1650	30,000
1715	123,500	1730	24,000
1750	123,600	1763	23,500
1800	134,500	1774	25,000

---

* All figures are approximate.

Cities

Pavia		*Como*	
1650	18,000	1650	12,000
1750	24,500	1730	13,500
1773	28,000	1774	13,500
1800	23,500	1800	15,000

Mantua		*Lodi*	
(part of Lombardy after 1708)		1619	14,000
1676	21,000	1730	9,500
1750	25,000	1750	15,500
1764	28,500	1800	11,500
1789	21,500		

		Novara	
Alessandria		1650	8,000
1650	13,000	1730	9,000
1734	11,500	1752	10,000
1774	18,500	1774	12,000

Duchy of Modena

1697	277,000
1770	308,500

Cities

Modena		*Reggio (Emilia)*	
1645	25,000	1628	13,500
1680	22,000	1695	15,500
1767	23,000	1767	16,500
1790	22,000	1788	18,000

Kingdom of Naples (Two Sicilies)

1600	3,100,000
1721	3,000,000
1750	3,700,000
1790	4,925,000

Sicily	
1652	1,121,000
1681	1,171,000
1737	1,307,000
1798	3,700,000

Sicilian Cities

Palermo		*Trapani*	
1625	128,000	1652	19,500
1713	100,000	1713	16,500
1737	102,000	1747	17,500
1798	140,500	1798	24,500

Catania		*Marsala*	
1652	11,500	1652	11,000
1713	16,000	1713	14,000
1747	25,500	1747	15,500
1798	45,000	1798	20,500

Messina		*Syracuse*	
1653	50,000	1652	13,500
1713	40,000	1713	17,000
1747	26,500	1748	18,000
1798	44,000	1798	19,500

Southern Italy

There are few population estimates for southern Italian cities other than Naples before the end of the 18th century.

Naples	
1606	280,000
1688	176,000
1707	215,500
1742	305,000
1796	426,616

Late 18th-century estimates for
southern Italian cities

Altamura	18,000 (1793/4)
Aquila	13,500 (1793/4)
Avellino	11,500 (1788)
Aversa	14,000 (1788)
Bari	18,000 (1793/4)
Barletta	16,000 (1793/4)
Chieti	12,500 (1793/4)
Cosenza	9,500 (1793/4)
Foggia	13,000 (1793/4)
Gaeta	13,500 (1788)
Gallipoli	13,000 (1793/4)

Lecce	20,000 (1793/4)
Matera	12,500 (1793/4)
Reggio Calabria	18,000 (1793/4)
Salerno	9,000 (1788)
San Severo	18,000 (1793/4)
Taranto	17,500 (1793/4)
Torre Annunziata	16,000 (1788)
Torre del Greco	14,000 (1788)

Papal States

1656	1,703,500
1701	1,969,000
1769	2,188,500
1790	2,552,000

Cities

Rome

1652	118,000
1702	138,500
1760	157,000
1794	170,000

Bologna

1645	58,500
1701	53,500
1759	69,000
1791	71,000

Ferrara

1656	28,000
1701	27,500
1740	30,000
1787	30,500

Benevento

1656	4,500
1701	11,500
1788	20,500

Perugia

1656	17,500
1701	16,000
1736	14,000

Ravenna

1656	13,000
1701	14,500
1736	13,500

Viterbo

1656	11,000
1701	12,000
1736	12,500
1782	13,000

Faenza

1656	10,500
1701	11,500
1736	12,500

Ancona

1656	9,500
1701	8,500
1736	10,000

Orvieto

1656	5,500
1701	6,000
1736	6,000
1782	8,000

Duchies of Parma and Piacenza

Parma

The Duchy

1700	180,000
1787	209,500

City of Parma

1650	28,000
1700	35,000
1787	34,000

Piacenza

The Duchy

1618	154,000
1758	200,000
1814	207,000

City of Piacenza

1618	33,000
1758	31,000
1814	28,000

Piedmont/Sardinia

Piedmont

1650	1,400,000
1700	1,671,000
1720	1,930,000
1790	2,774,000

Cities

Turin		*Asti*	
1631	40,000	1650	10,000
1702	42,500	1734	13,000
1750	58,000	1774	14,500
1790	76,500		

Cuneo		*Fossano*	
		1650	10,000
1650	11,000	1734	11,500
1734	12,500	1774	14,500
1774	18,000		

Sardinia

1688	230,000
1728	310,000
1751	360,000
1790	370,000

Cities

Cagliari		*Sassari*	
1688	16,000	1627	13,500
1728	17,000	1700	12,000
1750	19,000	1750	14,000
1783	19,000	1783	16,500

Tuscany

1650	920,000
1700	1,000,000
1750	1,078,000
1800	1,187,500

Cities

Florence		*Pisa*	
1641	69,500	1642	13,000
1672	70,500	1672	13,000
1751	74,000	1745	14,000
1794	81,000		

		Pistoia	
		1642	8,500
Livorno (Leghorn)		1672	8,000
1642	12,000	1745	9,500
1700	13,500		
1745	32,500	*Arezzo*	
1790	41,500	1642	7,000
		1745	7,500
Lucca			
1645	25,000		
1744	21,000	*Prato*	
		1642	5,500
Siena		1672	6,500
1642	16,000	1745	6,500
1717	16,000		
1645	15,500		
1784	16,000		

Republic of Venice

1620	1,821,000
1700	1,800,000
1766	2,335,000
1790	2,465,000

Cities

Venice		Bergamo	
1642	121,000	1650	28,000
1696	132,500	1700	30,000
1776	140,500	1766	33,000
1802	134,500	1785	36,000

Verona		Vicenza	
1627	53,500	1631	32,000
1650	33,000	1710	26,000
1738	48,000	1766	28,500
1785	53,000	1802	29,000

Padua		Udine	
1648	32,500	1632	10,000
1691	35,000	1766	14,500
1766	41,000	1780	15,500
1802	45,400	1802	16,000

Brescia		Treviso	
1642	30,000	1632	10,000
1730	35,000	1766	10,000
1764	39,000	1780	10,500
1785	38,000		

POLAND–LITHUANIA

National totals

1650	7,500,000
1700	9,000,000
1750	11,000,000
1772	12,000,000 (before first partition)
	7,500,000 (after first partition)
1793	9,000,000 (before second partition)
	6,000,000 (after second partition)

Cities

Warsaw		Krakow	
1700	30,000	1800	19,500
1790	120,000		

EUROPEAN RUSSIA

National totals

1650	15,000,000
1724	17,900,000
1750	22,000,000
1775	28,000,000
1800	35,000,000

Russian cities: Population estimates for Russian cities* before 1800 are extremely rare and probably very unreliable.

Moscow		*St Petersburg*	
1650	100,000	(Leningrad)	
1730	138,000	1730	68,000
1790	175,000	1800	220,000

Some other cities in 1800: *Riga*: 30,000; *Odessa*: 8,000.

PORTUGAL

National totals

1650	2,000,000
1700	2,000,000
1750	500,000
1790	2,750,000

Cities			
Lisbon		*Oporto*	
1650	165,000	1650	20,000
1700	150,000	1720	21,000
1750	150,000	1787	43,000
1790	165,000		

---

* Included in this term are all cities governed by Tsarist Russia.

SOUTHERN NETHERLANDS [Belgium and Luxemburg)

National totals

1650	1,500,000
1700	1,750,000
1750	2,250,000
1800	3,250,000

Belgian cities		*Ghent*	
Antwerp		1650	50,000
1650	80,000	1700	40,000
1700	67,000	1750	45,000
1750	50,000	1800	56,000
1800	62,000		
		Liege	
Brussels		1650	40,000
1755	54,000	1700	40,000
1800	66,000	1750	45,000
		1800	50,000

Population of some other Belgian cities in 1700:

Bruges:	25–35,000	Mons:	20,000
Tournai:	25–35,000	Ypres:	10,000
Louvain:	20,000		

SPAIN

National totals

1650	7,700,000
1700	7,500,000
1750	9,300,000
1787	10,541,000

Cities	*1650*	*1700*	*1787*
Madrid	75,000	100,000	160,000
Barcelona	65,000	40,000	90,000
Seville	80,000	60,000	80,000
Valencia	60–75,000	–	75,000
Granada	60–75,000	–	60,000
Cadiz	15,000	–	66,000
Malaga	35,000	–	50,000

Saragossa	25,000	–	55,000
Cordoba	35,000	–	35,000
Murcia	–	20,000	35,000
Toledo	25,000	–	20,000

SWEDEN–FINLAND

SWEDEN

1650	1,200,000
1700	1,500,000
1750	1,785,727
1775	2,020,847
1790	2,281,137

Cities

Stockholm		*Göteborg*	
1650	45,000	1670	5,000
1700	60,000	1800	12,000
1800	75,000		

FINLAND

1650	250,000
1700	300,000
1750	429,912
1775	610,145
1790	705,623

Helsinki

1800	4,000

SWITZERLAND

National totals

1650	1,100,000
1700	1,200,000
1750	1,400,000
1800	1,700,000

Cities

Geneva

1650	15,000
1700	17,000
1750	20,000
1790	22,000

Basel

1650	10,000
1700	12,000
1750	15,000
1790	15,500

Zurich

1637	8,500

1682	11,000
1762	11,500
1790	12,000

Bern

1650	6,000
1700	8,000
1750	10,000
1790	12,000

Lucerne

1650	3,500
1700	4,000
1800	4,500

TURKISH EUROPE

National totals

1650	7,150,000
1700	6,350,000
1750	8,520,000
1800	11,450,000

Romania

1650	2,250,000
1700	1,400,000*
1750	2,500,000
1800	4,000,000

Serbia–Bosnia

1650	1,500,000
1700	1,500,000
1750	1,950,000
1800	2,400,000

Greece

1650	1,500,000
1700	1,500,000
1750	1,800,000
1800	2,250,000

Bulgaria

1650	1,250,000
1700	1,250,000
1750	1,500,000
1800	2,000,000

Turkey-in-Europe

1650	400,000
1700	400,000
1750	500,000
1800	600,000

Albania

1650	250,000
1700	300,000
1750	350,000
1800	400,000

* Transylvania annexed by Habsburg Empire.

8 COLONIES AND DEPENDENCIES

The colonies and dependencies are arranged in alphabetical order. This is preceded by a listing of colonies and dependencies under the 'mother-country' – Brandenburg–Prussia, Denmark, France, Great Britain, Portugal, Russia, Spain, Sweden and the United Provinces.

Details of Governors, Residents and Administrators of the colonies and dependencies are listed in: Henige, D. P., *Colonial Governors from the Fifteenth Century to Present* (Madison: University of Wisconsin Press, 1970).

Brandenburg–Prussia
Gross-Freidrichsburg.

Denmark
Danish Gold Coast; Danish West Indies; Tranquebar.

France
Acadia; Fort-Dauphin; French Guiana; French India; Gorée; Grenada; Guadeloupe; Île de France (Mauritius); Île Royale (Cape Breton); Île St Jean (Prince Edward Island); Louisiana; Martinique; Montreal; Plaisance; Quebec; Réunion; St Barthelemy; St Christophe (St Kitts); St Dominique (Haiti); Ste Lucie; Ste Marie de Madagascar; St Pierre and Miquelon; Senegal.

Great Britain
Antigua; Bahama Islands; Barbados; Bengal; Bermuda; Bombay; British Honduras; British Virgin Islands; Canada; Cape Breton; Cayman Islands; Connecticut; Delaware; Dominica; Falkland Islands (Malvinas Islands); The Gambia; Georgia; Gibraltar; India; Jamaica; Leeward Islands; Maryland; Massachusetts Bay; Minorca; Montserrat; Nevis; New Brunswick; Newfoundland; New Hampshire; New Haven; New Jersey; New Plymouth; New South Wales; New York; Niue; Norfolk Island; North Carolina; Nova Scotia; Penang; Pennsylvania; Pitcairn Island; Rhode Island; Rupert's

Island; St Helena; St Vincent; Senegambia; South Carolina; Tangier; Tobago; Turks and Caicos Islands; Virginia.

Holland (United Provinces)

Berbice (British Guiana); Cape Colony; Ceylon; Coromandel Coast; Curaçao; Demerara (British Guiana); Essequibo (British Guiana); Formosa (Taiwan); Gold Coast; Malacca; Mauritius; Netherlands East Indies; New Amsterdam; Pomeroon; St Eustatius; Surinam.

Portugal

Angola; Azores; Brazil; Cape Verde Islands; Ceylon; Macao; Madeira; Maranhão; Mombasa; Mozambique; Nova Colônia do Sacramento (Uruguay); Portuguese Guinea; Portuguese India; São Tomé and Príncipe; Timor.

Russia

Russian America (Alaska).

Spain

Argentina (Río de la Plata); Bolivia (Upper Peru); California; Canary Islands; Ceuta and Melilla; Chile; Costa Rica; Cuba; El Salvador; Florida; Guam; Guatemala; Malvinas Islands (Falkland Islands); Margarita; Mexico; Nicaragua; Nueva Granada (Colombia); Orán; Panama; Paraguay; Peru; Philippine Islands; Puerto Rico; Santa Catalina; Santo Domingo; Spanish Guinea; Trinidad; Venezuela

Sweden

New Sweden; St Barthélemy

Acadia. Throughout the period of the 17th century the French and the British struggled for colonial rights in the region located at the eastern tip of Canada known as Acadia (Acadie) that included roughly the area now known as the Maritime provinces (New Brunswick, Nova Scotia and Prince Edward Island). The first settlement was made by a French expedition in 1604 at the mouth of the St Croix River. In 1654 an English force from Massachusetts captured Port Royal, but Acadia was returned to France under the Treaty of Breda in 1667. Port Royal was captured by New Englanders in 1690, but the Treaty of Ryswick in 1697 kept Acadia in French hands. The area was finally wrested from the French in 1710 during the War of the Spanish Succession. The British permanently occupied the area following confirmation by the Treaty of Utrecht (1713–4), although Île Royale (Cape Breton) remained in French hands. (See also New Brunswick, Nova Scotia and Île St Jean.)

Angola. Located in southwestern Africa, Angola was discovered by Diogo Cão in 1482. Portuguese colonisation began in 1575 with the founding of Luanda after Paulo Dias de Novais had been granted an area along the coast south of the Congo. In 1648 the Portuguese ejected the Dutch, who had occupied all the Portuguese settlements along the coast from 1641. After the Battle of Mbwila in 1665 the Portuguese were paramount in the area. Colonisation remained on a small scale until the middle of the 19th century, however, as greater profits were to be found in the slave trade, especially between 1648 and 1836, when Angolan slaves were transported to Brazil.

Antigua. An eastern Caribbean island located at the southern end of the Leeward Islands, Antigua was discovered by Columbus in 1493 and settled by the British from St Kitts in 1632. It was briefly occupied by the French in 1666–7, but was returned to Britain under the terms of the Treaty of Breda in 1667. Antigua, along with other scattered British possessions in the Lesser Antilles, was organised into the Leeward Islands government in 1671.

Argentina (Río de la Plata). The Spaniard Juan Díaz de Solís entered the area of the Río de la Plata in 1516 but was killed by Indians. Four years later Ferdinão de Magalhães wintered on the southern Patagonian Coast, and in 1526–8 Sebastian Cabot planted a temporary settlement on the Paraná River near Rosario. In 1536 the largest royal expedition ever used in the conquest of the New World arrived under the command of Pedro de Mendoza, but it gradually withdrew to Ascuncíon (Paraguay). The first permanent Spanish town on Argentine soil was planted in 1553 at Santiago del Estero, and the establishment of other towns in the interior, whose industries were dependent on the labour of Christianised Indians and Negro slaves, followed rapidly. The Spanish settlement of Buenos Aires, planted in 1536 and abandoned five years later, was re-established by Juan de Garay in 1580. In 1776 Spain established the viceroyalty of the Río de la Plata.

Azores. The Portuguese discovered the group of islands known as the Azores, located in the Atlantic Ocean 800 miles west of Lisbon, in 1427. Settlement began in 1432. From 1580 to 1640 the archipelago was under Spanish control. In 1831 the Azores were administratively regrouped into three metropolitan districts of Portugal.

Bahama Islands. Located off the southeastern coast of the US and north of Cuba, the Bahama Islands were occupied by England from 1629 but the first systematic colonisation was not undertaken until 1648 by the English company of Eleutherian Adventurers. In 1670 the Bahamas were granted to the lords' proprietors of Carolina. The islands then became a haven for piracy and this occasioned the assumption of direct crown control in 1717. In 1776 the Bahamas were taken by America, and in 1781 by Spain, but they were restored to Britain as a crown colony under the Treaty of Paris in 1783.

Barbados. Located in the Lesser Antilles, Barbados was discovered by the Spanish in 1519 and settled by the English in 1627, three years after English sailors laid claim to the island in the name of King James I. It became a crown colony in 1662.

Bengal. Located in the eastern part of the Indian subcontinent on the Bay of Bengal, this region was first settled for England in 1642 by the British East India Company. Having ousted the Dutch and French and conquered the native rulers, the Company was able to establish the nucleus of a presidency at Fort William in 1700. The British victories of Plassey in 1757 and Buxar in 1764 ended Moslem control of Bengal and added most of the Ganges plain, including Agra province, to the British-controlled territory. Bengal was granted the administration of the presidencies of Bombay and Madras in 1774.

Berbice (British Guiana). In 1627 the Dutch house of Van Pere was granted a concession in Berbice, on the coast of Guiana, and it privately administered this settlement from 1666 to 1714. In 1720 the settlement was governed by the Berbice Association and in 1732 it formed a separate colony. Along with other Dutch colonies in this area, Berbice was permanently occupied in 1803 by the British and was united with the Dutch Guianese settlements of Demerara and Essequibo in 1831 to form British Guiana.

Bermuda. Located in the west Atlantic, Bermuda was discovered in about 1515 by the Spaniard Juan Bermúdez. Comprising a group of over 300 coral islands, Bermuda, also known as Somers' Islands, was uninhabited until the English Admiral Sir George Somers was shipwrecked there in 1609. It received 60 settlers in 1612 when included in the Virginia Company's third charter, remaining under company administration until acquired by the British crown in 1684. However, Bermuda never became solely a crown colony: government was the joint responsibility of the Virginia Company and the Sovereign. In 1767 Bermuda was made a base for the British fleet.

Bolivia (Upper Peru). Modern Bolivia was once a part of the ancient Inca Empire. After the Spaniards defeated the Incas in the 16th century, the predominantly Indian population of Bolivia (or Upper Peru as it was called during the colonial period) was reduced to slavery. The colony won its independence in 1825 and was named after the liberator Simón Bolívar.

357

Bombay. Portugal ceded Bombay to England in 1661 as part of the dowry of Catherine of Braganza, wife of Charles II. In 1668 Bombay passed to the control of the British East India Company. After 1708 it was the main centre of British authority in India until replaced by Bengal later in the century.

Brazil. Pedro Alvares Cabral discovered Brazil for the Portuguese in 1500. During the next 150 years other European powers, especially France and the United Provinces, attempted to conquer and settle parts of the area but were ultimately unsuccessful. Preoccupied with colonial expansion in Africa and India, the Portuguese showed little interest in Brazil until 1530, when they began to expand their economic activities and settlements in the country. At the same time large-scale importation of black slaves from Africa began, and a vast trade grew up between Brazil and West Africa based on exchange of tobacco for slaves and gold. The colony declared its independence in 1822, and, in the following year, after some resistance, the Portuguese were expelled.

British Honduras. This Central American colony was founded in the early 17th century by British buccaneers, but possession was disputed with Spain until the Battle of St George's Cay in 1798, after which the British settlers were unchallenged until 1821, when the area was claimed by Guatemala.

British Virgin Islands. A group of 36 islands lying between the Caribbean Sea and the Atlantic Ocean, this colony has been in British possession since 1666, at which time the British expelled the Dutch.

California. Although Baja California was discovered by the Spanish in 1533 and the entire coast of Baja and Alta California was explored by 1543, no settlement took place until 1697. Serious Spanish occupation began in 1769. In 1822 California became part of the Republic of Mexico.

Canada. British interest in the area was manifested almost as early as that of the French. John Cabot reached the east coast of Canada in 1497, but France established the first Canadian settlements. Port Royal was attacked in 1614 by the British, who captured Quebec and Champlain in 1629. Three years later Quebec was restored to the French. Under the terms of the Treaty of Utrecht in 1713, Britain gained Acadia, the Hudson Bay area and Newfoundland, and in 1759 retook Quebec, founded in 1608 by Champlain. In 1763 Britain had acquired all of France's North American possessions except Louisiana under the terms of the Treaty of Paris.

Canary Islands. Spanish sovereignty over the islands, an archipelago in the North Atlantic off the northwestern coast of Africa, was recognised in 1479 under the terms of the Treaty of Alcáçovas, and settlement began shortly thereafter. The most important islands were Gran Canaria and Tenerife, but other islands were also settled, including La Palma.

Cape Colony. Located at the southern tip of Africa, Cape Colony was established by the Dutch East India Company in 1652 to serve as a way-station on voyages to the East Indies, but rapidly became a colony of settlement extending its boundaries eastward along the cape. Company rule was ended in 1794 after the colony became resentful of efforts to control its growth. Cape Colony was seized by the British in 1795, but was returned to the Dutch in 1803 under terms of the Treaty of Amiens. In 1806 it was seized again, and permanently retained, by the British.

Cape Verde Islands. Located in the Atlantic Ocean 320 miles west of Cape Verde, the westernmost point of Africa, the Cape Verde Islands were discovered in 1455 by Alvise da Cadamasto and Antonio Noli, explorers in the service of Prince Henry of Portugal, and soon settled by Portuguese colonists and African slaves from Guinea. The islands first came under the control of a single governor in 1587. Portuguese Guinea was settled from the Cape Verde Islands in the 16th century, but the posts established at Cacher and Bissau remained under the government of the Cape Verde Islands until 1879, when Portuguese Guinea became a separate province.

Cayman Islands. Located about 200 miles northwest of Jamaica, the Cayman Islands were ceded by Spain to England in 1670 but were not settled until 1734. Until 1900 they were locally governed by justices of the peace.

Ceuta and Melilla. Located in North Africa, Ceuta was conquered by the Portuguese in 1415 and remained loyal to the Spanish crown after Portugal broke with Spain in 1640. The Treaty of Lisbon in 1668 confirmed the Spanish possession of Ceuta. The neighbouring *plaza* of Melilla had been occupied by the Duke of Medina Sidonia in 1497 and came under the control of the Spanish crown in 1556. Ceuta and Melilla were governed separately until 1847.

Ceylon. The Portuguese arrived in Ceylon in the early 16th century at the behest of the ruler of Kotte, one of the three warring states into which Ceylon was then divided. The Portuguese remained and in 1518 appointed a captain to Colombo, centre of the Kotte kingdom. By 1619 the Portuguese controlled most of Ceylon's coastal area, though little of the interior. Hoping to use the Dutch to drive the Portuguese from the island, the ruler of Kandy invited the United Provinces to Ceylon in 1638. The Portuguese were expelled by 1658, but the Dutch remained and, by 1765, controlled the entire coastline. In 1795–6 the British seized the Dutch possessions in Ceylon, which were retained by them under the Treaty of Amiens in 1802.

Chile. Although Chile was settled from Peru after about 1540, Spanish settlement of the southern part of the colony did not take place until the 18th century due to the resistance offered by the Araucanian Indians. The end of Spanish colonial dominion came in 1817.

Connecticut. Founded in 1639 by settlers from Massachusetts Bay, Connecticut absorbed its small neighbour New Haven in 1664. Two years earlier it was granted a charter giving it an unusual degree of self-government, and from 1687 to 1690 it formed part of the Dominion of New England. In 1776 it severed its connection with Britain.

Coromandel Coast. The Dutch established themselves along the Coromandel Coast in south-eastern India early in the 17th century, with the first governor appointed in 1608. Posts were established by the Dutch to exploit the textile trade for use in their intercoastal Asian trade. These prospered until the advent of the English and French during the last quarter of the 17th century, when Dutch trade declined. Although the Dutch were able to occupy the French posts in the area from 1639 to 1699, they were no longer a serious factor by the 18th century. From 1795 to 1818 the Dutch posts on the Coromandel Coast were occupied by the British, to whom they were finally ceded in 1825.

Costa Rica. Discovered by Columbus in 1502, it was not until 1563 that the region was completely conquered by the Spanish and brought under the captaincy general of Guatemala. Originally called Nuevo Cartago, it was not regarded as an important colony and was frequently attacked by British, French and Dutch buccaneers. Costa Rica obtained its independence from Spain in 1821.

Cuba. Spain began the conquest of Cuba in 1511 as a convenient base from which to launch exploratory expeditions to the Americas. Britain captured Havana in August 1762, but Spain agreed to exchange Florida for Havana at the Peace Preliminaries of Fontainebleau in November of the same year. With the exception of this brief period, Cuba remained a Spanish possession until 1898, when it was occupied by American forces.

Curaçao. Along with the neighbouring islands of Aruba and Bonaire, Curaçao was captured from the Spanish by the Dutch in 1634. Prior to coming under direct state control in 1792, the islands were administered by the first West India Company (to 1674) and the second West India Company (to 1792).

Danish Gold Coast. After expelling Sweden from its posts on the Gold Coast in 1657, Denmark established itself in the fort of Osu, renamed Christianborg, which became the headquarters for Danish commercial activities along the Guinea coast. Further trading centres were established, all of them situated to the east of Accra along the coast, and the prosperity of which depended largely on the slave trade, abolished in 1792 (in force from 1803).

Danish West Indies. St Thomas, St Johns and St Croix are the three islands comprising the Danish West Indies. The Danish West India Company began the settlement of St Thomas in 1672, and, in 1684, took possession of St Johns, colonising the island in 1716. Denmark bought St Croix, abandoned after a slave rebellion, from the French in 1733. St Thomas and St Johns were administered as a unit from 1734 to 1756, while St Croix was administered separately, but a governor-general administered all three islands from 1736 to 1744. The group was made a Danish royal colony in 1755. In the following year the office of governor-general was reinstated with St Croix being the seat of the governor-general until 1871, with the other two islands retaining a separate but subordinate administration.

Delaware. In 1638 the Swedes made the first permanent settlement in this Atlantic coastal state of the US. It was originally called New Sweden, which was conquered by the Dutch in 1655 and added to the New Netherlands colony, which, in turn, was conquered in 1664 by the English and became New York. In Aug 1682 the Duke of York transferred the three counties of Delaware (named by the English in honour of an early governor of Virginia) to the province of Pennsylvania, under William Penn. Delaware received the right to elect its own assembly – and thus became a separate colony from Pennsylvania – in 1703. The colony became the sovereign state of Delaware in 1776.

Demerara (British Guiana). Located in western Guiana, Demerara was developed from Essequibo in 1750 and remained subject to the latter when it was captured by the British. The French occupied the colony from 1782 to 1784, when it was returned to the Dutch. Between 1796 and 1802 the British again held Demerara. It was returned to the Dutch in 1802, only to be finally occupied by the British from 1803. In 1831 it was united with the former Dutch colonies of Essequibo and Berbice to form British Guiana.

Dominica. In early 1627 the Earl of Carlisle was granted this island, located in the Lesser Antilles, but early efforts to occupy it were thwarted by the Carib Indian inhabitants. Attempted settlement by the French was prevented by the British in 1759, and in 1763 the Treaty of Paris formally ceded the island to Britain, though it was 1815 before Dominica passed to the British.

El Salvador. In 1524 Pedro de Alvarado began the Spanish conquest of Cuscatlán (now western El Salvador) and, four years later, the city of San Salvador was founded. The district of El Salvador was ruled by the Audiencia de Guatemala from 1570 to 1821. It declared its independence from both Spain and Guatemala in 1821.

Essequibo (British Guiana). Located in western Guiana, Essequibo was settled by the Dutch West India Company in 1624. It was briefly captured by the British in 1666, but retaken. The Demerara area was settled from Essequibo in 1750, and, in 1784, following brief French and British occupations, the colony became subordinate to Demerara. In 1803, the British again occupied the island, and in 1831 it was united with the former Dutch colonies of Berbice and Demerara to form British Guiana.

Falkland Islands (Malvinas Islands). Located in the south Atlantic off the coast of Argentina, the islands were probably discovered by the Englishman John Davies in 1592 and were later named the Falkland Islands. The French were the first to settle the islands in 1764, establishing a post on East Falkland which they abandoned in 1767. Commodore John Bryon claimed West Falkland for Britain in 1765 and the British planted a garrison there in the following year. In May 1770 a Spanish force ejected the British, but the settlement was formally restored to Britain on 16 September 1771, being abandoned three years later due to the high cost of maintenance. In 1811 the Spanish also evacuated East Falkland, and both islands remained uninhabited.

Florida. In 1565 the Spanish destroyed a French colony planted in 1562 on the east coast of the Florida peninsula and established a colony of their own. Spain held Florida until the Treaty of Paris in 1763, at which time it went to Britain, which then divided the colony into West Florida and East Florida. During the American Revolution Spain occupied British West Florida (1780–1) and was ceded the two Floridas by the Treaty of Versailles in 1783. Prompted by United States expansionism and recurring boundary disputes, Spain sold the Floridas to the US in 1819.

Formosa (Taiwan). Having been driven from the Pescadores Islands by the

362

Chinese, the Dutch occupied the southern section of Formosa (now Taiwan) in 1624. Two years later the Spanish founded a colony in the northern part of the island, but this was abandoned two years later, after which the Dutch controlled the entire island. Formosa became autonomous in 1662 when the large Chinese immigrant population expelled the Dutch completely.

Fort-Dauphin. Located on the southeastern tip of Madagascar, Fort-Dauphin was founded by the French in 1642 and abandoned in 1674 because its original purpose, as a base from which to compete with the English and Dutch in the Indian Ocean, was never achieved, besides which it was exposed to the attacks of hostile Malagasy. From 1667 to 1671 the colony briefly served as the headquarters of the Compagnie des Indes Orientales.

French Guiana. Initial attempts at colonisation by the French from 1604 onwards failed, and the colonists were ousted by the Dutch who were, in turn, evicted by the French in 1664. In the Dutch Wars of Louis XIV, the port of Cayenne was captured by the Dutch (in 1676) but then retaken. By about 1700 the French had a more secure grip on the territory, and although a further attempt at colonisation in 1763–5 was abortive, the colony grew in population and prosperity.

French India. After previous failures in 1603 and 1642, France secured a foothold in India in 1672. Two years later the site of Pondichéry was acquired, and this became the capital in 1683. By 1750, under the administration of Joseph-François Dupleix, France was the strongest European power in India. A French policy of non-intervention resulted in British occupation of French possessions from 1761 to 1765, 1778 to 1783, 1793 to 1803 and 1803 to 1816, after which they were permanently returned to the French.

The Gambia. The Duke of Courland purchased an island and other nearby plots of land at the mouth of the Gambia River in 1651, after which trading posts were established. In 1659 the Gambia was leased to the Dutch West India Company due to the captivity of the Duke and the consequent inability of the Kurland government to administer it. Although the Kurland commandant was expelled in the same year, he returned in 1660. In 1661 the Kurlanders were finally expelled by the British, who had won trading rights in the area from Portugal as early as 1588, but had been unable to establish settlements. By 1776 the British establishments in the Gambia fell under the new colony of Senegambia. The French captured the British posts in the area in 1779 and no further settlement was made there until 1816.

363

Georgia. In 1732 General James Oglethorpe and others were granted a royal charter to establish a colony in Georgia, as an experiment in debtor rehabilitation and in order to provide a buffer between the other English colonies and the Spaniards in Florida. The first colonists arrived in 1733 when James Oglethorpe founded the colony of Georgia and the city of Savannah. Until 1754, when it became a crown province upon surrender of its Charter by the Trustees, Georgia was a proprietary colony. It expelled the royal governor in 1776, but the British reoccupied most of the colony in 1779. Three years later the British were finally forced to abandon Georgia.

Gibraltar. Located at the end of a promontory at the western entrance to the Mediterranean Sea, Gibraltar was captured from the Spanish by the British under Sir George Rooke in 1704 during the War of the Spanish Succession, and finally ceded by Spain to Britain in 1713 by the Treaty of Utrecht. The Spanish made several abortive attempts to retake Gibraltar, notably in the famous siege from 1779 to 1783, but the Treaty of Versailles in 1783 reconfirmed Britain's possession. In 1830 it became a crown colony.

Gold Coast. In 1637 the United Provinces made its first inroad into the Portuguese monopoly along the western coast of Africa by capturing the fort at Elmina. By 1642 the Dutch had totally driven Portugal out and controlled the ports of Accra, Axim, Kormantin and Takoradi, in addition to Elmina, as well as partaking of the extensive trade at Ouidah. It remained in the area until 1872, by which time the posts had been sold for cash or for concessions in Sumatra to Britain, which had established trading forts along the Guinea coast of West Africa as early as 1632.

Gorée. An island in Senegal, Gorée was captured from the Dutch by the French in 1677, after which it became a centre of the slave trade.

Grenada. Settled from Martinique in 1649, this Windward island of the Lesser Antilles was owned by various private individuals until 1664, when it was purchased by the Compagnie des Indes Occidentales. In 1674 Grenada came under royal control, subject to the authority of the governor-general of the French Antilles. The island was captured in 1762 by the British who, under the Treaty of Paris in 1763, retained possession of the island. French forces seized Grenada in 1779, but the island was returned to Britain in 1783.

Gross-Friedrichsburg. Several posts were established by Brandenburg–Prussia along the Guinea coast of West Africa (today, the Republic of Ghana), with headquarters at Gross-Friedrichsburg established in 1683. Unable to compete commercially with the Danes, Dutch and English, already established in this area, and beset by the incompetence of their own directors-general, the posts were largely abandoned by 1716 and were sold to the United Provinces in 1720.

Guadeloupe. Located in the Lesser Antilles, Guadeloupe was discovered by Columbus in 1493 but it was not settled by Europeans until the arrival in 1635 of the French, who gradually eliminated the native Carib Indians and imported large numbers of slaves from Africa. From 1674, when the island came under the direct administration of the crown, Guadeloupe was subordinated to the governor-general of the French Antilles at Martinique, but retained a governor of its own. Occupied by the British in 1759 in the course of the Seven Years' War, Guadeloupe was restored to France in 1763 under the terms of the Peace of Paris. The British occupied the colony again during the French Revolution, but were expelled by Revolutionary forces from France. Briefly occupied by Britain from 1810 to 1814 and 1815 to 1816, it was finally restored to France in 1816.

Guam. The southernmost of the Mariana Islands in the western Pacific, Guam was discovered by Magellan in 1521. Serious settlement was only begun by the Spanish in 1668 in order to safeguard the shipping routes from Mexico to the Philippines.

Guatemala. In 1524, under the leadership of Pedro de Alvarado, the Spanish conquered the Mayan and other indigenous populations of this area. In 1570 the captaincy general of Guatemala was created to govern the area from Chiapas and the Yucatán to the Costa Rica settlements. With the break-up of the Spanish Empire in the New World in the early 19th century, Guatemala and the rest of Central America fell under Mexican rule (1821–3), becoming an independent republic in 1840.

Île Royale (Cape Breton). Located at the mouth of the St Lawrence River, Île Royale was occupied by the French after the British conquest of Acadia in 1710. It was occupied by the British from 1745 to 1749 and in 1758, when all of New France was taken from the French. Britain's possession of the area was secured under the terms of the Treaty of Paris in 1763. Settlement was at first discouraged by the British, and it was only in 1784 that Loyalists from the former American colonies were allowed to settle there. It was at this time that Cape Breton (as it was now called) was created a separate government, being detached from Nova Scotia, to which it was reunited in 1820.

Île St Jean (Prince Edward Island). Located off the coast of Nova Scotia in the Gulf of St Lawrence, Île St Jean was discovered by Jacques Cartier in

1534. After 1713 it was an outpost of Louisbourg on Cape Breton Island and the location of several settlements. It fell to the British in 1745; to the French, again, three years later; and back, finally, to the British in 1758. It formally became a British colony under the terms of the Treaty of Paris in 1763, being placed under the governor of Nova Scotia. It was given a government of its own in 1769. The British renamed the island Prince Edward Island.

India. British interest in India began early in the 17th century when the East India Company established the trading post of Surat (1613) and then acquired Bombay (1661) and Calcutta (1691). The beginning of the British Raj in India dates from 1757. Between 1757 and 1765 all of Bengal and Bihar came under British control.

Jamaica. This island in the western Caribbean was discovered by Columbus in 1494 and subsequently granted to him and to his descendants, the Dukes of Verágua. Despite its location, it was of little interest to Spain. An English force under Sir William Penn and Robert Venables attacked Jamaica in 1655, and by 1660 the Spanish had been driven from the island. An Anglo-Spanish treaty of 1670 recognised Britain's title to Jamaica and all other *de facto* possessions in America, in return for which the British promised to cease their buccaneering activities.

Leeward Islands. Located in the eastern West Indies, the first British settlement here was on St Kitts in 1623. By 1632 the neighbouring islands were also colonised. The scattered British possessions in the Lesser Antilles were organised into the Leeward Islands government in 1671, including the islands of Antigua, Montserrat, British Virgin Islands, St Kitts, Nevis, Barbuda and Anguilla. France and Spain disputed British possession in the 17th century and the islands changed hands frequently until finally granted to Britain in 1815.

Louisiana. The area was first claimed for France by La Salle in 1682, but serious colonisation only began in 1699 when Pierre d'Iberville founded Biloxi. New Orleans was established, and became the capital, in 1718. Although several posts were created along the Mississippi as far north as the Illinois, there was little settlement beyond the southern reaches of the river. Louisiana was under crown rule from 1699 to 1713. From 1713 to 1716 it was a proprietary colony of Antoine Crozat, and from 1716 to 1733 it was administered by the Compagnie de l'Ouest. After 1733 it was again under the direct rule of the French crown. In 1762, in order to forestall a British takeover, Louisiana was ceded to Spain by the Treaty of Fontainbleau. In 1800 it was restored to France under the secret treaty of San Ildefonso and sold in 1803 to the United States.

Macao. Located on the coast of Kwangtung province in southwest China, Macao was leased from China by Portugal in 1557, at which time a trading post was established. From 1623 to 1844 Macao was governed by a resident governor who was subordinate to the viceroy or governor-general of Portuguese India.

Madeira. Located 360 miles off the northwest coast of Africa, Maderia was settled by the Portuguese in 1418–20. British influence has been considerable in Madeira, which was occupied by Britain in 1801 to 1802 and 1807 to 1814, although nominal Portuguese control was maintained. Madeira became a metropolitan district of Portugal in 1834.

Malacca. Malacca fell to the Portuguese in 1511 and was captured by the Dutch in 1641. It had a strategic value which made it the most important Dutch post on the Malay Peninsula. Occupied by the British from 1795 to 1818, it was finally ceded to Britain in 1825.

Maranhão. Located on the north coast of Brazil east of the Amazon estuary, Maranhão was first settled by the Portuguese in 1615 in response to French efforts at colonisation in the area. In 1621, Maranhão, then embracing all known land north and west of Ceará, became one of two states (the other called Brazil) which constituted Portuguese holdings in South America. This colonial state was broken up in the 18th century into captaincies.

Margarita. An island located off the northeast coast of Venezuela in the Caribbean Sea, Margarita was discovered by Columbus in 1498 and settled by the Spanish from about 1525. It came under the control of the crown in 1600.

Martinique. Forming part of the Windward Islands and of the Lesser Antilles island chain in the eastern Caribbean Sea, Martinique was discovered by Columbus in 1502 but subsequently ignored by the Spanish, partly because of the hostility of the native Carib inhabitants. A group of French settlers under Pierre Belain settled at St Pierre in 1635 and, after the Caribs had been nearly eliminated by the end of the 17th century, other settlements were established and black slaves were imported. In 1674 Martinique was made part of the French crown domain. There were several brief occupations by the British, from 1762 to 1763, 1794 to 1802 and 1809 to 1814, after which the island was finally restored to France.

Maryland. First explored in 1608 by Captain John Smith from the Virginia colony of Jamestown, Maryland was granted to George Calvert in 1632 from territory granted to Virginia under its royal charter. Colonised in 1634, the colony was the first in British North America to establish freedom of worship. When the colony of Pennsylvania was created in 1681, part of Maryland was lost. It remained a proprietary colony from 1632 to 1691 and from 1716 to 1776, when it terminated its status as a British colony.

Massachusetts Bay. In 1629 a group of merchants and others under the auspices of the Massachusetts Bay Company colonised the area known as Massachusetts Bay. After 1668 it governed Maine. In 1684 its Charter was revoked and it became a royal colony. From 1686 to 1689 it was part of the Dominion of New England, absorbing its neighbour New Plymouth in 1692, when it became known as Massachusetts. In 1775 it expelled the last of its royal governors.

Mauritius (Île de France). First occupied by the Dutch in 1638 to serve as a way-station on the route to the East Indies, this Indian Ocean island was abandoned in 1658 when the Cape Colony proved superior in this respect. Although partially resettled in 1664, it was finally abandoned in 1710, being occupied by the French from 1722 and renamed Île de France. Valued for its strategic location on the route to French possessions in India, Île de France was first administered by the Compagnie des Indes and, after 1767, by the French government. Britain occupied the island in 1810 and retained possession of it at the Treaty of Paris in 1814.

Mexico. The Spanish conquest of Mexico started from Cuba in 1517 when the unsuccessful expedition by Francisco Hernández de Córdoba reached Yucátan. Another expedition took place in the following year under Juan Grijalva, encouraging other adventurers who, headed by Hernán Cortés, took part in an expedition which was converted into an occupation in 1519. Spanish expansion quickly followed. Spain maintained a tight political grip on the colony until the Napoleonic invasion of Spain in 1808.

Minorca. One of the Balearic Islands in the western Mediterranean, Minorca was seized from Spain by Britain in 1708 during the War of the Spanish Succession and retained by the Treaty of Utrecht in 1713. The French seized the island in 1756 but returned it to Britain under the Treaty of Paris in 1763. Minorca was surrendered to the Spanish in 1782, recovered in 1798 and finally ceded to Spain in 1802.

Mombasa. Located on the east coast of Africa 1300 miles north of Mozambique, Mombasa was visited by Vasco da Gama in 1497. It was held by the Portuguese from 1593 to 1698, when it was recaptured by the Omanis. Mombasa remained under Arab rule until 1728, when the Portuguese regained it. In the following year the Portuguese abandoned Mombasa after a seige by Omani forces.

Montreal. In 1535 the French discoverer Jacques Cartier was the first known European to reach this area. The first permanent French settlement was founded on the island in May 1642. Montreal was captured by British troops under Jeffrey Amherst in 1760, which marked the end of French rule in Canada. It was ceded to Britain, with the rest of French Canada, at the end of the French and Indian War in 1763.

Montserrat. Located in the Lesser Antilles, Montserrat was discovered by Columbus in 1493 and settled by the British in 1632. It was occupied by the French in February 1667 but returned to the British in July of the same year under the terms of the Treaty of Breda. It was again occupied by the French in 1782 and returned in the following year under the terms of the Treaty of Versailles.

Mozambique. Located in southeast Africa, Mozambique was first sighted by Vasco da Gama in 1498. But the Portuguese did not begin to settle here until 1505 when a fort was built at Sofala. During the 16th century the Portuguese extended their influence inland, establishing trading posts along the Zambesi. Until the early 19th century the extensive slave trade of the area was responsible for whatever prosperity Mozambique attained. In 1752 Mozambique, which had hitherto been ruled as part of Goa (India), became a separate province under a governor or captain-general.

Netherlands East Indies. Occuptation of the territory of Indonesia was begun in 1596, but the Dutch did not gain complete control until they finally ousted the British in 1623. The Dutch East India Company then extended its influence throughout the area, but its holdings were taken over by the Dutch government in 1798 and became known as the Netherlands (or Dutch) East Indies. From 1811 to 1815 the British occupied Java and most of the other islands, but by an agreement of 1824 with the Dutch were left with a free hand in the East Indies.

Nevis. Located in the Lesser Antilles, Nevis was discovered by Columbus in 1493 and settled by the British in 1628. It was briefly occupied by the French in 1706 and again from 1782 to 1784.

New Brunswick. Located on the Atlantic coast in the southeastern part of Canada, New Brunswick was first sighted by the Frenchman Jacques Cartier in 1534. In 1604 the first settlement was made within its borders by a French expedition. The British captured a fort built in St John harbour in 1654, but this was returned to France by the Treaty of Breda in 1667. By the Treaty of Utrecht in 1713 all of Acadia was ceded to Britain, although the French insisted that this did not include the New Brunswick area, which they sporadically attempted to regain forcefully until their final defeat in Canada c. 1760. The area was separated in 1784 from Nova Scotia, under which it had been administered, and was given the name New Brunswick.

Newfoundland. A small colony was established by Britain on the island in 1611 after a first attempt failed in 1583. In 1705 St John's in Newfoundland was captured by St Ovide, governor of the French colony of Plaisance (or Placentia), but the French ceded Newfoundland to Britain after the War of the Spanish Succession at the Treaty of Utrecht in 1713. In 1762, during a raid on Newfoundland, the French captured St John's. Expelled at the end of the same year, the French remained in St Pierre and the Miquelon Islands. It was not until the Treaty of Paris in 1763 that Newfoundland and Labrador (included in the government of Newfoundland in the same year) were granted to Britain, although in 1783 the French regained the west coast.

New Hampshire. First settled by colonists of Massachusetts Bay from 1630, it was governed from Massachusetts until 1679 and, again, from 1692 to 1741. It was a separate colony from 1679 to 1692 and from 1741 to 1776, at which time New Hampshire broke its ties with Britain.

New Haven. It was settled from Massachusetts Bay in 1638 by John Davenport, a Puritan divine, and Theophilus Eaton, a merchant. As a result of the formation of the United Colonies of New England in 1643, a colonial government was established and the New Haven Colony took its place as the smallest of the Puritan colonies of New England. The small size of the colony led to its absorption into Connecticut in 1664.

New Jersey. This area in the middle Atlantic region of the United States was included in the grant given to James, Duke of York, in 1664. There had previously been settlements by the Dutch and Swedes in the area. From 1676 to 1702 West Jersey was held by William Penn, while East Jersey was granted as a proprietary colony to Philip Carteret. In 1702 the two provinces were united under royal authority. In 1776 the last royal governor was expelled.

New Plymouth. Settled in 1620 by English Puritans, New Plymouth failed to prosper because of its poor location and its lack of good harbours. It was absorbed into Massachusetts in 1692.

New South Wales. Claimed by the British in 1770, New South Wales became the site of the first British colony in Australia in 1788. However, it was not until 1810 that effective settlement took place.

New Sweden. Located on the Delaware River in what became the state of New Jersey, New Sweden was fostered and initially governed from 1638 by disaffected Dutchmen who had left the service of the Dutch West India Company's colony of New Netherlands. In 1655 the Dutch under Pieter Stuijvesant captured all of the Swedish posts and put an end to the colony of New Sweden. In 1674 under the terms of the Treaty of Westminster, New Sweden was definitely recognised as British.

New York (New Amsterdam). Originally settled by the Dutch West Indies in 1624 and called New Netherlands, the colony was taken by the English in 1664 and retained three years later under the terms of the Treaty of Breda. It was briefly recaptured by the Dutch in 1673 and surrendered to the British in the following year under the terms of the Treaty of Westminster in return for British acceptance of Dutch rule in Surinam. The conquered colony was granted to James, Duke of York, the brother of Charles II, in 1674. The grant also included the areas of what were to become known as New Jersey and Pennsylvania. New York formed part of the Dominion of New England from 1688 to 1689, when it fell under royal control. The colony rapidly expanded and prospered during the 18th century. In 1783 it became part of the United States.

Nicaragua. Discovered by Columbus in 1502, Nicaragua was first settled in 1522. The Moskito Coast, located on the eastern coast, was subject to British control until 1782, after which British interests in Central America focused at Belize. Spanish authority came to an end in 1821, and in 1839 Nicaragua became an independent republic.

Niue. Located in the South Pacific about 300 miles east of Tonga, Niue was discovered in 1774 by Captain James Cook, and from 1861 it was the scene of British missionary activities. In 1900 a protectorate was claimed, and in the following year the island was annexed to New Zealand.

Norfolk Island. Located in the South Pacific between New Zealand and New Caledonia, Norfolk Island was discovered by James Cook in 1774 and was colonised in 1788, after which it was used as a convict colony by New South Wales.

North Carolina. Although the French first discovered the North Carolina coast in 1524 and the Spanish planted a temporary colony near the mouth of the 'Rio Jordan' two years later, it was the British who permanently colonised the area. Colonists sent by Sir Walter Raleigh landed on Roanoke Island in 1585, but the first lasting settlements were made in the late 1650s around Albermarle Sound by colonials from Virginia. In 1663 Charles II granted Carolina to eight lords proprietors. Two settled areas soon developed, Albermarle County and Craven County (later Charleston), and these gradually came to be known as North Carolina and South Carolina. A reorganisation in 1691 provided for a governor of all Carolina; then, from 1712 to 1729, the proprietors appointed governors to rule North Carolina as a separate colony. In 1729 proprietary control was forfeited due to the misrule of the proprietors and North and South Carolina became crown colonies. They remained so until 1775, when they ended their allegiance to Britain.

Nova Colônia do Sacramento (Uruguay). In 1680 the Portuguese established a colony on the north bank of the Plate estuary which was called Nova Colônia do Sacramento. This was immediately occupied by the Spaniards and only returned in 1683. The colony was again occupied by Spain in 1705 and returned in 1715 under the terms of the Treaty of Utrecht. In 1750, under the terms of the Treaty of Madrid, the Portuguese agreed to abandon the colony, but the plan was not implemented until 1777 under the terms of the Treaty of San Ildefonso in which Portugal received assurances of Spain's acceptance of Portuguese sovereignty in the Amazon hinterland.

Nova Scotia. Located in eastern Canada, Nova Scotia was discovered by John Cabot in 1497 and first settled by the French under Pierre du Guast and Samuel de Champlain in 1605 at Port Royal. It changed hands eight times between the French and British in the 17th century and early 18th century. Finally Britain was ceded Nova Scotia under the Treaty of Utrecht in 1713, which wrested all of Acadia, excluding Cape Breton, from France. In 1763 Prince Edward Island was joined to Nova Scotia, but was separated once more in 1769.

Nueva Granada (Colombia). In 1500 a Spanish expedition under Alonso de Ojeda undertook the exploration of the northern coast of South America in what is now Colombian territory. The first permanent settlement of Santa Marta was made in 1525, by which time Balboa had discovered the Pacific and several Spanish explorers had begun to probe the inlets and rivers along the western shore. The region was named Nueva Granada in the 1540s. The Comunero Revolt of 1781 was the first serious uprising against Spanish authority. Although it failed, various forces and events conspired during the next 30 years to increase separatist sentiment.

Orán. Located on the northern coast of Africa, Orán was occupied by Spanish forces in 1509. Except for the period 1708–32 when it was under the control of the Ottoman Empire, Orán remained a Spanish possession until 1792, when it was abandoned.

Panama. Discovered in 1501 by the Spaniard Rodrigo de Bastidas, the colony remained under Spanish control until 1821, when it became free and adhered to the Gran Colombia of Simón Bolívar.

Paraguay. The first permanent settlement in Paraguay, situated in the south central part of the South American continent, was made in 1537 when the Spaniard Juan de Salazar founded a fort on the present site of Asunción. In this early period Paraguay included the entire Plata–Paraná–Paraguay river region. The Buenos Aires region was detached in 1617, when Paraguay became a colony separate from Argentina and was placed immediately under the viceroyalty of Peru until the viceroyalty of La Plata was set up in 1776 with Buenos Aires as capital. In 1811 Paraguay became independent of Spanish control.

Penang. Located off the northwestern coast of the Malay Peninsula, this island was ceded to the British East India Company in 1786 by the Sultan of Kedah. From 1791 the British paid annual sums to the Sultan in return for the territory, to which the mainland province of Wellesby was added in 1800. In 1826, Penang, Singapore and Malacca were brought under a joint administration and became known as the Straits Settlements.

Pennsylvania. Parts of present-day Pennysylvania were settled by the Swedes and Dutch prior to the middle of the 17th century. Henry Hudson entered Delaware Bay for the Dutch in 1609 and the Swedes established their first settlement on Tinicum Island in the Delaware River. In 1655 Dutch forces conquered the Swedish territory and nine years later English forces conquered Dutch territory in America, including the Delaware Valley. Pennsylvania was included in the Charter given in 1664 to James, Duke of York, but was detached from New York in Aug 1682 and granted to William Penn as a proprietary colony. In 1703 Delaware became a separate colony from Pennsylvania, a separation which was approved by the Privy Council. In 1776 the last proprietary governor was expelled.

Peru. The Spanish under Francisco Pizarro invaded the Inca state in 1532 and began their conquest of the kingdom, which the Spaniards named Peru. Spanish authority was first seriously threatened in 1820 when patriot forces invaded Peru from Chile. In the following year the independence of Peru was proclaimed and, in 1825, it became a republic.

Philippine Islands. Discovered by Magellan in 1521, Spain began the occupation of the islands in 1565. Except for Mindanao and the Sulu archipelago, which were not effectively settled until the mid-19th century, all the major islands were firmly under Spanish control by 1600. The British gained possession of the Philippines in 1762 but restored them under the Treaty of Fontainebleau in 1764, after which the islands remained in Spanish hands until the Spanish–American War when they were ceded to the United States following the Battle of Manila Bay in 1898.

Pitcairn Island. Located in the east-central Pacific Ocean, Pitcairn Island was discovered in 1767 by a British navigator and was settled in 1790 by mutineers from the *Bounty*.

Plaisance. Situated on an inlet in southern Newfoundland, Plaisance was established by the French c. 1640 and colonised on a small scale in 1662. The colony was ceded to Britain in 1713 under the terms of the Treaty of Utrecht and its inhabitants emigrated to Île Royale.

Pomeroon. Located in western Guiana, Pomeroon was created in 1657 as a separate post subordinated to the main Dutch settlement in the area of Essequibo, and was populated principally by fugitives from Netherlands Brazil. In 1666 the English briefly occupied the colony, which was not resettled until 1679. Following the devastation of Pomeroon by a French – Carib attack in 1689, the colony existed simply as a frontier post under Essequibo.

Portuguese Guinea. Located on the west coast of Africa, this area was discovered in 1446–7 by explorers in the service of Prince Henry the Navigator and was settled by the Portuguese in the 16th century from the Cape Verde Islands. Captaincies were created at Cacheu in 1614 and Bessau in 1687, but the area was administered by the Cape Verde Islands until 1879 when the colony of Portuguese Guinea was established.

Portuguese India. This consisted of three enclaves: Goa, on the western coast of India, seized in 1510 from the ruler of Bijapur; Diu and Damão, located several hundred miles to the north, occupied in 1535 and 1538, respectively. There were numerous juntas throughout the second half of the 17th and 18th centuries. About 1760 the seat of government was transferred from Goa to Pangim.

Puerto Rico. Located in the eastern Caribbean, Puerto Rico was discovered by Columbus in 1493 and settlement began in 1509. The island was subjected to frequent attacks by the British, French and Dutch in the 16th century and in 1597 England held the territory for five months. Slavery in the colony continued to exist until 1873. Like Cuba, Puerto Rico was occupied by American troops during the Spanish–American War in 1898 and formally ceded to the United States under the Treaty of Paris in the same year.

Quebec. First visited by Jacques Cartier in 1535, the first successful efforts at colonisation in the area began in 1608. In 1629 Samuel de Champlain, a geographer for Henry IV who had founded the city of Quebec in 1608, was forced to surrender the colony to a British force under Sir David Kirke. But by the Treaty of St Germain-en-Laye (1632), Canada was restored to France and Champlain returned as governor of the colony of Quebec. In 1759, after an attack by the British, Quebec, the stronghold of the French Empire in North America, surrendered to Britain. By the Treaty of Paris in 1763, Canada became a British colony.

Réunion. Lying about 400 miles east of Madagascar in the Mascarene archipelago, this island was claimed on 26 Jun 1638 by the French, who named it Bourbon. Originally administered by the French East India Company, it passed to the French crown in 1764–7, after which it was subject to the authority of the governor-general at Île de France. Renamed Réunion in 1793, Bonaparte in 1806, Bourbon in 1815 and, finally, Réunion once more in 1848.

Rhode Island. Settled in 1638 by religious dissidents from Massachusetts Bay, the colony was granted a charter in 1663 by Charles II. From 1686 to 1689 Rhode Island was part of the Dominion of New England, and on 4 May 1776, the General Assembly declared the colony independent of the British crown. On 29 May 1790 it ratified the United States Constitution.

Rupert's Land. This was the name given to the area granted by the British to the Hudson's Bay Company in 1670. It includes, broadly, all the lands draining into Hudson's Bay. Posts were established at York Fort, Albany and Churchill between 1672 and 1719. York Fort was occupied by the French from 1694 to 1696 and 1697 to 1714 (restored under the terms of the Treaty of Utrecht) and Albany from 1686 to 1693. The conquest of Canada by the British prompted the Hudson's Bay Company to build fur-trading posts inland, the first such post being Cumberland House, established in 1774.

Russian America (Alaska). In 1741, the Russian navigator Vitus Bering explored the coasts of Russian Alaska located in the northwest corner of North America, bounded on the east by Canada. The first trading post was established on Kodiak Island in 1784 by the Shelekhov-Golikov company in order to exploit the fur trade. Other posts were established along the coast as far south as California, but the interior was not explored until after 1833. It was purchased from Russia by the United States in 1867 and renamed Alaska.

St Barthélemy. One of the Leeward Islands in the northern Lesser Antilles 200 miles east of Puerto Rico, St Barthélemy was owned, but never occupied, by France in the 17th and 18th centuries. In 1784 France sold it to Sweden and the island flourished as a neutral port during the wars of the French Revolution.

St Christophe (St Kitts). Located in the West Indies, the island was a bone of contention between France and Britain, both of whom established settlements there in the 1620s. In 1702 the French were finally expelled, Britain's sole possession being confirmed by the Treaty of Utrecht in 1713. In 1782, during the American Revolution, the French seized the island, which was returned to Britain in the following year under the terms of the Treaty of Versailles.

St Dominique (Haiti). Located in the West Indies, it occupies the western third of Hispaniola island. It was discovered in 1492 by Columbus. Neglected by the Spaniards during the early colonial era, the region was subjected to incursions in the 17th century by French and British privateers based on Tortuga Island. In 1697, the Treaty of Ryswick recognised French authority over the western third of Hispaniola Island, which came to be known as St Dominique (present-day Haiti). The colony, with the aid of black slave labour, became th world's largest sugar producer by the 18th century, but after a decade of strife the French withdrew in 1803. The colony declared its independence in 1804.

Sainte-Lucie (St Lucia). Located in the Lesser Antilles, this is the largest of the Windward Islands. It was unsuccessfuly settled by the British in 1605 and 1638. French claims to the island were confirmed by treaty with the Caribs in 1660. Sainte-Lucie subsequently switched hands several times between the French and British from 1638 to 1803 and was officially declared neutral from 1723 to 1743 and 1748 to 1756. It was occupied by the French in 1756, lost to Britain in 1762 and regained in 1763 at the Treaty of Fontainebleau. The French then held the colony until 1781, when it was again lost to the British and regained under the Treaty of Versailles in 1783, after which it remained in French hands, except for a brief period from 1794 to 1795. It was again captured by the British in 1803 and ceded to them by the Treaty of Paris in 1814.

Ste Marie de Madagascar. Located off the northeastern coast of Madagascar, this small island was ceded to the French by its Malagasy ruler in 1750, but it remained unoccupied until 1819.

St Eustatius. Located at the northern end of the Lesser Antilles, it was settled by the Dutch West Indies Company in 1636, but occupied at various times by the English (1665–8, 1672 to after 1674, 1690–6, 1781) and by the French (1689–90, 1781–4). The nearby islands of St Martin and Saba were first occupied by the Dutch at about the same time as St Eustatius and were attached to it administratively.

St Helena. Located in the South Atlantic Ocean 1200 miles west of Africa, this small island was discovered by the Portuguese in 1502. The Dutch claimed it in 1633 but did not take possession. The British held it from 1651 except for a brief Dutch occupation in 1673. The island remained under the administration of the British East India Company until 1834, except for the period of Napoleon's exile there from 1815 to 1821, when it was directly administered by the crown.

St Pierre and Miquelon. Located off the southern coast of Newfoundland, these islands were claimed for France by Jacques Cartier in 1535, but were probably colonised by France in 1604. They were occupied by the British in 1713, but restored to France in 1763 under the terms of the Treaty of Paris. Britain again occupied the islands in 1778, but they were restored under the terms of the Treaty of Versailles in 1778. After a third occupation by the British in 1793, the islands were permanently restored to France under the Treaty of Paris in 1814.

St Vincent. One of the Lesser Antilles, it was granted by Charles I to the Earl of Carlisle in 1627 but remained unoccupied by Europeans until the British captured it under the command of General Monkton in 1762. It was ceded to Britain under the terms of the Treaty of Paris in 1763 and, though French forces seized the island in 1779, it was restored to the British in 1783 under the terms of the Treaty of Versailles. The Carib Indians, who had long since used St Vincent as a refuge, were deported in 1797.

Santa Catalina. Located in the Caribbean Sea about 100 miles off the coast of Nicaragua, this island was settled by an offshoot of the Somers Islands Company, the Providence Company, in 1630, whereupon it was named Providence. In 1641 it was captured by the Spanish and renamed Santa Catalina. From 1665 to 1666 and, briefly, in 1670, the island was again occupied by the British. Although Spain reoccupied the island in 1688 it was not constituted a separate province.

377

Santo Domingo. Situated on the island of Hispaniola's southern coast, it was established by Bartholomew Columbus in 1496. It is the oldest continuously settled community founded by Europeans in the Western hemisphere.

São Tomé and Príncipe. Located in the Gulf of Guinea near the coast of Africa, these islands were discovered by the Portuguese in 1470–1. The larger of the two, São Tomé, was established in 1485 and proclaimed a colony in 1522. It was occupied by the Dutch from 1641 to 1644. Until the establishment of plantations during the 18th century, the islands were of considerable importance as supply stations.

Senegal. French presence along the Senegal coast began in 1628 when the Compagnie Normand took control of the activities there. A post was established at the mouth of the Senegal River in 1638 and in 1659 the French built St Louis. With the capture of Gorée from the Dutch in 1677, the French gained an important naval base in West Africa and their influence was extended to the interior. In 1758 the British captured all the French ports, returning only Gorée in 1763. France retook its possessions in 1775, but returned Gorée under the terms of the Treaty of Versailles in 1783.

Senegambia. This colony consisted of British posts on the Gambia River as well as the French colony of Senegal, minus the islet of Gorée. It was formed in 1765, the first British crown colony in Africa. Disputes among the British administrators facilitated the recapture of Senegal by the French in 1775 and in 1783 under the terms of the Treaty of Versailles, Britain returned only her former posts on the Gambia, which came under the authority of the Company of Merchants trading to Africa, when Senegambia officially came to an end as a colony.

South Carolina. In 1526 the Spanish founded an unsuccessful colony along the coast of South Carolina, located in the southeast United States. A second shortlived settlement was established by the French in 1562 on what is now known as Parris Island, near Beaufort. The failure of the French and the Spanish (the latter attempted two further settlements between 1566 and 1580) opened the way for British settlement, the first being established at Albermarle Point on the Ashley River in 1670. In 1719 the settlers, annoyed because the proprietors did little to aid in fighting pirates and Indians, declared themselves free of proprietary rule and elected their own governor. Parliament purchased the proprietors' interest, and, in 1729, South Carolina became a royal colony. It remained so until 1775 when it ended its allegiance to Britain.

Spanish Guinea. Located in West Africa on the Gulf of Guinea, Spanish Guinea comprises the islands of Fernando Po and Annobón and the small coastal enclave known as Río Muni. The islands were discovered by the Portuguese in 1472. Ceded to Spain by Portugal in 1777 by the Treaty of San Ildefonso, the territory was abandoned in 1781 because of yellow fever.

Surinam. The colony of Willoughby at the mouth of the Surinam River was planted by the British in 1651 and captured in 1657 by the Dutch, who retained it at the Treaty of Breda in the same year in return for New Netherlands.

Tangier. Located at the northwest tip of Africa at the entrance to the Strait of Gibraltar, Tangier was seized by the Portuguese in 1471. Under Spanish rule for 60 years after 1580, it later reverted to Portugal. In 1661 it was ceded to Charles II in the dowry of his Queen, Catherine of Braganza. After a long siege by Moroccans in 1684 the British, after destroying their fortifications, abandoned Tangier.

Timor. One of the Lesser Sunda Islands of Indonesia, it was first settled by the Portuguese in 1520. The western part of the island was seized by the Dutch in 1618 and the Portuguese thereafter occupied only the eastern part of the island and a small enclave on the northwest coast. Until 1844 Timor was under Portuguese India and from then until 1896, when it became a separate colony, under Macao.

Tobago. Located off the coast of Venezuela, it was settled briefly in 1616 by the British, who were driven out by the native Carib Indians. It was then held by the Dutch from 1658 to 1677. Possession of the island shifted frequently between Britain and France from 1677 to 1762. It was secured by the British at the Treaty of Paris in 1763 and became part of the South Caribbee Islands from 1763 to 1781, whereupon it was captured by Comte de Grasse and held by France until 1793, having been ceded to France ten years earlier under the terms of the Treaty of Versailles. Britain regained Tobago in 1793, but the island again came under French control from 1802 to 1803, when the British finally regained it.

Tranquebar. Located on the Coromandel coast of southeastern Indian, Tranquebar was purchased from the Raja of Tanjore by the Danish East India Company in 1620 and remained the headquarters for Danish commercial activities in the area. It remained under the Danes from 1620, except for British occupation from 1801 to 1814, until sold in 1845 to Great Britain.

Trinidad. Located off the coast of Venezuela, it was discovered by Columbus in 1598. The Spanish made only feeble attempts at colonisation. Throughout the 17th century the island was a source of contention between Spain, Britain, France, the United Provinces and the Duchy of Kurland. In 1735 Trinidad, hitherto a province of Guyana, was created a separate province. In 1797 it was captured by British forces, who retained Trinidad under the terms of the Treaty of Amiens in 1802.

Turks and Caicos Islands. Located at the southern end of the Bahamas, the Turks Islands were occupied by Britain in 1766 and annexed to the Bahamas in 1804. The Caicos Islands were administered by the Bahamas from 1799.

Venezuela. First explored by the Spanish in 1499, it remained under the authority of Spain until 1810 when control of the area alternated between the Spanish and patriot forces. In 1820 the Spanish were finally expelled.

Virginia. Established in 1607 under the auspices of the Virginia Company of London, this was the first permanent British settlement in North America. It came under royal control in 1624, and eight years later Maryland was created from territory granted to Virginia under its charter. In 1775 the last royal governor was forced to flee.

INDEX

Most of the chapters in this book run in alphabetical sequence and for this reason we have not attempted to produce a completely detailed index. The main aim has been to allow the reader to locate the country, event or personage by page for any major subject included in this publication.

BRISTOL CITY COUNCIL
LIBRARY SERVICE

BRISTOL
REFERENCE LIBRARY

COLLEGE GREEN

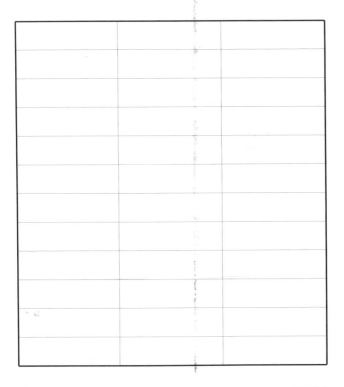